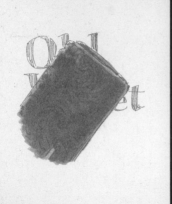

My wallet broke.
Half of me is in shock for
having lost my favorite wallet,
but the other half of me is
happy that I get to search for
a new one. Now that I think
about it, that's how I usually
feel when I lose stuff.

-Tite Kubo

BLEACH is author Tite Kubo's second title. Kubo made his debut
with ZOMBIEPOWDER., a four-volume series for WEEKLY SHONEN
JUMP. To date, BLEACH has been translated into numerous
languages and has also inspired an animated TV series that
began airing in the U.S. in 2006. Beginning its serialization in
2001, BLEACH is still a mainstay in the pages of WEEKLY SHONEN
JUMP. In 2005, BLEACH was awarded the prestigious Shogakukan
Manga Award in the shonen (boys) category.

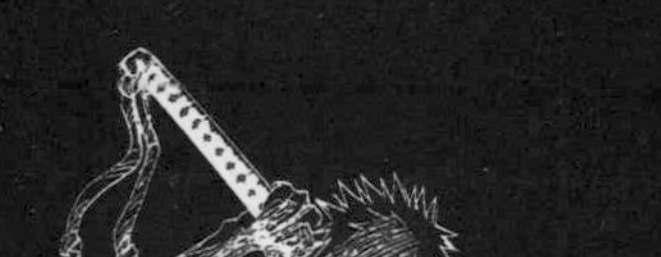

BLEACH
VOL. 56: MARCH OF THE STARCROSS
SHONEN JUMP Manga Edition

STORY AND ART BY
TITE KUBO

Translation/Joe Yamazaki
Touch-up Art & Lettering/Mark McMurray
Design/Kam Li
Editor/Alexis Kirsch

Printed in the U.S.A.

Published by VIZ Media, LLC
P.O. Box 77010
San Francisco, CA 94107

10 9 8 7 6 5 4 3 2 1
First printing, April 2013

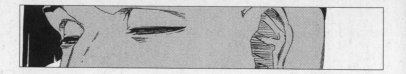

The soldiers blow their trumpets
Like stars shooting by the ear
The soldiers stomp their feet
Like thunder in the air

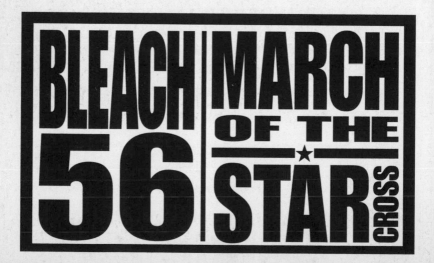

BLEACH 56 | MARCH OF THE ★ STAR CROSS

ALL STARS ★ AND

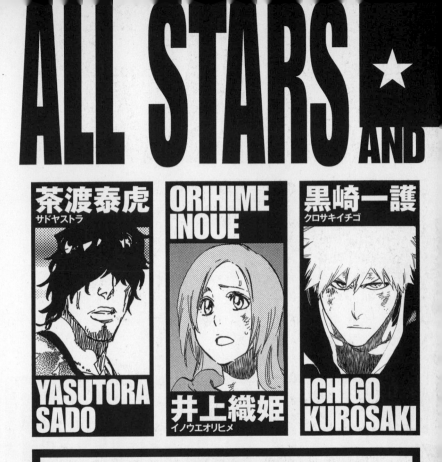

茶渡泰虎
サドヤストラ

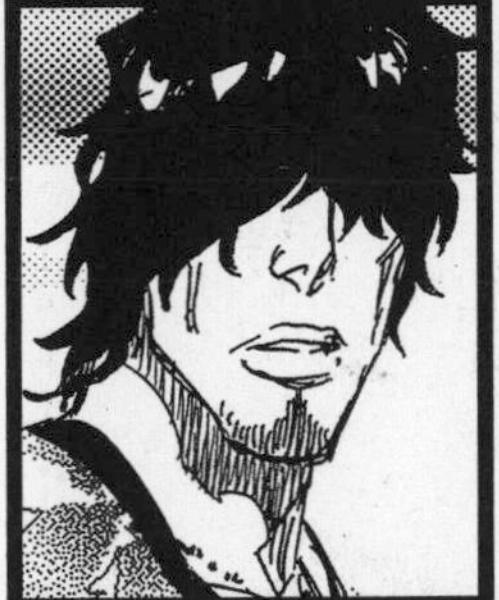

YASUTORA SADO

ORIHIME INOUE

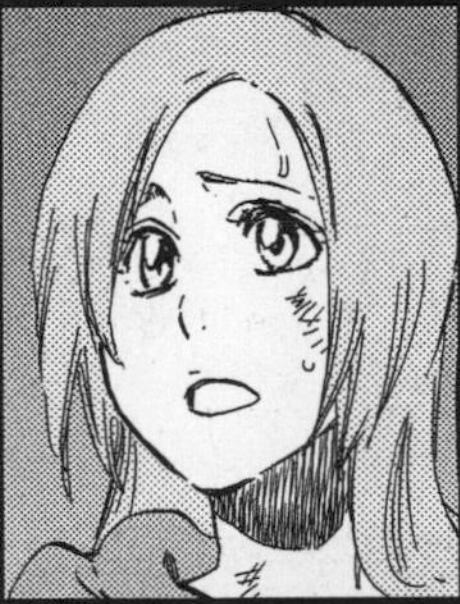

井上織姫
イノウエオリヒメ

黒崎一護
クロサキイチゴ

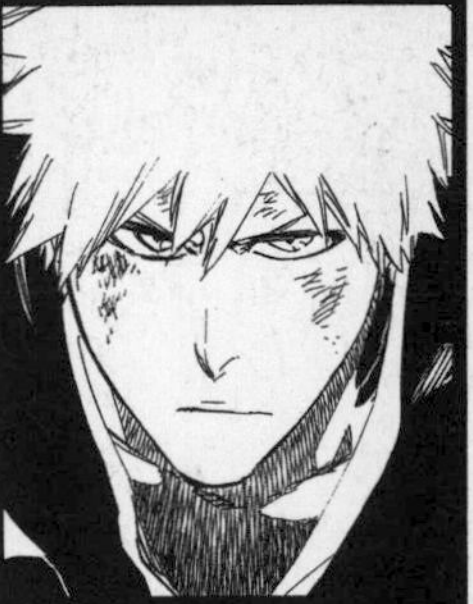

ICHIGO KUROSAKI

★ plot

Ichigo Kurosaki meets Soul Reaper Rukia Kuchiki and ends up helping her eradicate Hollows. After developing his powers as a Soul Reaper, Ichigo enters battle against Aizen and his dark ambitions! Ichigo finally defeats Aizen in exchange for his powers as a Soul Reaper.

With the battle over, Ichigo regains his normal life. But his tranquil days end when he meets Ginjo, who offers to help Ichigo get his powers back. But it was all a plot by Ginjo to steal Ichigo's new powers! Ginjo, who was the first ever Deputy Soul Reaper, then reveals to Ichigo the truth behind the deputy badge. However, even after learning of the Soul Society's plans for him, Ichigo chooses to continue protecting his friends and defeats Ginjo.

Now a Deputy Soul Reaper once again, Ichigo is suddenly attacked by a mysterious Arrancar and heads to Hueco Mundo to help his friend Nel!

BLEACH

KISUKE URAHARA

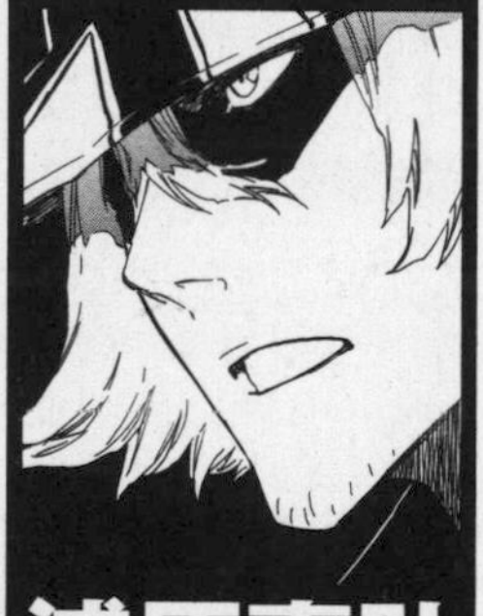

浦原喜助
ウラハラキスケ

ネル・トゥ

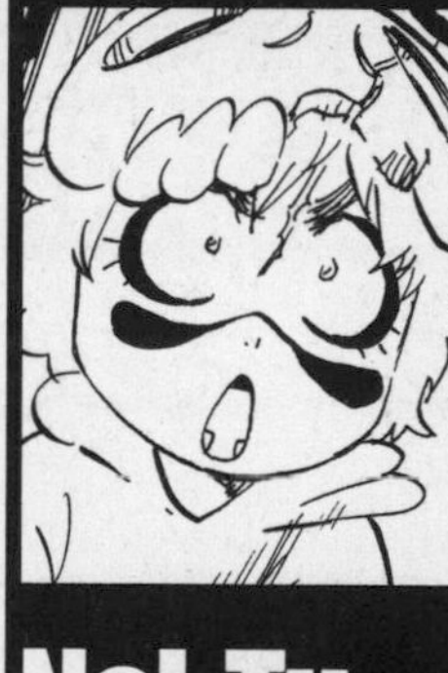

Nel Tu

Quilge Opie

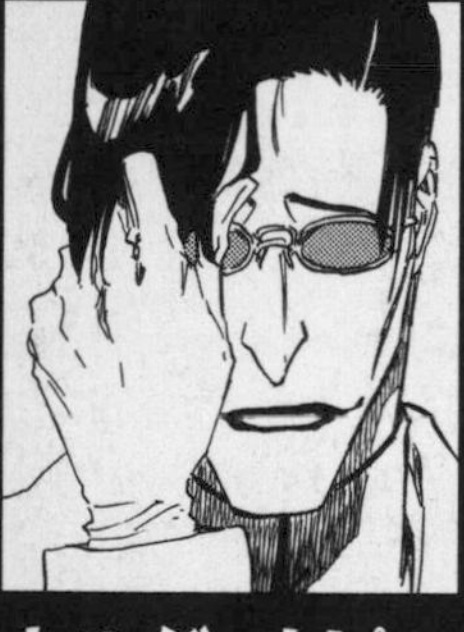

キルゲ・オピー

STORIES

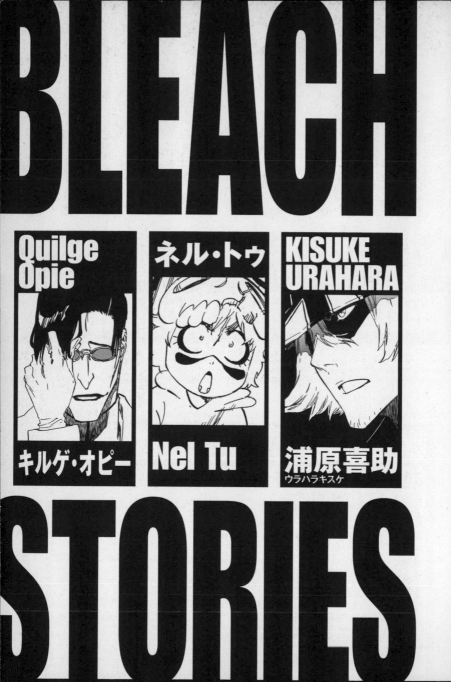

BLEACH 56

MARCH OF THE STARCROSS

CONTENTS

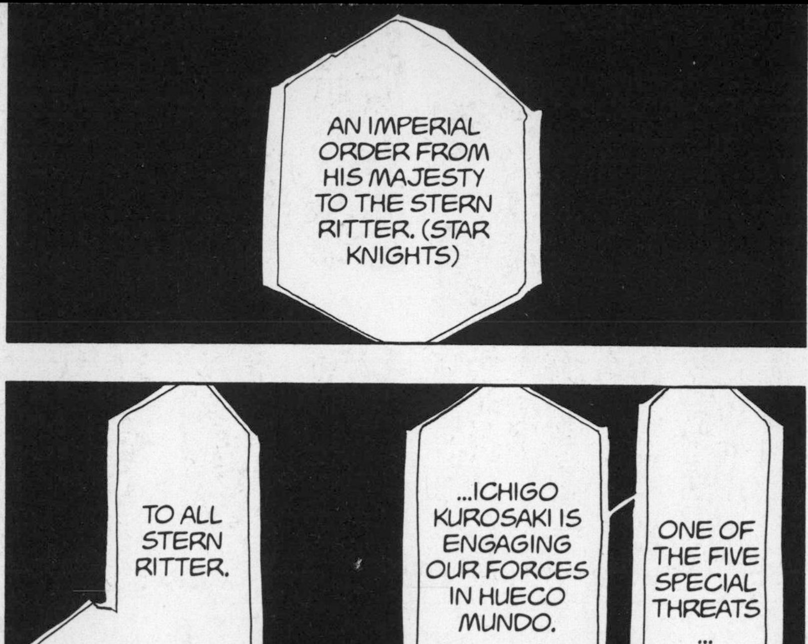
AN IMPERIAL ORDER FROM HIS MAJESTY TO THE STERN RITTER. (STAR KNIGHTS)
ONE OF THE FIVE SPECIAL THREATS...
...ICHIGO KUROSAKI IS ENGAGING OUR FORCES IN HUECO MUNDO.
TO ALL STERN RITTER.
EQUIP YOURSELVES AND ASSEMBLE AT THE GATE OF THE SUN IMMEDIATELY.

490.MARCH OF THE STARCROSS 2

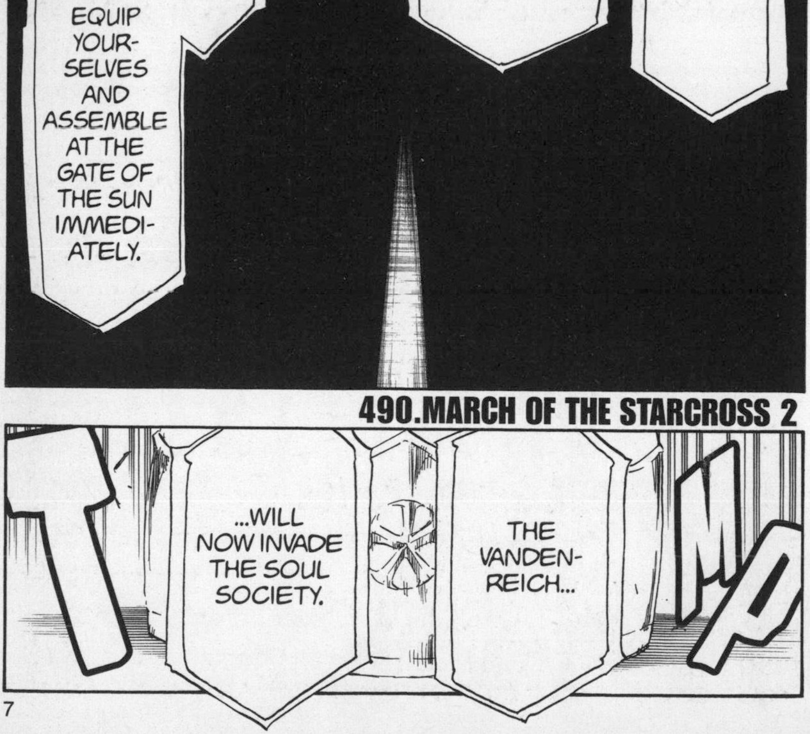
MP
THE VANDENREICH...
...WILL NOW INVADE THE SOUL SOCIETY.
T

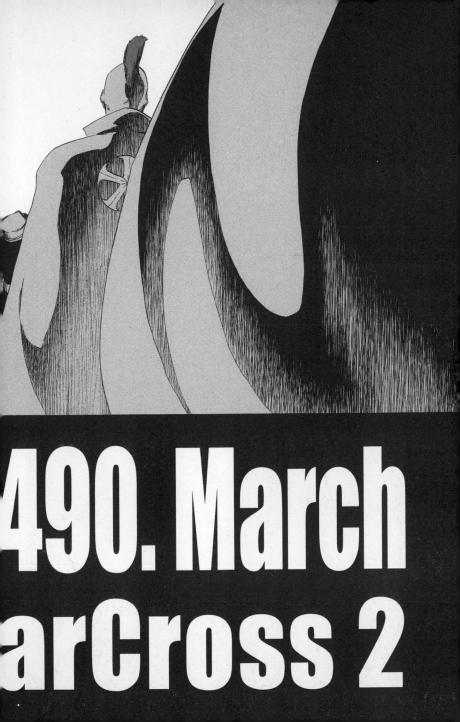

490. March
arCross 2

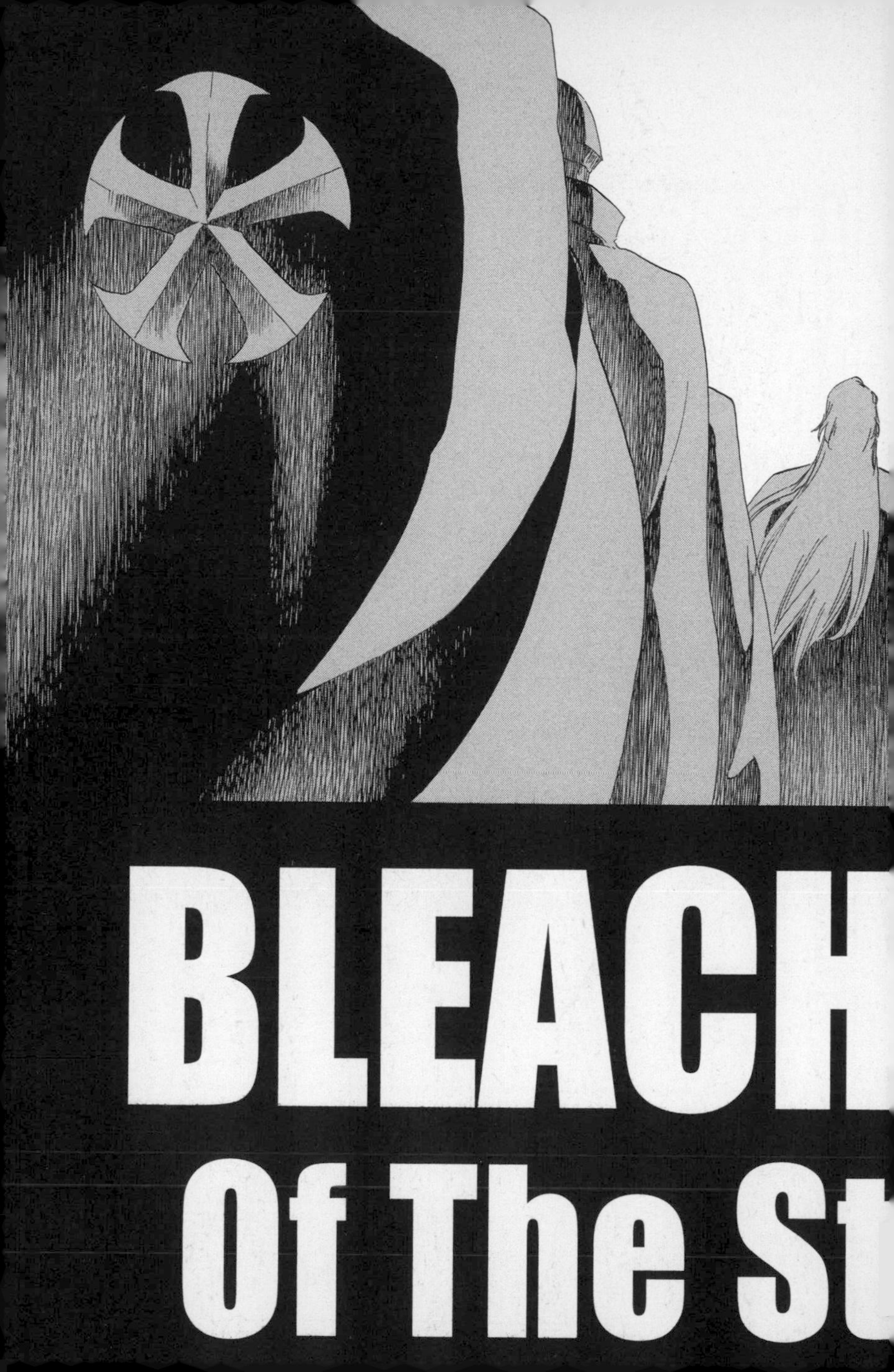
BLEACH
Of The St

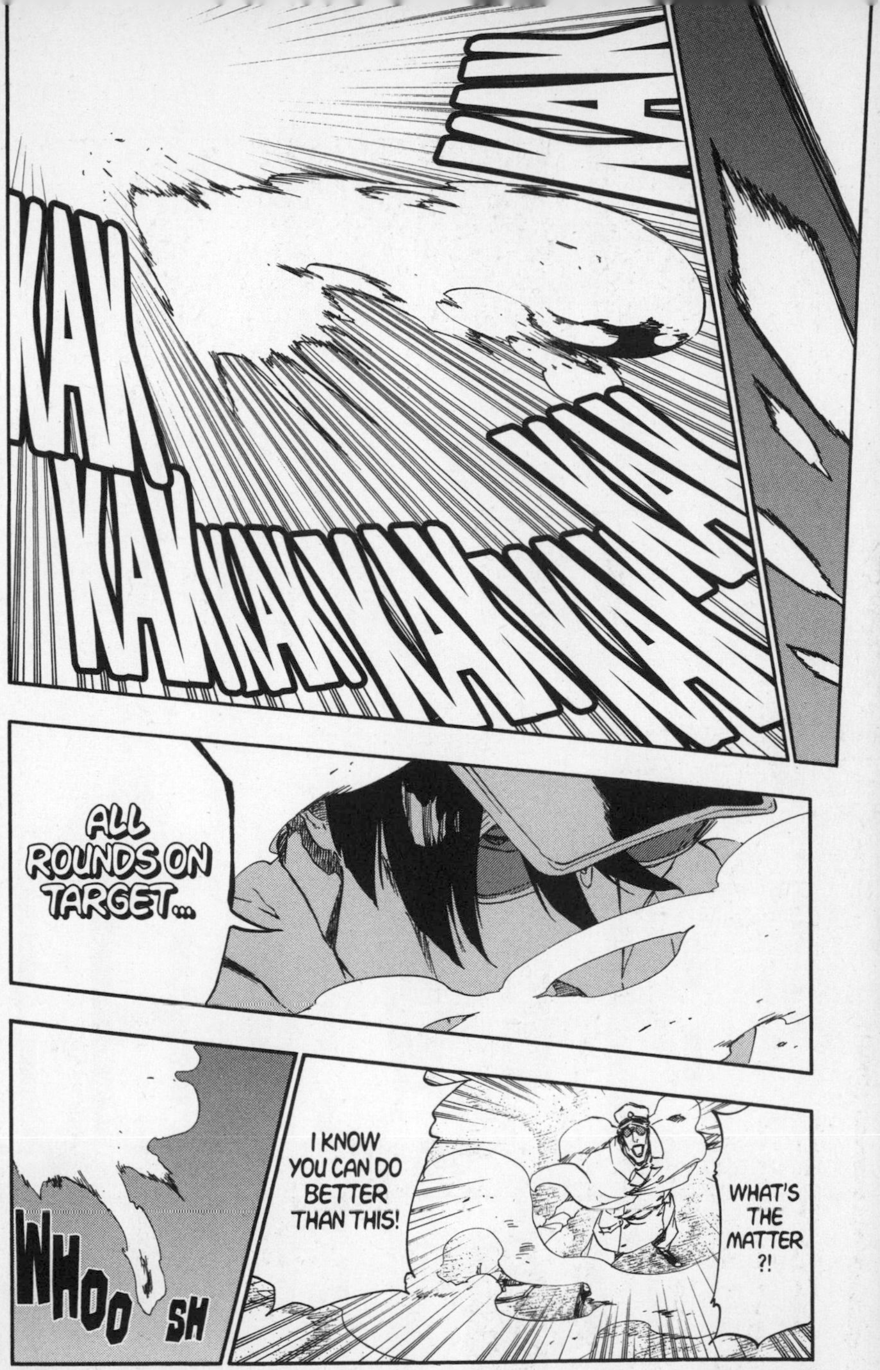
KAN
KAN
KAN KAN KAN KAN
ALL ROUNDS ON TARGET...
WHAT'S THE MATTER ?!
I KNOW YOU CAN DO BETTER THAN THIS!
WHOOSH

READ THIS WAY

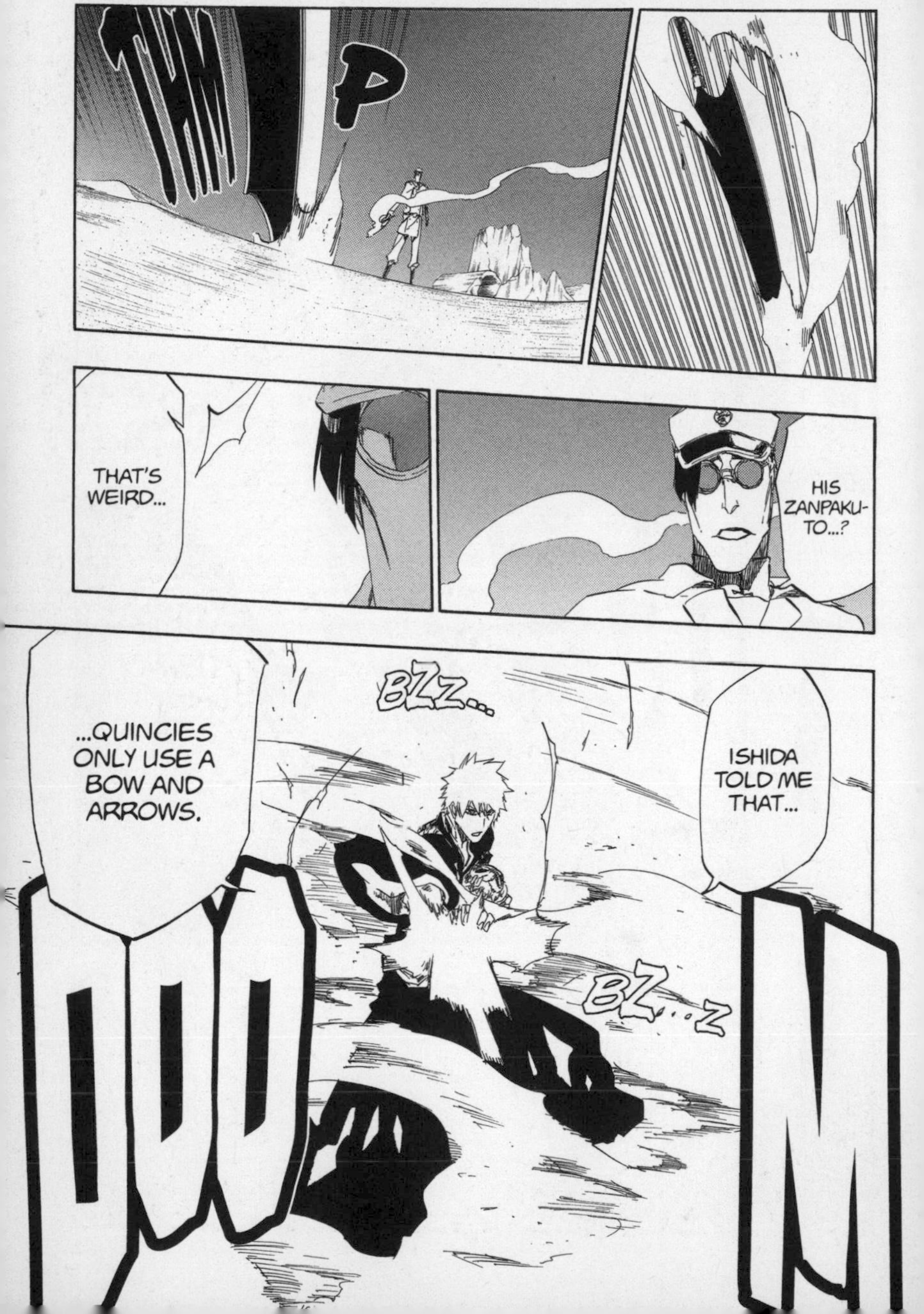
THMP
HIS ZANPAKU-TO...?
THAT'S WEIRD...
ISHIDA TOLD ME THAT...
...QUINCIES ONLY USE A BOW AND ARROWS.
BZZ...
BZ...Z
DOOM

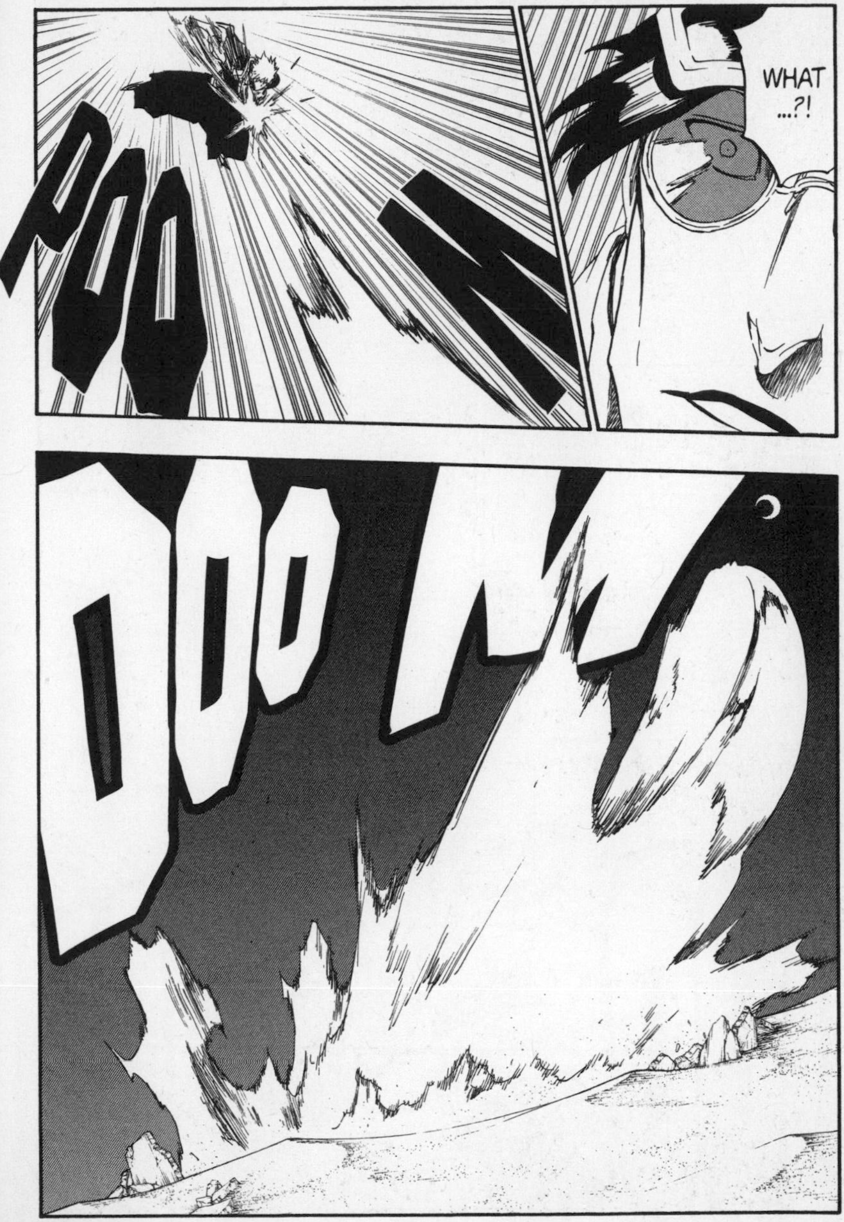
WHAT
...?!
DOOM

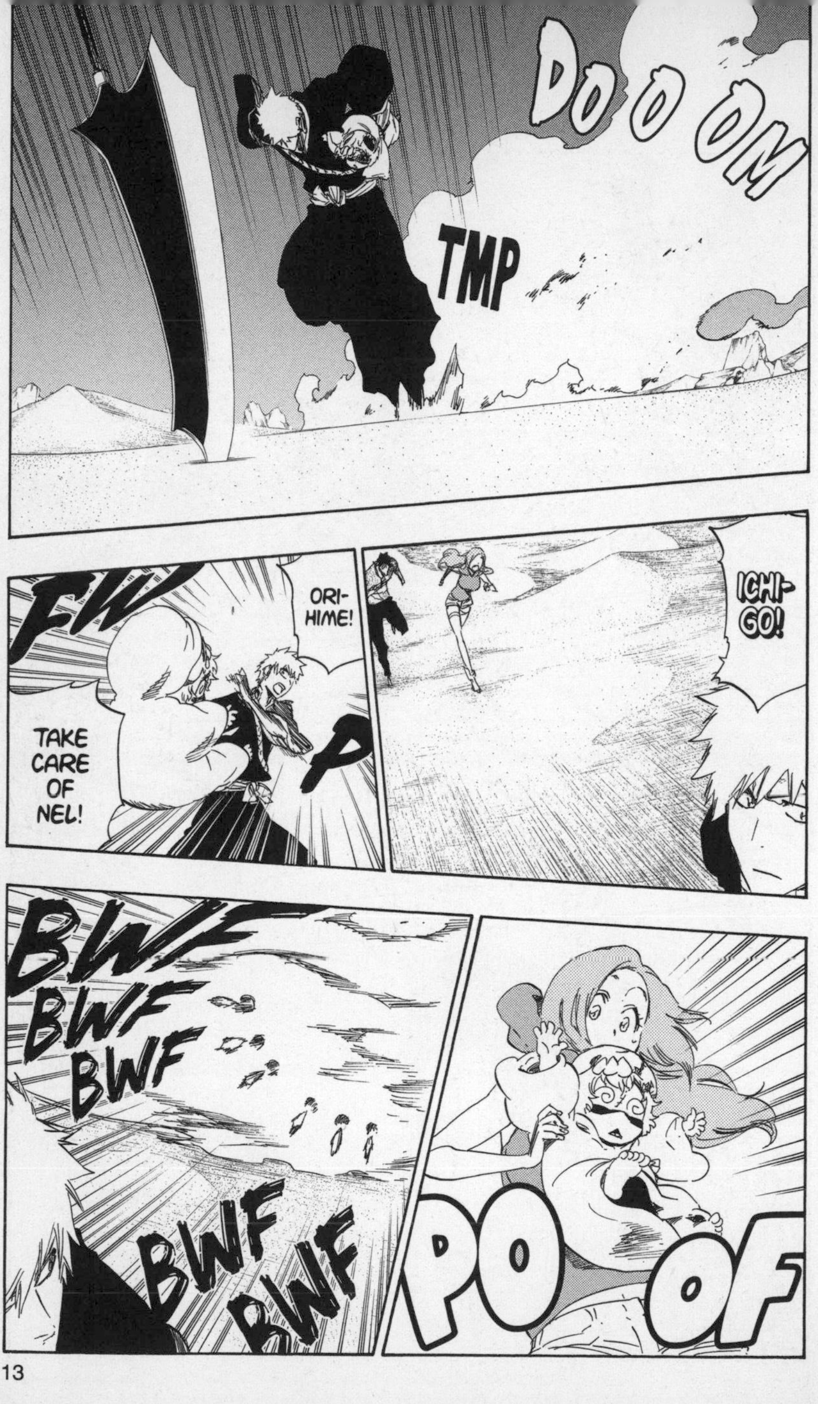
DOOOM
TMP
ICHI-GO!
ORI-HIME!
TAKE CARE OF NEL!
POOF
BWF
BWF
BWF
BWF
BWF

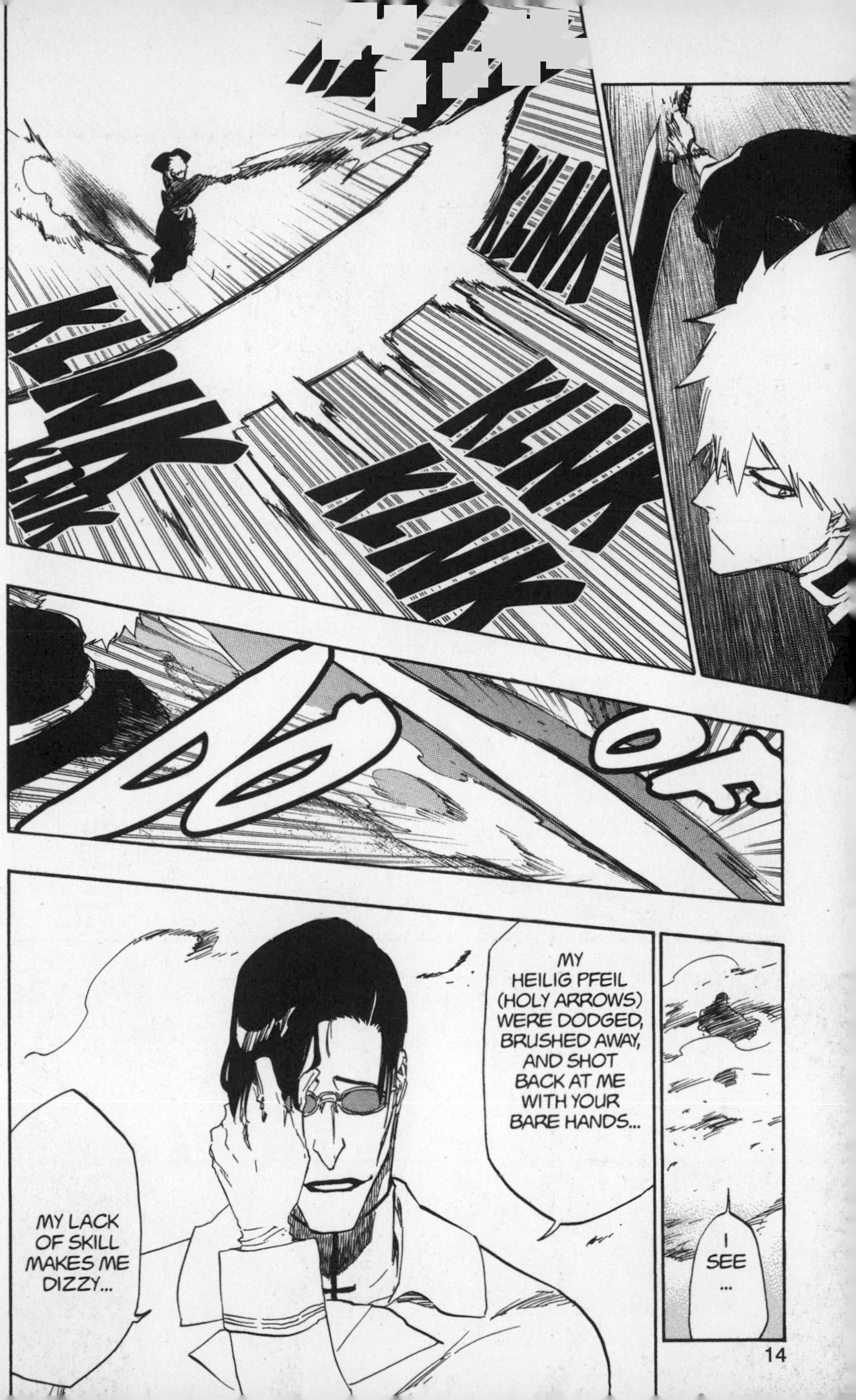
KLNK
I SEE...
MY HEILIG PFEIL (HOLY ARROWS) WERE DODGED, BRUSHED AWAY, AND SHOT BACK AT ME WITH YOUR BARE HANDS...
MY LACK OF SKILL MAKES ME DIZZY...

READ THIS WAY

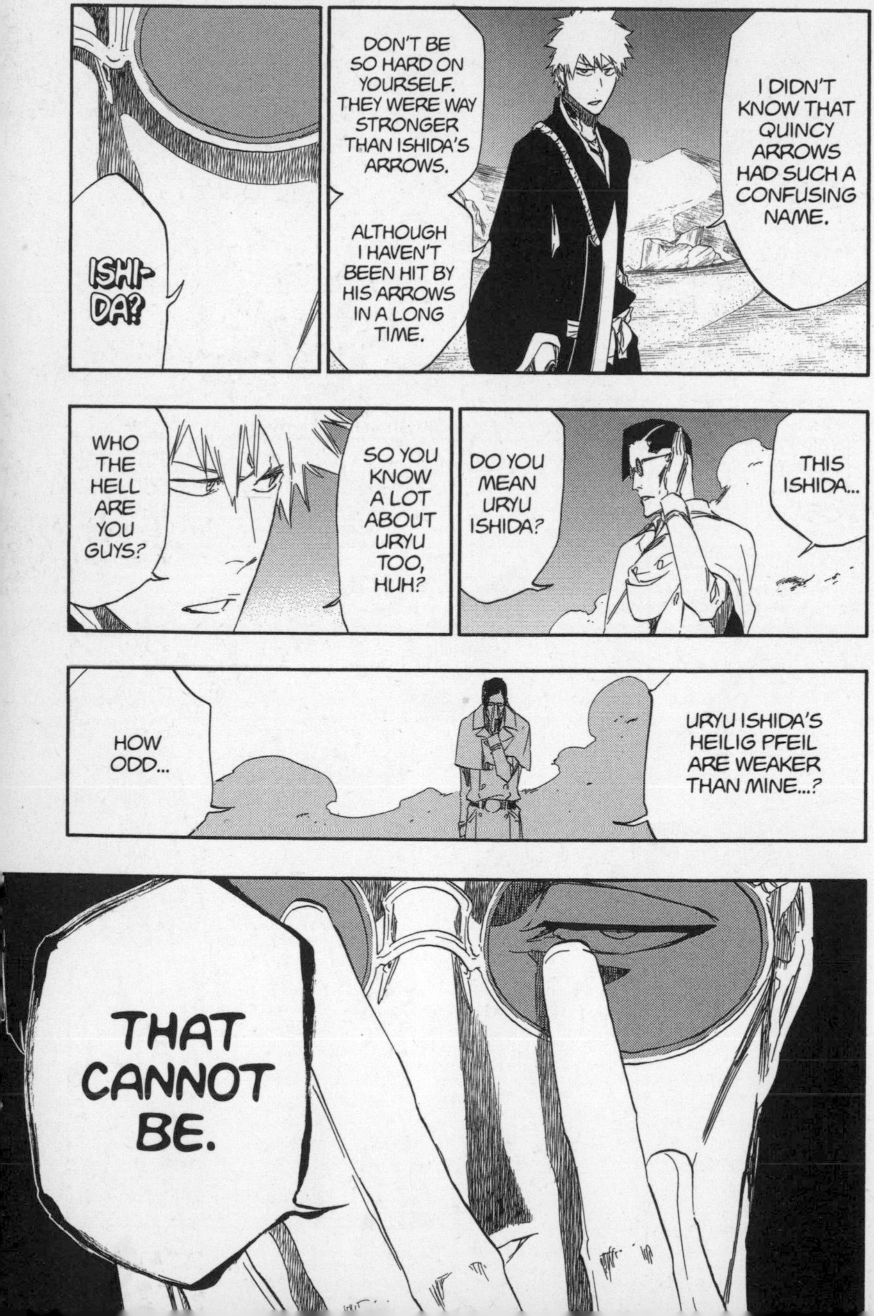
I DIDN'T KNOW THAT QUINCY ARROWS HAD SUCH A CONFUSING NAME.
DON'T BE SO HARD ON YOURSELF. THEY WERE WAY STRONGER THAN ISHIDA'S ARROWS.
ALTHOUGH I HAVEN'T BEEN HIT BY HIS ARROWS IN A LONG TIME.
ISHI-DA?
THIS ISHIDA...
DO YOU MEAN URYU ISHIDA?
SO YOU KNOW A LOT ABOUT URYU TOO, HUH?
WHO THE HELL ARE YOU GUYS?
URYU ISHIDA'S HEILIG PFEIL ARE WEAKER THAN MINE...?
HOW ODD...
THAT CANNOT BE.

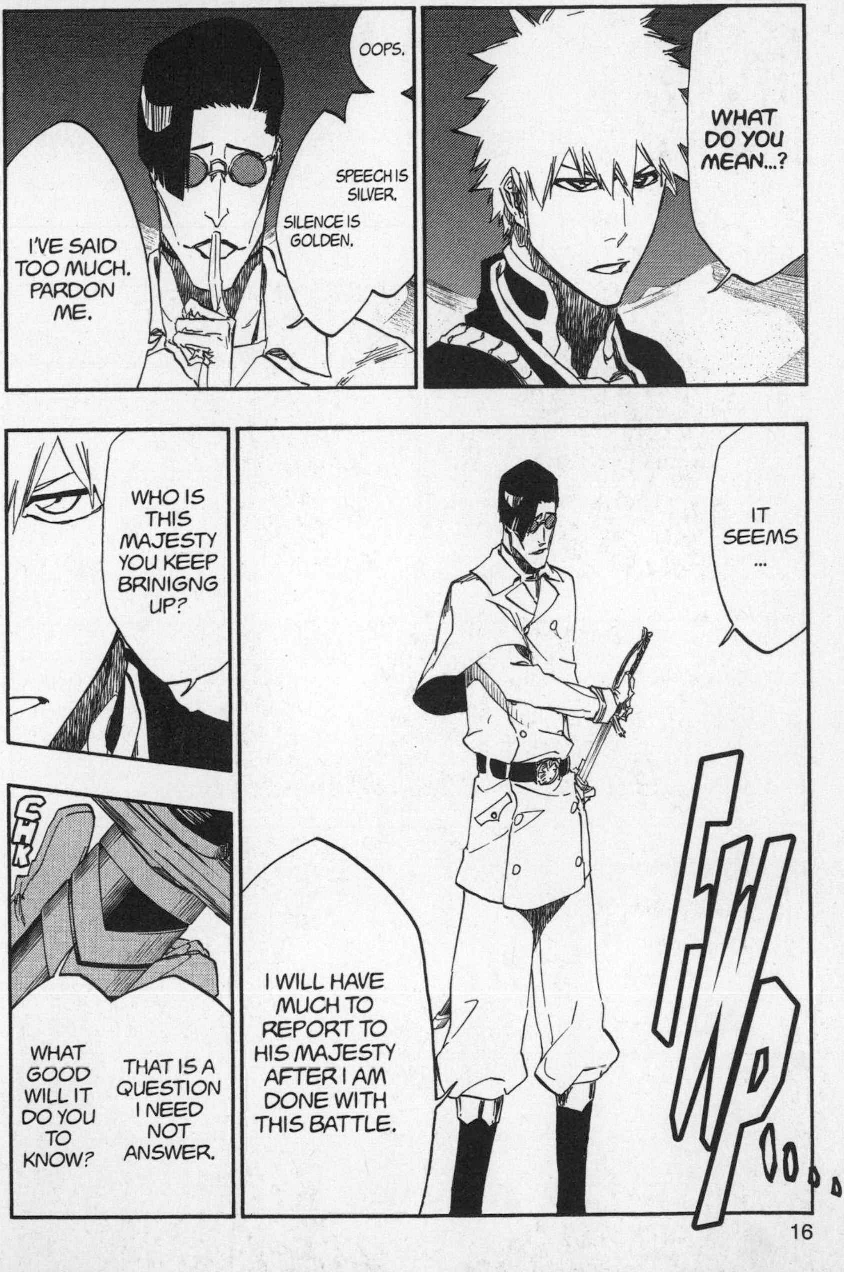
WHAT DO YOU MEAN...?
OOPS.
SPEECH IS SILVER.
SILENCE IS GOLDEN.
I'VE SAID TOO MUCH. PARDON ME.
IT SEEMS...
I WILL HAVE MUCH TO REPORT TO HIS MAJESTY AFTER I AM DONE WITH THIS BATTLE.
WHO IS THIS MAJESTY YOU KEEP BRINIGNG UP?
CHK
THAT IS A QUESTION I NEED NOT ANSWER.
WHAT GOOD WILL IT DO YOU TO KNOW?

READ THIS WAY

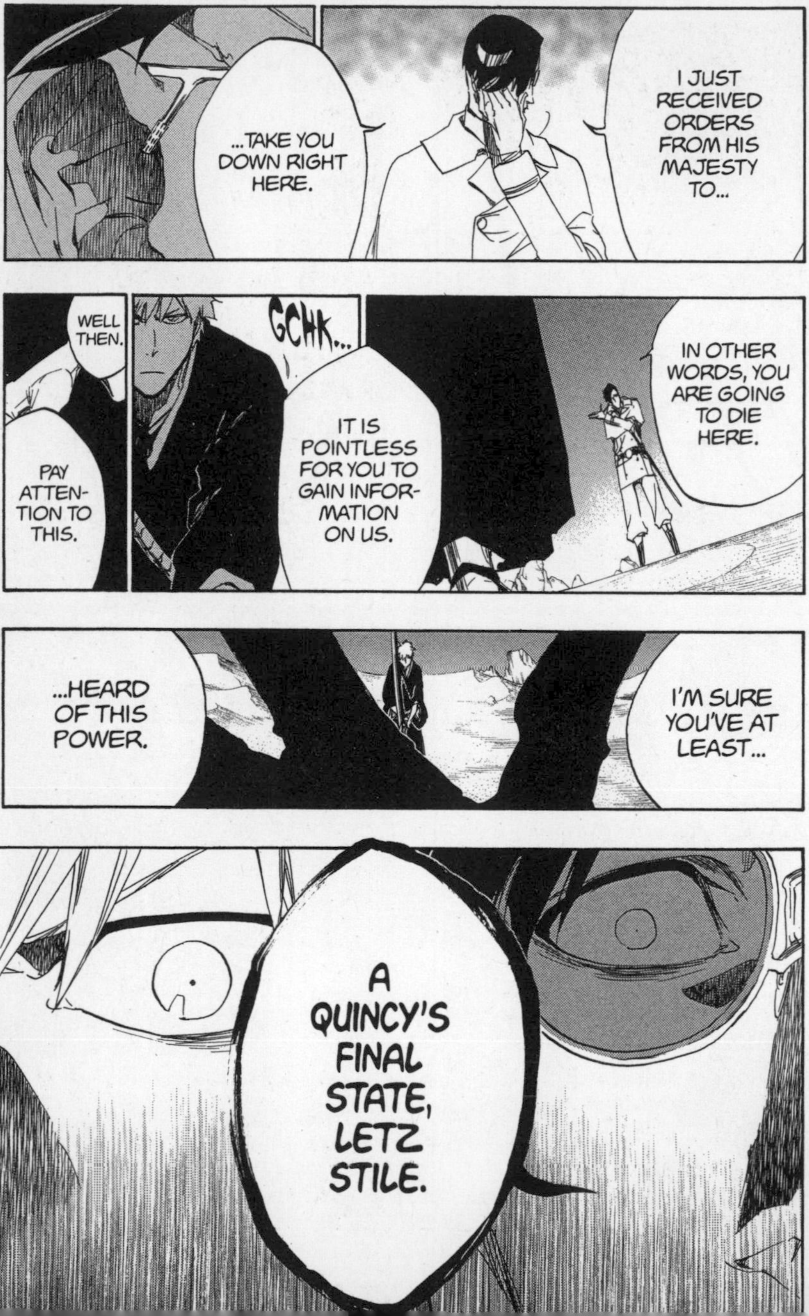
I JUST RECEIVED ORDERS FROM HIS MAJESTY TO...
...TAKE YOU DOWN RIGHT HERE.
IN OTHER WORDS, YOU ARE GOING TO DIE HERE.
GCHK...
IT IS POINTLESS FOR YOU TO GAIN INFORMATION ON US.
WELL THEN.
PAY ATTENTION TO THIS.
I'M SURE YOU'VE AT LEAST...
...HEARD OF THIS POWER.
A QUINCY'S FINAL STATE, LETZ STILE.

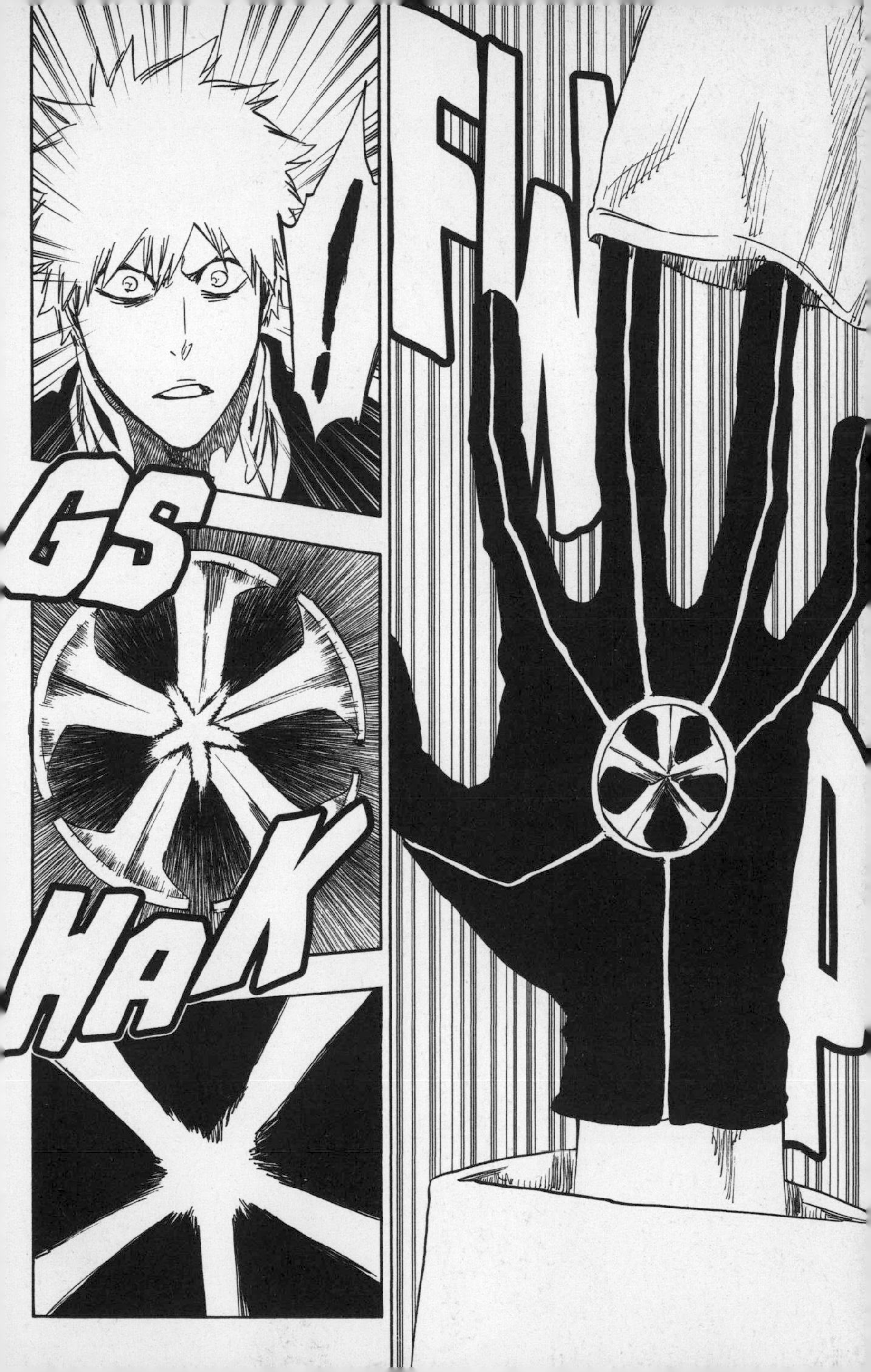
FWUP
!
GS
HAK

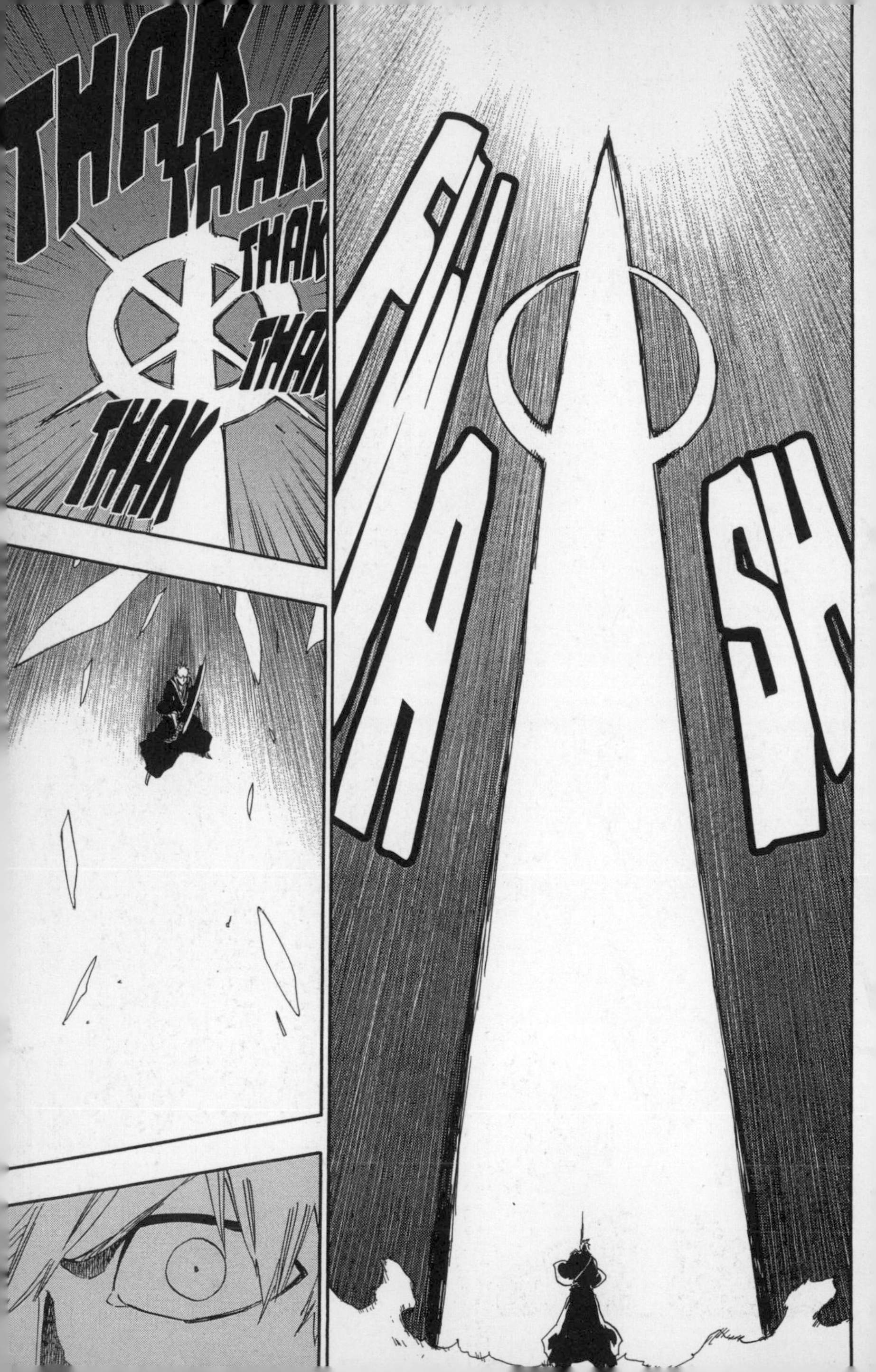
SH
THAK
THAK
THAK
THAK
THAK

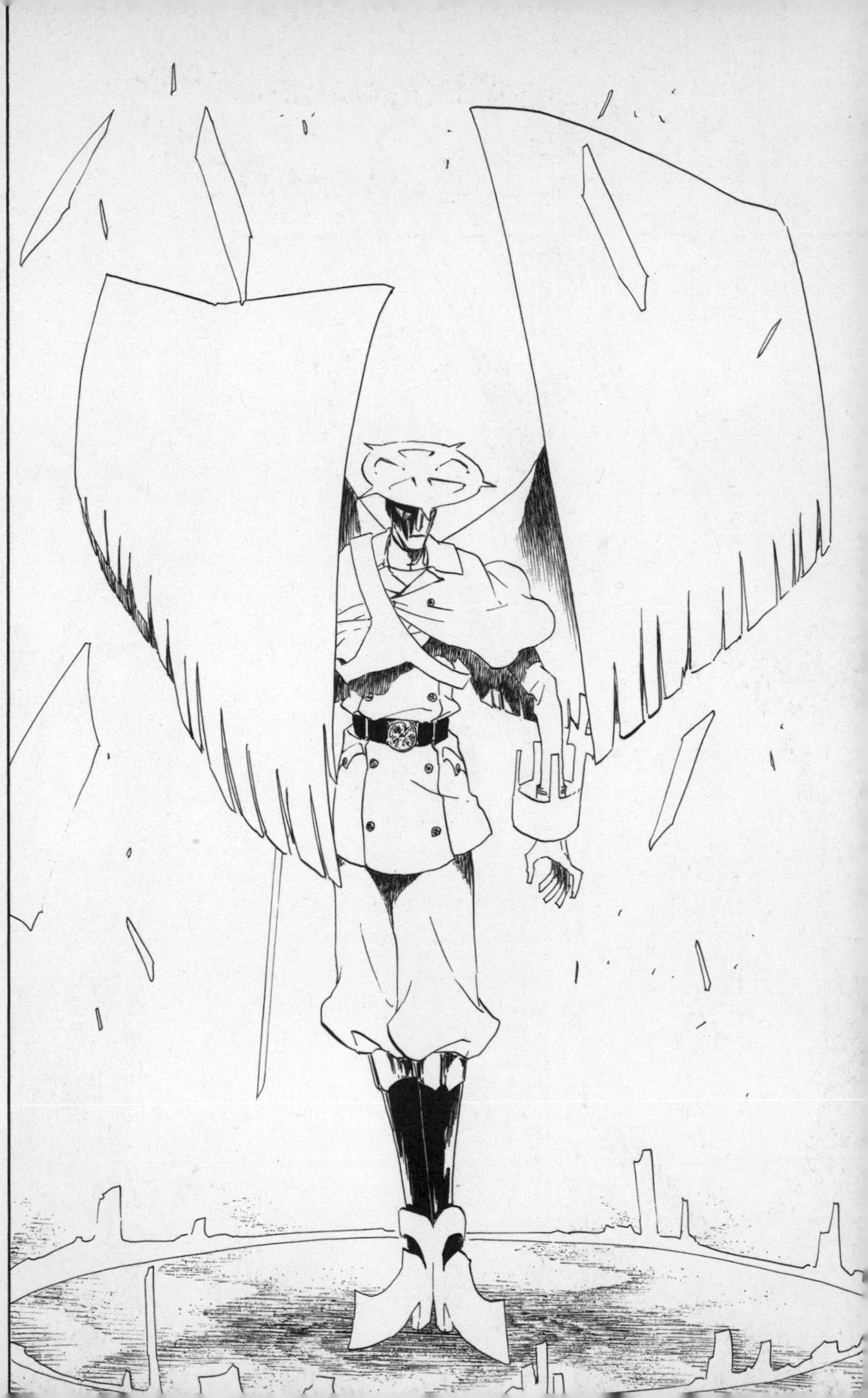

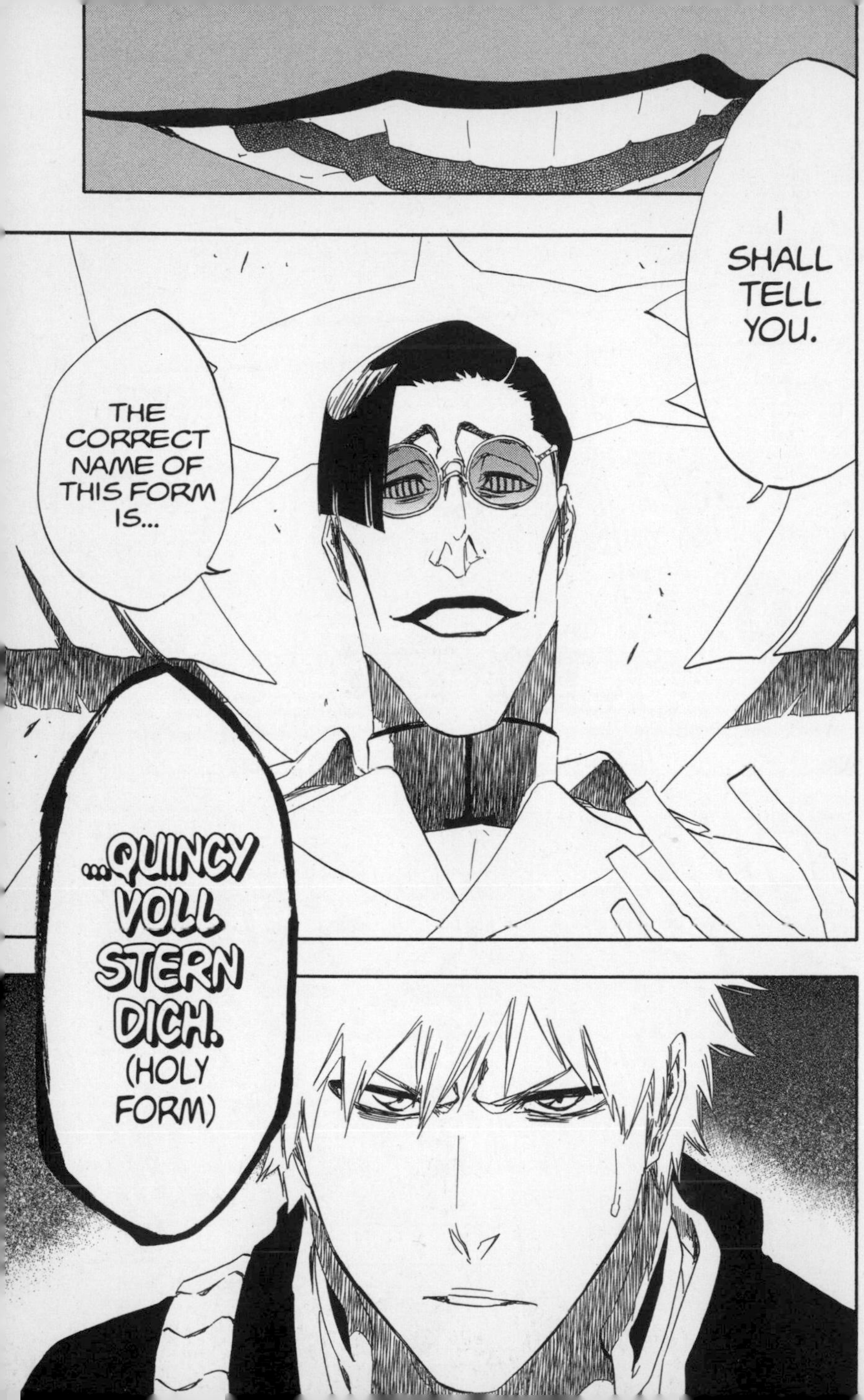
I SHALL TELL YOU.
THE CORRECT NAME OF THIS FORM IS...
...QUINCY VOLL STERN DICH. (HOLY FORM)

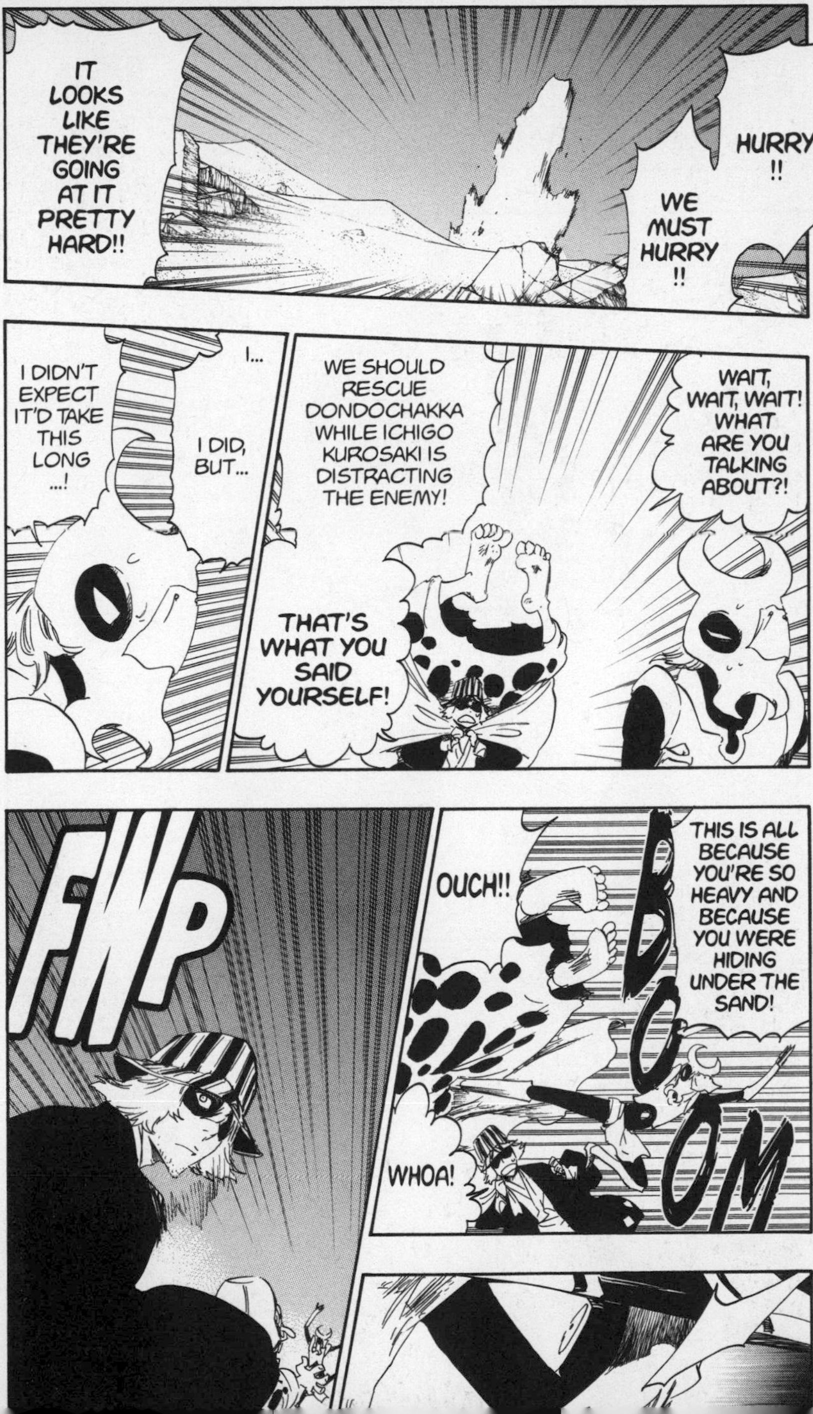
HURRY!!
WE MUST HURRY!!
IT LOOKS LIKE THEY'RE GOING AT IT PRETTY HARD!!
WAIT, WAIT, WAIT! WHAT ARE YOU TALKING ABOUT?!
WE SHOULD RESCUE DONDOCHAKKA WHILE ICHIGO KUROSAKI IS DISTRACTING THE ENEMY!
THAT'S WHAT YOU SAID YOURSELF!
I...
I DID, BUT...
I DIDN'T EXPECT IT'D TAKE THIS LONG...!
THIS IS ALL BECAUSE YOU'RE SO HEAVY AND BECAUSE YOU WERE HIDING UNDER THE SAND!
BOOM
OUCH!!
WHOA!
FNP

READ THIS WAY

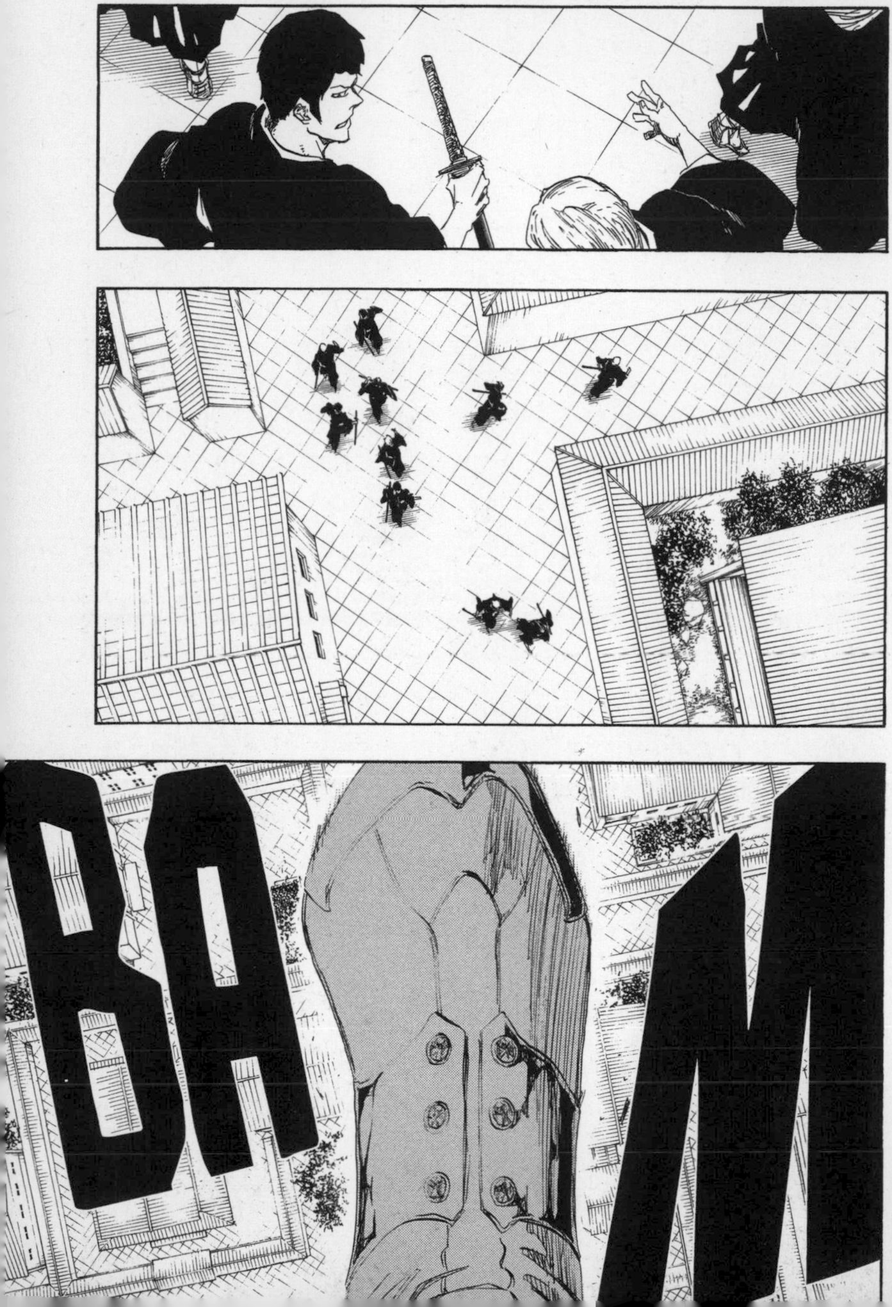
BAM

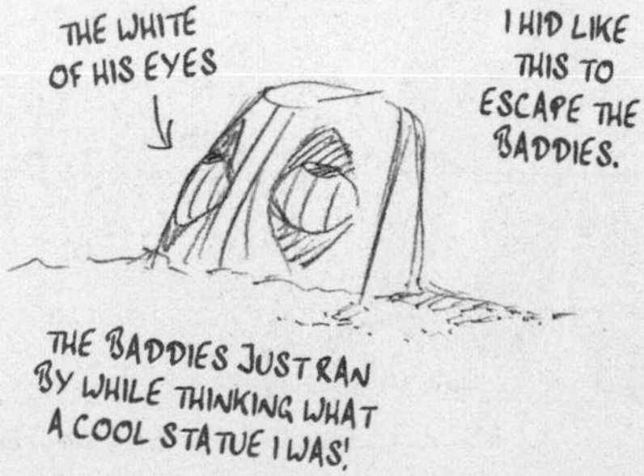
THE WHITE OF HIS EYES
I HID LIKE THIS TO ESCAPE THE BADDIES.
THE BADDIES JUST RAN BY WHILE THINKING WHAT A COOL STATUE I WAS!

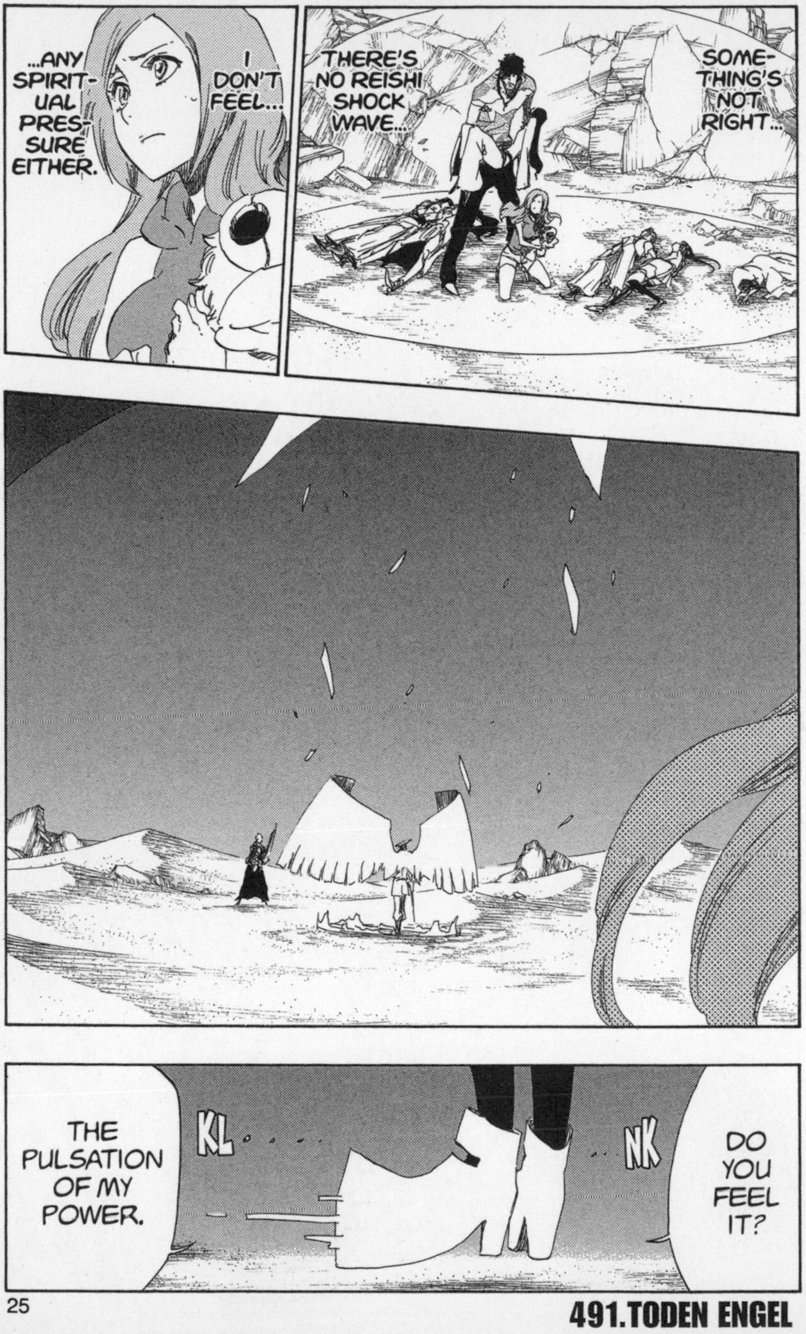
SOMETHING'S NOT RIGHT...
THERE'S NO REISHI SHOCK WAVE...
I DON'T FEEL...
...ANY SPIRITUAL PRESSURE EITHER.
DO YOU FEEL IT?
KL...NK
THE PULSATION OF MY POWER.

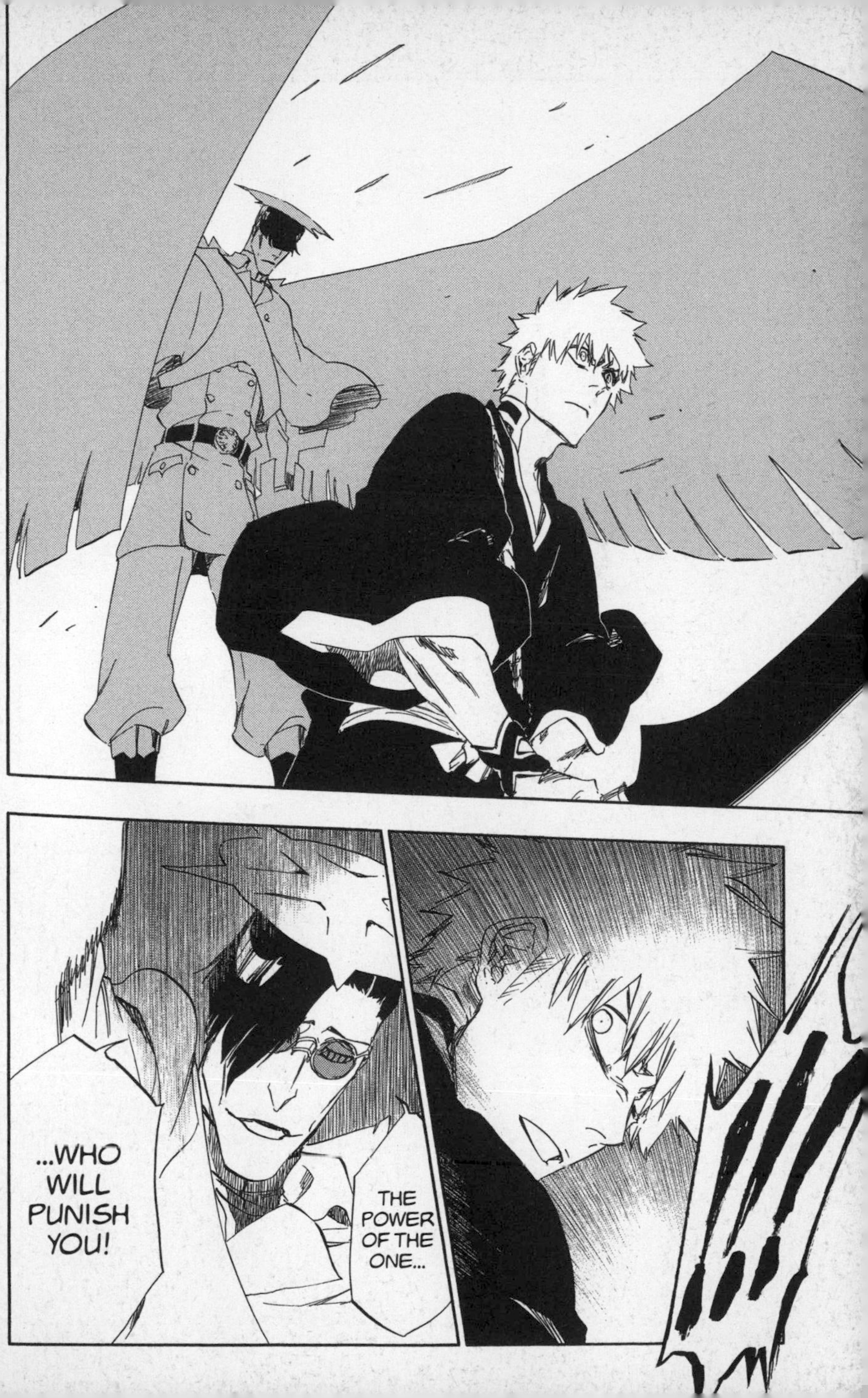
THE POWER OF THE ONE...
...WHO WILL PUNISH YOU!

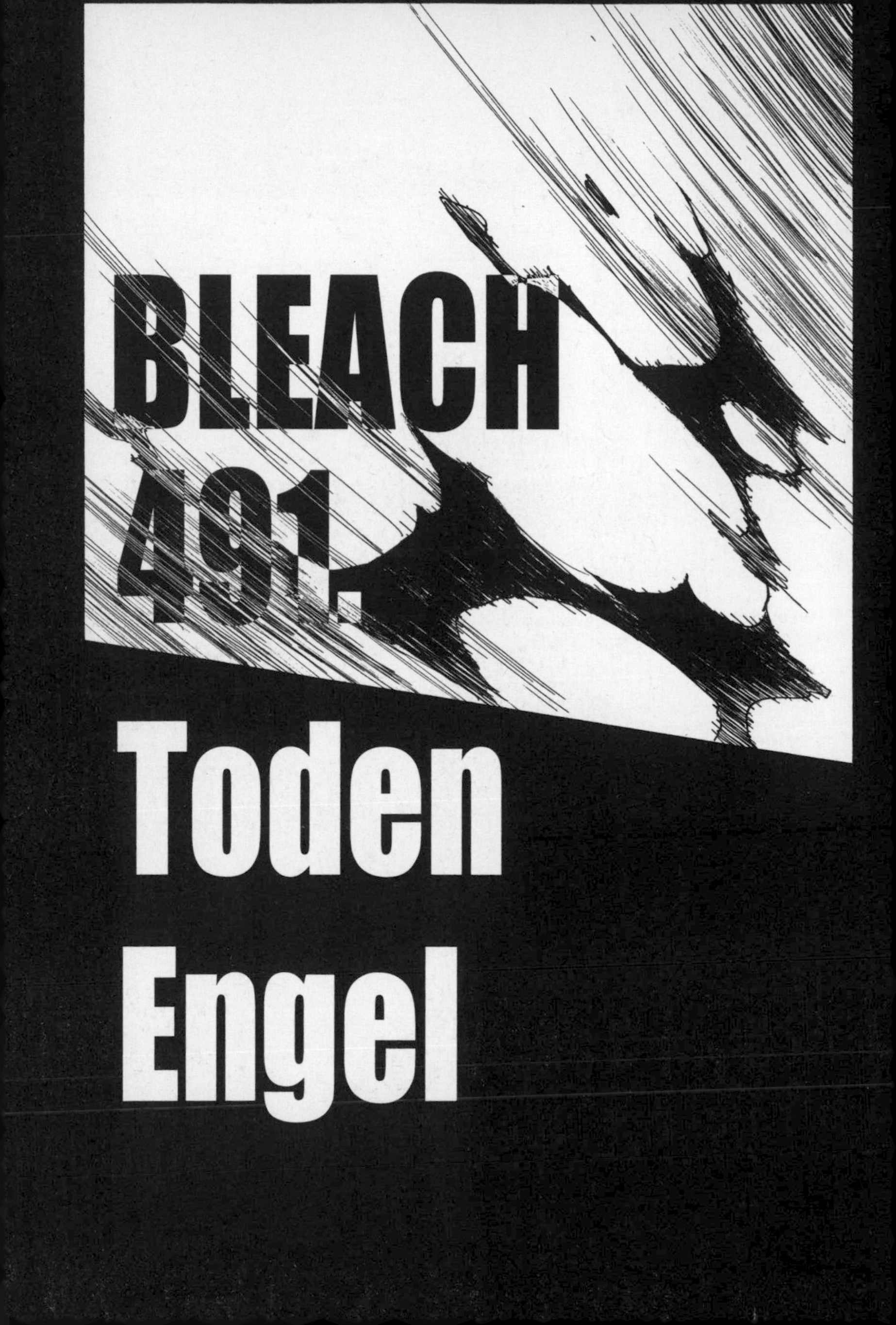

BLEACH 491. Toden Engel

QUINCY LETZ STILE

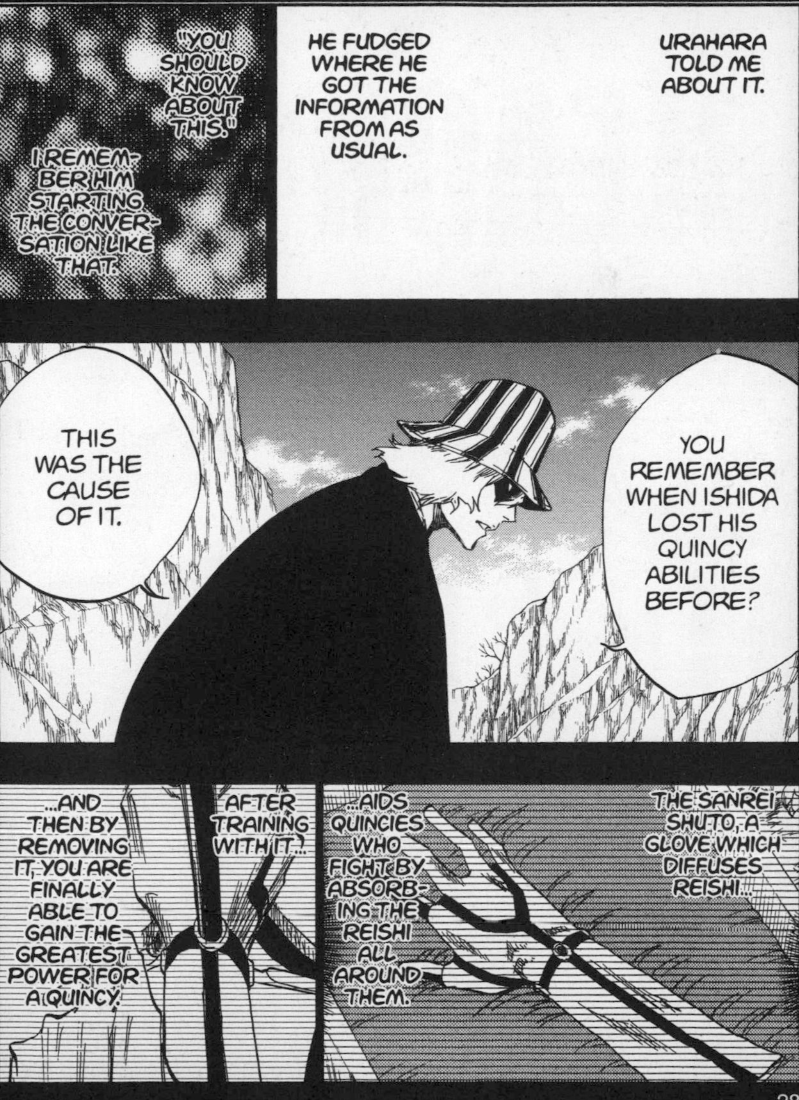
URAHARA TOLD ME ABOUT IT.
HE FUDGED WHERE HE GOT THE INFORMATION FROM AS USUAL.
"YOU SHOULD KNOW ABOUT THIS."
I REMEMBER HIM STARTING THE CONVERSATION LIKE THAT.
YOU REMEMBER WHEN ISHIDA LOST HIS QUINCY ABILITIES BEFORE?
THIS WAS THE CAUSE OF IT.
THE SANREI SHUTO, A GLOVE WHICH DIFFUSES REISHI...
...AIDS QUINCIES WHO FIGHT BY ABSORBING THE REISHI ALL AROUND THEM.
AFTER TRAINING WITH IT...
...AND THEN BY REMOVING IT, YOU ARE FINALLY ABLE TO GAIN THE GREATEST POWER FOR A QUINCY.

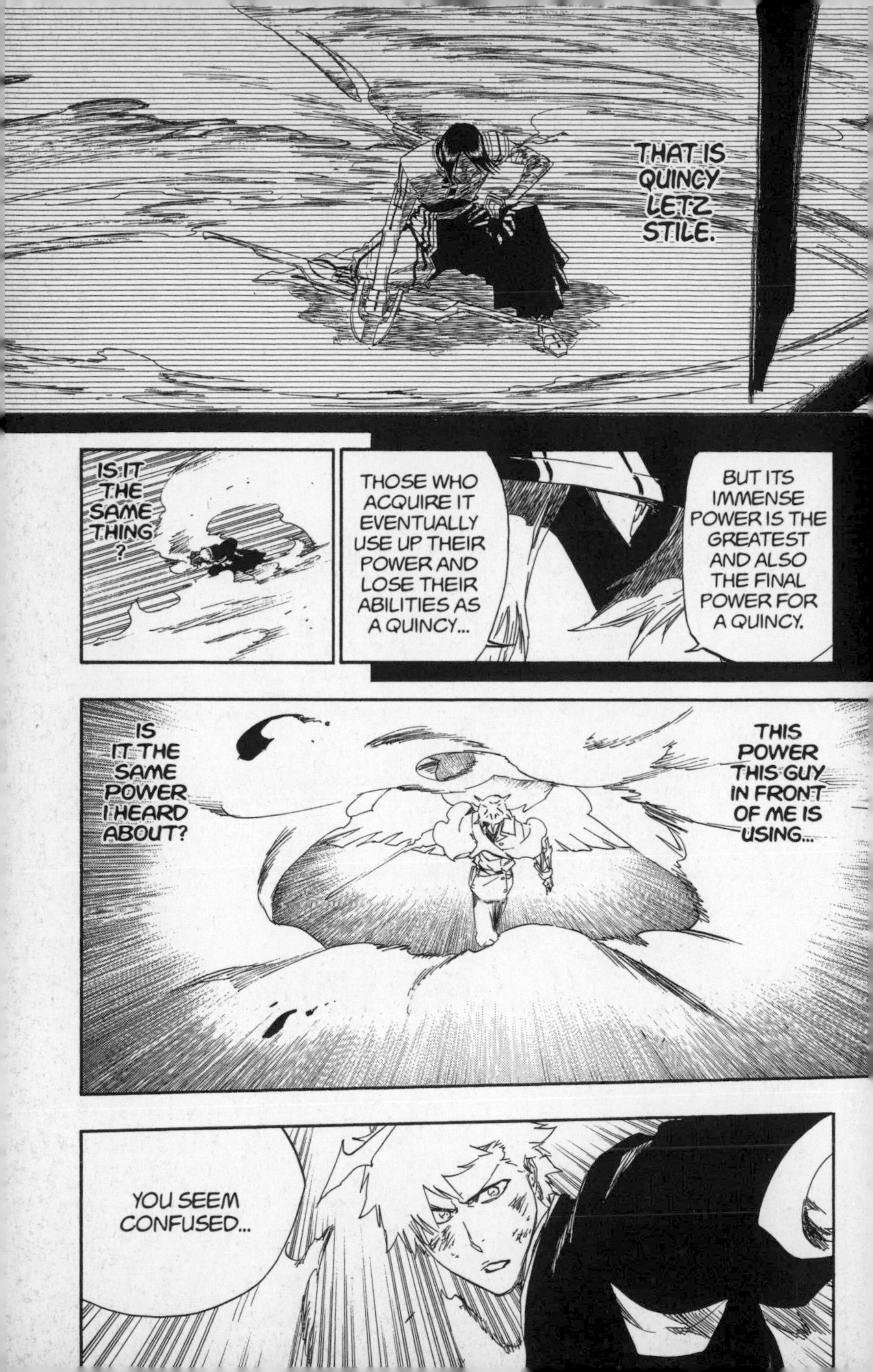
THAT IS QUINCY LETZ STILE.
BUT ITS IMMENSE POWER IS THE GREATEST AND ALSO THE FINAL POWER FOR A QUINCY.
THOSE WHO ACQUIRE IT EVENTUALLY USE UP THEIR POWER AND LOSE THEIR ABILITIES AS A QUINCY...
IS IT THE SAME THING?
THIS POWER THIS GUY IN FRONT OF ME IS USING...
IS IT THE SAME POWER I HEARD ABOUT?
YOU SEEM CONFUSED...

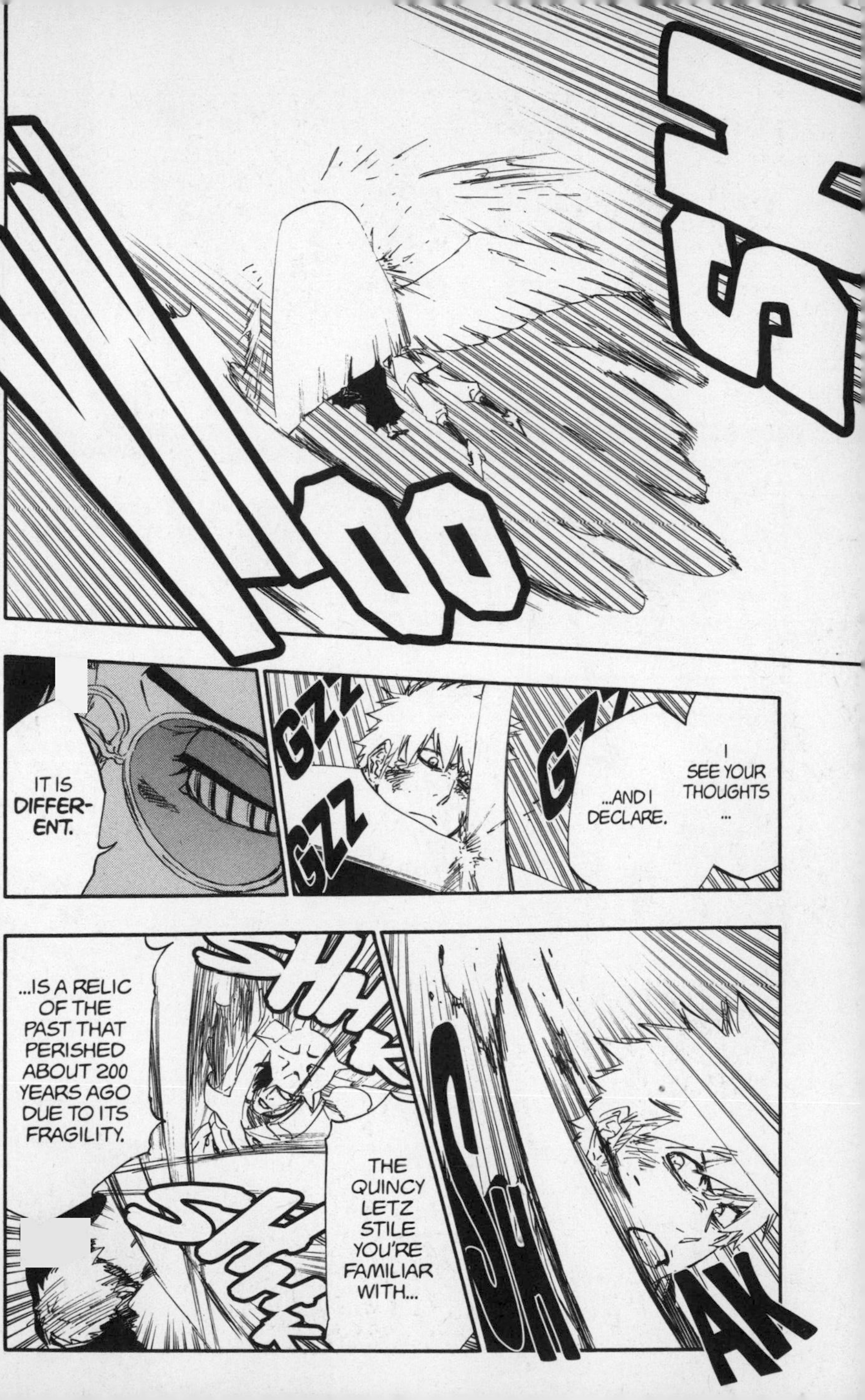
I SEE YOUR THOUGHTS ...
...AND I DECLARE.
GZZ GZZ
IT IS DIFFERENT.
THE QUINCY LETZ STILE YOU'RE FAMILIAR WITH...
...IS A RELIC OF THE PAST THAT PERISHED ABOUT 200 YEARS AGO DUE TO ITS FRAGILITY.

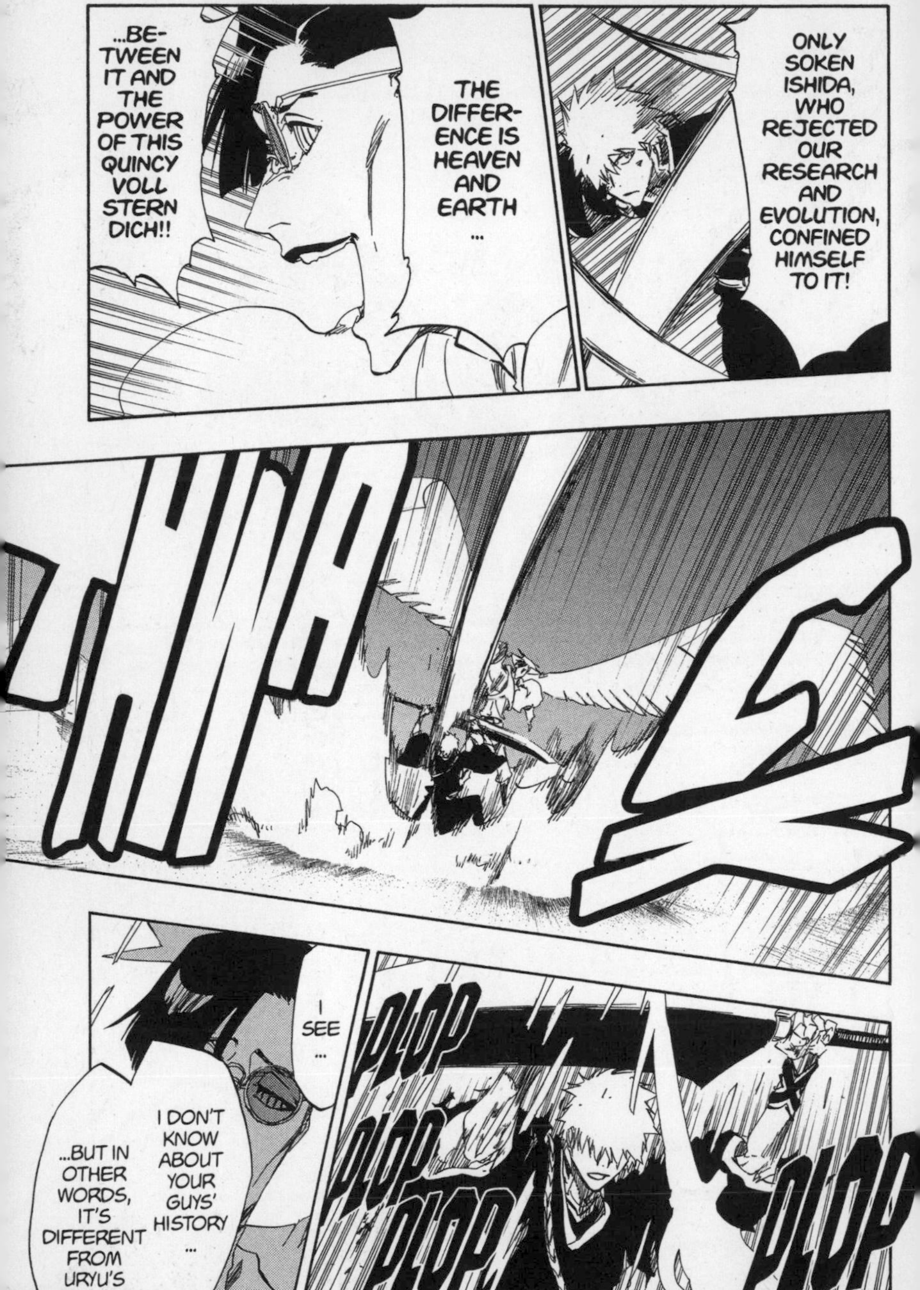
ONLY SOKEN ISHIDA, WHO REJECTED OUR RESEARCH AND EVOLUTION, CONFINED HIMSELF TO IT!
THE DIFFERENCE IS HEAVEN AND EARTH ...
...BETWEEN IT AND THE POWER OF THIS QUINCY VOLLSTERNDICH!!
PLOP
PLOP
PLOP
PLOP
PLOP
I SEE ...
I DON'T KNOW ABOUT YOUR GUYS' HISTORY ...
...BUT IN OTHER WORDS, IT'S DIFFERENT FROM URYU'S POWER.

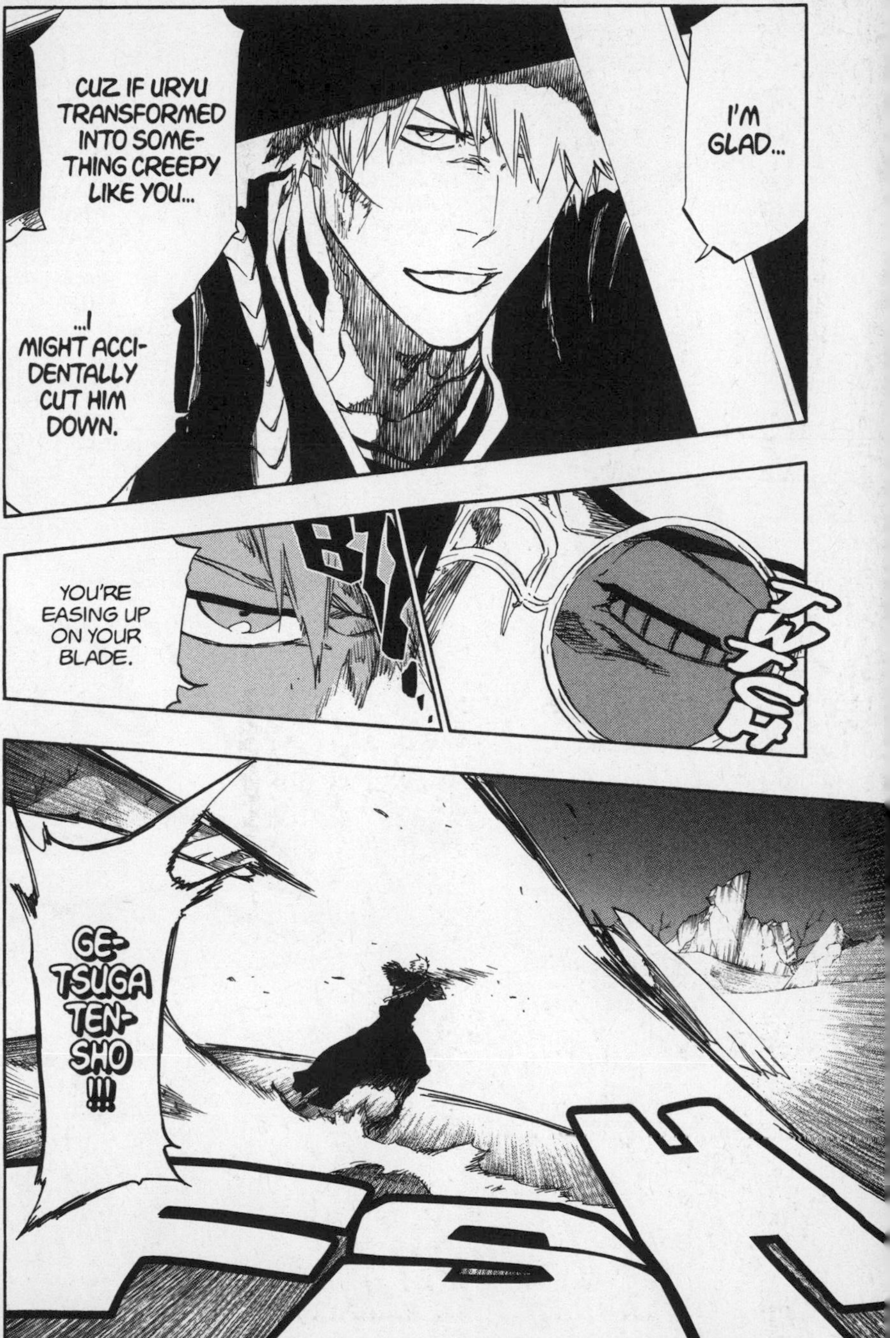
I'M GLAD...
CUZ IF URYU TRANSFORMED INTO SOMETHING CREEPY LIKE YOU...
...I MIGHT ACCIDENTALLY CUT HIM DOWN.
YOU'RE EASING UP ON YOUR BLADE.
GETSUGA TENSHO!!!

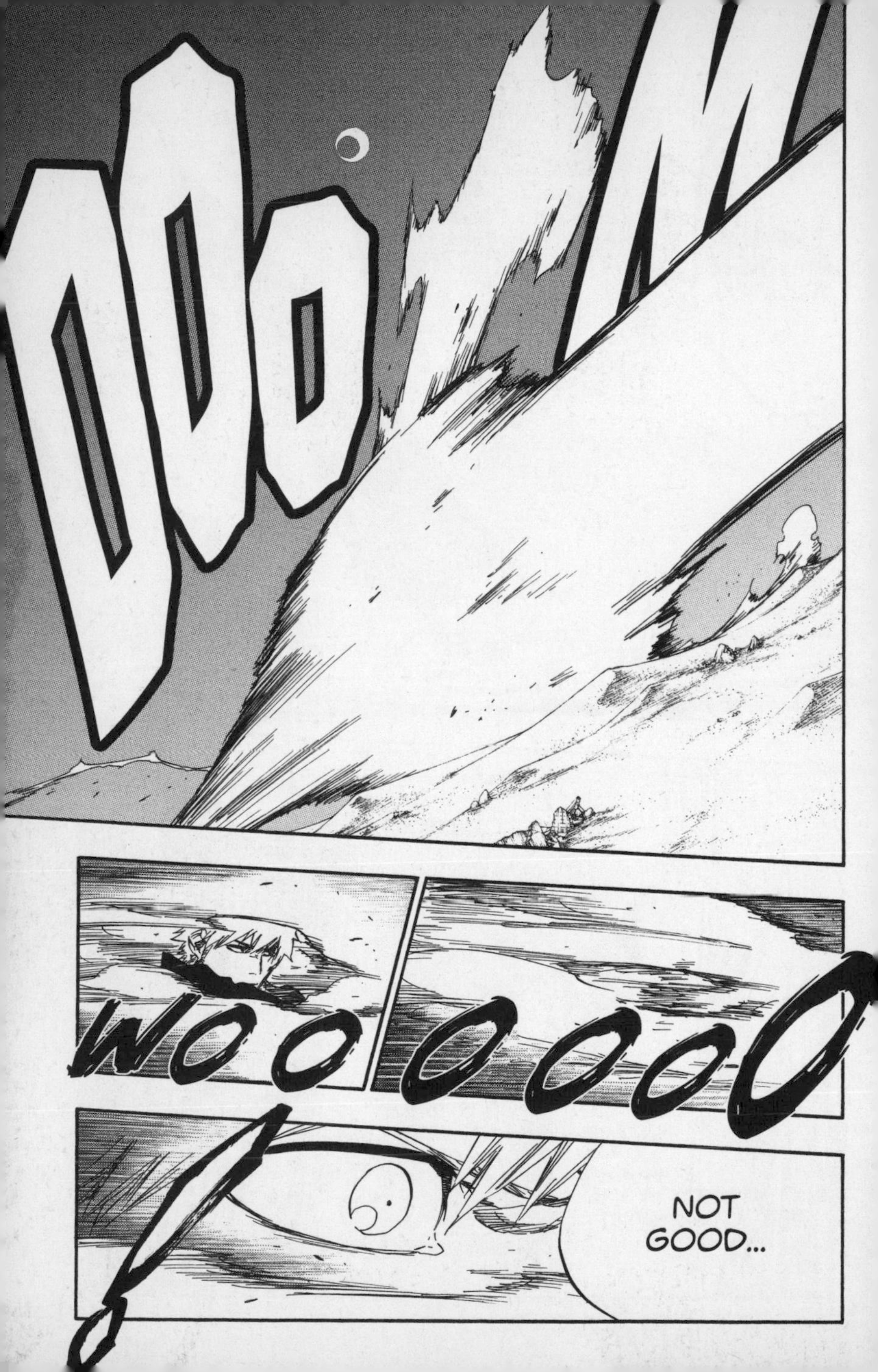
DOOM
WOOOOOO!
NOT GOOD...

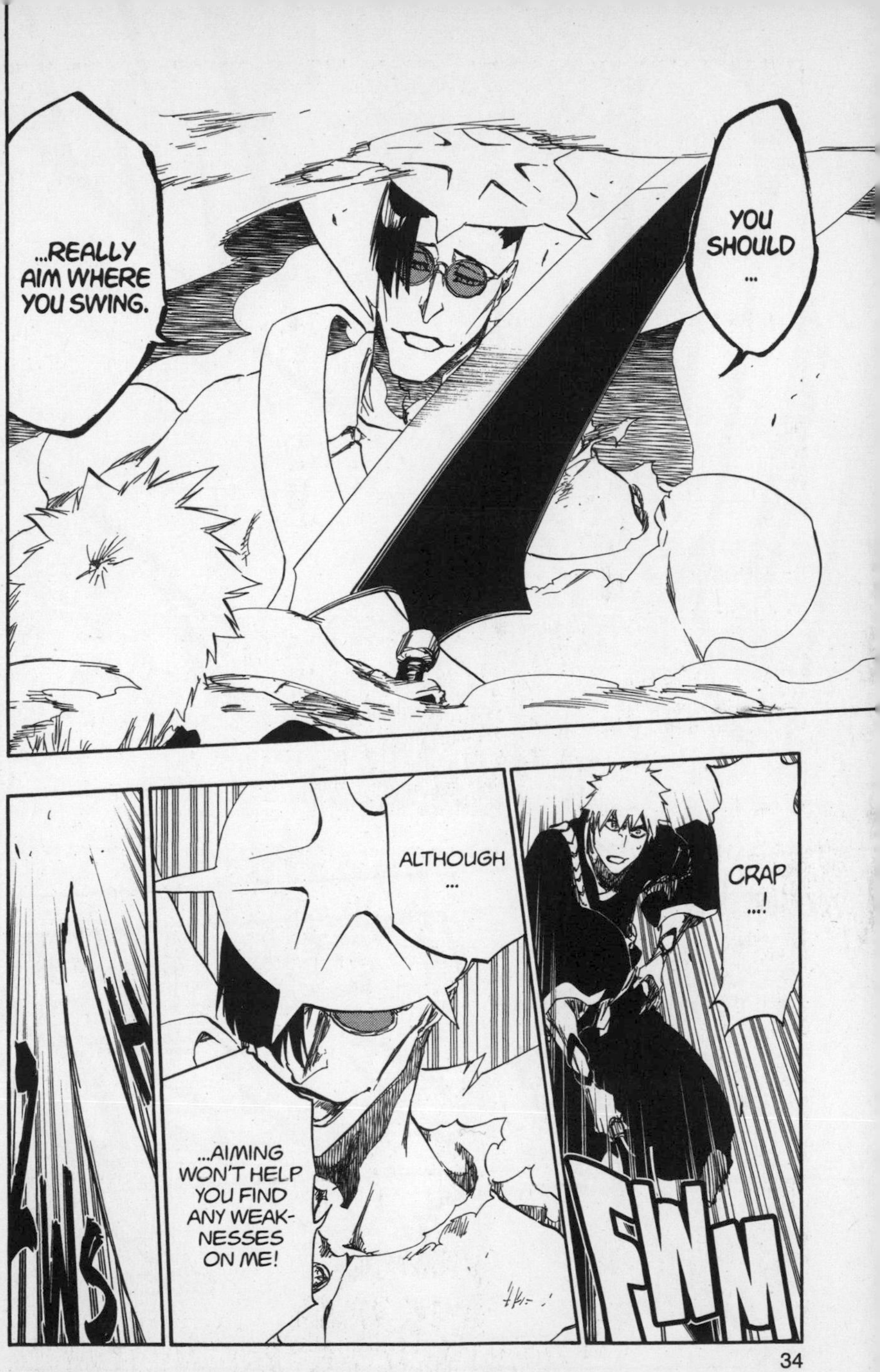
YOU SHOULD ...
...REALLY AIM WHERE YOU SWING.
CRAP ...!
ALTHOUGH ...
...AIMING WON'T HELP YOU FIND ANY WEAK-NESSES ON ME!

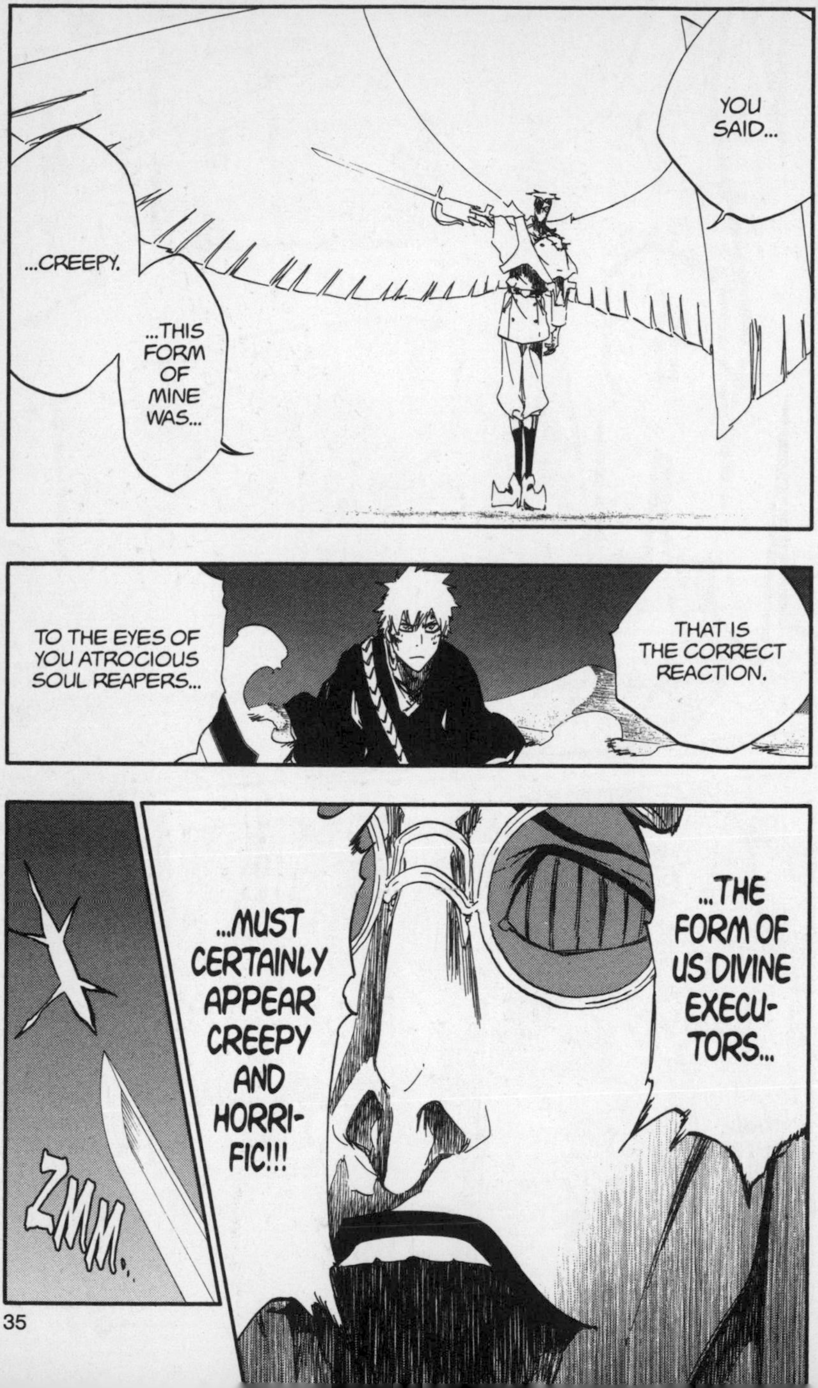
YOU SAID...
...THIS FORM OF MINE WAS...
...CREEPY.
THAT IS THE CORRECT REACTION.
TO THE EYES OF YOU ATROCIOUS SOUL REAPERS...
...THE FORM OF US DIVINE EXECUTORS...
...MUST CERTAINLY APPEAR CREEPY AND HORRIFIC!!!
ZMM..

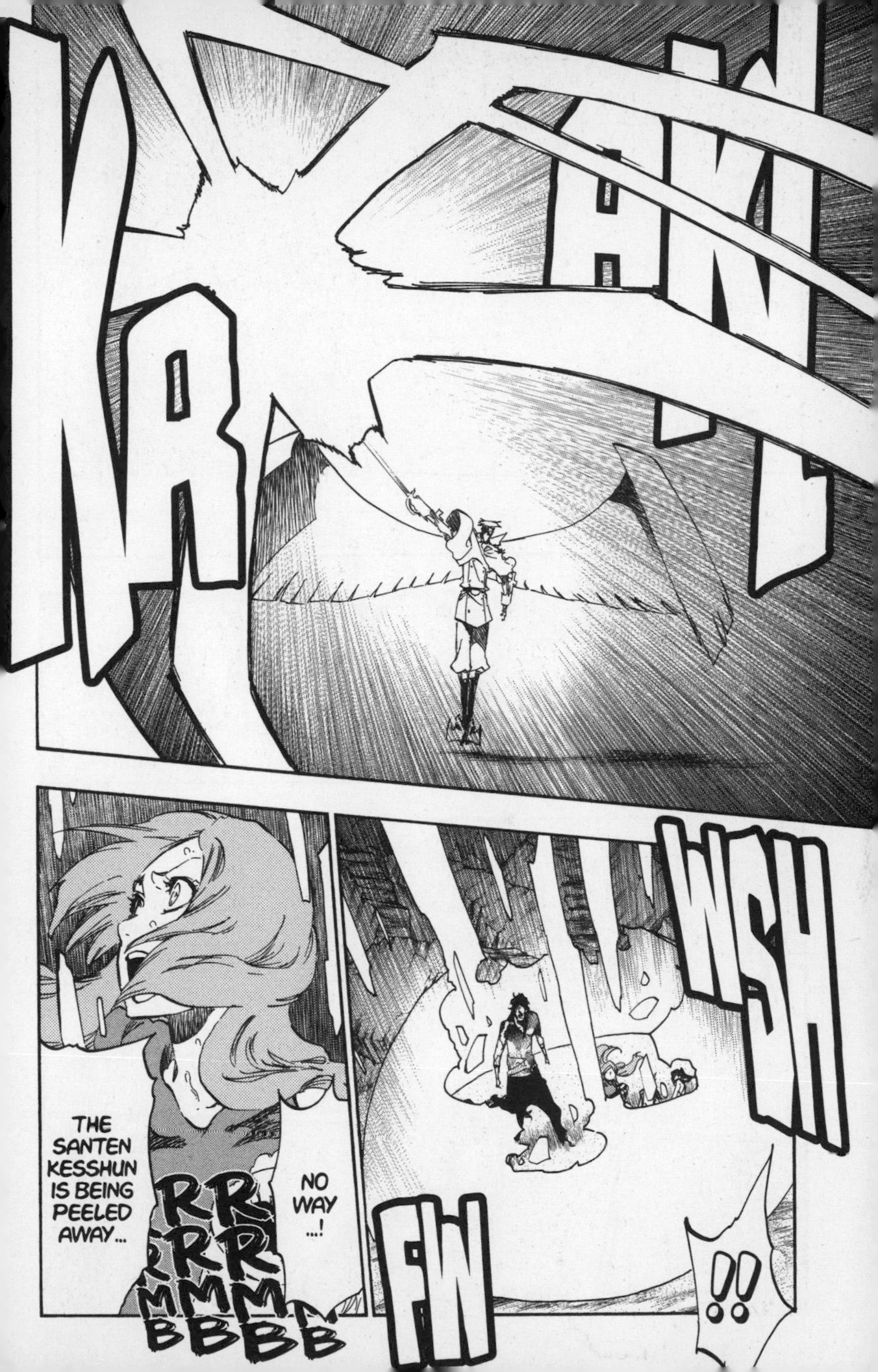

WSH
!!
NO WAY...!
THE SANTEN KESSHUN IS BEING PEELED AWAY...
RRRRMMMMBBBB

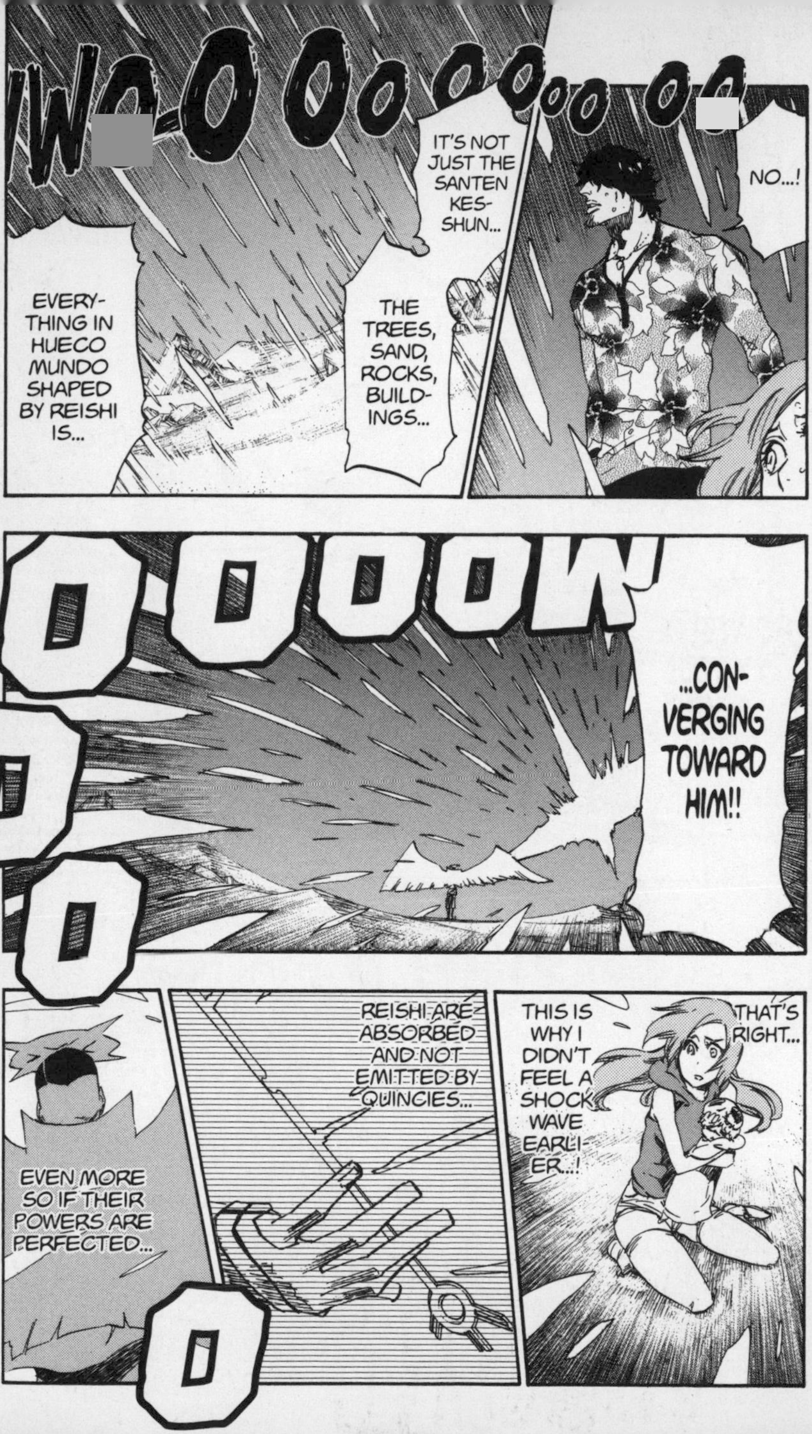
WOOOOOOOOOO
NO...!
IT'S NOT JUST THE SANTEN KES-SHUN...
THE TREES, SAND, ROCKS, BUILD-INGS...
EVERY-THING IN HUECO MUNDO SHAPED BY REISHI IS...
OOOOW
...CON-VERGING TOWARD HIM!!
OOO
THAT'S RIGHT...
THIS IS WHY I DIDN'T FEEL A SHOCK WAVE EARLI-ER...!
REISHI ARE ABSORBED AND NOT EMITTED BY QUINCIES...
EVEN MORE SO IF THEIR POWERS ARE PERFECTED...
O

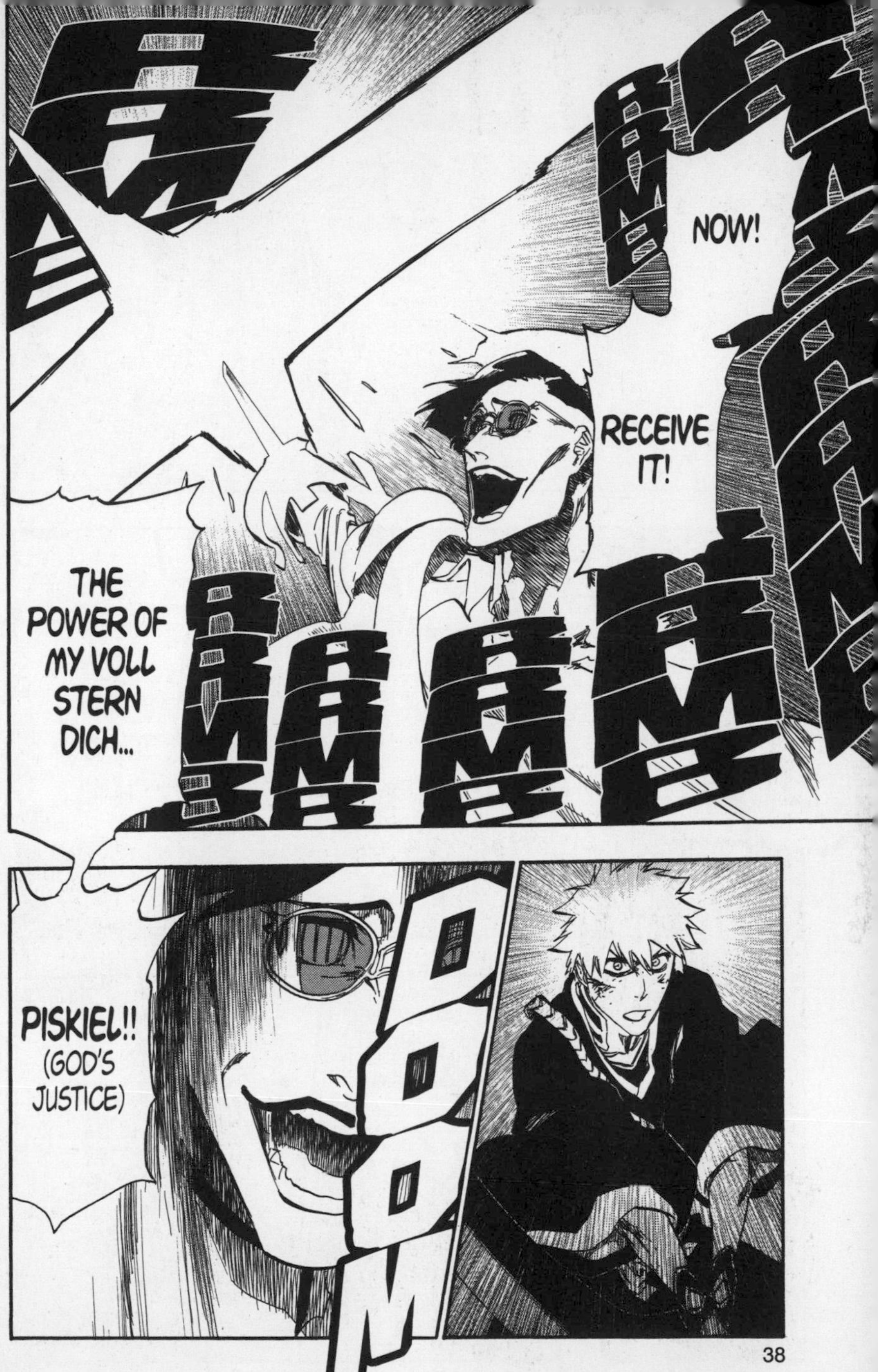
NOW!
RECEIVE IT!
THE POWER OF MY VOLL STERN DICH...
PISKIEL!! (GOD'S JUSTICE)
DOOOM

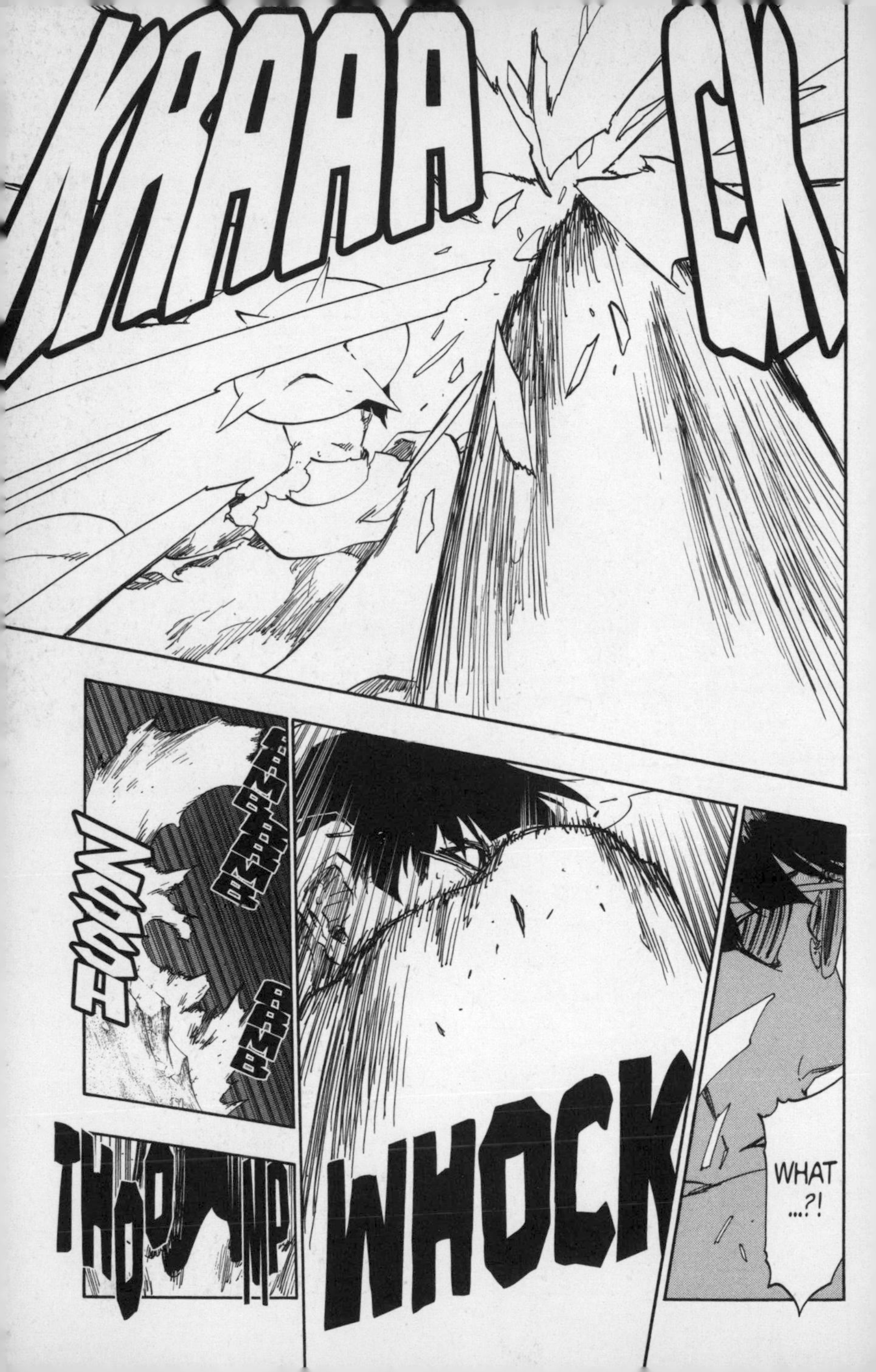
KRAAA-CK
WHAT ...?!
WHOCK

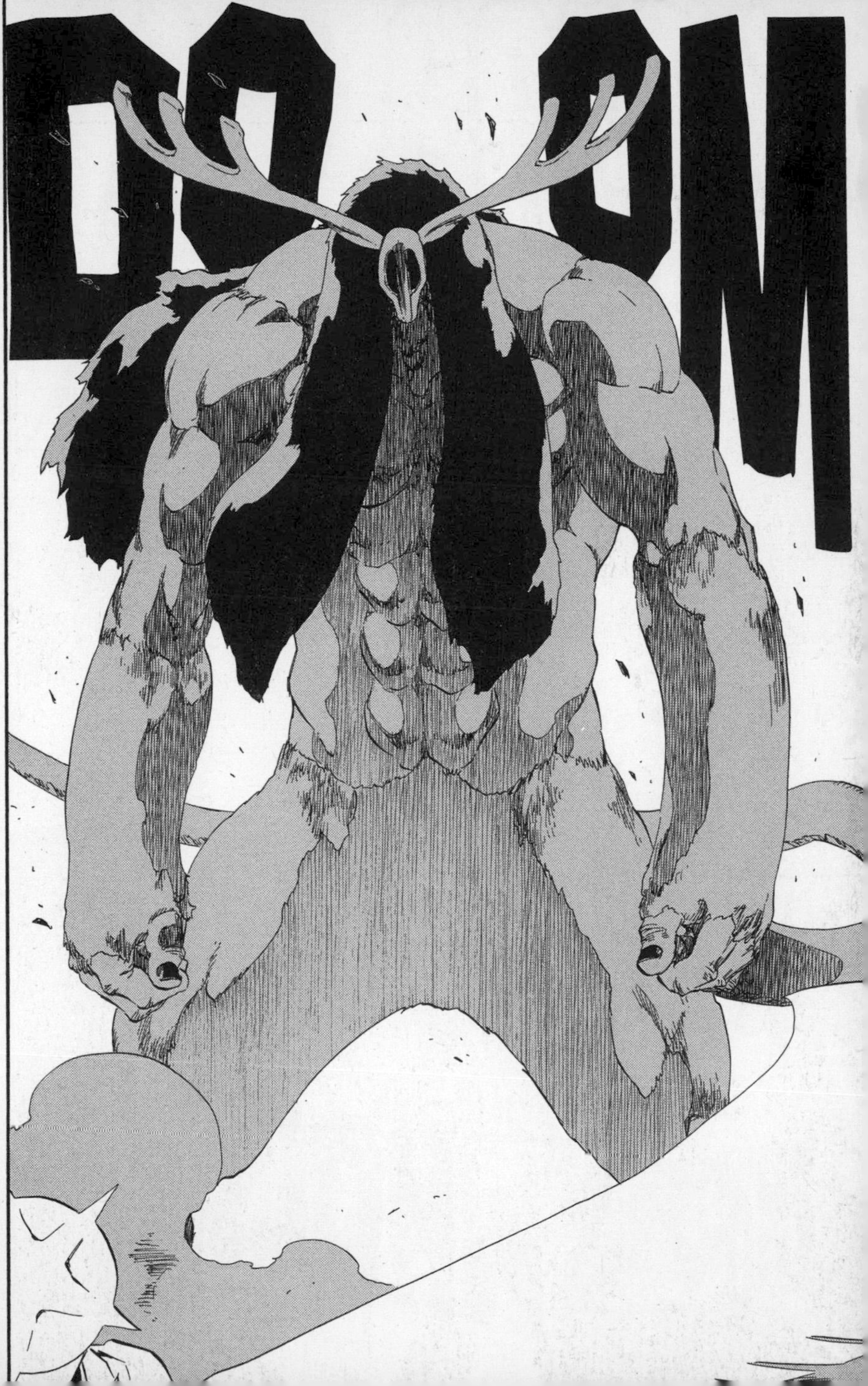
DOOM

READ THIS WAY

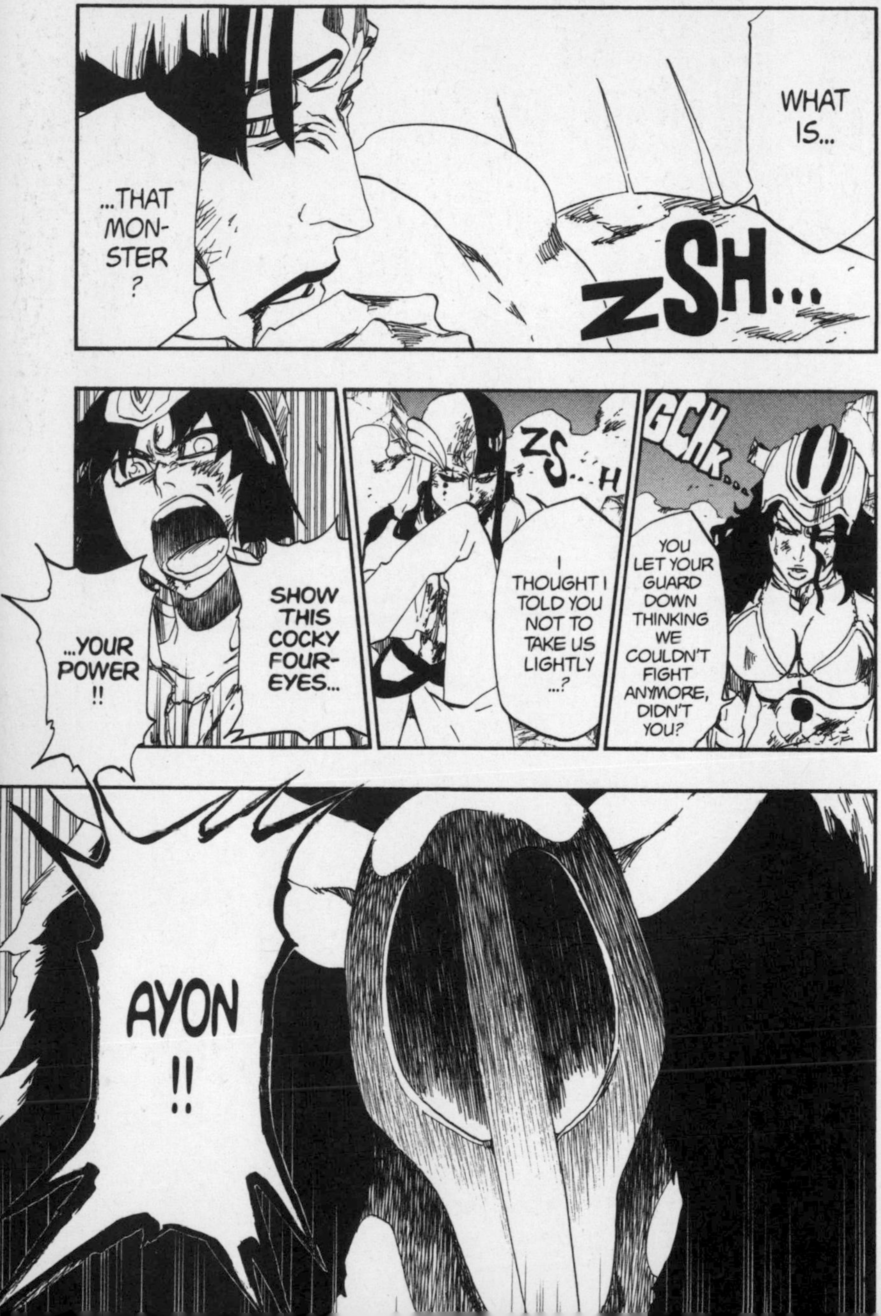
WHAT IS...
ZSH...
...THAT MONSTER?
GCHK...
YOU LET YOUR GUARD DOWN THINKING WE COULDN'T FIGHT ANYMORE, DIDN'T YOU?
ZS...H
I THOUGHT I TOLD YOU NOT TO TAKE US LIGHTLY...?
SHOW THIS COCKY FOUR-EYES...
...YOUR POWER!!
AYON!!

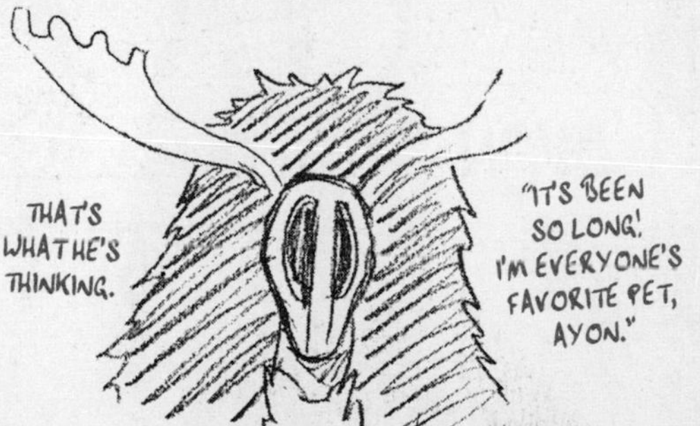
"IT'S BEEN SO LONG! I'M EVERYONE'S FAVORITE PET, AYON."
THAT'S WHAT HE'S THINKING.

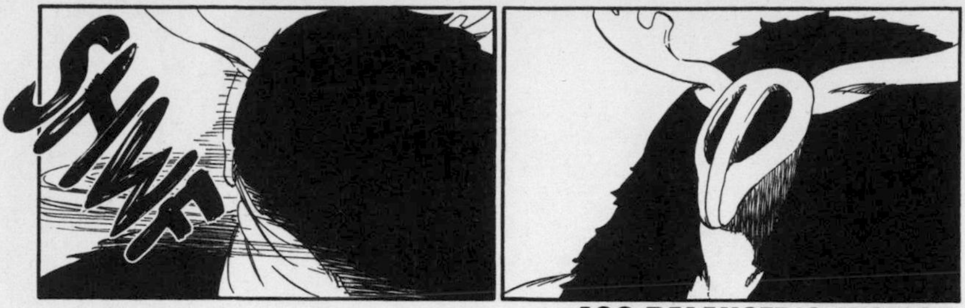
SHWF

492.BALANCER'S JUSTICE

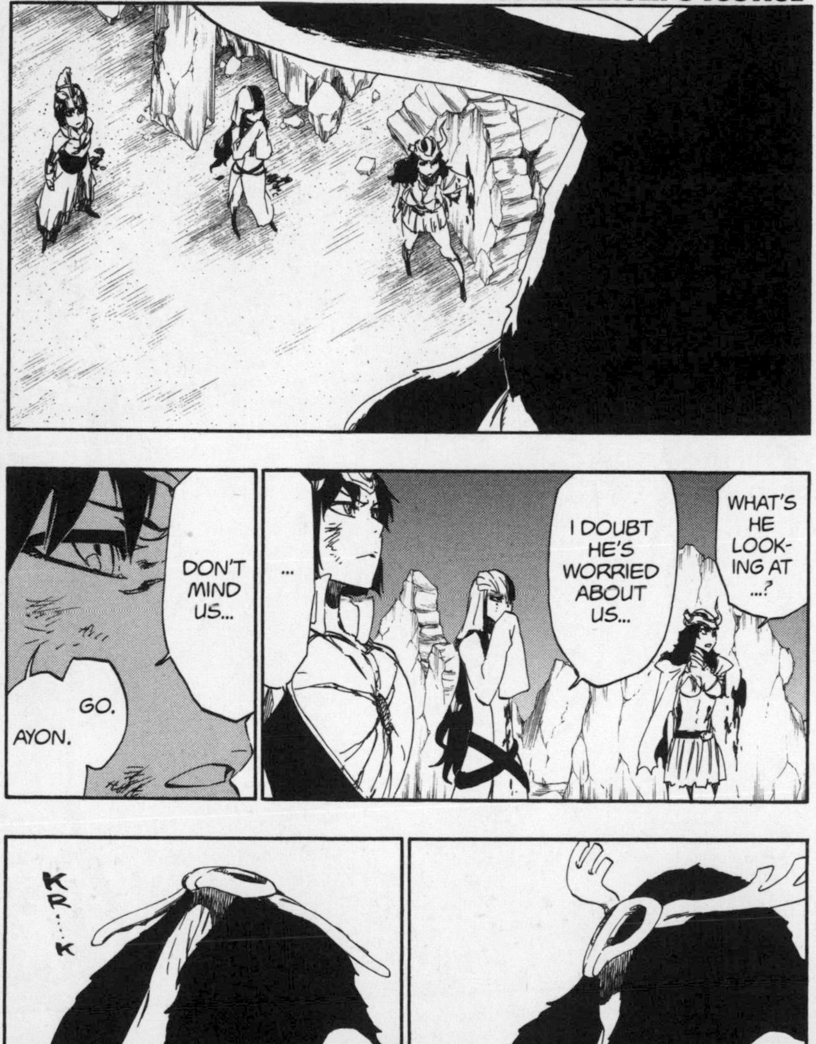
WHAT'S HE LOOKING AT ...?
I DOUBT HE'S WORRIED ABOUT US...
...
DON'T MIND US...
GO.
AYON.
KR....K

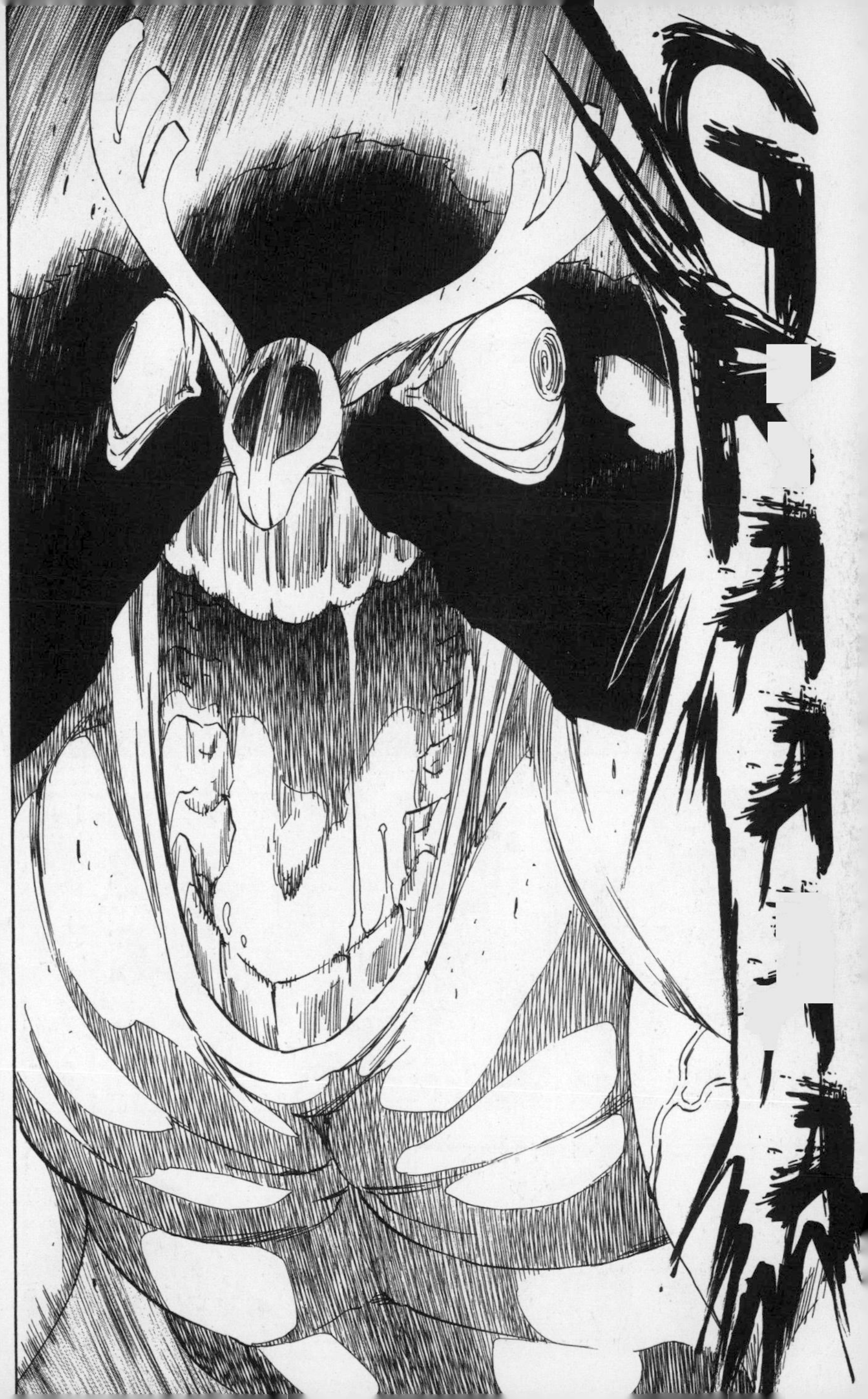

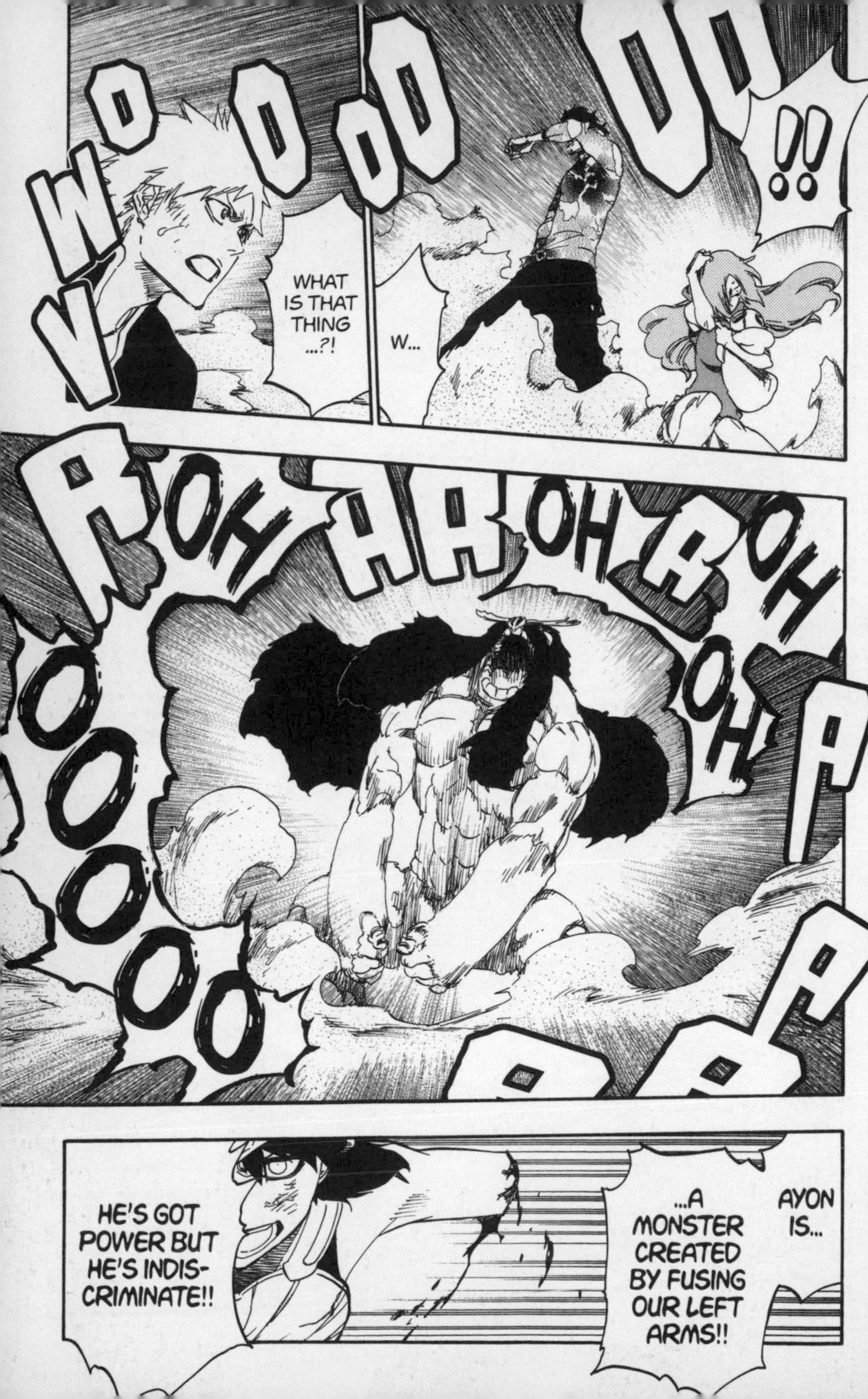
W...
WHAT IS THAT THING ...?!
AYON IS...
...A MONSTER CREATED BY FUSING OUR LEFT ARMS!!
HE'S GOT POWER BUT HE'S INDIS-CRIMINATE!!

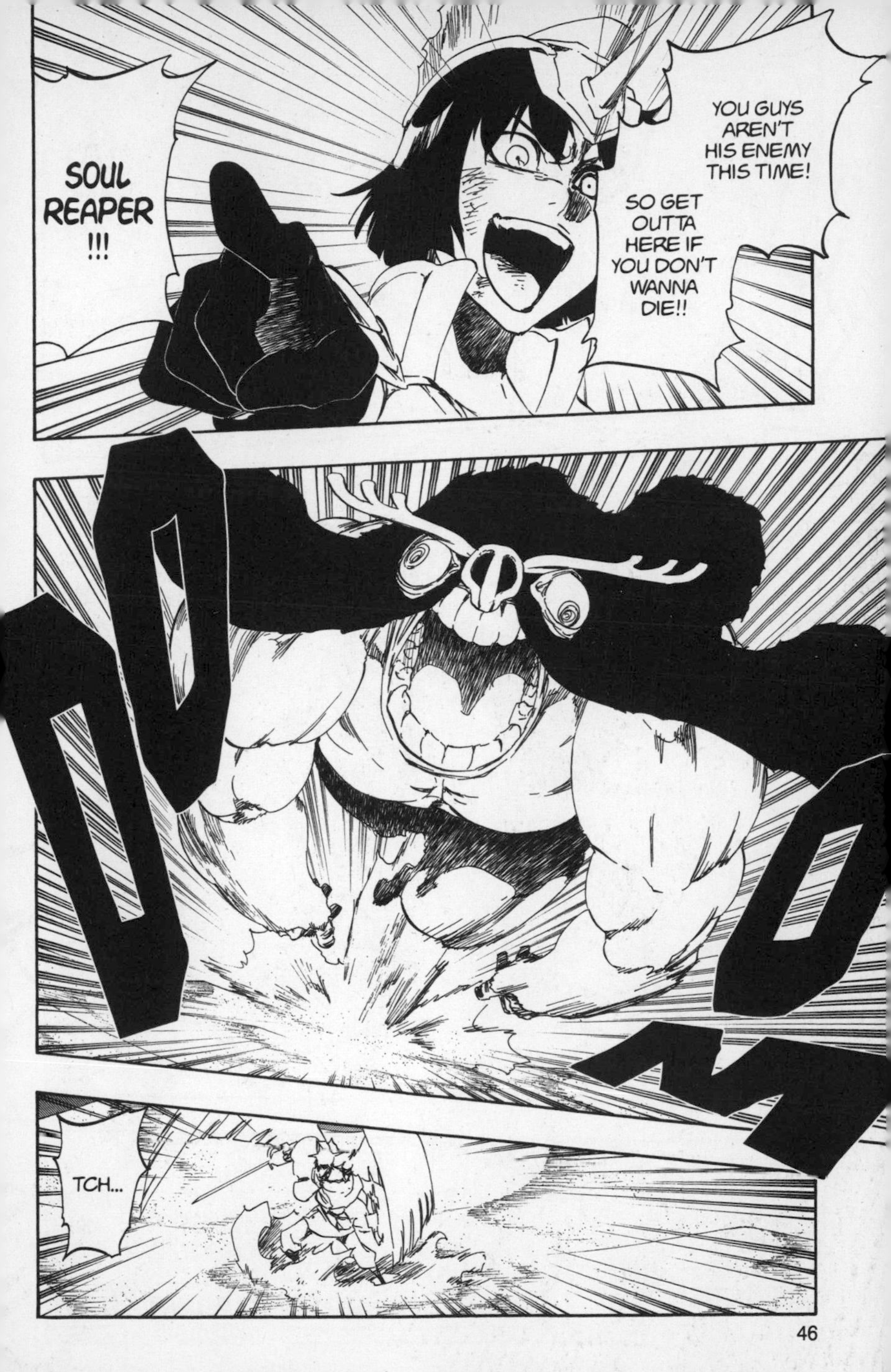
YOU GUYS AREN'T HIS ENEMY THIS TIME!
SO GET OUTTA HERE IF YOU DON'T WANNA DIE!!
SOUL REAPER !!!
DOOM
TCH...

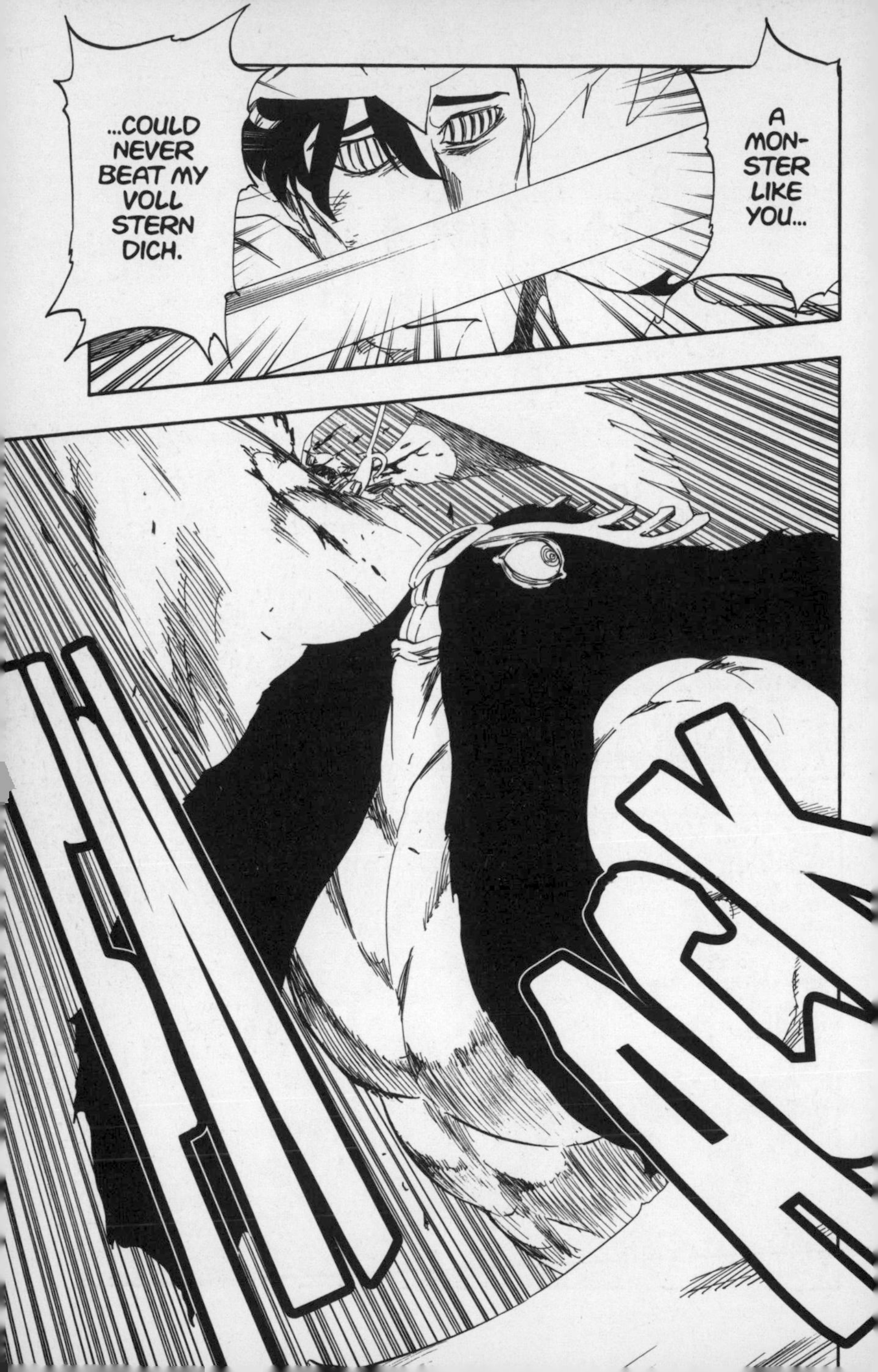
A MON-
STER
LIKE
YOU...
...COULD
NEVER
BEAT MY
VOLL
STERN
DICH.

BLEACH 492.

Balancer's Justice

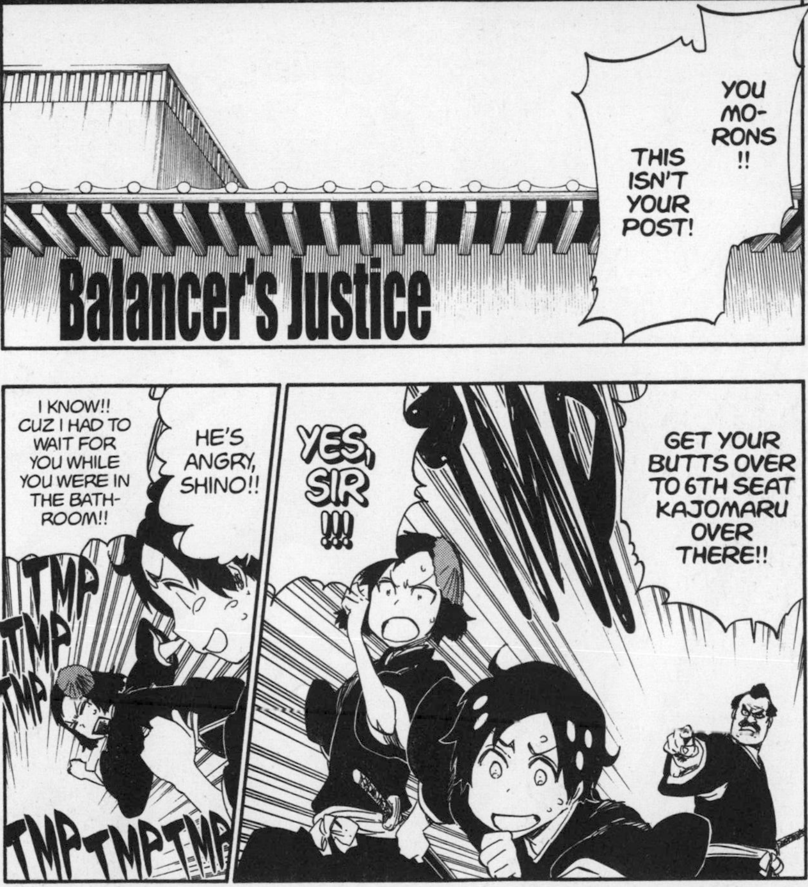
YOU MO-RONS!!
THIS ISN'T YOUR POST!
GET YOUR BUTTS OVER TO 6TH SEAT KAJOMARU OVER THERE!!
YES, SIR!!!
HE'S ANGRY, SHINO!!
I KNOW!! CUZ I HAD TO WAIT FOR YOU WHILE YOU WERE IN THE BATH-ROOM!!
TMP TMP TMP
TMP TMP TMP

READ THIS WAY

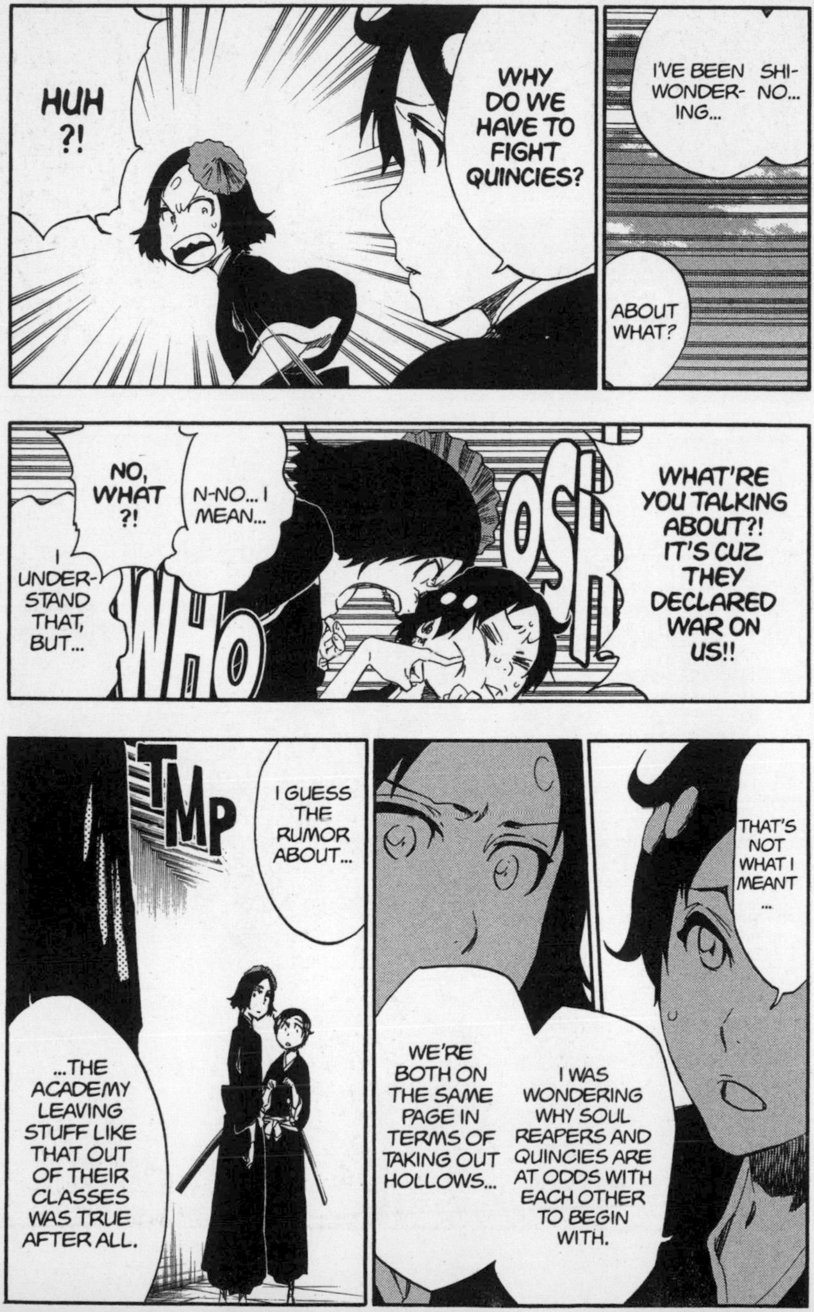
SHI-NO...
I'VE BEEN WONDERING...
ABOUT WHAT?
WHY DO WE HAVE TO FIGHT QUINCIES?
HUH ?!
WHAT'RE YOU TALKING ABOUT?! IT'S CUZ THEY DECLARED WAR ON US!!
WHOOSH
N-NO... I MEAN...
NO, WHAT ?!
I UNDERSTAND THAT, BUT...
THAT'S NOT WHAT I MEANT ...
I WAS WONDERING WHY SOUL REAPERS AND QUINCIES ARE AT ODDS WITH EACH OTHER TO BEGIN WITH.
WE'RE BOTH ON THE SAME PAGE IN TERMS OF TAKING OUT HOLLOWS...
TMP
I GUESS THE RUMOR ABOUT...
...THE ACADEMY LEAVING STUFF LIKE THAT OUT OF THEIR CLASSES WAS TRUE AFTER ALL.

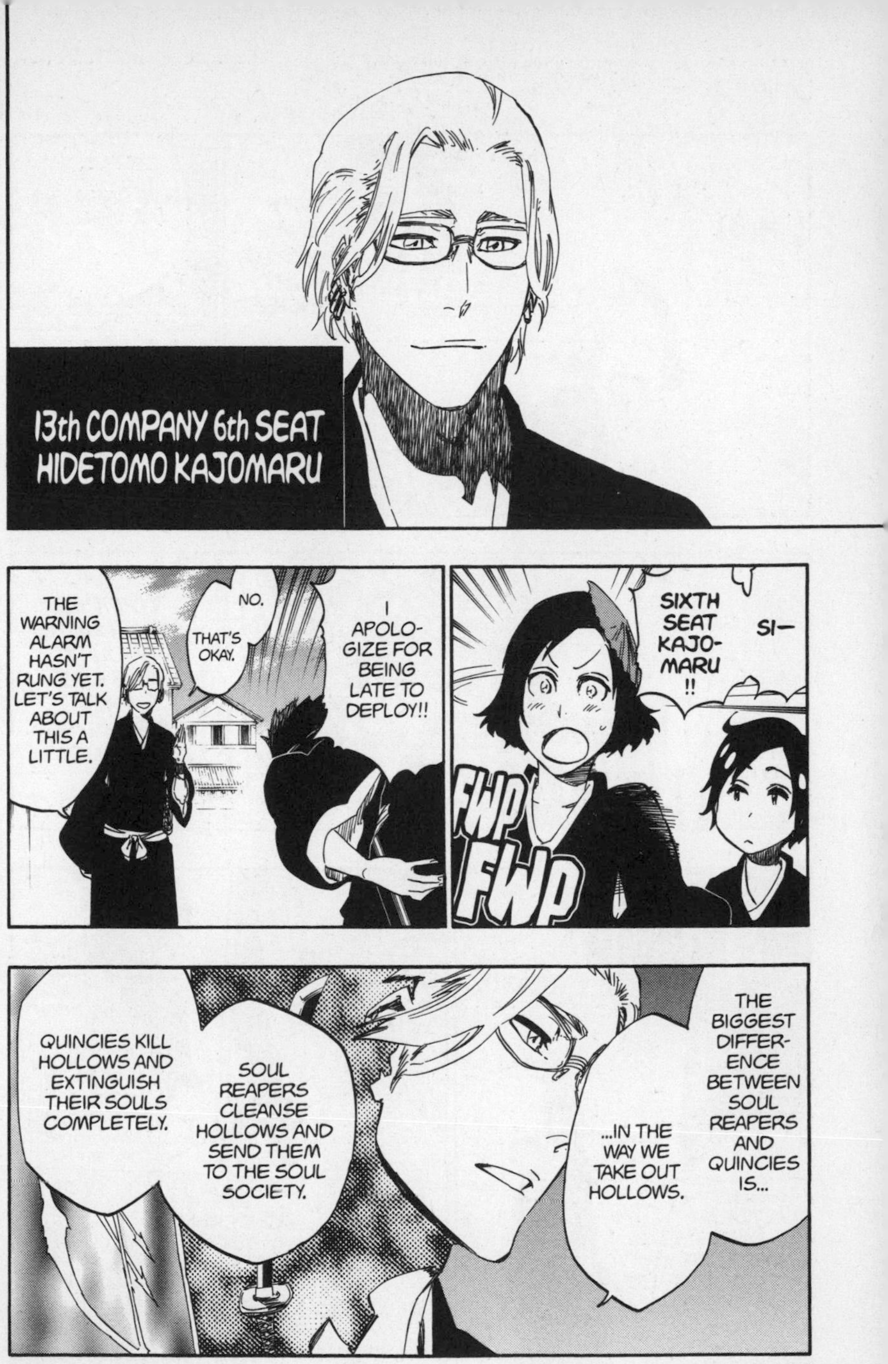
13th COMPANY 6th SEAT
HIDETOMO KAJOMARU
SI—
SIXTH SEAT KAJO-MARU!!
FWP FWP
I APOLO-GIZE FOR BEING LATE TO DEPLOY!!
NO.
THAT'S OKAY.
THE WARNING ALARM HASN'T RUNG YET. LET'S TALK ABOUT THIS A LITTLE.
THE BIGGEST DIFFER-ENCE BETWEEN SOUL REAPERS AND QUINCIES IS...
...IN THE WAY WE TAKE OUT HOLLOWS.
SOUL REAPERS CLEANSE HOLLOWS AND SEND THEM TO THE SOUL SOCIETY.
QUINCIES KILL HOLLOWS AND EXTINGUISH THEIR SOULS COMPLETELY.

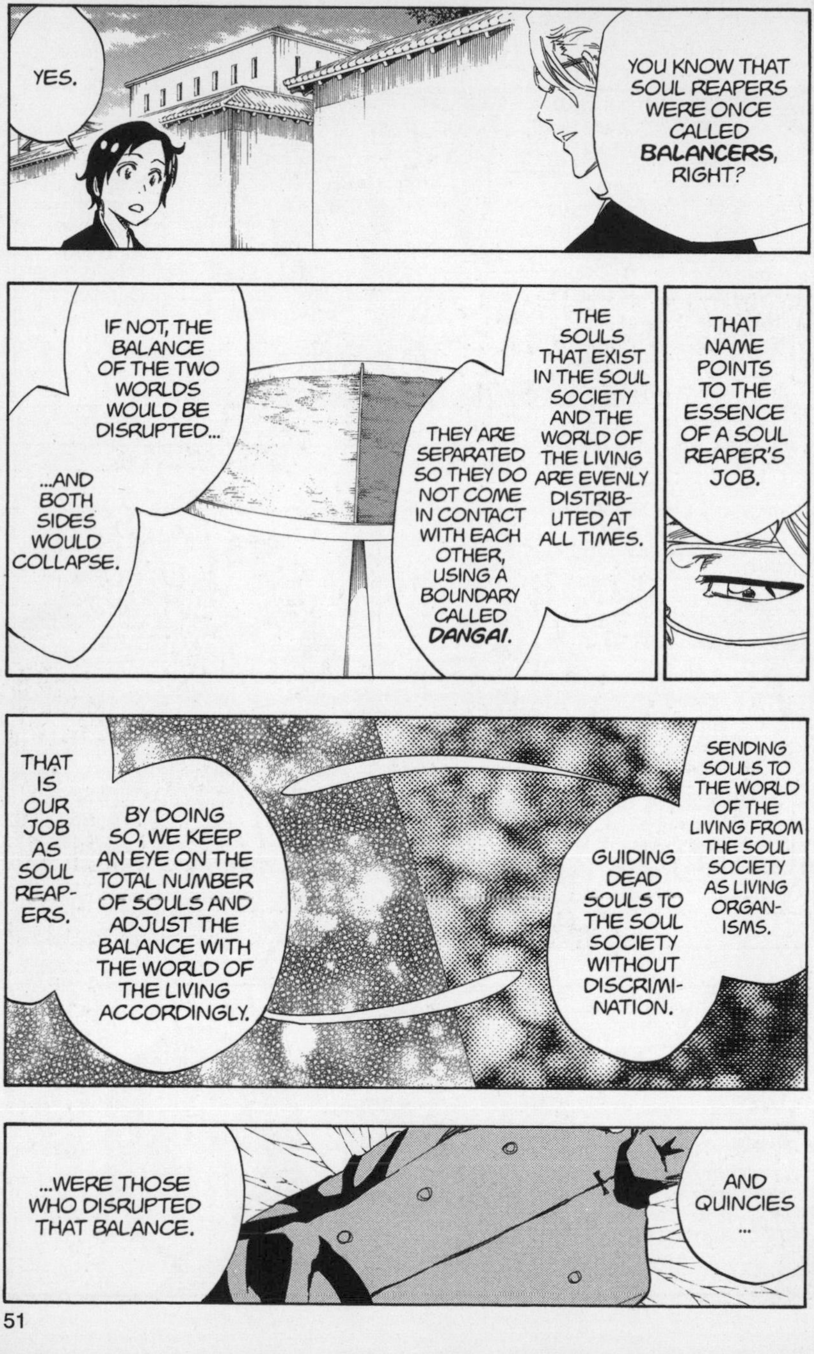
YOU KNOW THAT SOUL REAPERS WERE ONCE CALLED **BALANCERS**, RIGHT?
YES.
THAT NAME POINTS TO THE ESSENCE OF A SOUL REAPER'S JOB.
THE SOULS THAT EXIST IN THE SOUL SOCIETY AND THE WORLD OF THE LIVING ARE EVENLY DISTRIB-UTED AT ALL TIMES.
THEY ARE SEPARATED SO THEY DO NOT COME IN CONTACT WITH EACH OTHER, USING A BOUNDARY CALLED ***DANGAI***.
IF NOT, THE BALANCE OF THE TWO WORLDS WOULD BE DISRUPTED...
...AND BOTH SIDES WOULD COLLAPSE.
SENDING SOULS TO THE WORLD OF THE LIVING FROM THE SOUL SOCIETY AS LIVING ORGAN-ISMS.
GUIDING DEAD SOULS TO THE SOUL SOCIETY WITHOUT DISCRIMI-NATION.
BY DOING SO, WE KEEP AN EYE ON THE TOTAL NUMBER OF SOULS AND ADJUST THE BALANCE WITH THE WORLD OF THE LIVING ACCORDINGLY.
THAT IS OUR JOB AS SOUL REAP-ERS.
AND QUINCIES ...
...WERE THOSE WHO DISRUPTED THAT BALANCE.

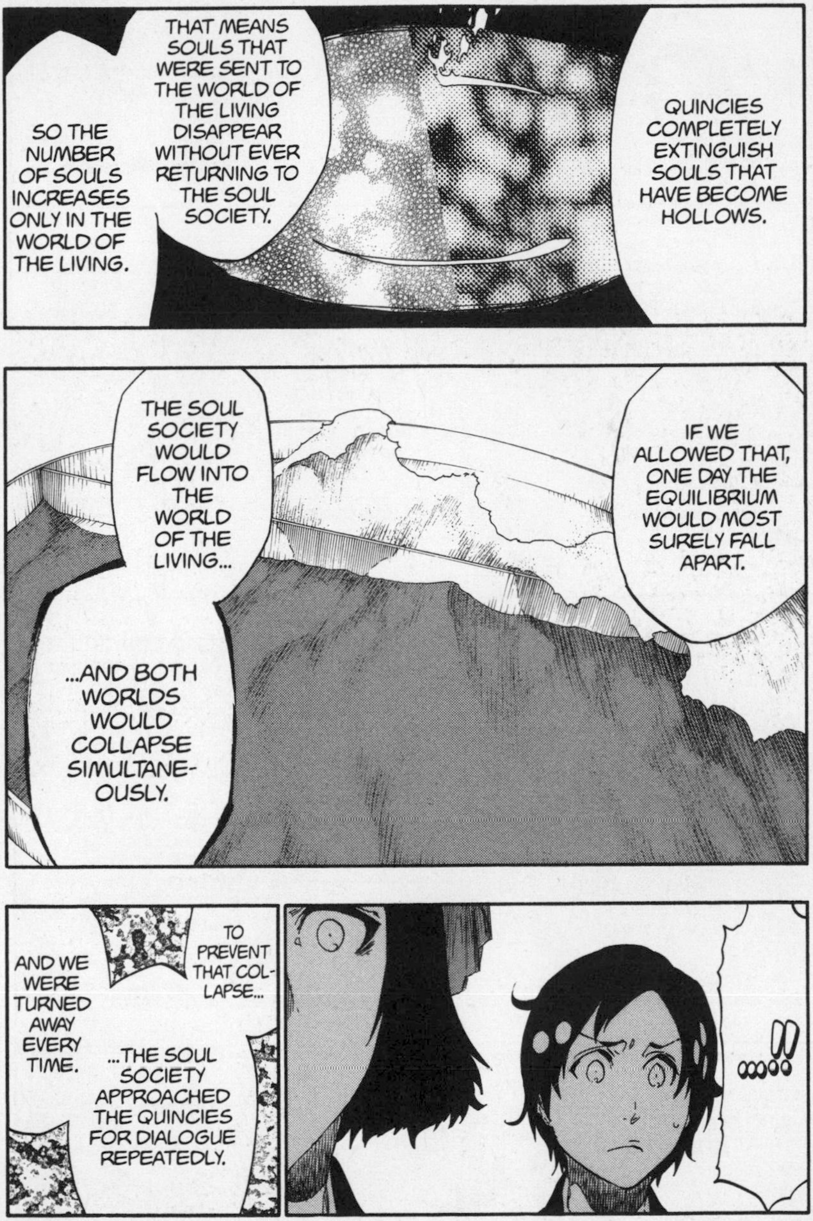
QUINCIES COMPLETELY EXTINGUISH SOULS THAT HAVE BECOME HOLLOWS.
THAT MEANS SOULS THAT WERE SENT TO THE WORLD OF THE LIVING DISAPPEAR WITHOUT EVER RETURNING TO THE SOUL SOCIETY.
SO THE NUMBER OF SOULS INCREASES ONLY IN THE WORLD OF THE LIVING.
IF WE ALLOWED THAT, ONE DAY THE EQUILIBRIUM WOULD MOST SURELY FALL APART.
THE SOUL SOCIETY WOULD FLOW INTO THE WORLD OF THE LIVING...
...AND BOTH WORLDS WOULD COLLAPSE SIMULTANE-OUSLY.
TO PREVENT THAT COL-LAPSE...
...THE SOUL SOCIETY APPROACHED THE QUINCIES FOR DIALOGUE REPEATEDLY.
AND WE WERE TURNED AWAY EVERY TIME.

READ THIS WAY

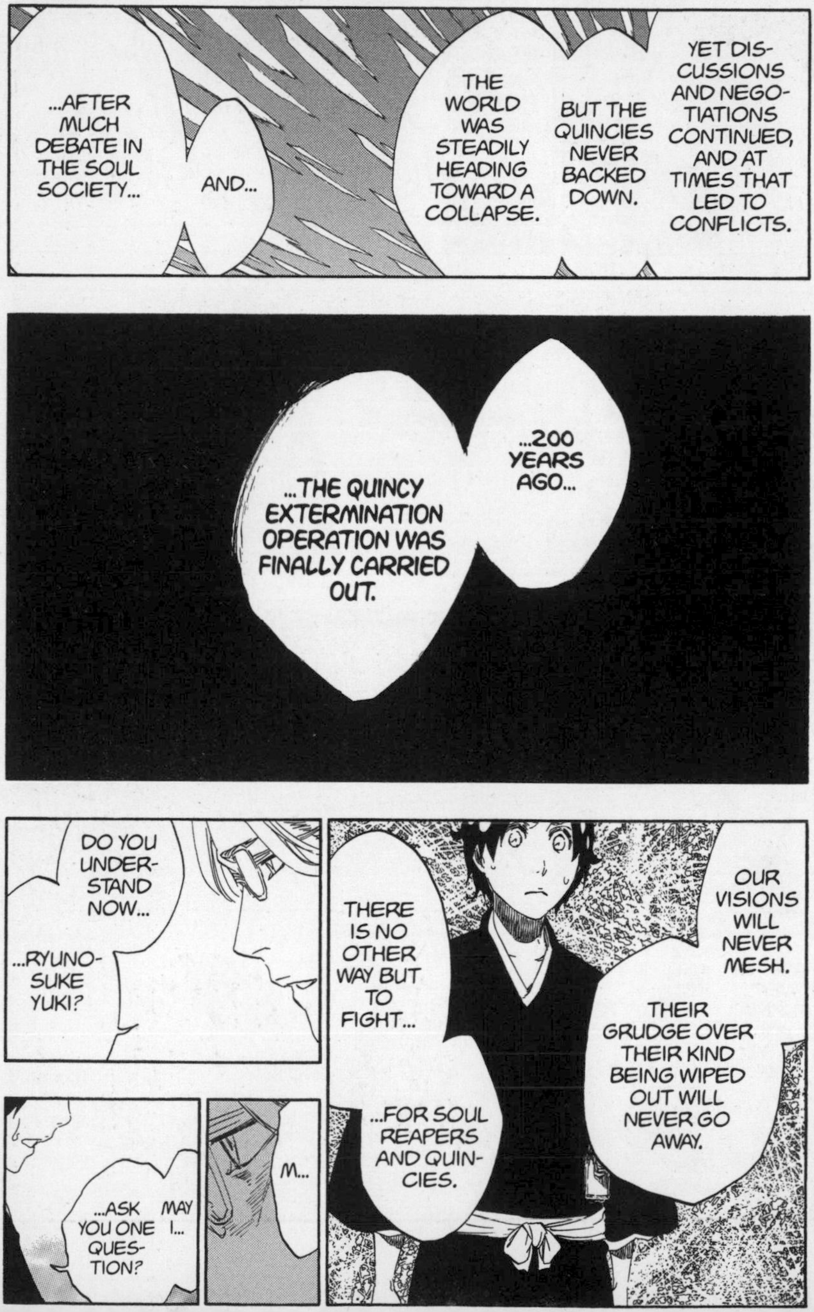
YET DIS-CUSSIONS AND NEGO-TIATIONS CONTINUED, AND AT TIMES THAT LED TO CONFLICTS.
BUT THE QUINCIES NEVER BACKED DOWN.
THE WORLD WAS STEADILY HEADING TOWARD A COLLAPSE.
AND...
...AFTER MUCH DEBATE IN THE SOUL SOCIETY...
...200 YEARS AGO...
...THE QUINCY EXTERMINATION OPERATION WAS FINALLY CARRIED OUT.
OUR VISIONS WILL NEVER MESH.
THEIR GRUDGE OVER THEIR KIND BEING WIPED OUT WILL NEVER GO AWAY.
THERE IS NO OTHER WAY BUT TO FIGHT...
...FOR SOUL REAPERS AND QUIN-CIES.
DO YOU UNDER-STAND NOW...
...RYUNO-SUKE YUKI?
M...
MAY I...
...ASK YOU ONE QUES-TION?

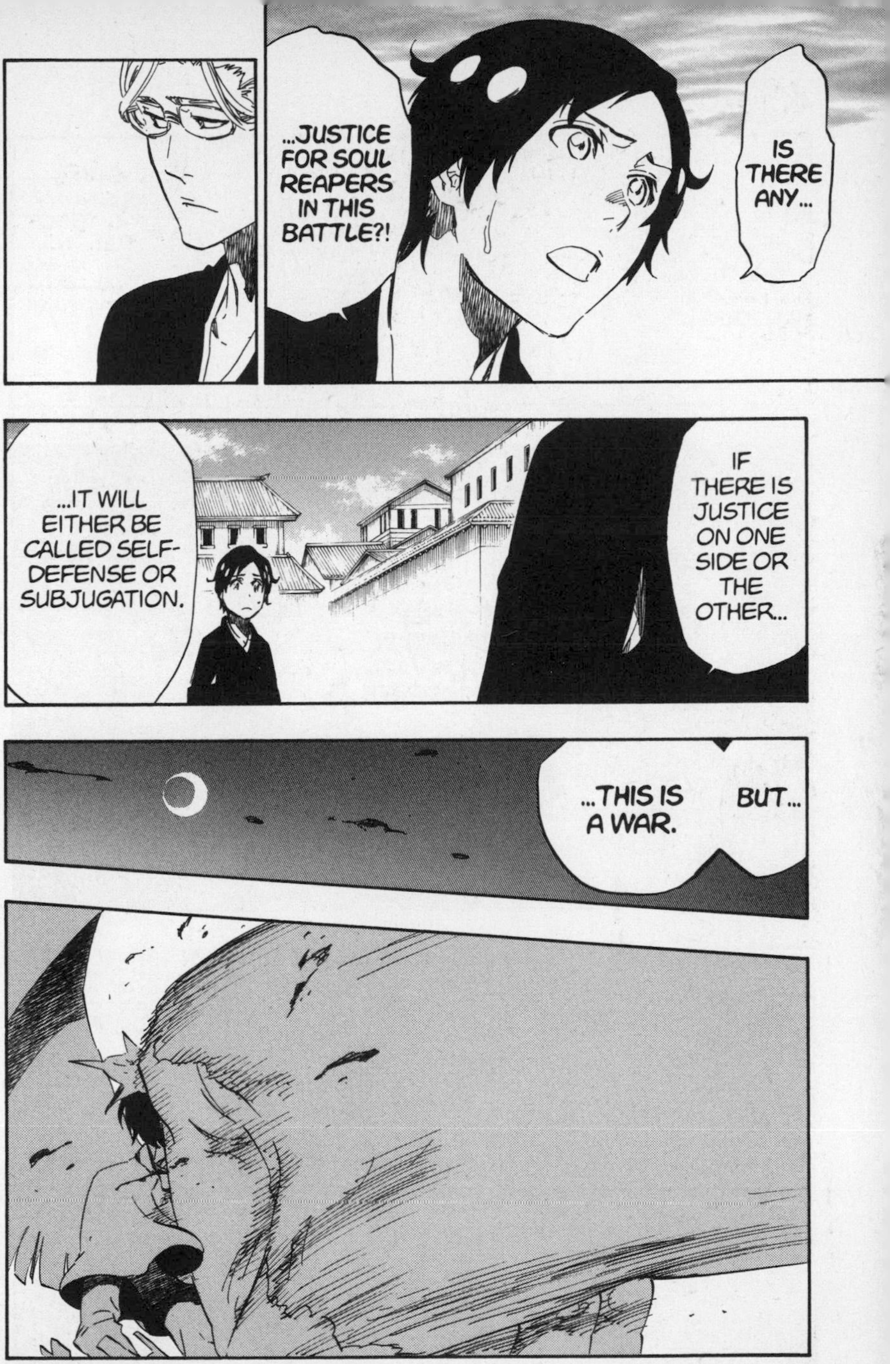
IS THERE ANY...
...JUSTICE FOR SOUL REAPERS IN THIS BATTLE?!
IF THERE IS JUSTICE ON ONE SIDE OR THE OTHER...
...IT WILL EITHER BE CALLED SELF-DEFENSE OR SUBJUGATION.
BUT...
...THIS IS A WAR.

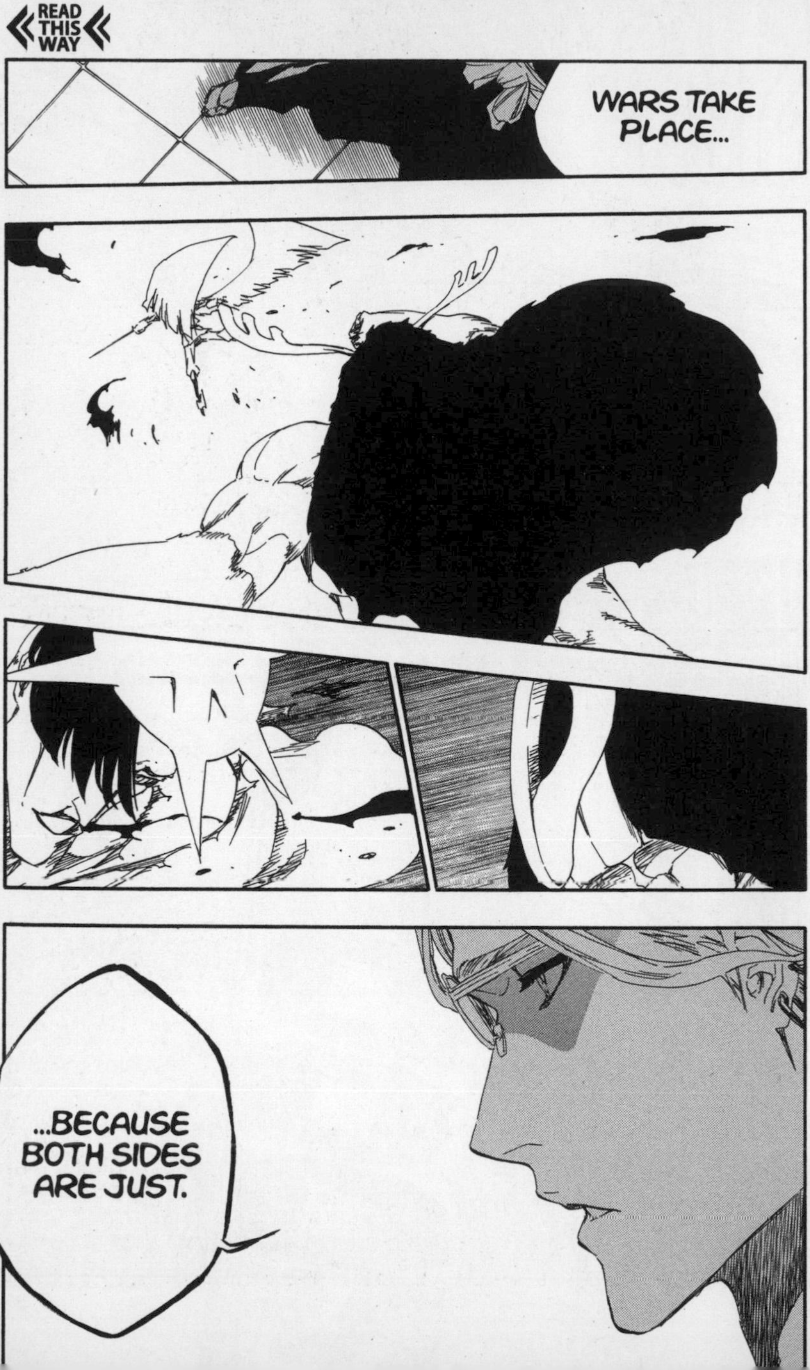
READ THIS WAY
WARS TAKE PLACE...
...BECAUSE BOTH SIDES ARE JUST.

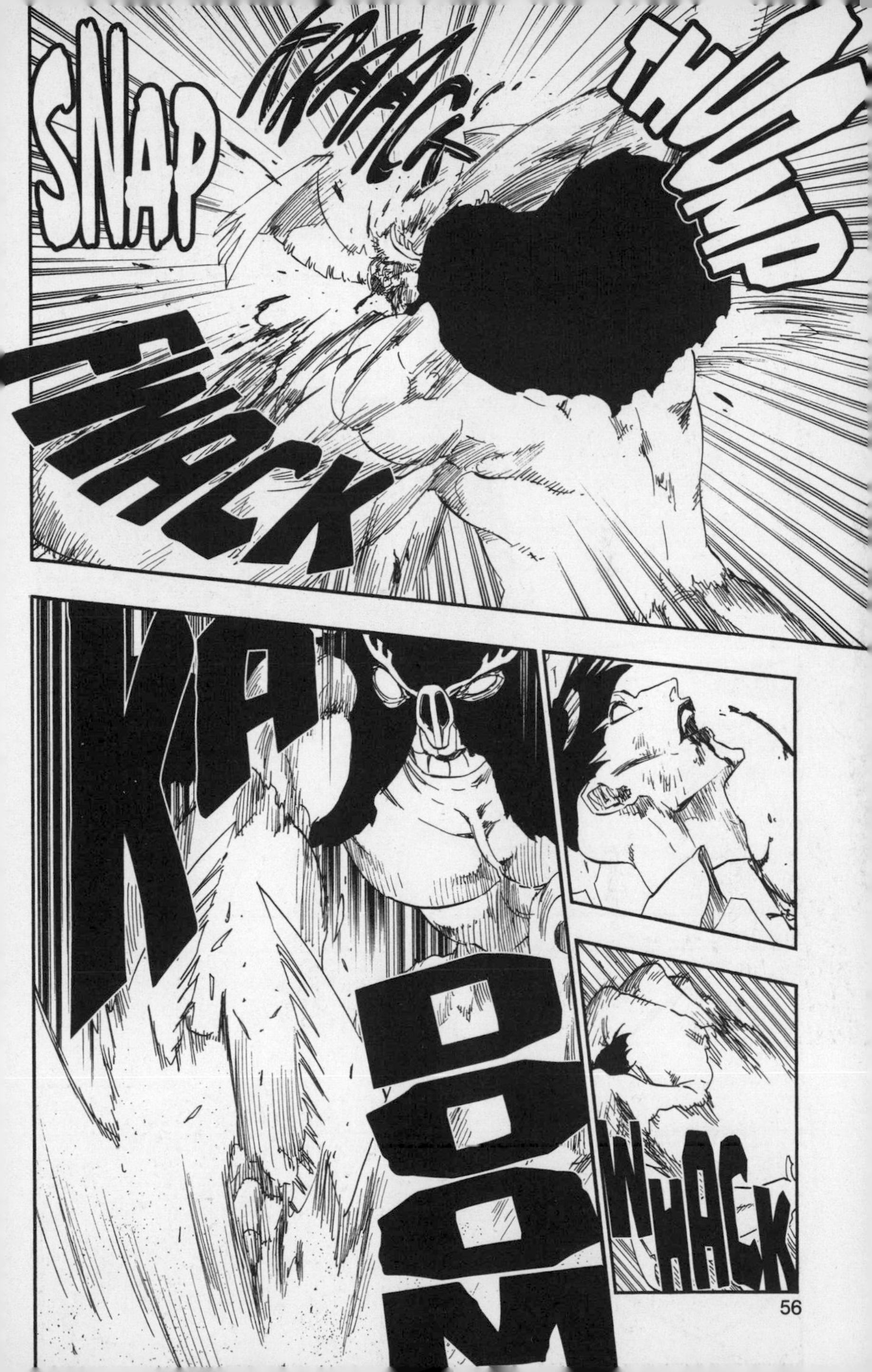
THUMP
KRAACK
SNAP
CRACK
WHACK
KA
BOOM

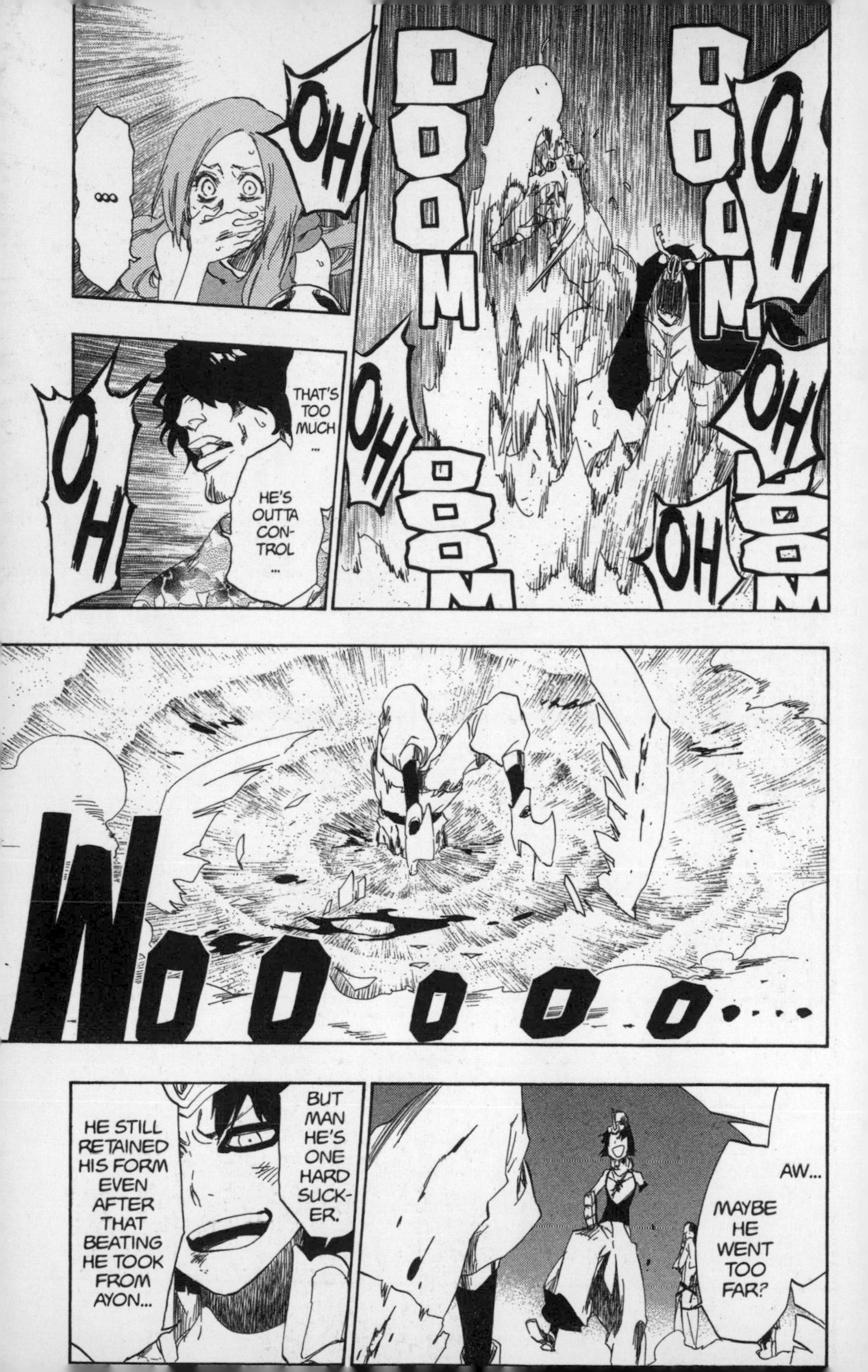

DOOM
OH
DOOM
OH
OH
DOOM
OH
DOOM
OH
...
OH
OH
THAT'S TOO MUCH...
HE'S OUTTA CON-TROL...
WOOOOOO...
AW...
MAYBE HE WENT TOO FAR?
BUT MAN HE'S ONE HARD SUCK-ER.
HE STILL RETAINED HIS FORM EVEN AFTER THAT BEATING HE TOOK FROM AYON...

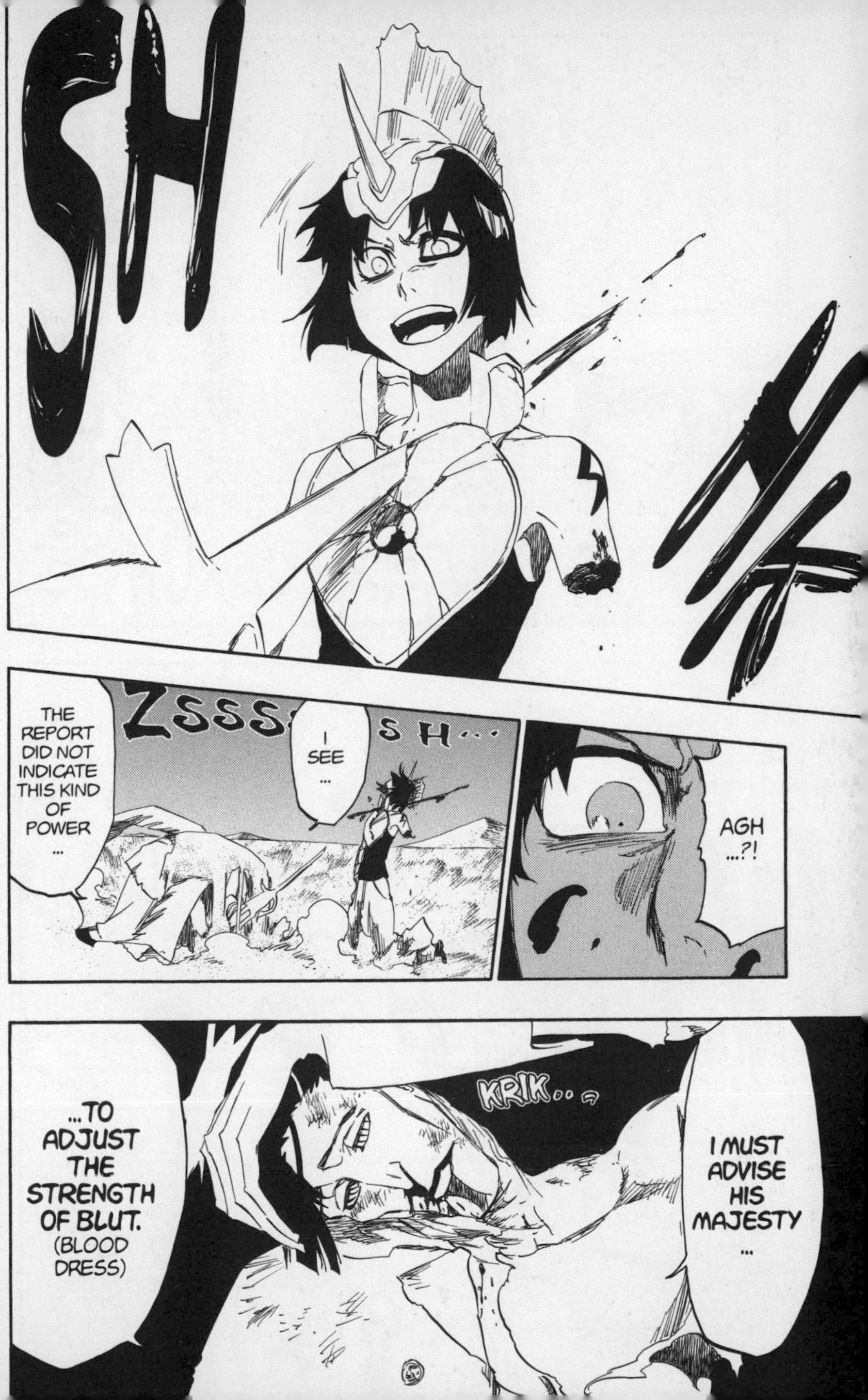
SH
AGH ...?!
ZSSS
SH...
I SEE ...
THE REPORT DID NOT INDICATE THIS KIND OF POWER ...
I MUST ADVISE HIS MAJESTY ...
KRIK...
...TO ADJUST THE STRENGTH OF BLUT. (BLOOD DRESS)

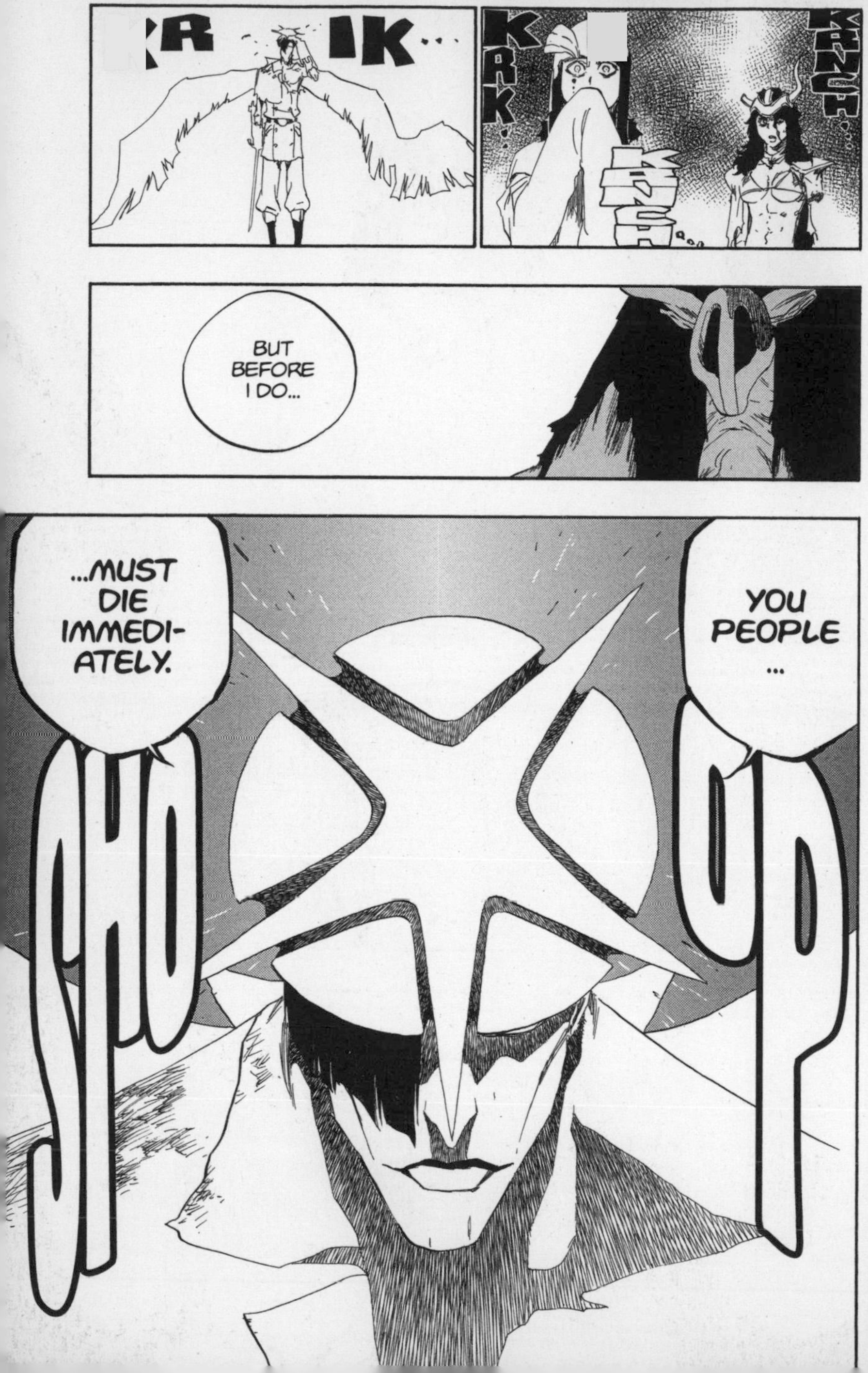
KRK...
KRNCH...
KRNCH...
KR
IK...
BUT BEFORE I DO...
YOU PEOPLE ...
...MUST DIE IMMEDI-ATELY.
SHO
OP

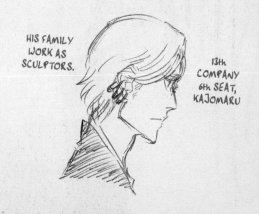

13th COMPANY 6th SEAT, KAJOMARU
HIS FAMILY WORK AS SCULPTORS.

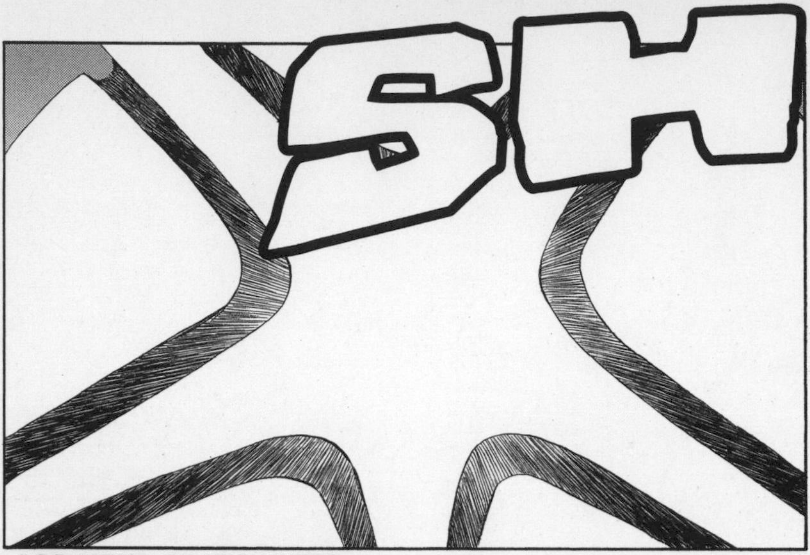
SH

493.LIGHT OF HAPPINESS

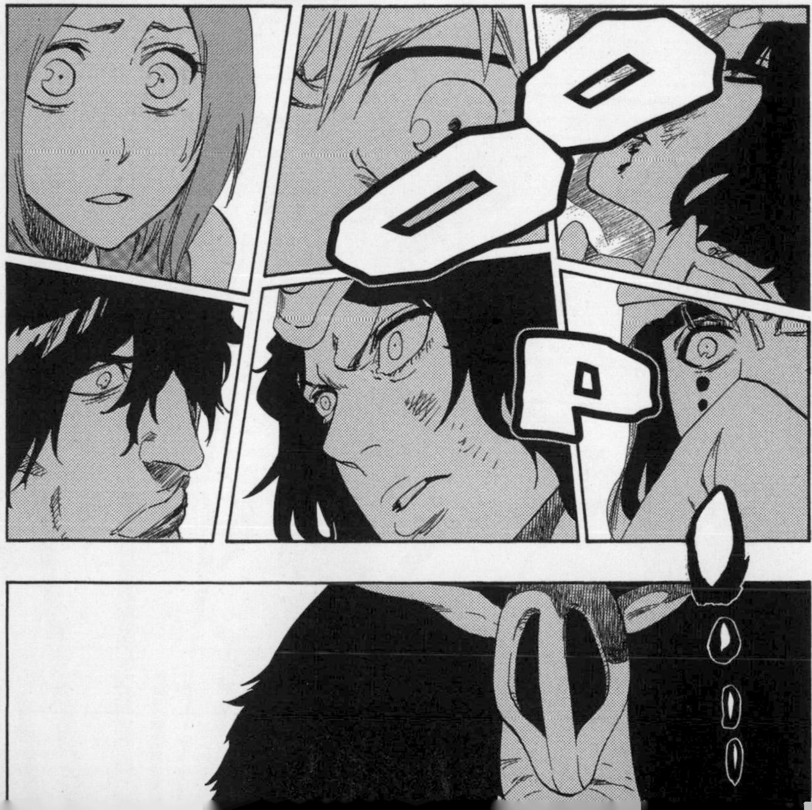
OOP

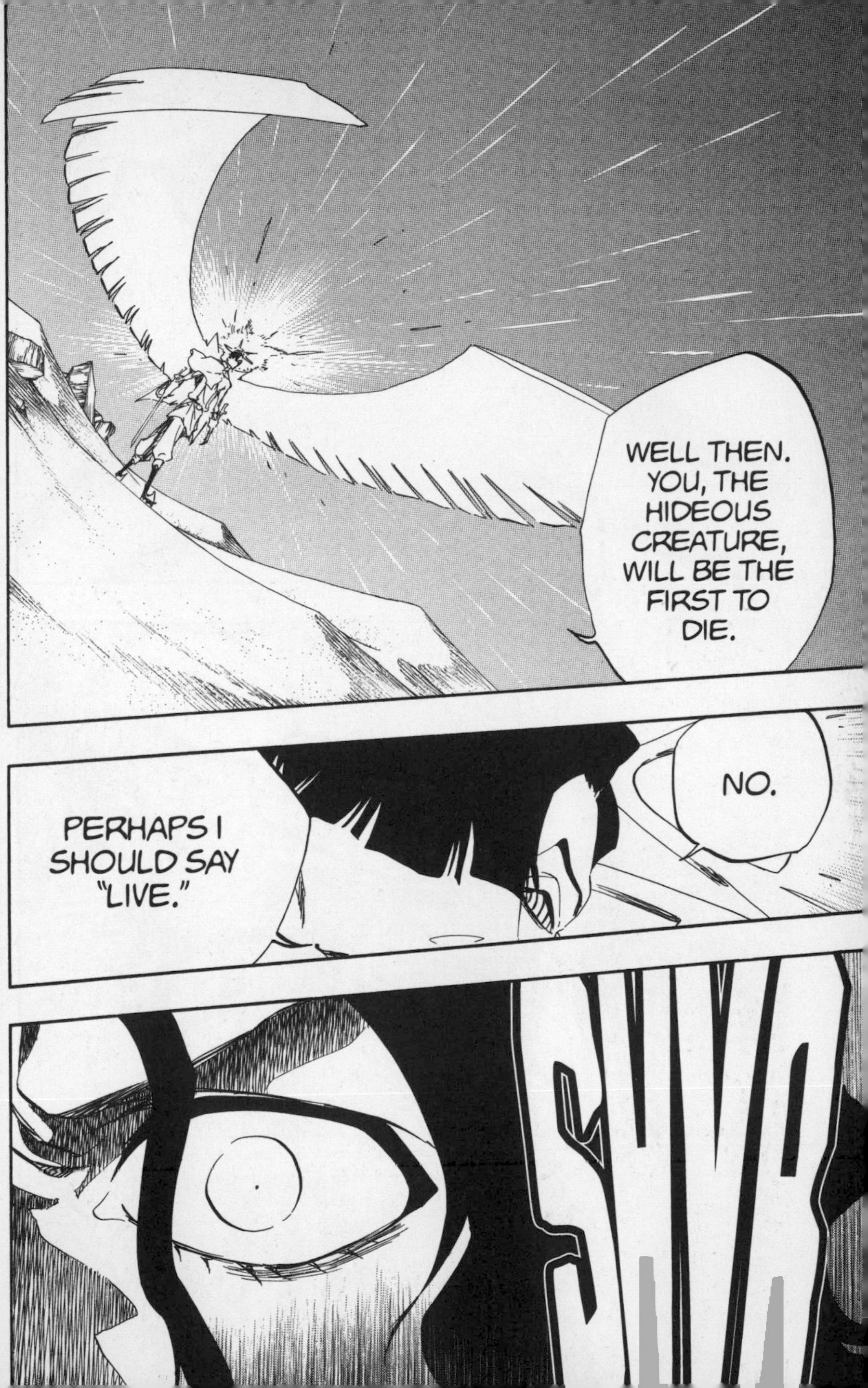
WELL THEN. YOU, THE HIDEOUS CREATURE, WILL BE THE FIRST TO DIE.
NO.
PERHAPS I SHOULD SAY "LIVE."
SHVR

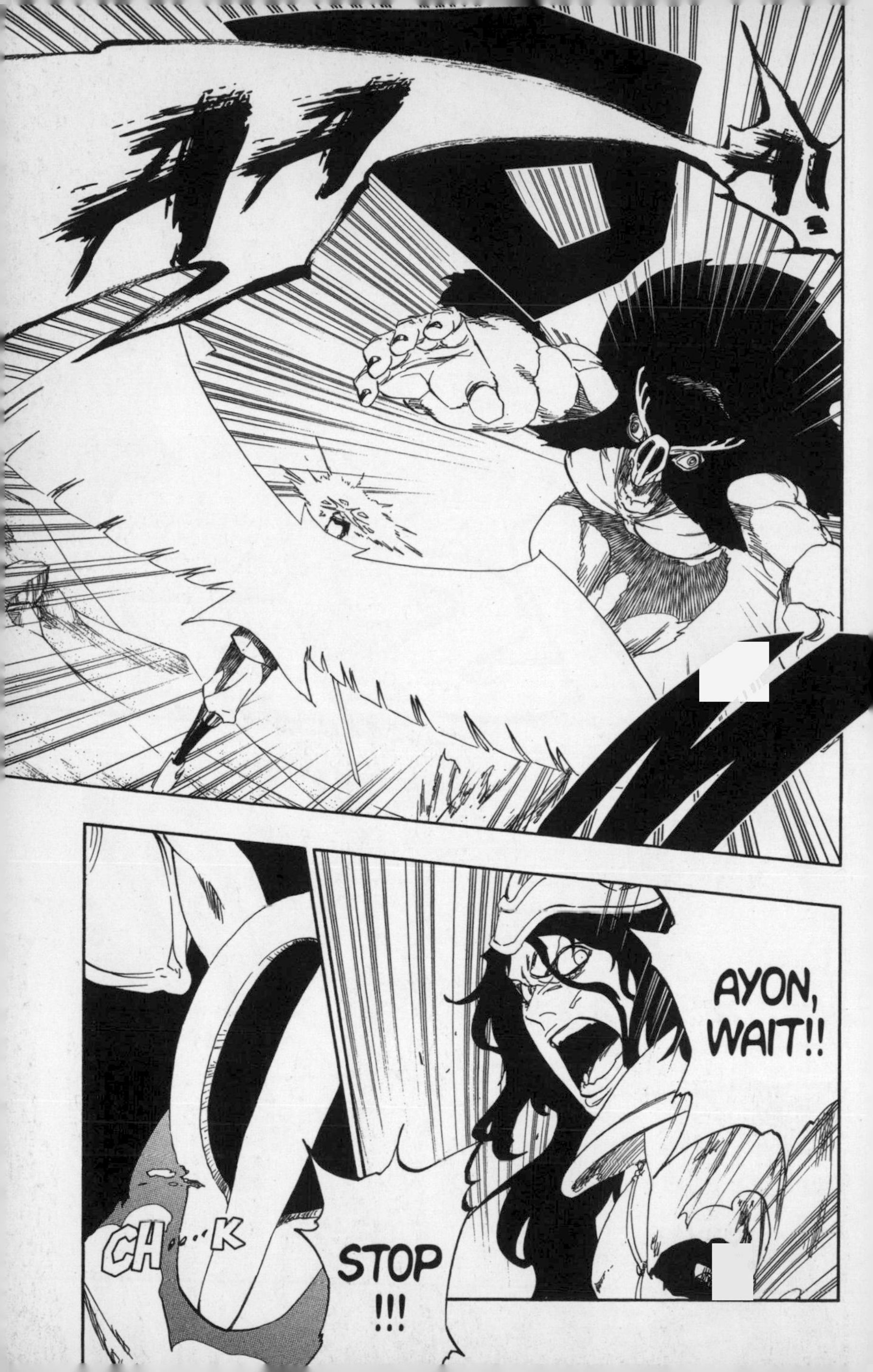
AYON, WAIT!!
STOP !!!
CH...K

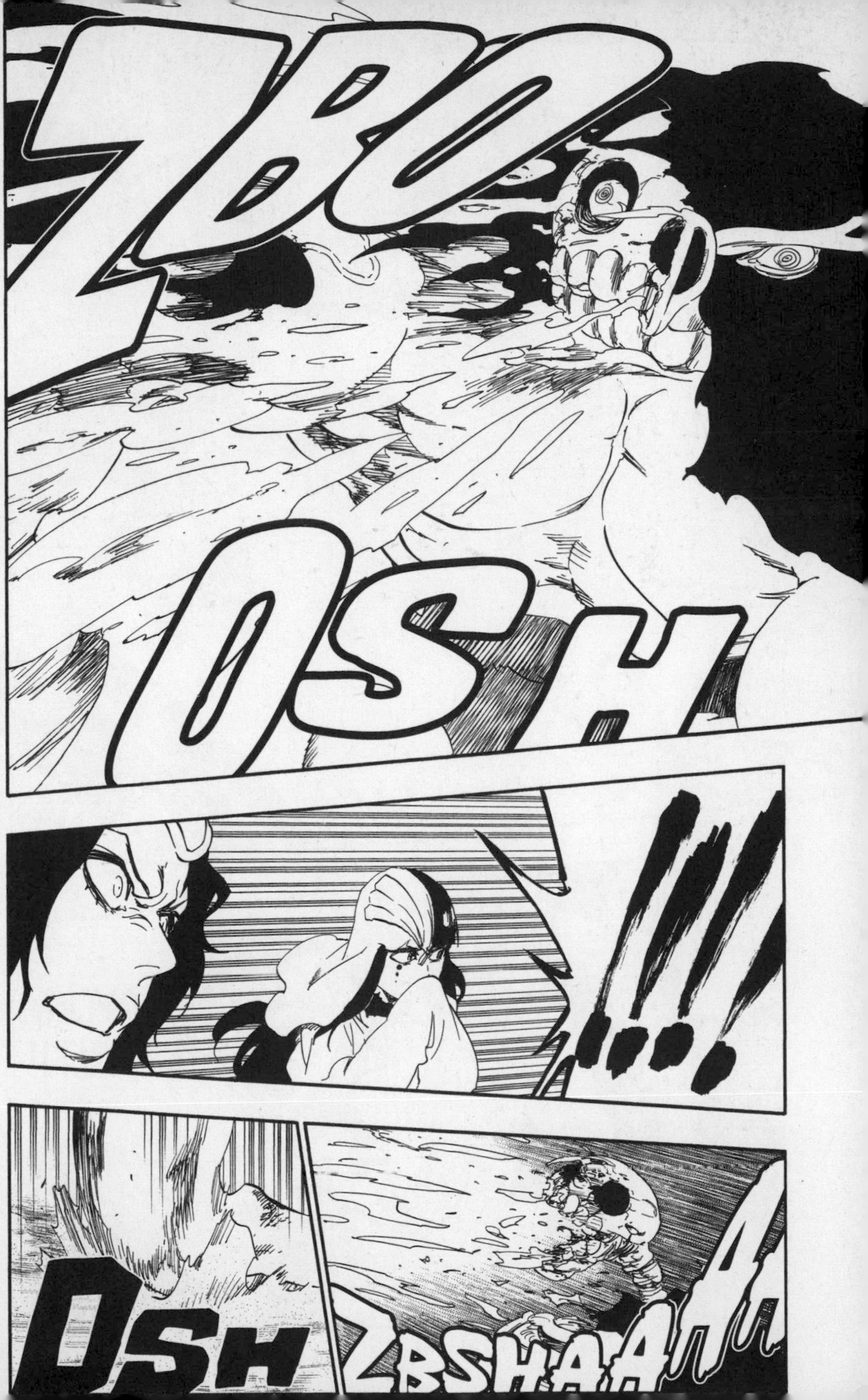
ZBO
OSH
!!!
ZBSHAAA
OSH

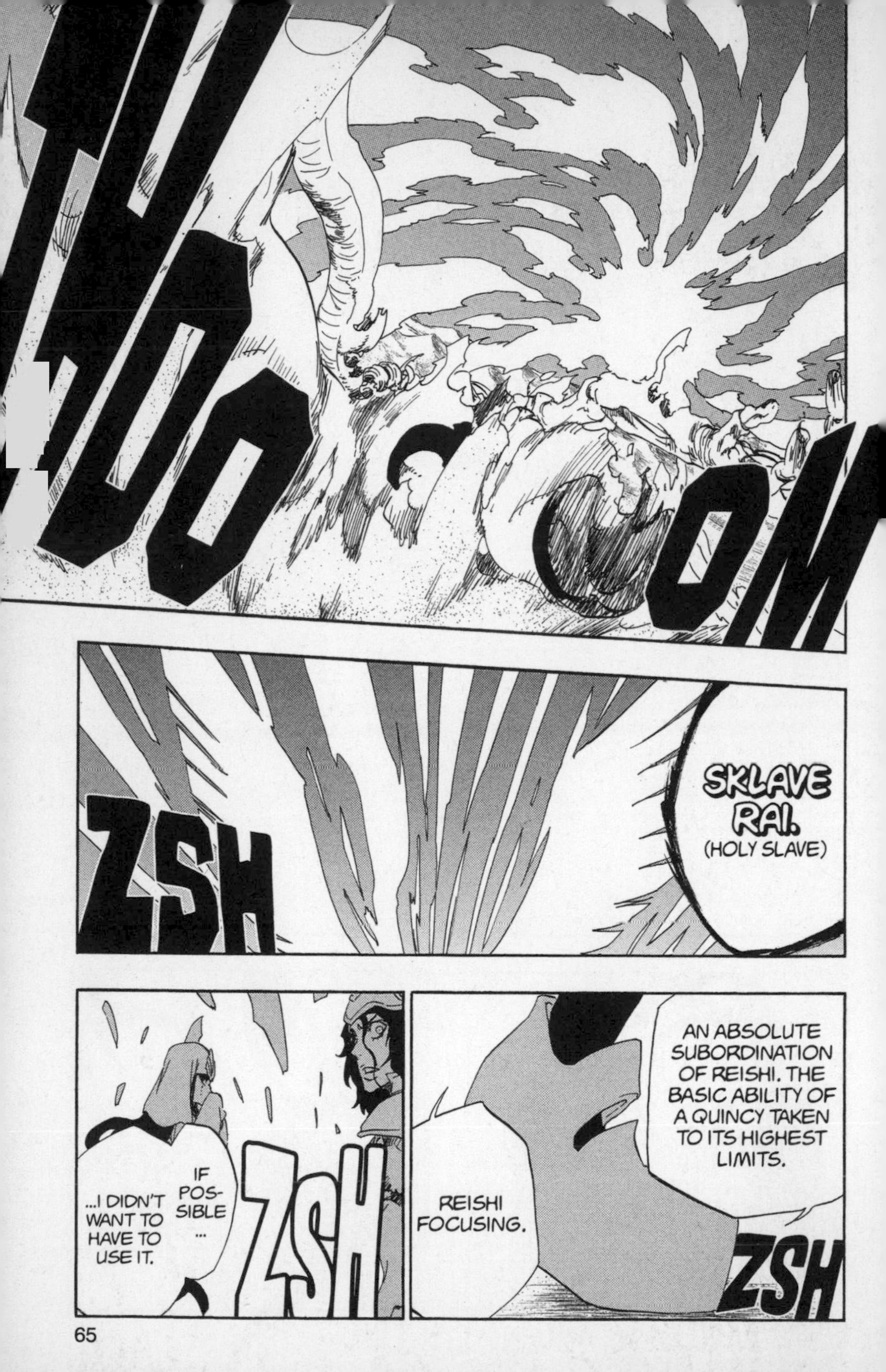
SKLAVE RAI.
(HOLY SLAVE)
ZSH
AN ABSOLUTE SUBORDINATION OF REISHI. THE BASIC ABILITY OF A QUINCY TAKEN TO ITS HIGHEST LIMITS.
REISHI FOCUSING.
ZSH
IF POSSIBLE...
...I DIDN'T WANT TO HAVE TO USE IT.
ZSH

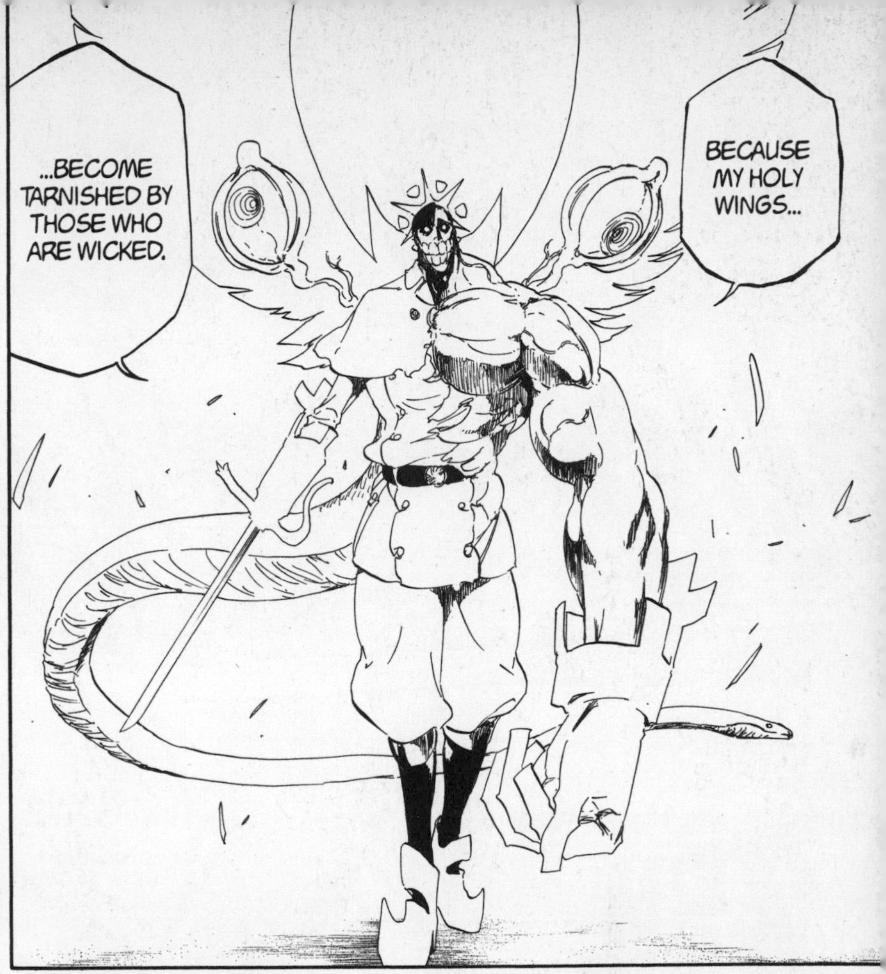
BECAUSE MY HOLY WINGS...
...BECOME TARNISHED BY THOSE WHO ARE WICKED.

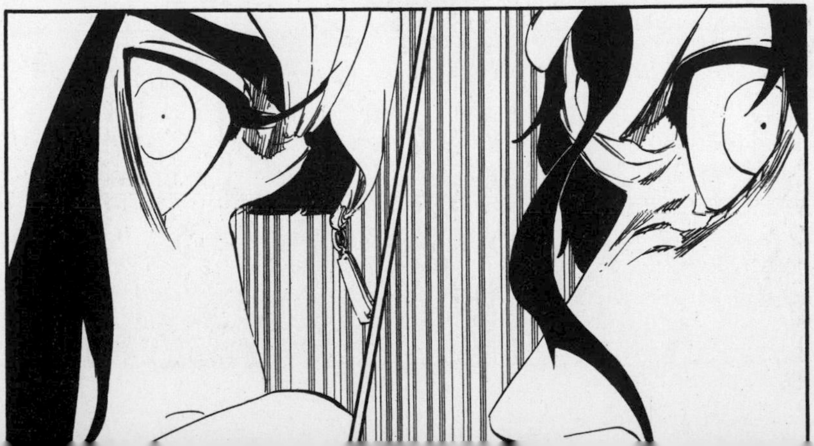

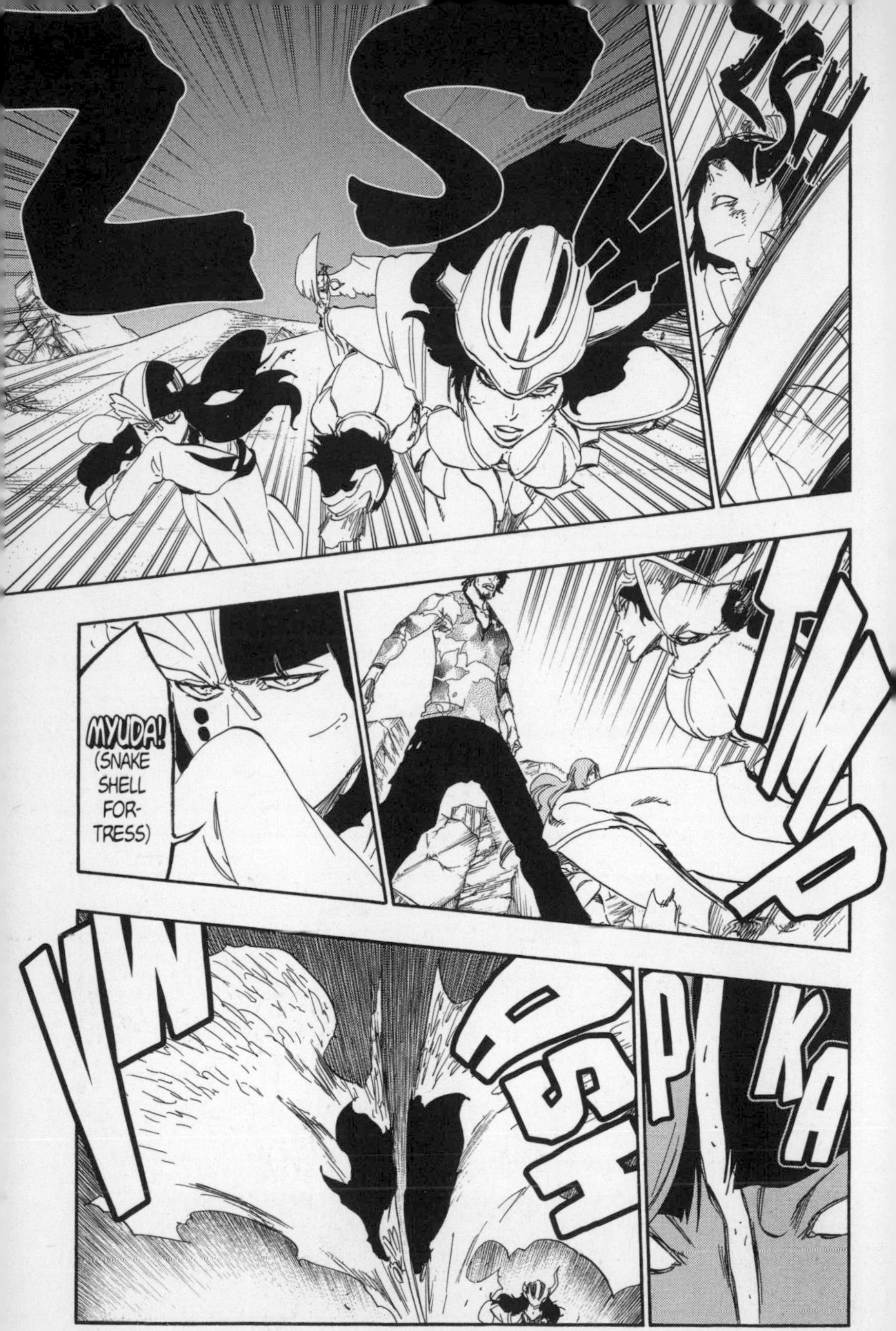
ZSH
ZSH
TMP
MYUDA!
(SNAKE SHELL FOR-TRESS)
KA
PI
ASH
VWN

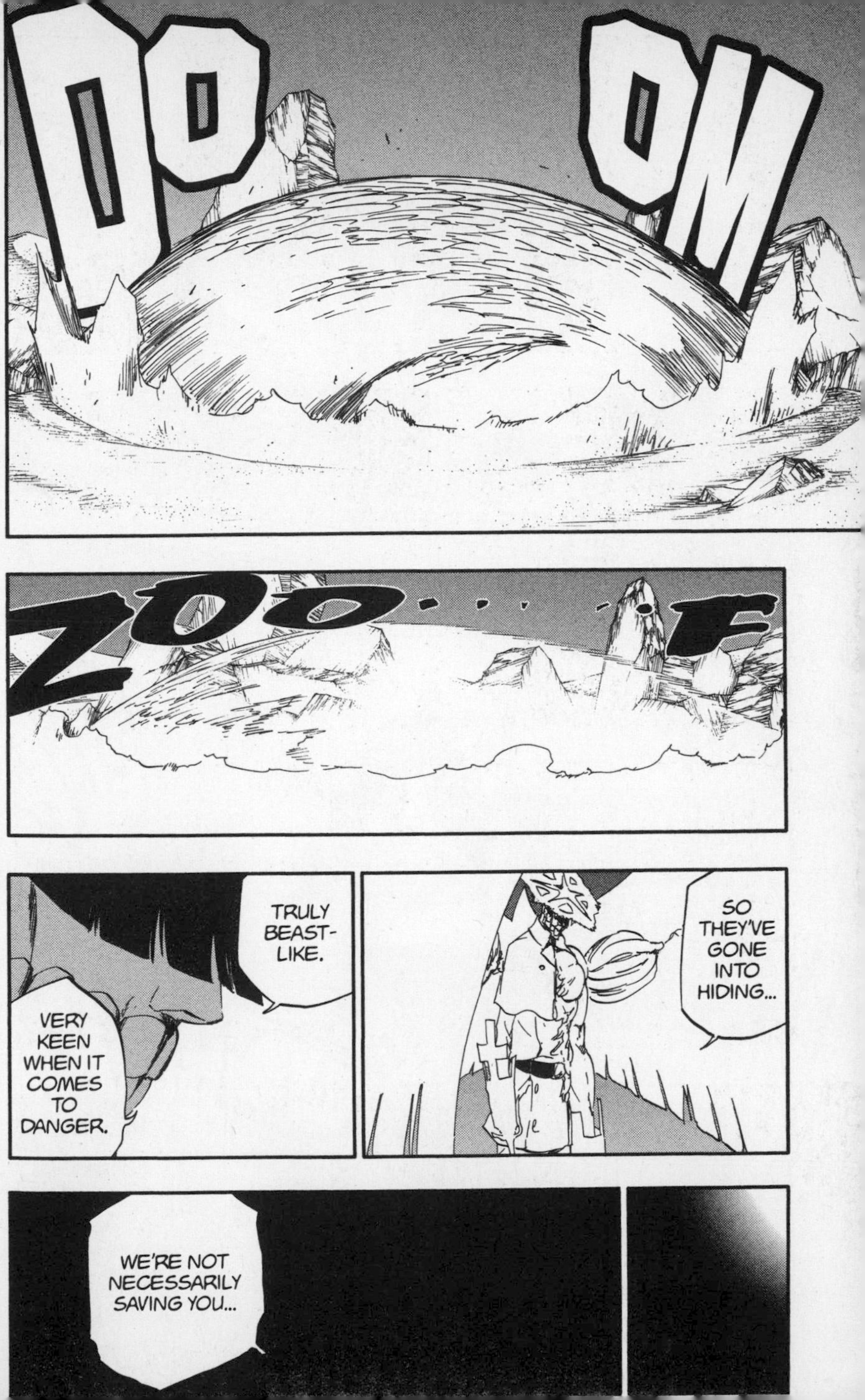
DOOM
ZOO...F
SO THEY'VE GONE INTO HIDING...
TRULY BEAST-LIKE.
VERY KEEN WHEN IT COMES TO DANGER.
WE'RE NOT NECESSARILY SAVING YOU...

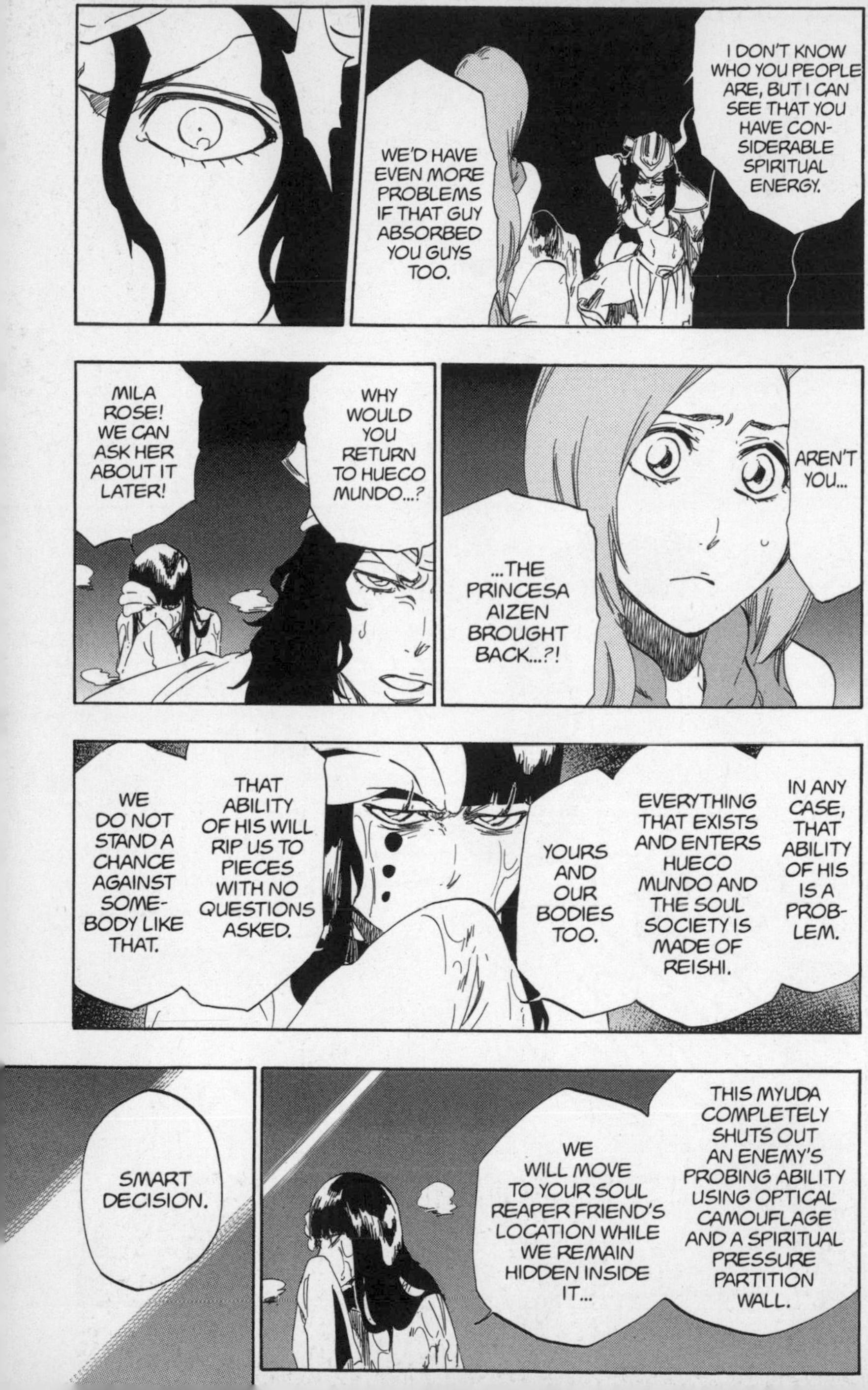
I DON'T KNOW WHO YOU PEOPLE ARE, BUT I CAN SEE THAT YOU HAVE CON-SIDERABLE SPIRITUAL ENERGY.
WE'D HAVE EVEN MORE PROBLEMS IF THAT GUY ABSORBED YOU GUYS TOO.
AREN'T YOU...
...THE PRINCESA AIZEN BROUGHT BACK...?!
WHY WOULD YOU RETURN TO HUECO MUNDO...?
MILA ROSE! WE CAN ASK HER ABOUT IT LATER!
IN ANY CASE, THAT ABILITY OF HIS IS A PROB-LEM.
EVERYTHING THAT EXISTS AND ENTERS HUECO MUNDO AND THE SOUL SOCIETY IS MADE OF REISHI.
YOURS AND OUR BODIES TOO.
THAT ABILITY OF HIS WILL RIP US TO PIECES WITH NO QUESTIONS ASKED.
WE DO NOT STAND A CHANCE AGAINST SOME-BODY LIKE THAT.
THIS MYUDA COMPLETELY SHUTS OUT AN ENEMY'S PROBING ABILITY USING OPTICAL CAMOUFLAGE AND A SPIRITUAL PRESSURE PARTITION WALL.
WE WILL MOVE TO YOUR SOUL REAPER FRIEND'S LOCATION WHILE WE REMAIN HIDDEN INSIDE IT...
SMART DECISION.

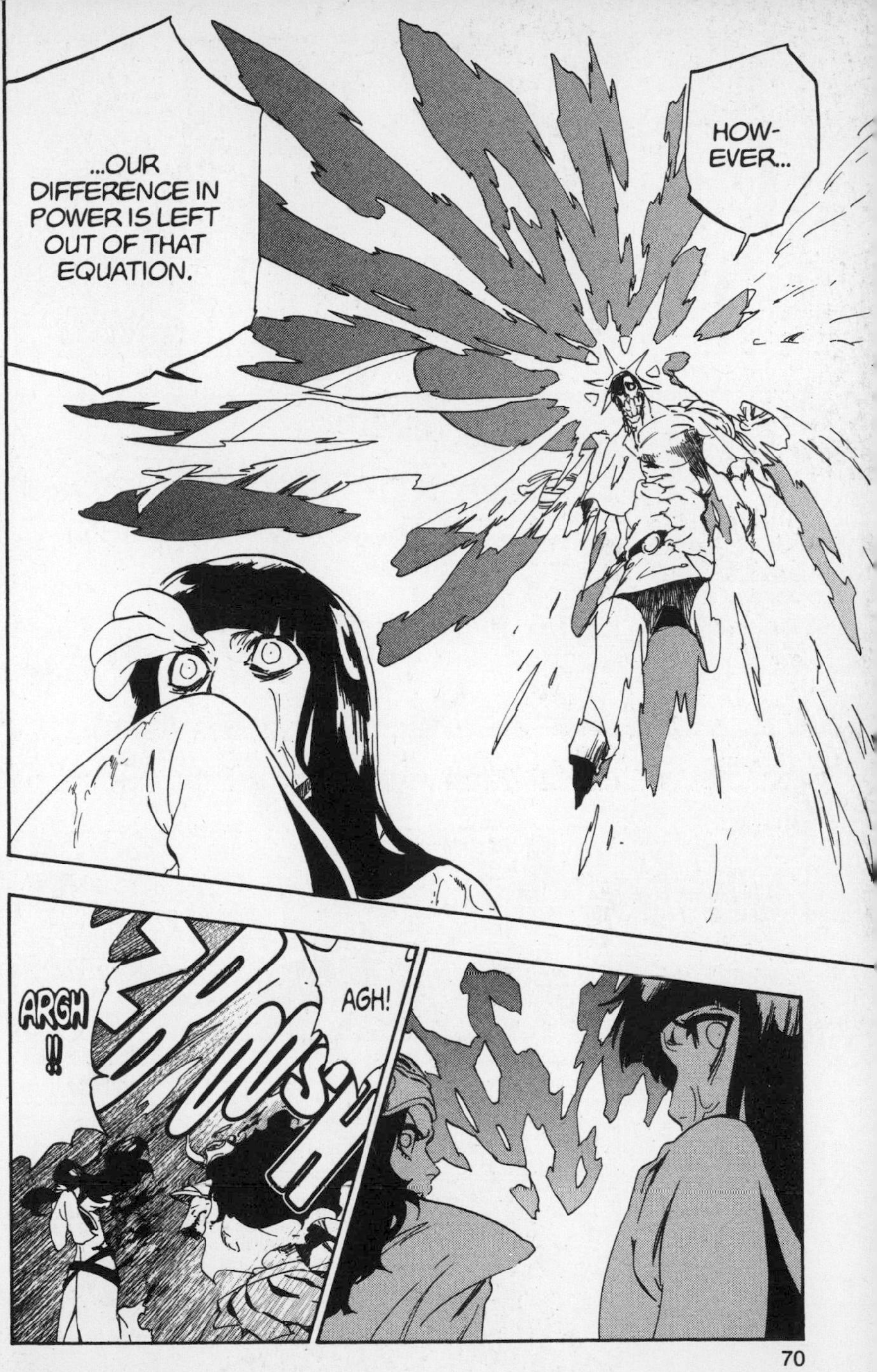
HOW-EVER...
...OUR DIFFERENCE IN POWER IS LEFT OUT OF THAT EQUATION.
AGH!
ARGH!!

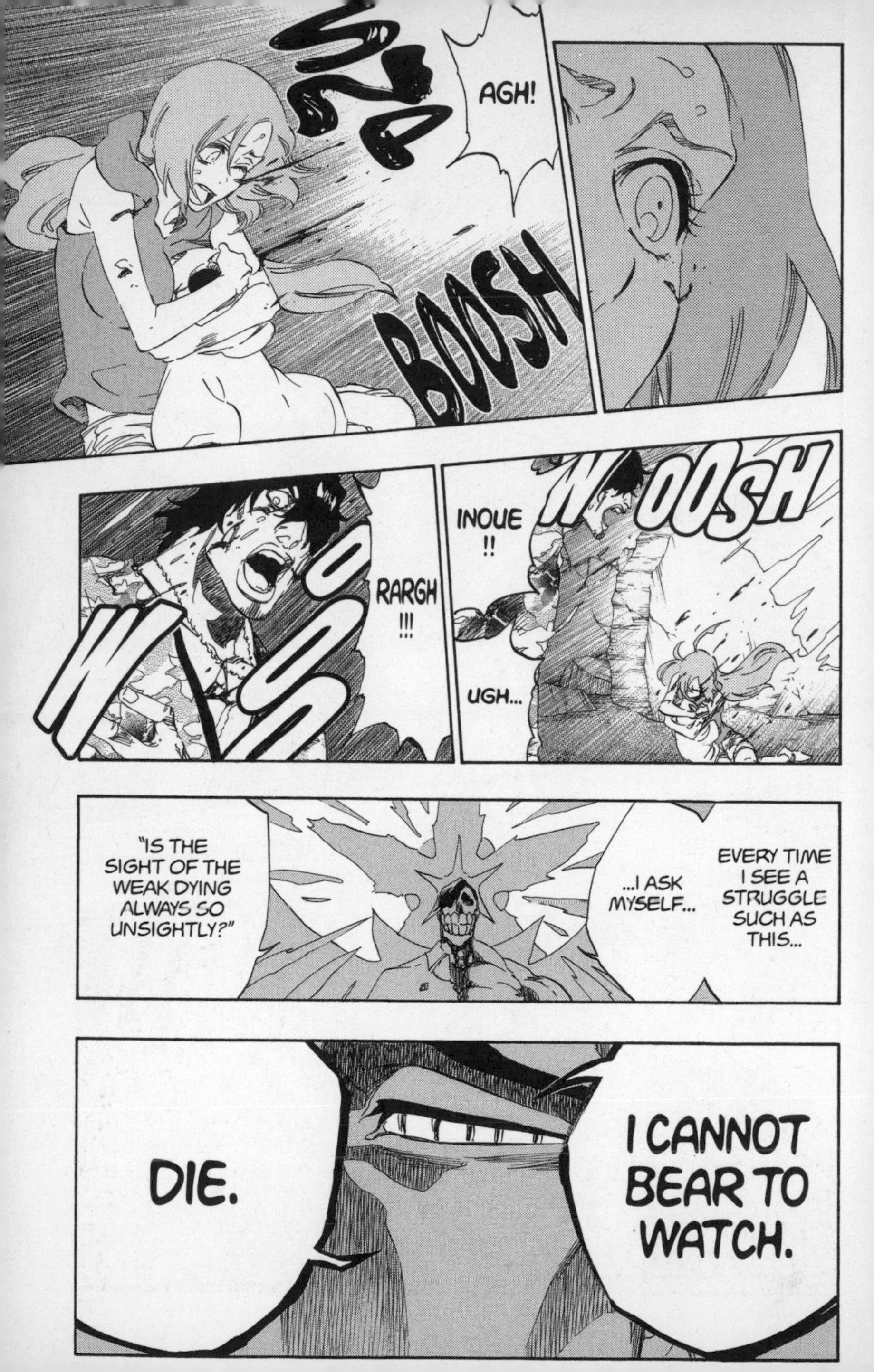
AGH!
BOOSH
INOUE!!
WOOSH
UGH...
RARGH!!!
EVERY TIME I SEE A STRUGGLE SUCH AS THIS...
...I ASK MYSELF...
"IS THE SIGHT OF THE WEAK DYING ALWAYS SO UNSIGHTLY?"
I CANNOT BEAR TO WATCH.
DIE.

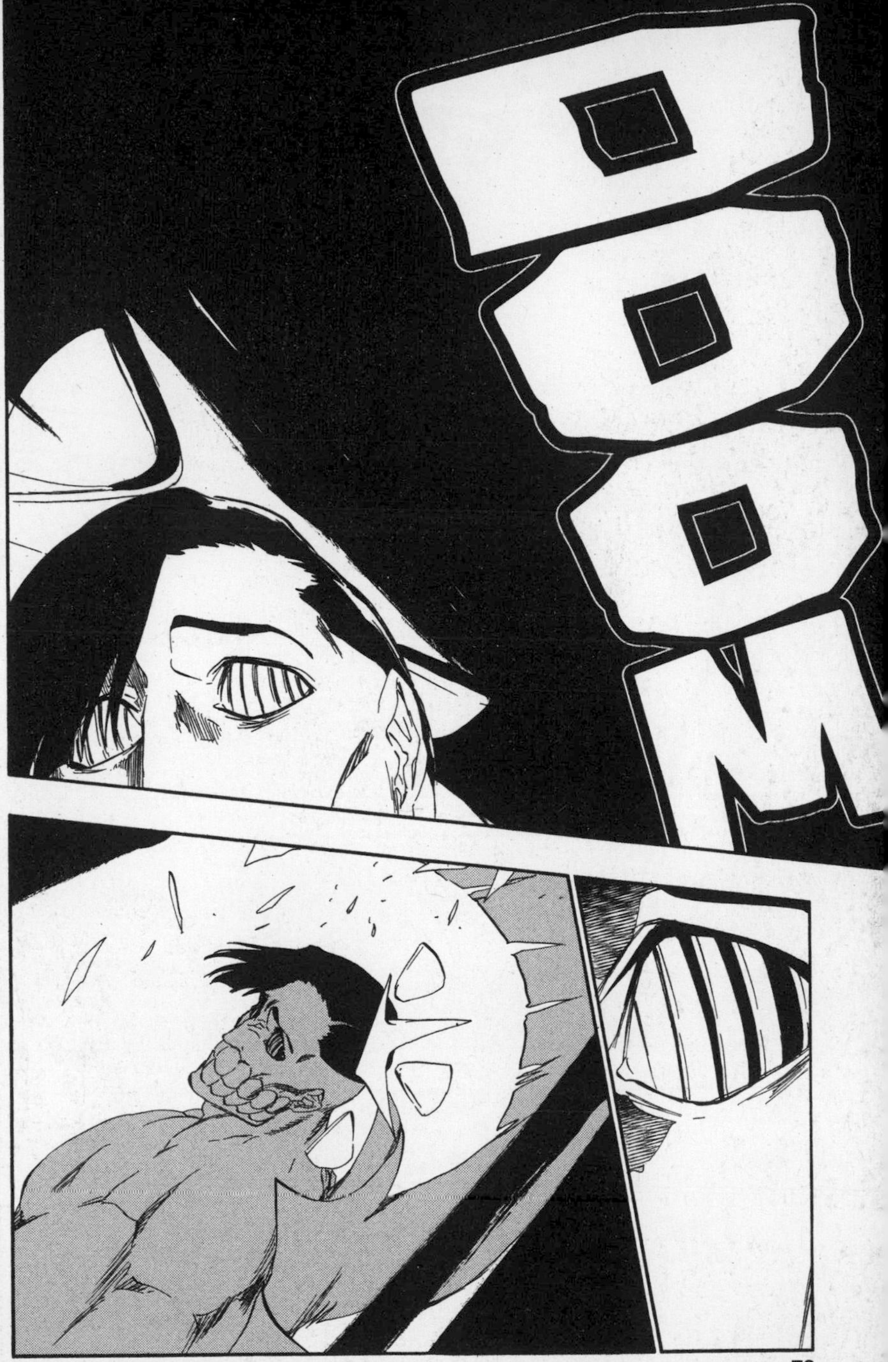
DOOM

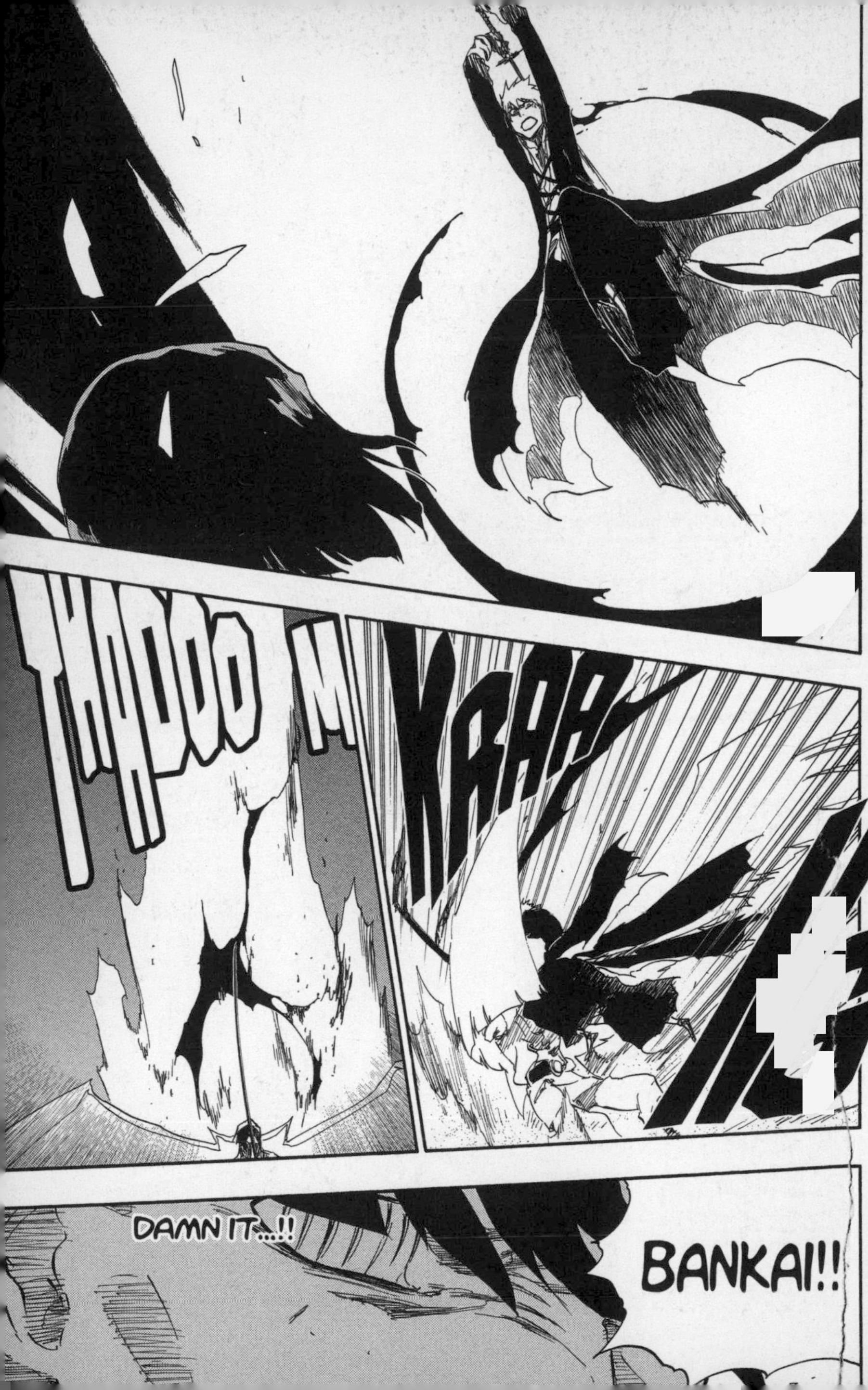
BANKAI!!
DAMN IT...!!

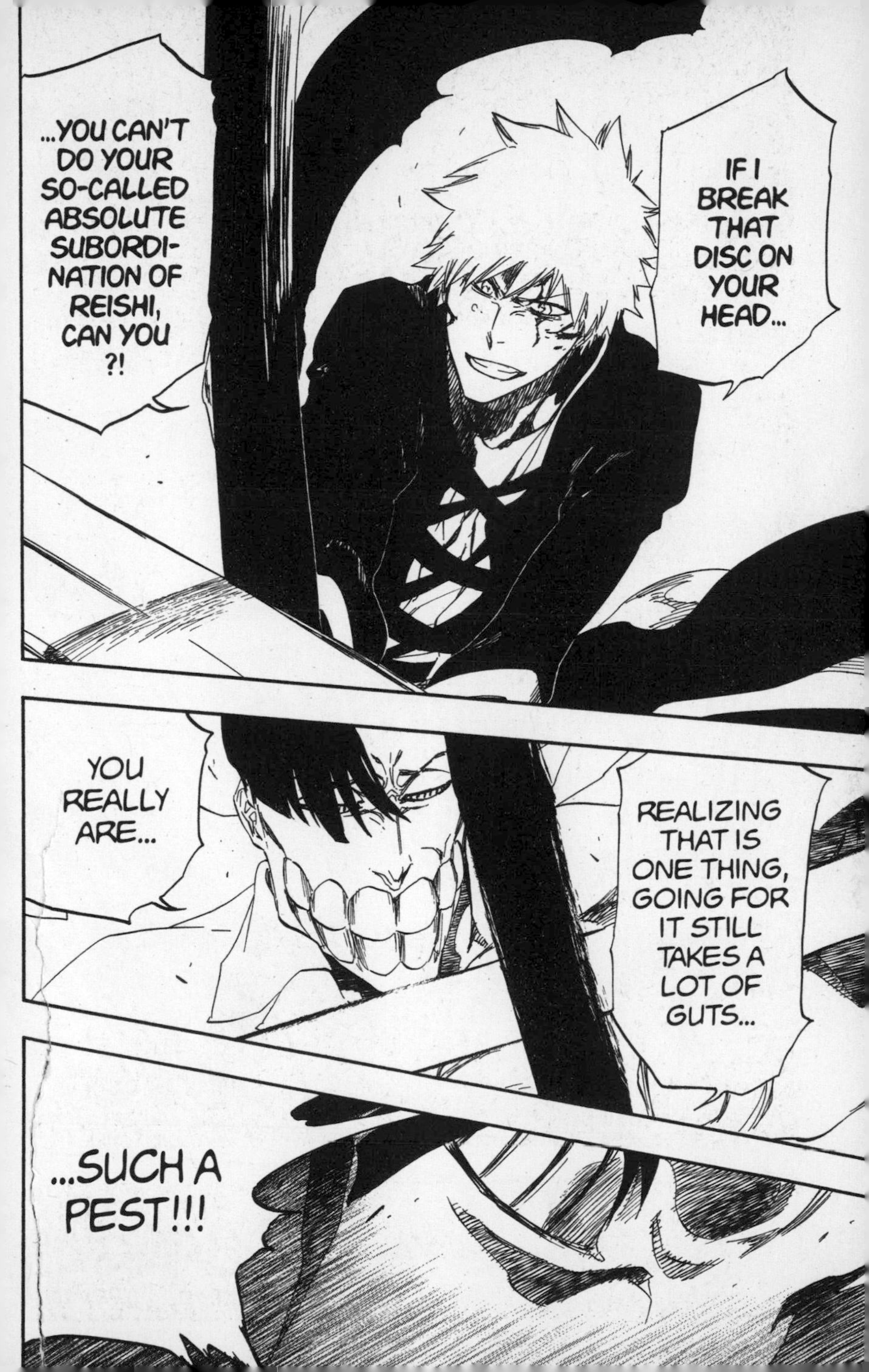
IF I BREAK THAT DISC ON YOUR HEAD...
...YOU CAN'T DO YOUR SO-CALLED ABSOLUTE SUBORDI-NATION OF REISHI, CAN YOU ?!
REALIZING THAT IS ONE THING, GOING FOR IT STILL TAKES A LOT OF GUTS...
YOU REALLY ARE...
...SUCH A PEST!!!

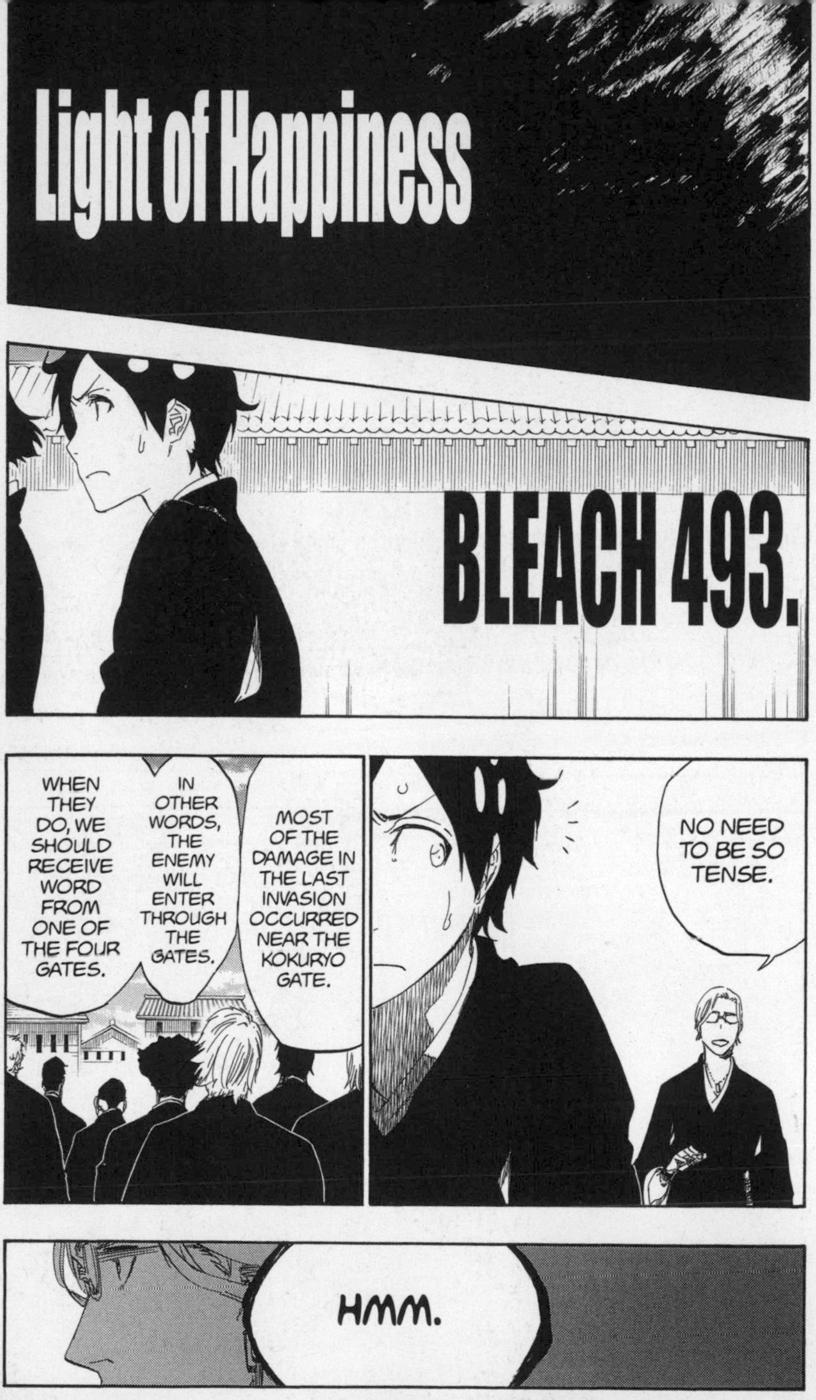
Light of Happiness
BLEACH 493.
NO NEED TO BE SO TENSE.
MOST OF THE DAMAGE IN THE LAST INVASION OCCURRED NEAR THE KOKURYO GATE.
IN OTHER WORDS, THE ENEMY WILL ENTER THROUGH THE GATES.
WHEN THEY DO, WE SHOULD RECEIVE WORD FROM ONE OF THE FOUR GATES.
HMM.

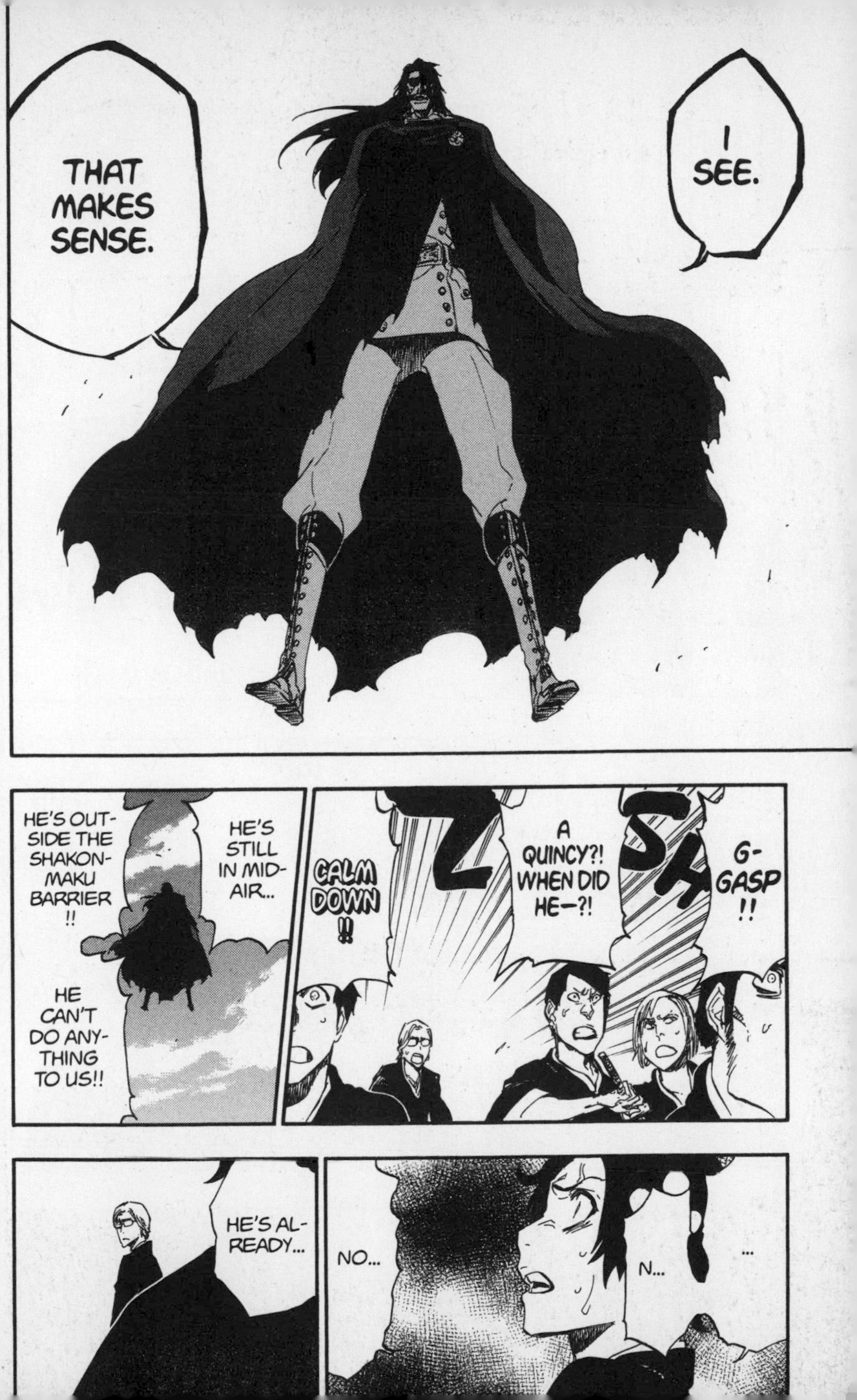
I SEE.
THAT MAKES SENSE.
G-GASP!!
ZSH
A QUINCY?! WHEN DID HE—?!
CALM DOWN!!
HE'S STILL IN MID-AIR...
HE'S OUTSIDE THE SHAKONMAKU BARRIER!!
HE CAN'T DO ANYTHING TO US!!
...
N...
NO...
HE'S ALREADY...

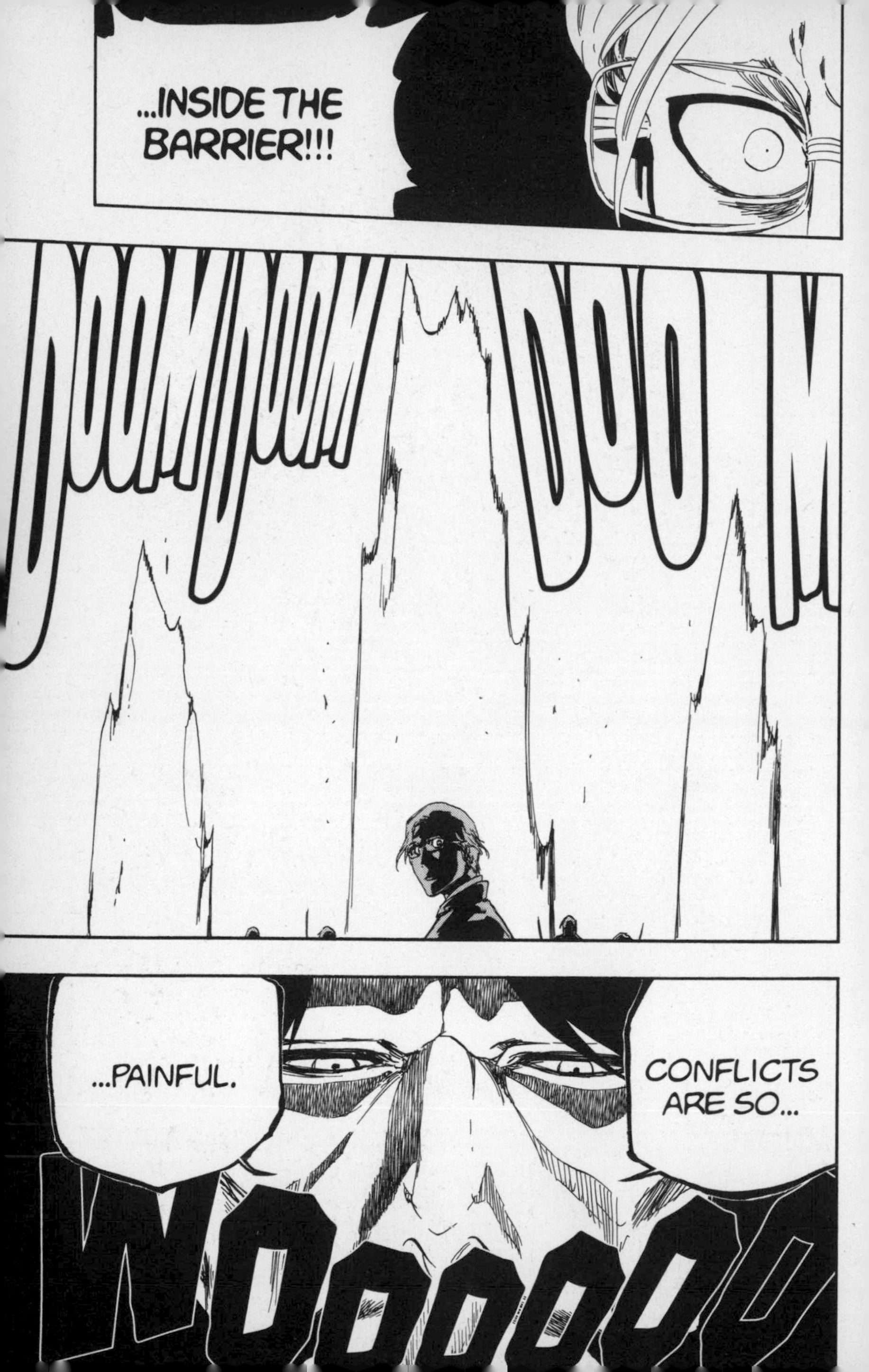
...INSIDE THE BARRIER!!!
CONFLICTS ARE SO...
...PAINFUL.

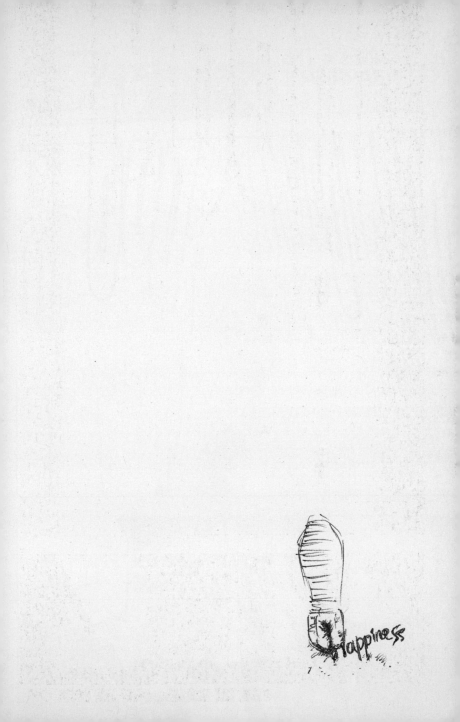

Happiness

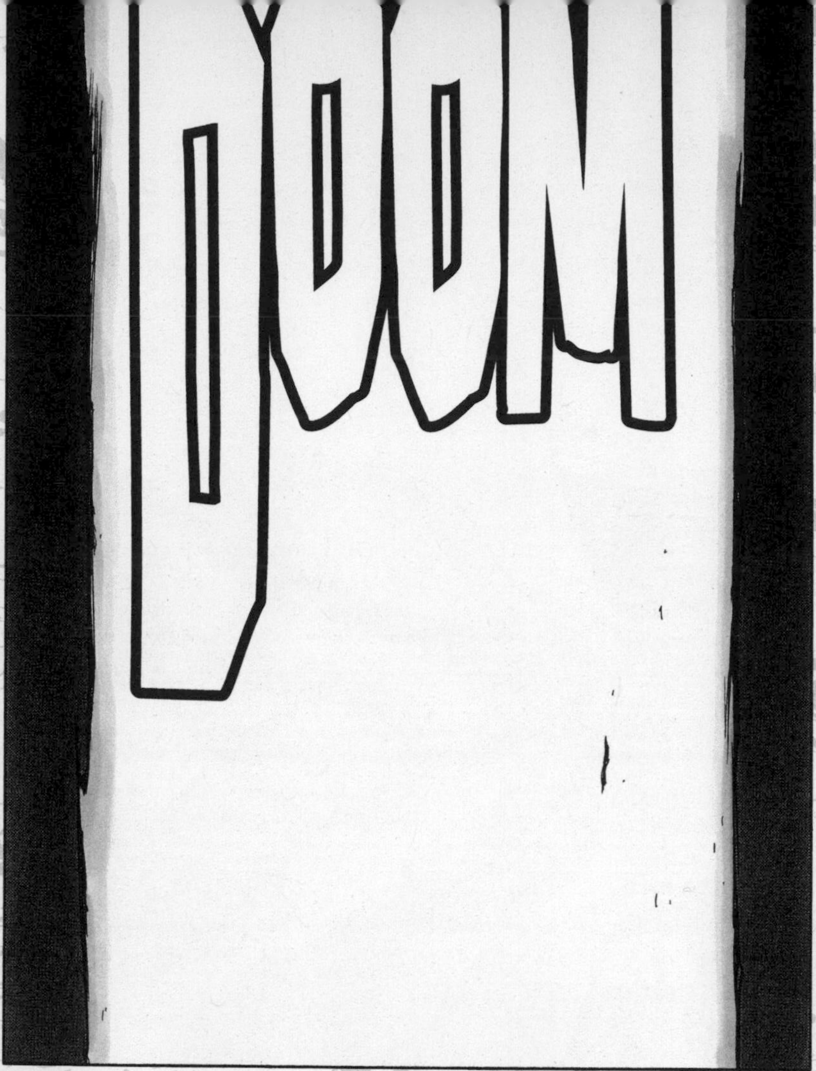
DOOM

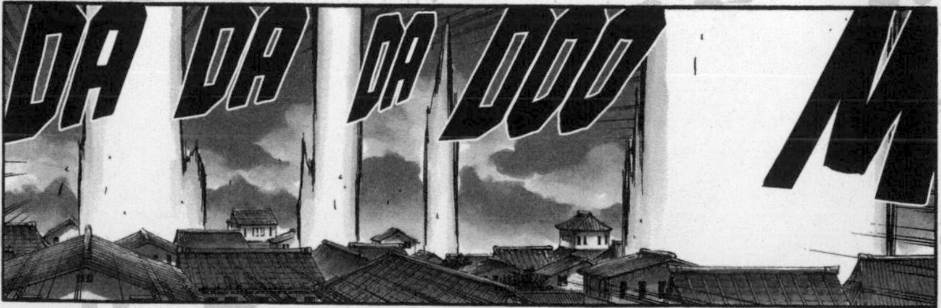
DA DA DA DOOOM

494. THE CLOSING CHAPTER PART ONE

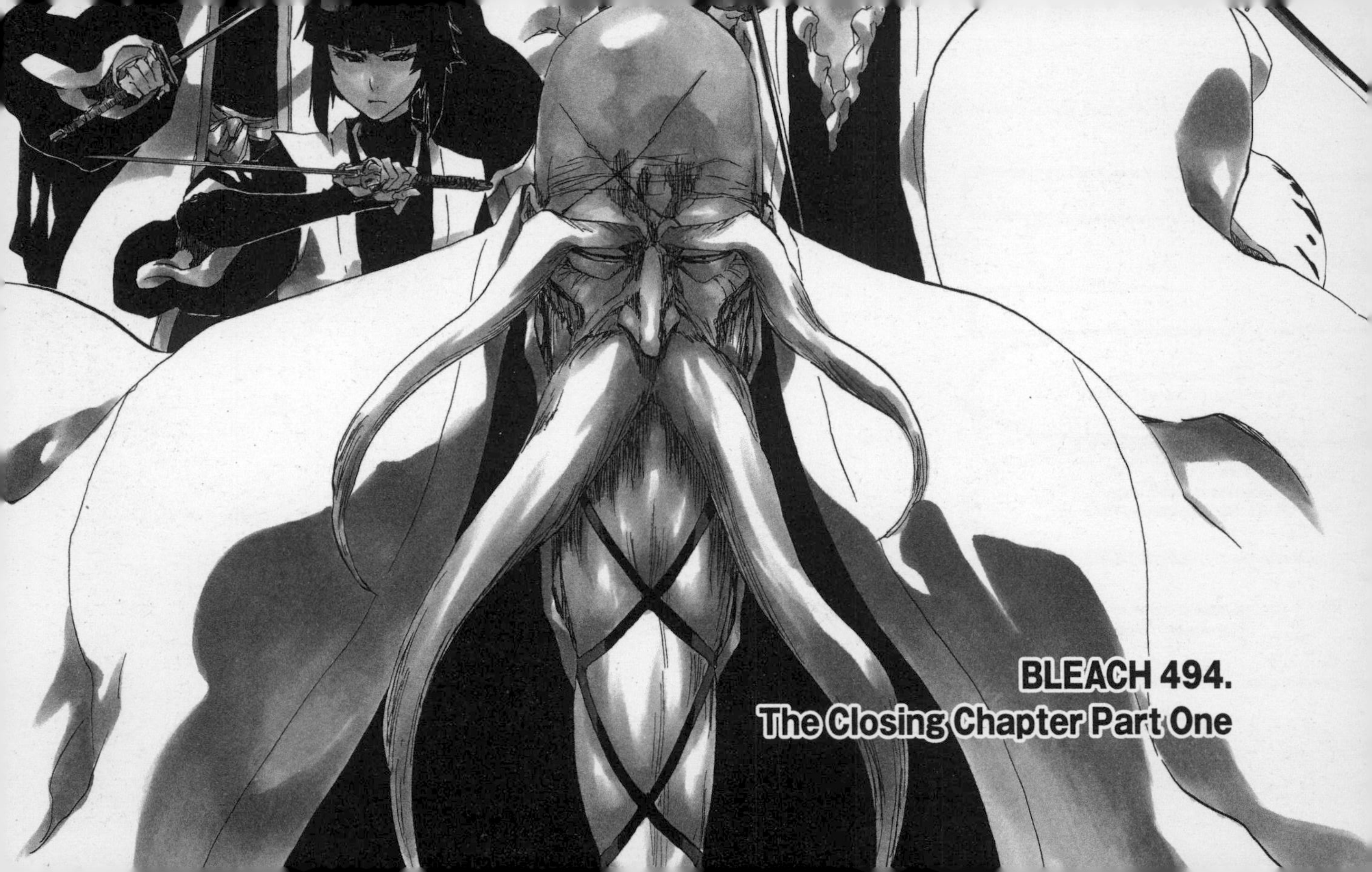
BLEACH 494.
The Closing Chapter Part One

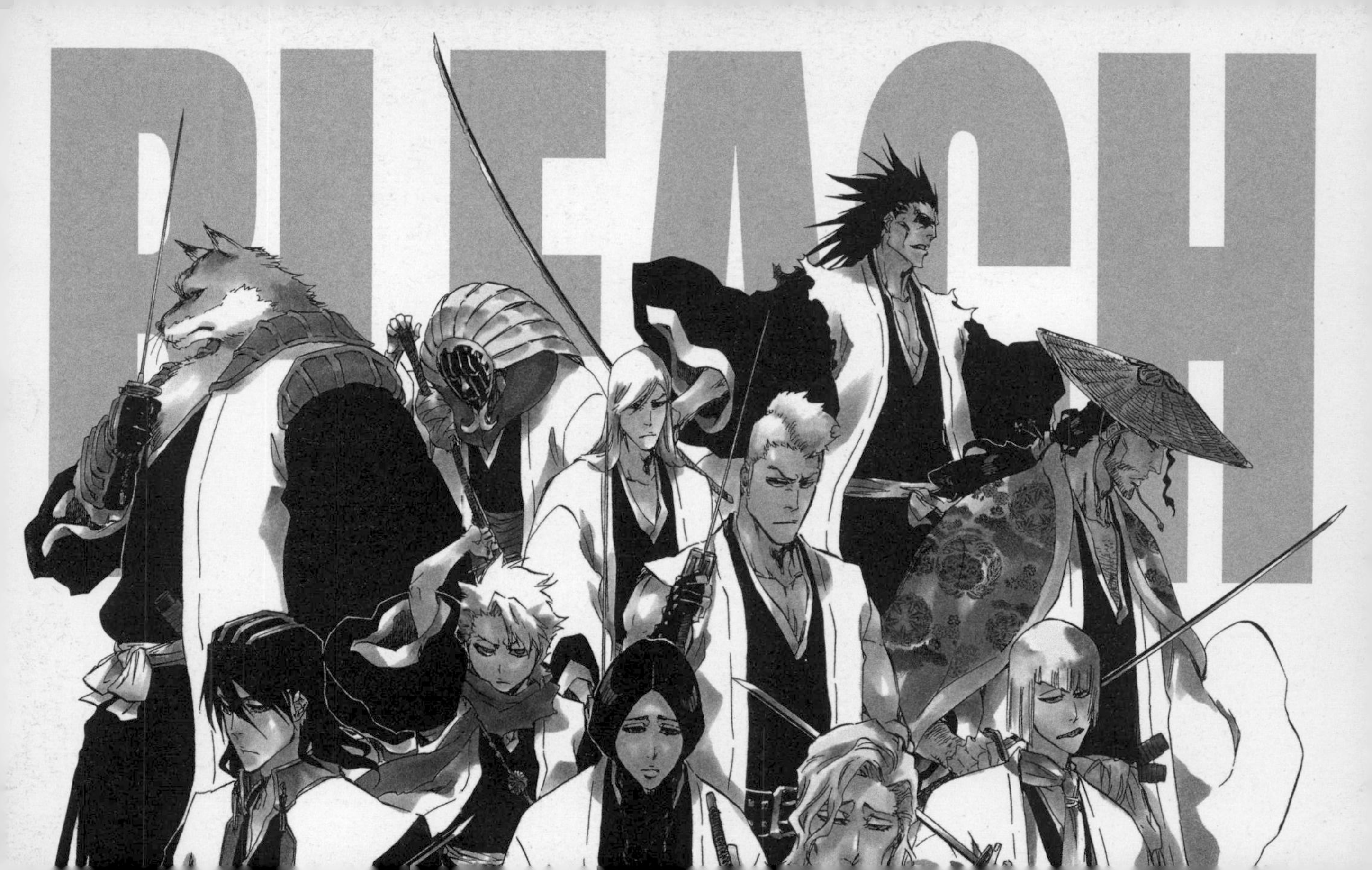
BLEACH

BLEACH
ブリーチ

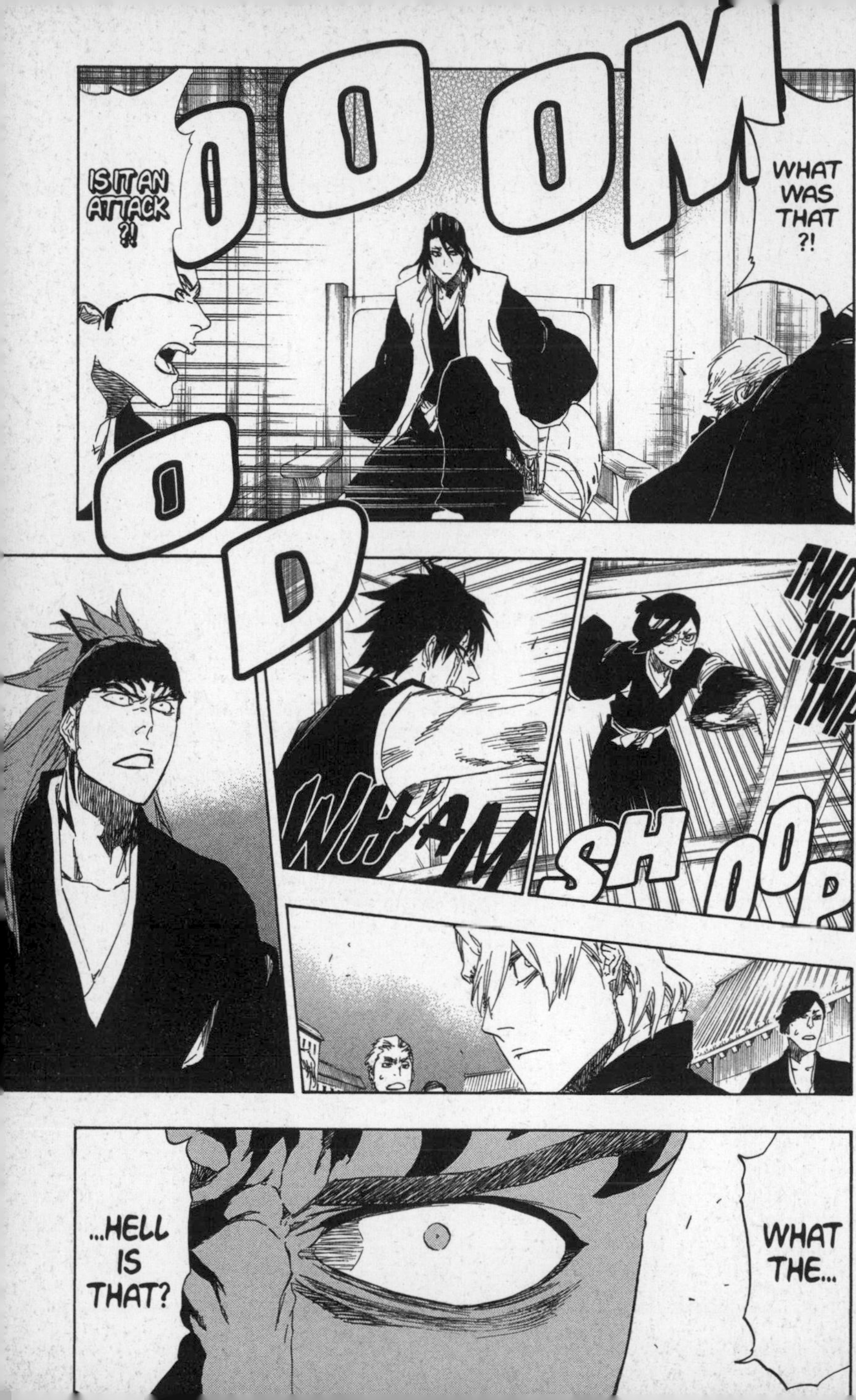
WHAT WAS THAT ?!
IS IT AN ATTACK ?!
DOOOOM
TMP TMP TMP
SHOOP
WHAM
WHAT THE...
...HELL IS THAT?

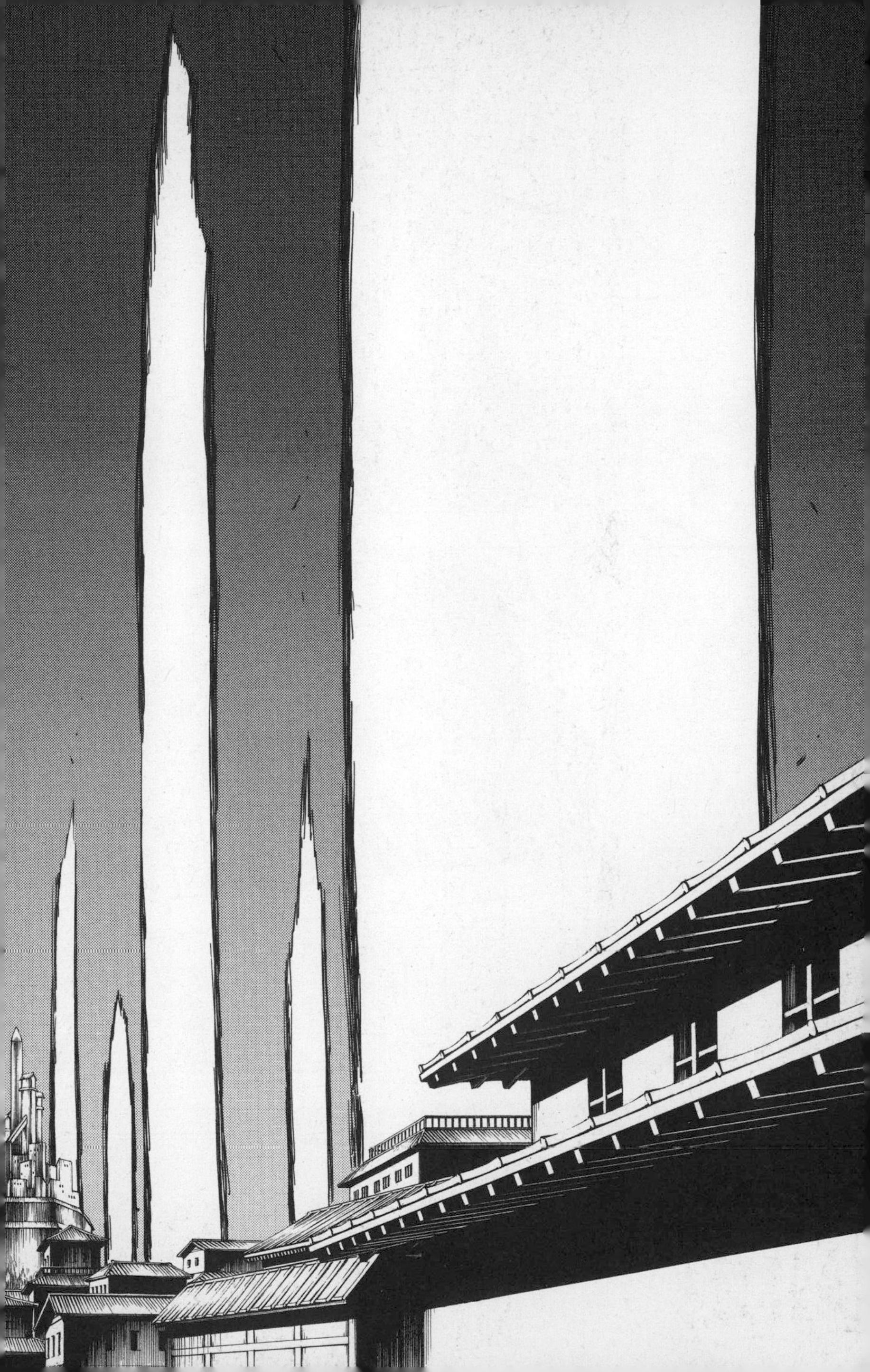

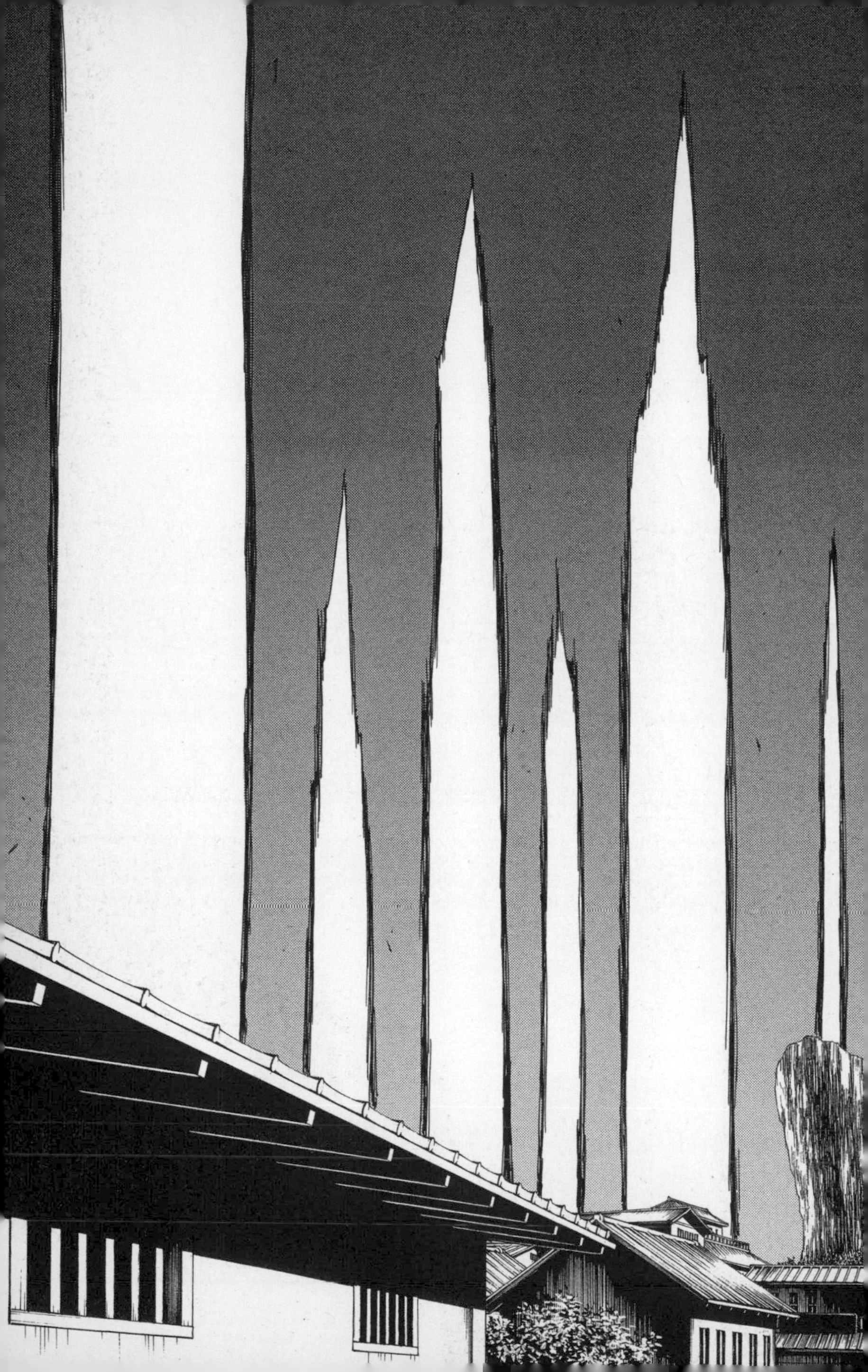

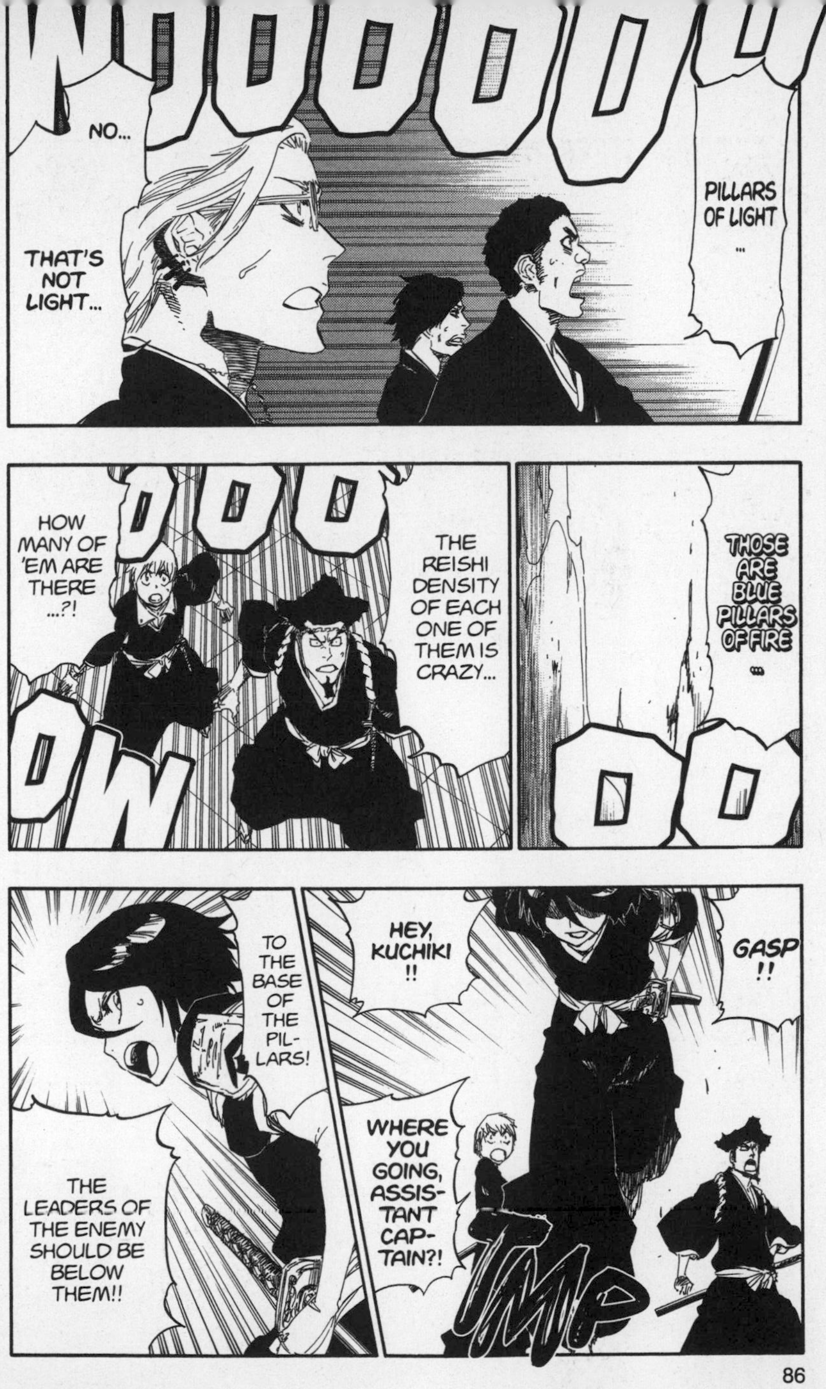
PILLARS OF LIGHT ...
NO...
THAT'S NOT LIGHT...
THOSE ARE BLUE PILLARS OF FIRE ...
THE REISHI DENSITY OF EACH ONE OF THEM IS CRAZY...
HOW MANY OF 'EM ARE THERE ...?!
GASP !!
HEY, KUCHIKI !!
WHERE YOU GOING, ASSISTANT CAPTAIN?!
TO THE BASE OF THE PILLARS!
THE LEADERS OF THE ENEMY SHOULD BE BELOW THEM!!

READ THIS WAY

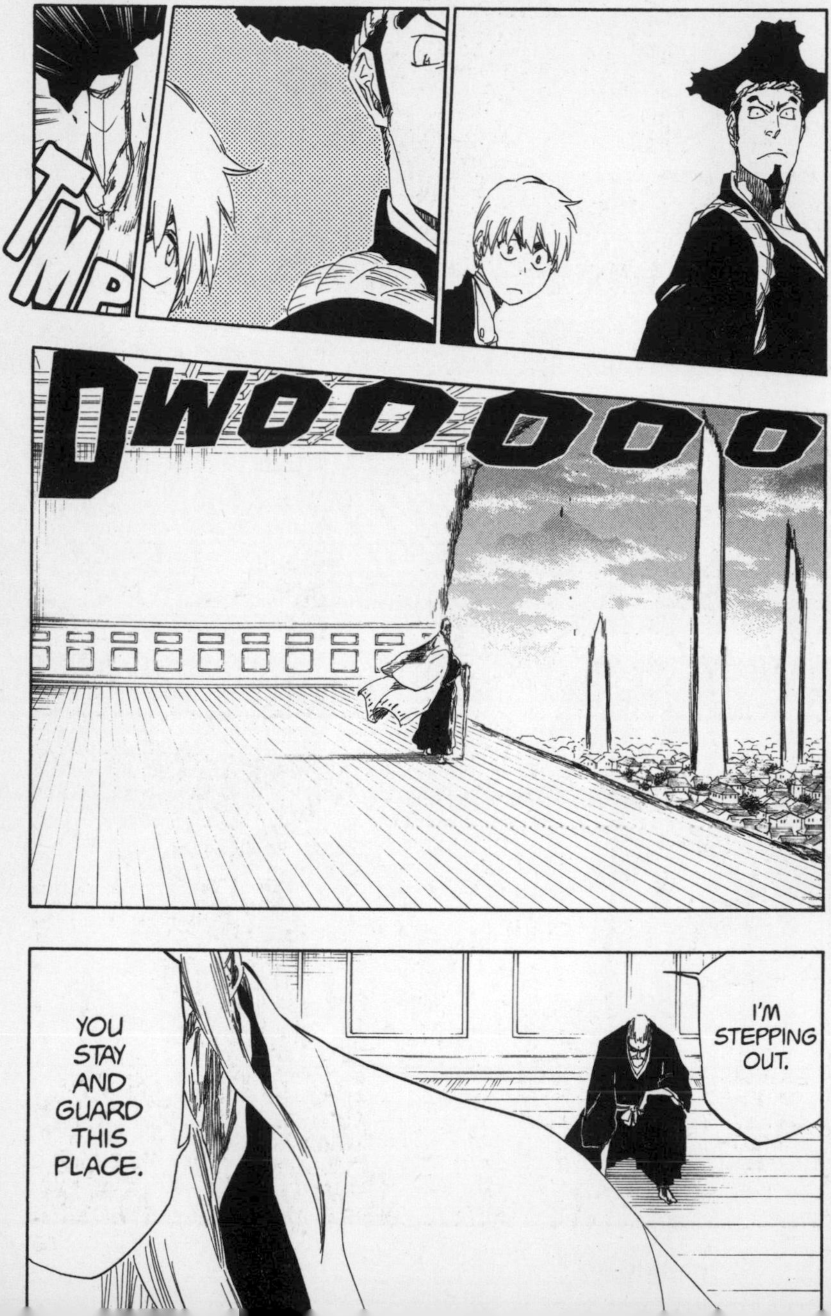
TMP
DWOOOOO
I'M STEPPING OUT.
YOU STAY AND GUARD THIS PLACE.

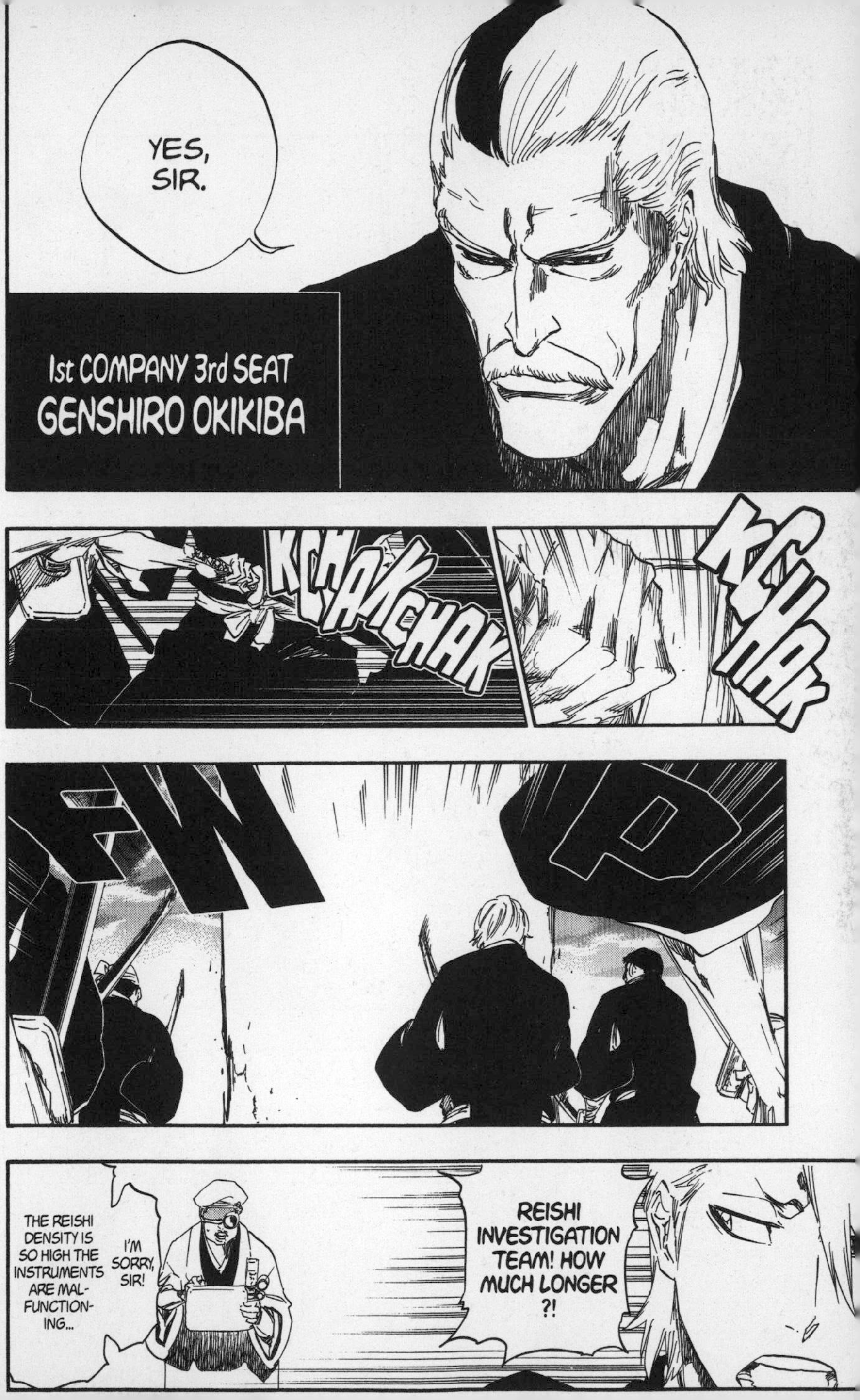
YES, SIR.
1st COMPANY 3rd SEAT GENSHIRO OKIKIBA
KCHAK
KCHAKCHAK
FWP
REISHI INVESTIGATION TEAM! HOW MUCH LONGER?!
I'M SORRY, SIR!
THE REISHI DENSITY IS SO HIGH THE INSTRUMENTS ARE MAL-FUNCTION-ING...

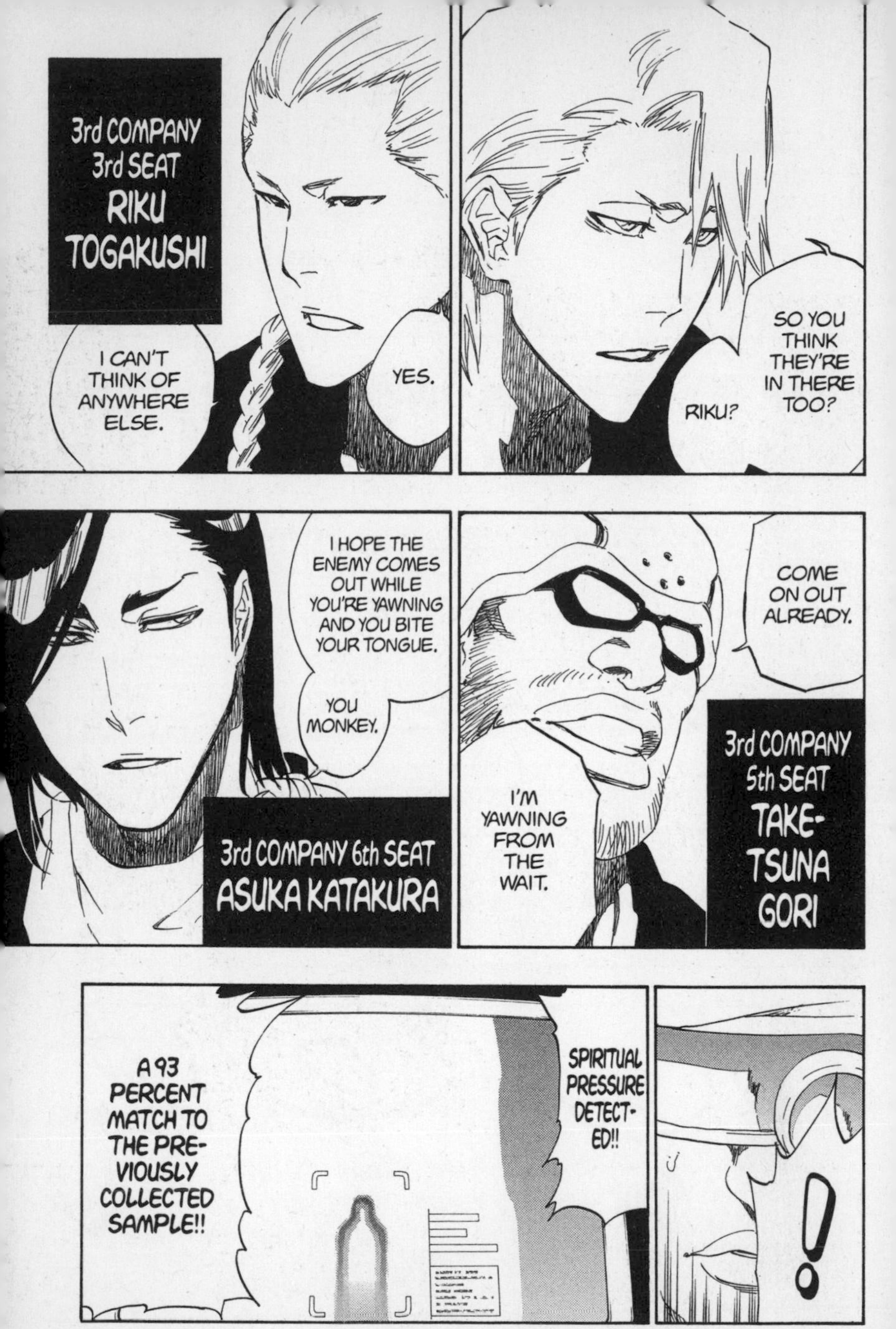
SO YOU THINK THEY'RE IN THERE TOO?
RIKU?
3rd COMPANY 3rd SEAT RIKU TOGAKUSHI
YES.
I CAN'T THINK OF ANYWHERE ELSE.
COME ON OUT ALREADY.
3rd COMPANY 5th SEAT TAKE-TSUNA GORI
I'M YAWNING FROM THE WAIT.
I HOPE THE ENEMY COMES OUT WHILE YOU'RE YAWNING AND YOU BITE YOUR TONGUE.
YOU MONKEY.
3rd COMPANY 6th SEAT ASUKA KATAKURA
!
SPIRITUAL PRESSURE DETECT-ED!!
A 93 PERCENT MATCH TO THE PRE-VIOUSLY COLLECTED SAMPLE!!

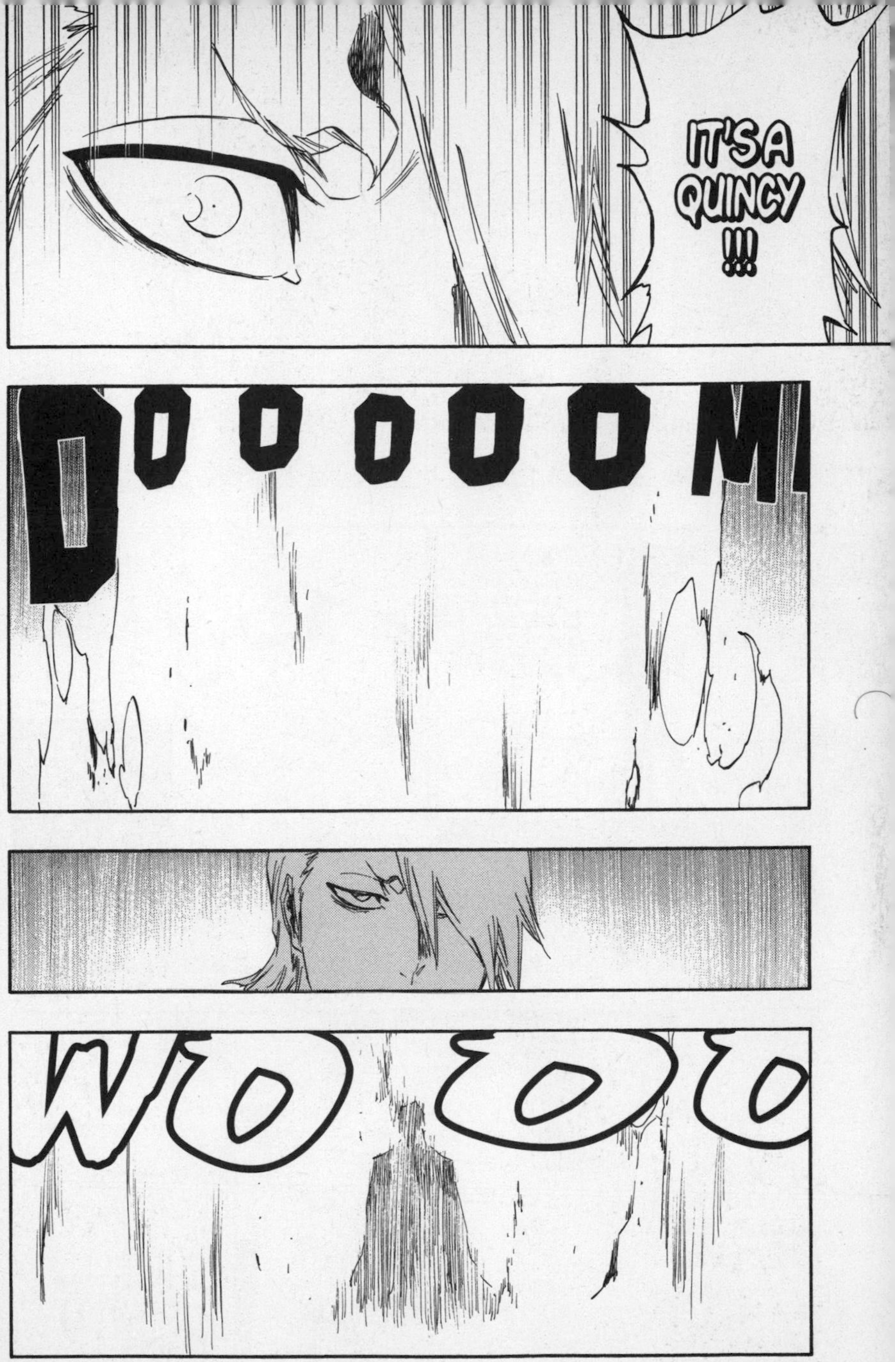
IT'S A QUINCY !!!
DOOOOOM
WOOOO

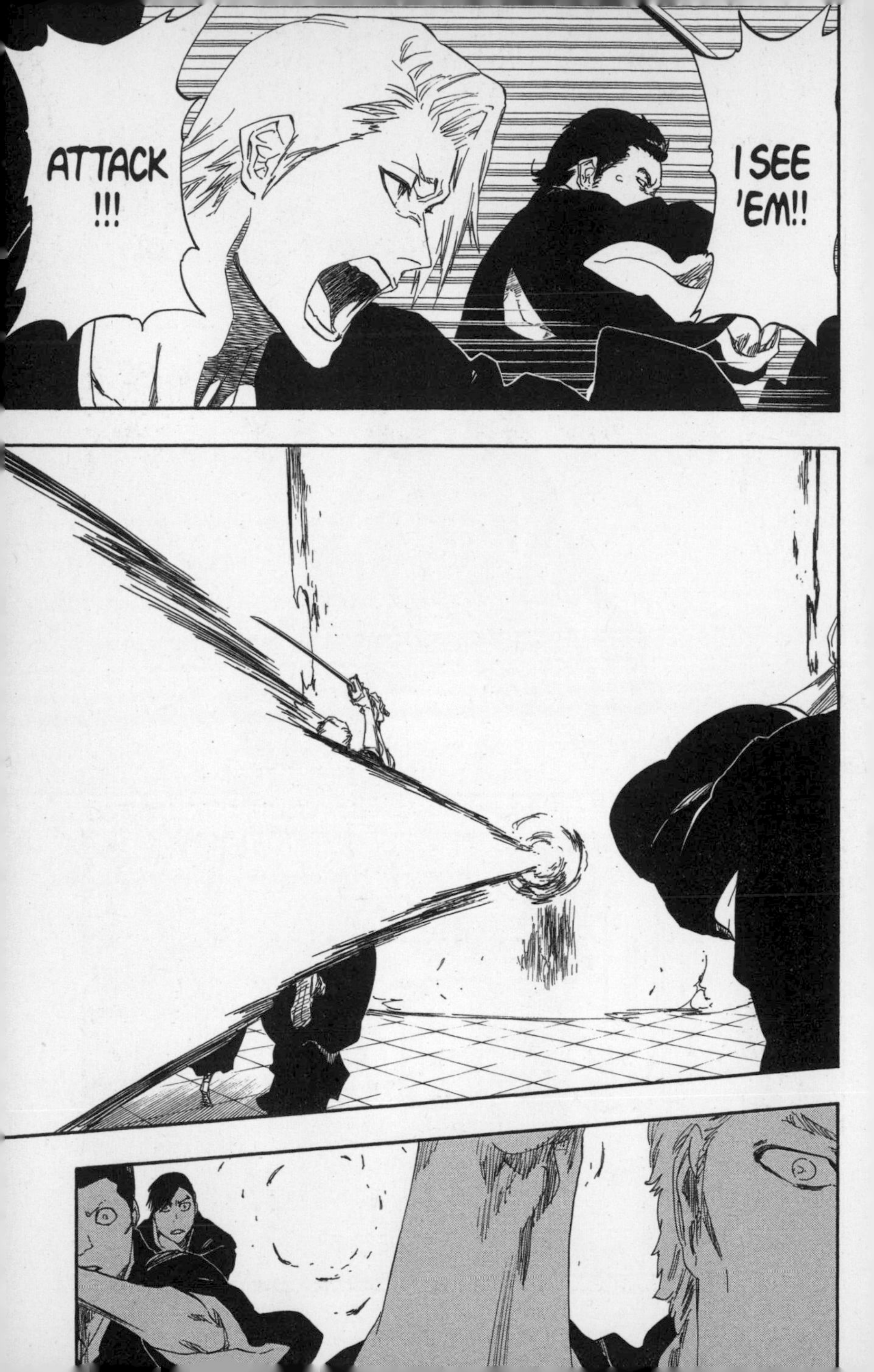
I SEE 'EM!!
ATTACK !!!

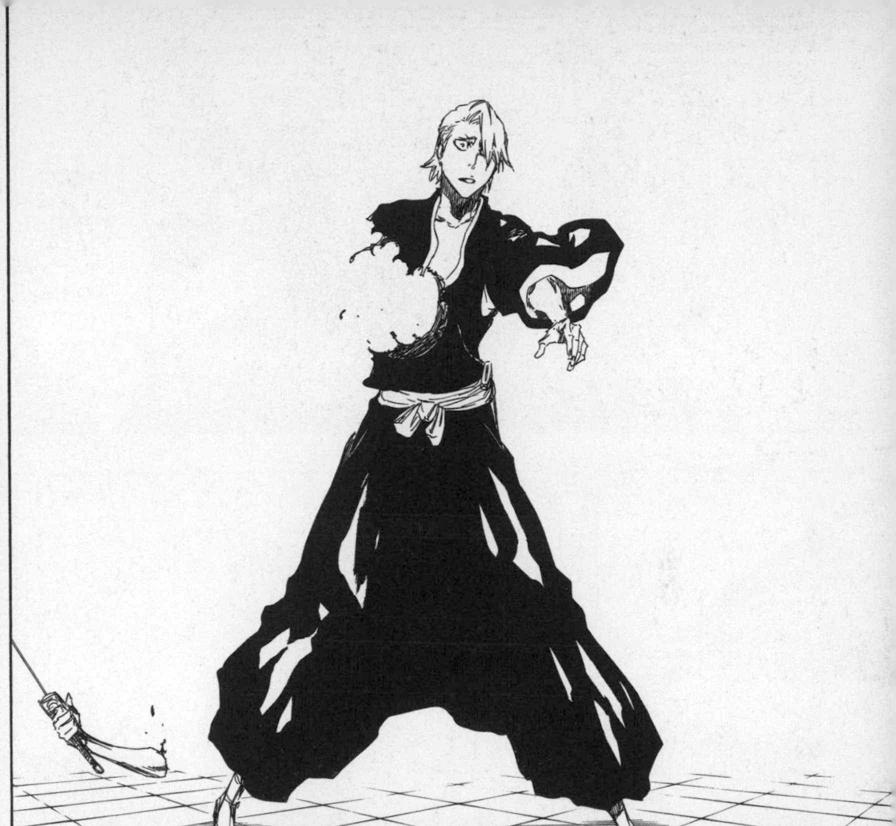

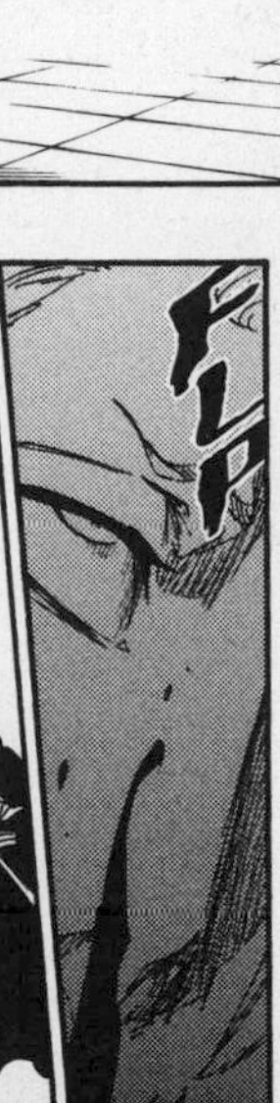

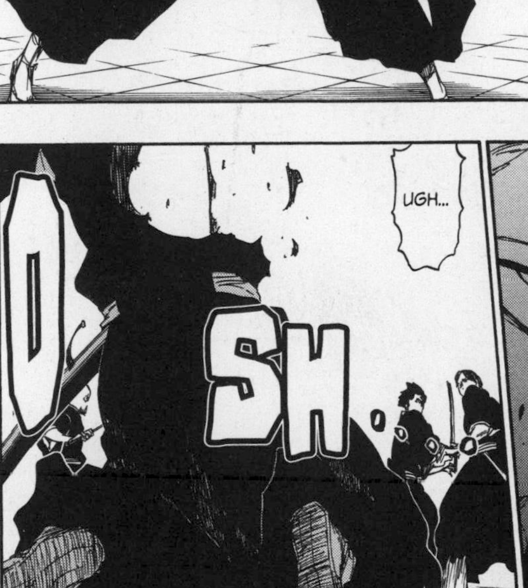
UGH...
D
SH

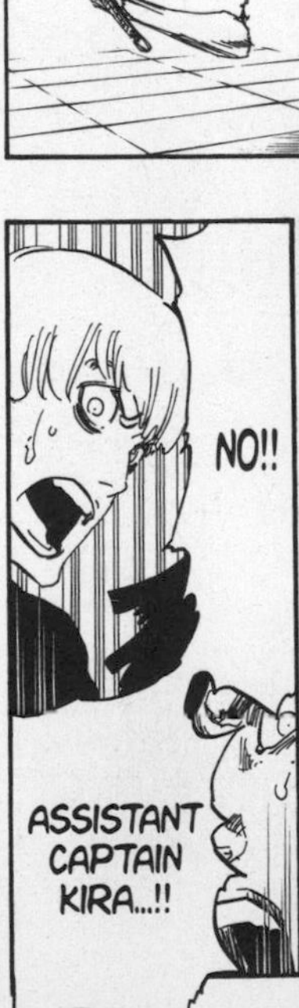
NO!!
ASSISTANT CAPTAIN KIRA...!!

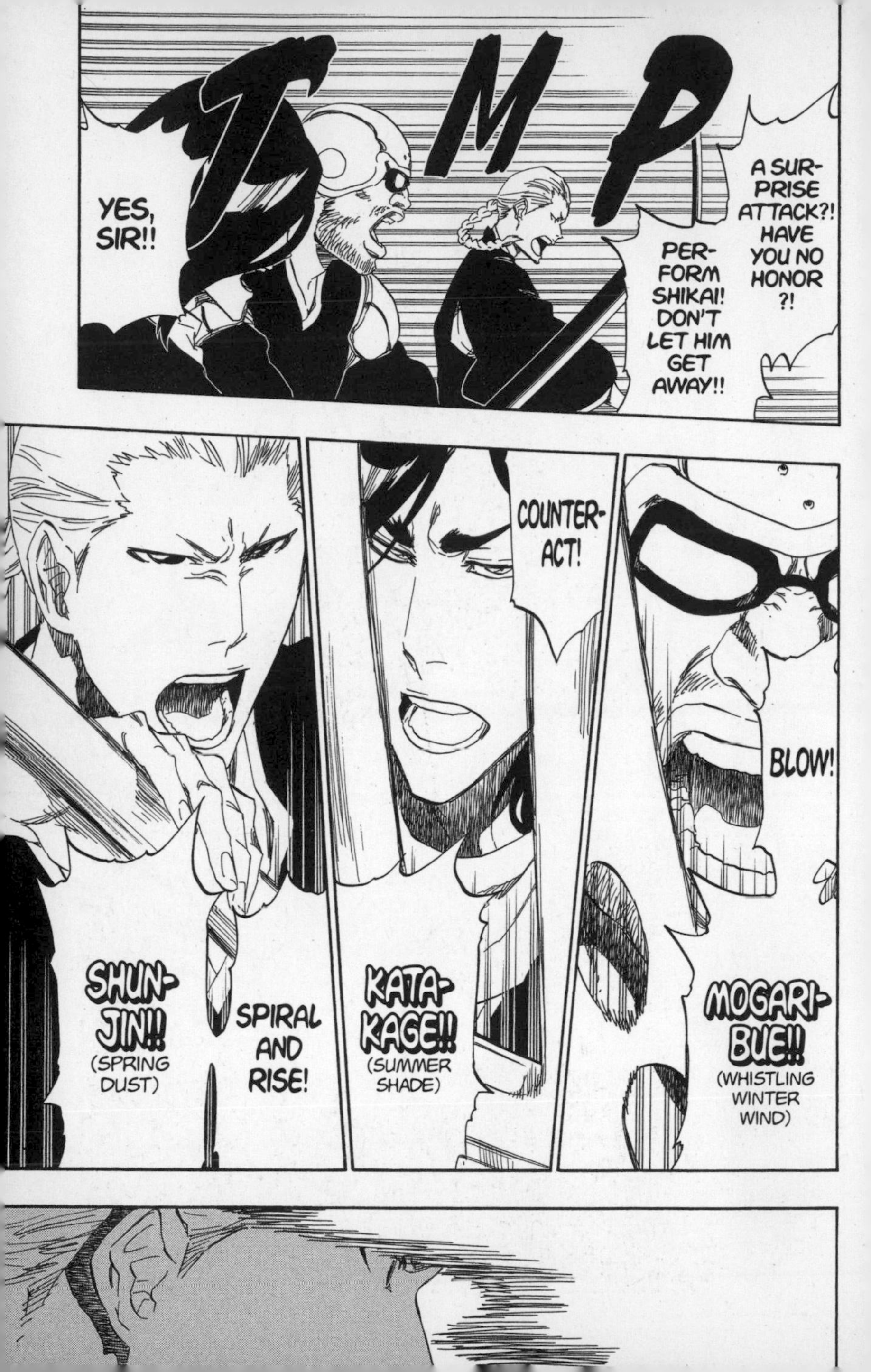
A SURPRISE ATTACK?! HAVE YOU NO HONOR?!
PERFORM SHIKAI! DON'T LET HIM GET AWAY!!
YES, SIR!!
BLOW!
MOGARI-BUE!! (WHISTLING WINTER WIND)
COUNTER-ACT!
KATA-KAGE!! (SUMMER SHADE)
SPIRAL AND RISE!
SHUN-JIN!! (SPRING DUST)

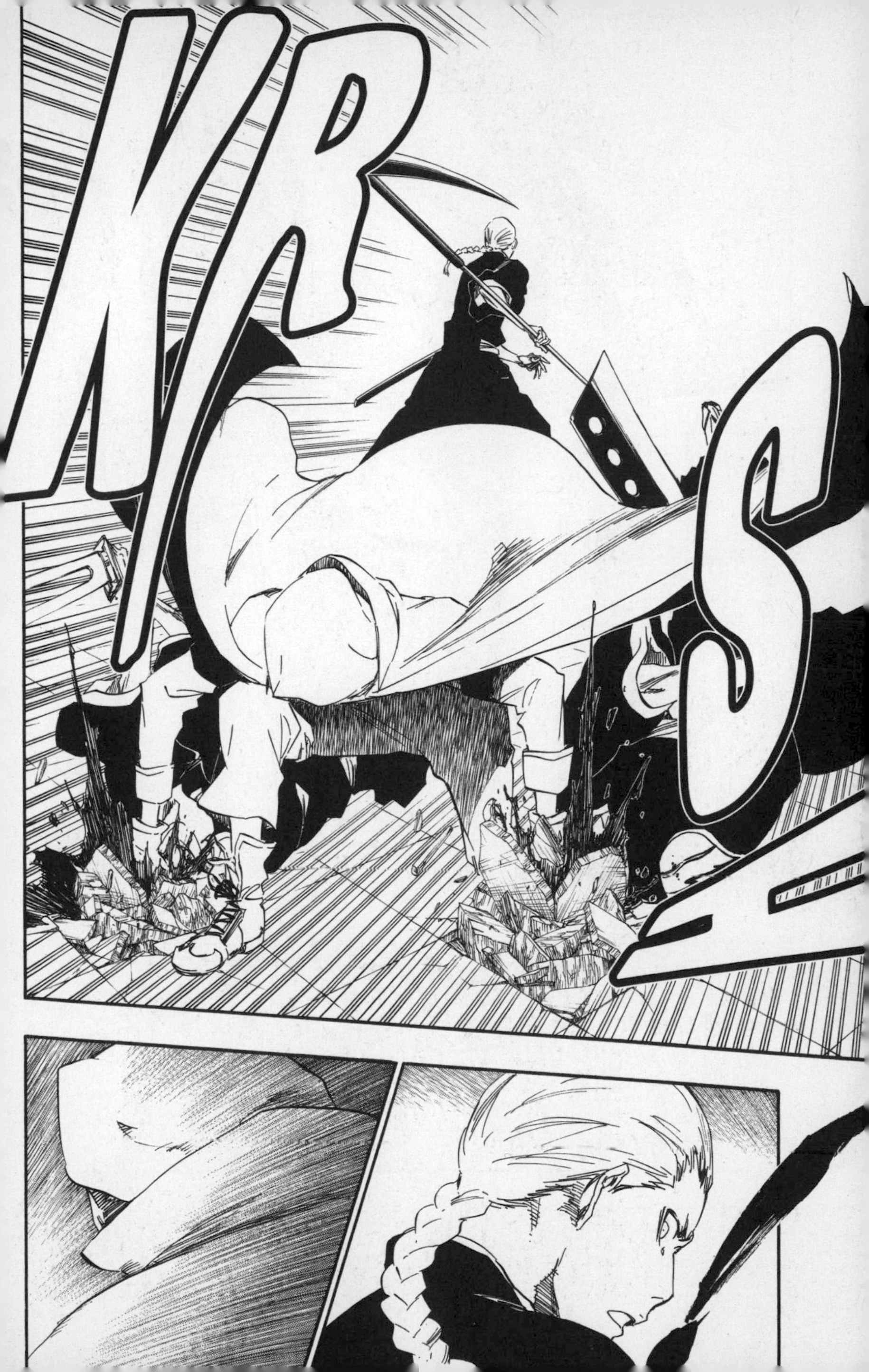
KRSSH

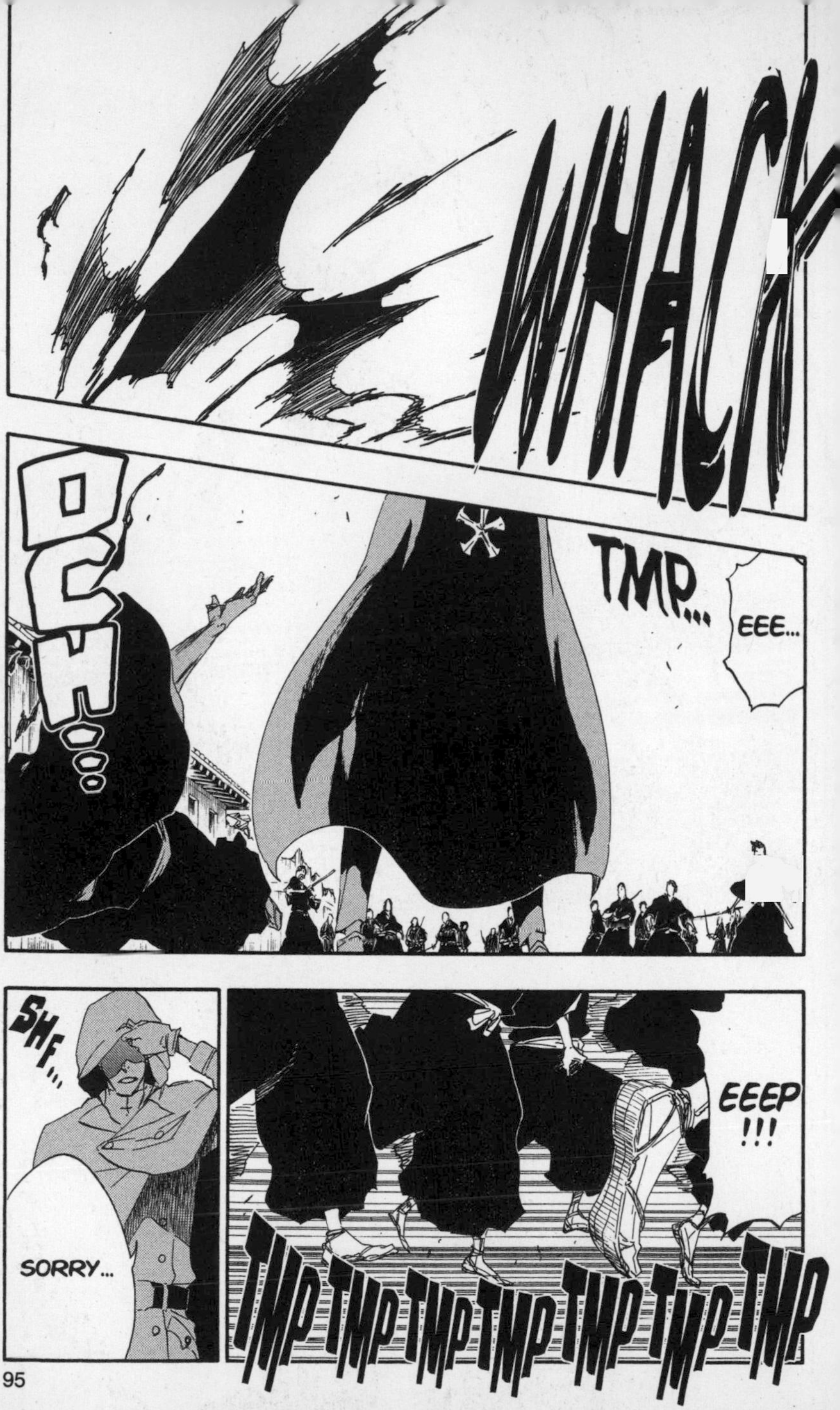
WHACK
EEE...
TMP...
OCH...
EEEP !!!
TMP TMP TMP TMP TMP TMP TMP
SHF...
SORRY...

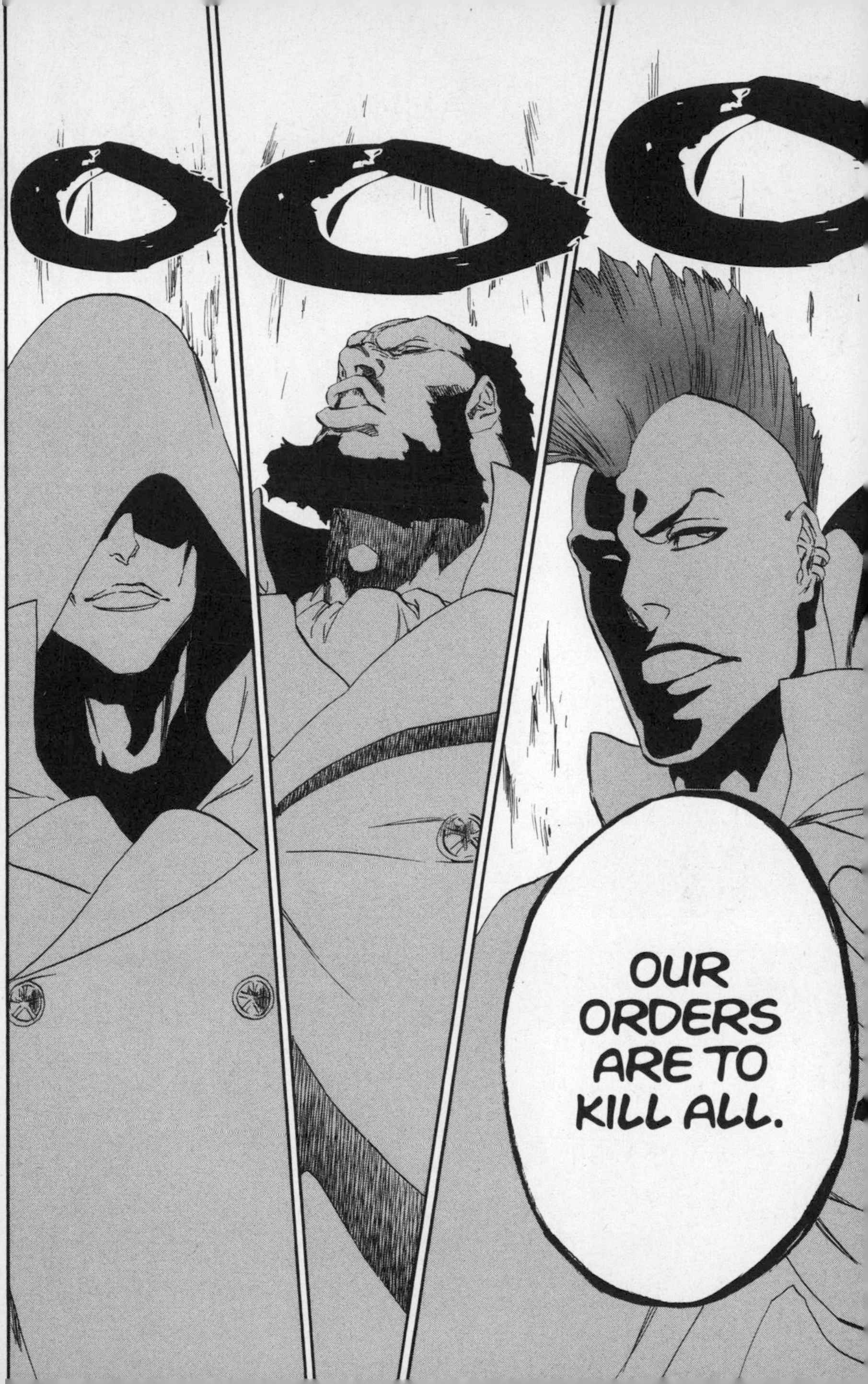
OUR ORDERS ARE TO KILL ALL.

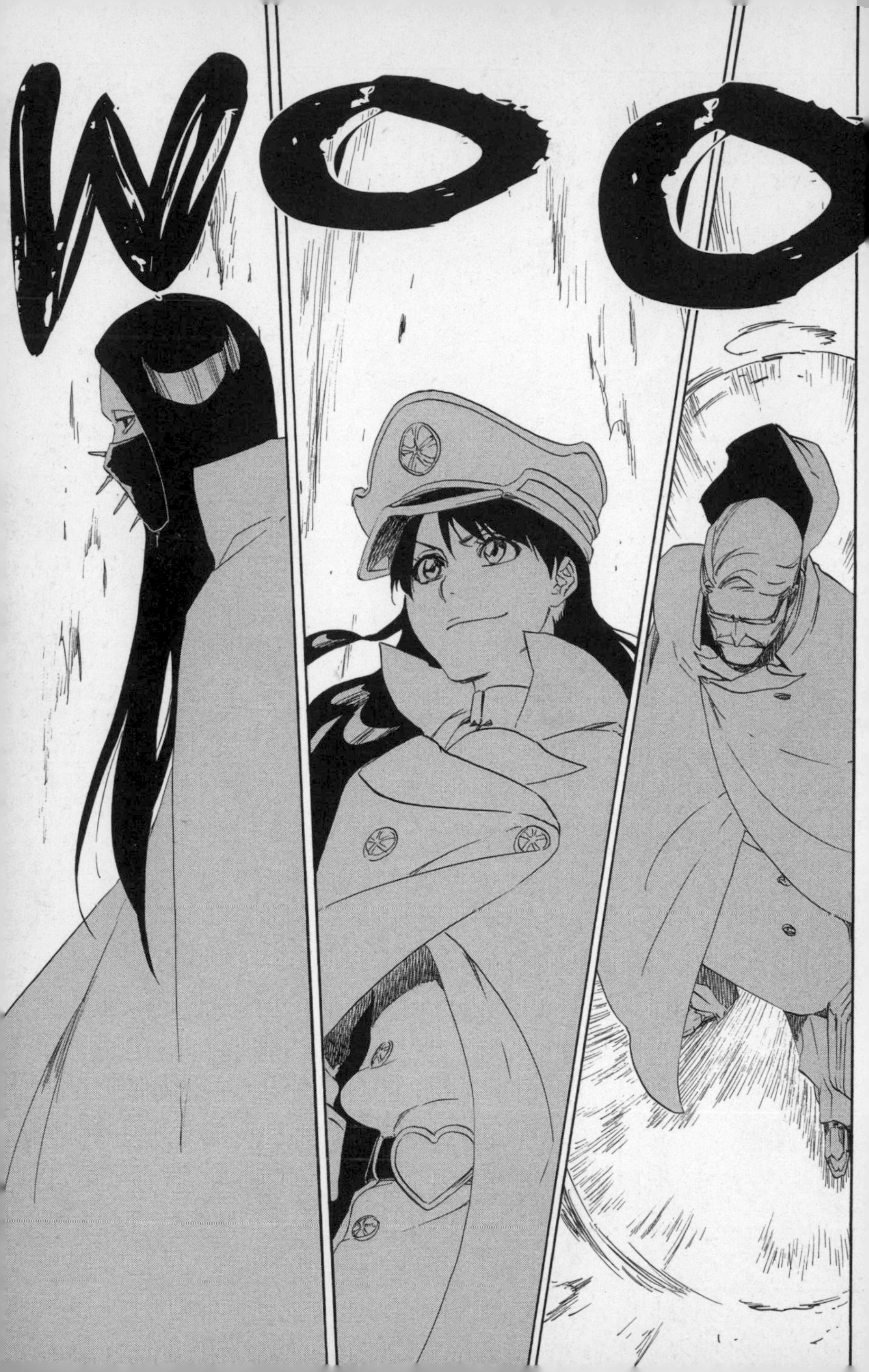
WOOO

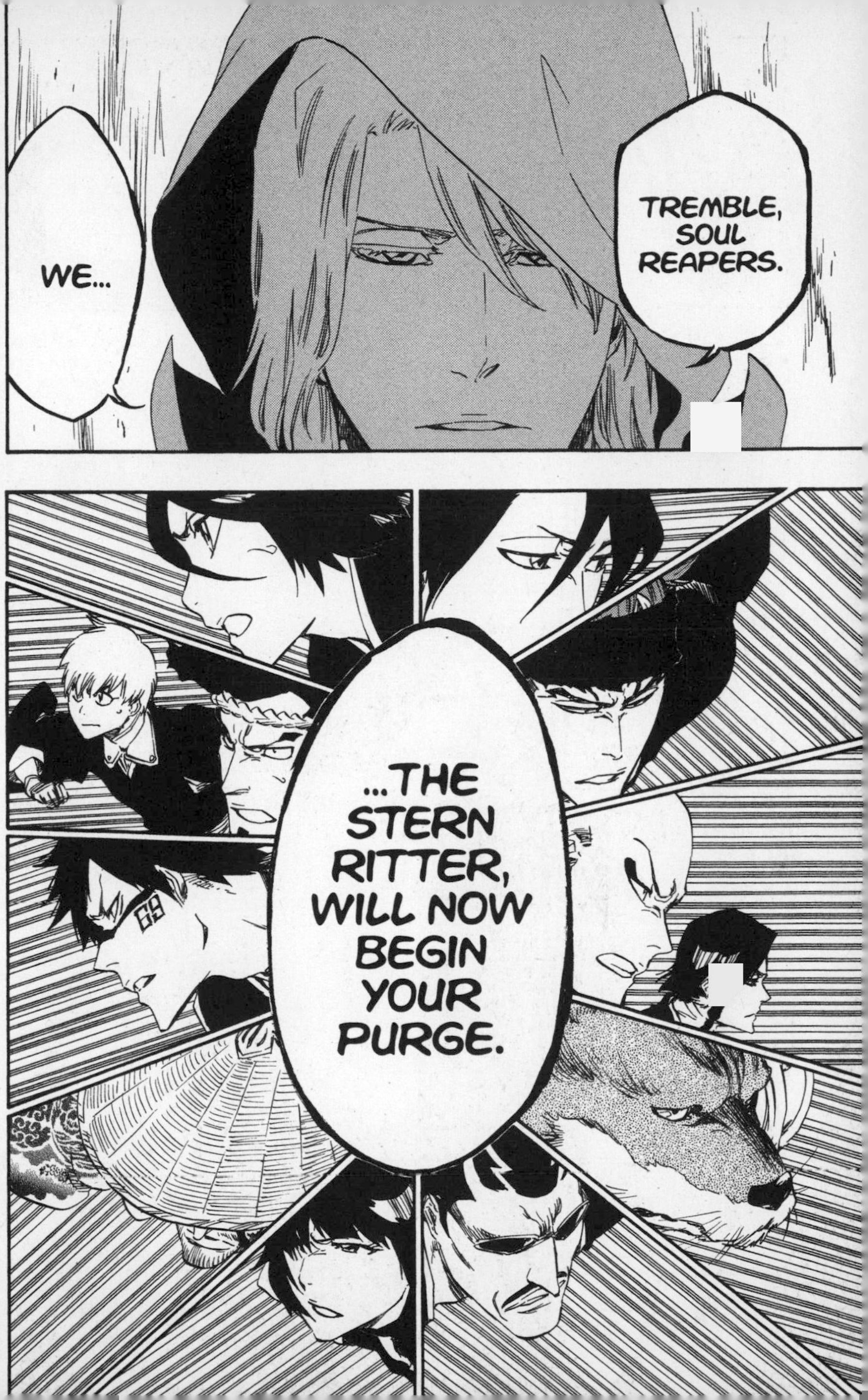
TREMBLE, SOUL REAPERS.
WE...
...THE STERN RITTER, WILL NOW BEGIN YOUR PURGE.

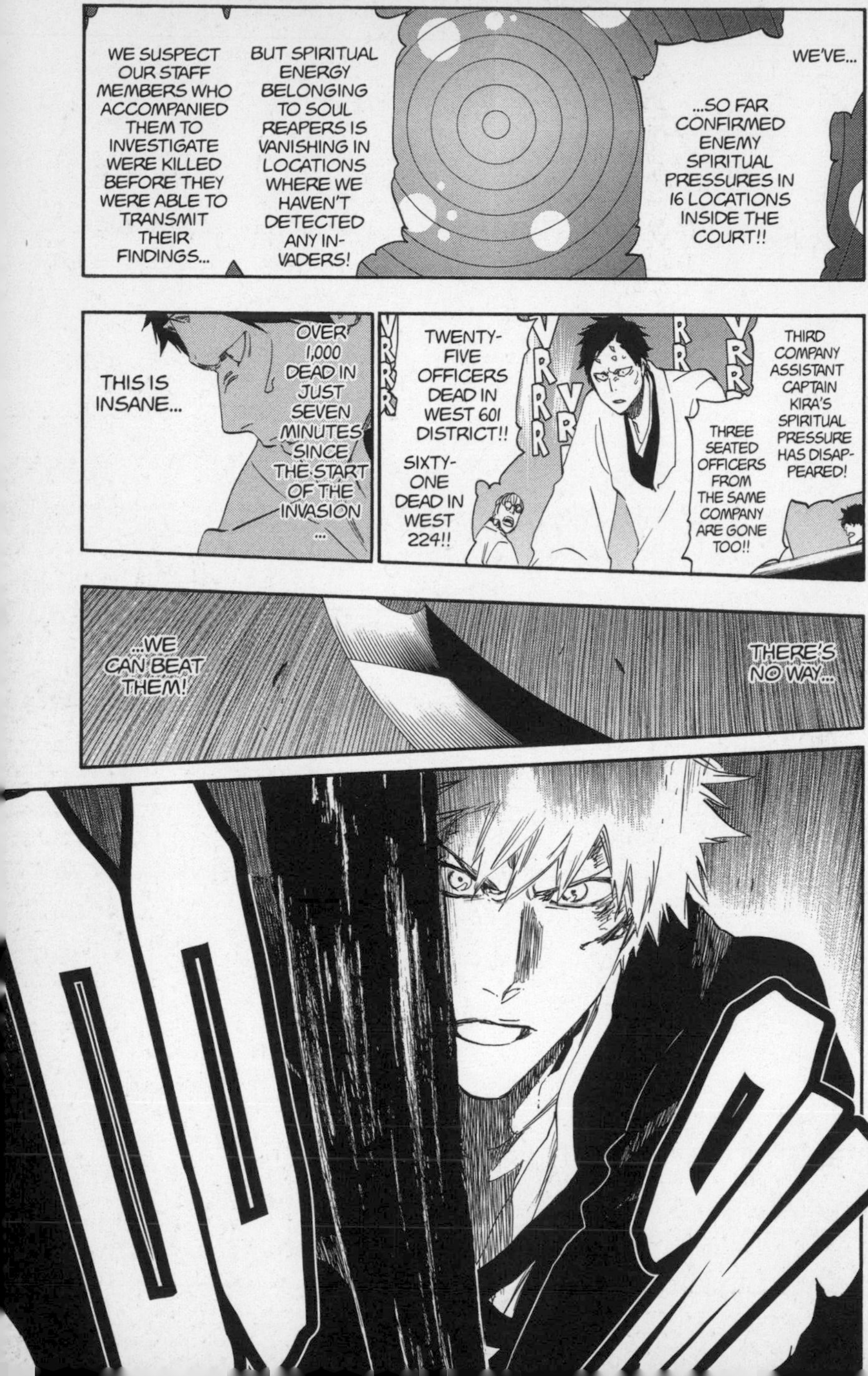
WE'VE...
...SO FAR CONFIRMED ENEMY SPIRITUAL PRESSURES IN 16 LOCATIONS INSIDE THE COURT!!
BUT SPIRITUAL ENERGY BELONGING TO SOUL REAPERS IS VANISHING IN LOCATIONS WHERE WE HAVEN'T DETECTED ANY INVADERS!
WE SUSPECT OUR STAFF MEMBERS WHO ACCOMPANIED THEM TO INVESTIGATE WERE KILLED BEFORE THEY WERE ABLE TO TRANSMIT THEIR FINDINGS...
THIRD COMPANY ASSISTANT CAPTAIN KIRA'S SPIRITUAL PRESSURE HAS DISAPPEARED!
THREE SEATED OFFICERS FROM THE SAME COMPANY ARE GONE TOO!!
VRRR
TWENTY-FIVE OFFICERS DEAD IN WEST 601 DISTRICT!!
SIXTY-ONE DEAD IN WEST 224!!
OVER 1,000 DEAD IN JUST SEVEN MINUTES SINCE THE START OF THE INVASION...
THIS IS INSANE...
THERE'S NO WAY...
...WE CAN BEAT THEM!

3rd COMPANY, 3rd SEAT, TOGAKUSHI
HIS FIRST APPEARANCE WAS ACTUALLY VOLUME 10.

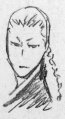

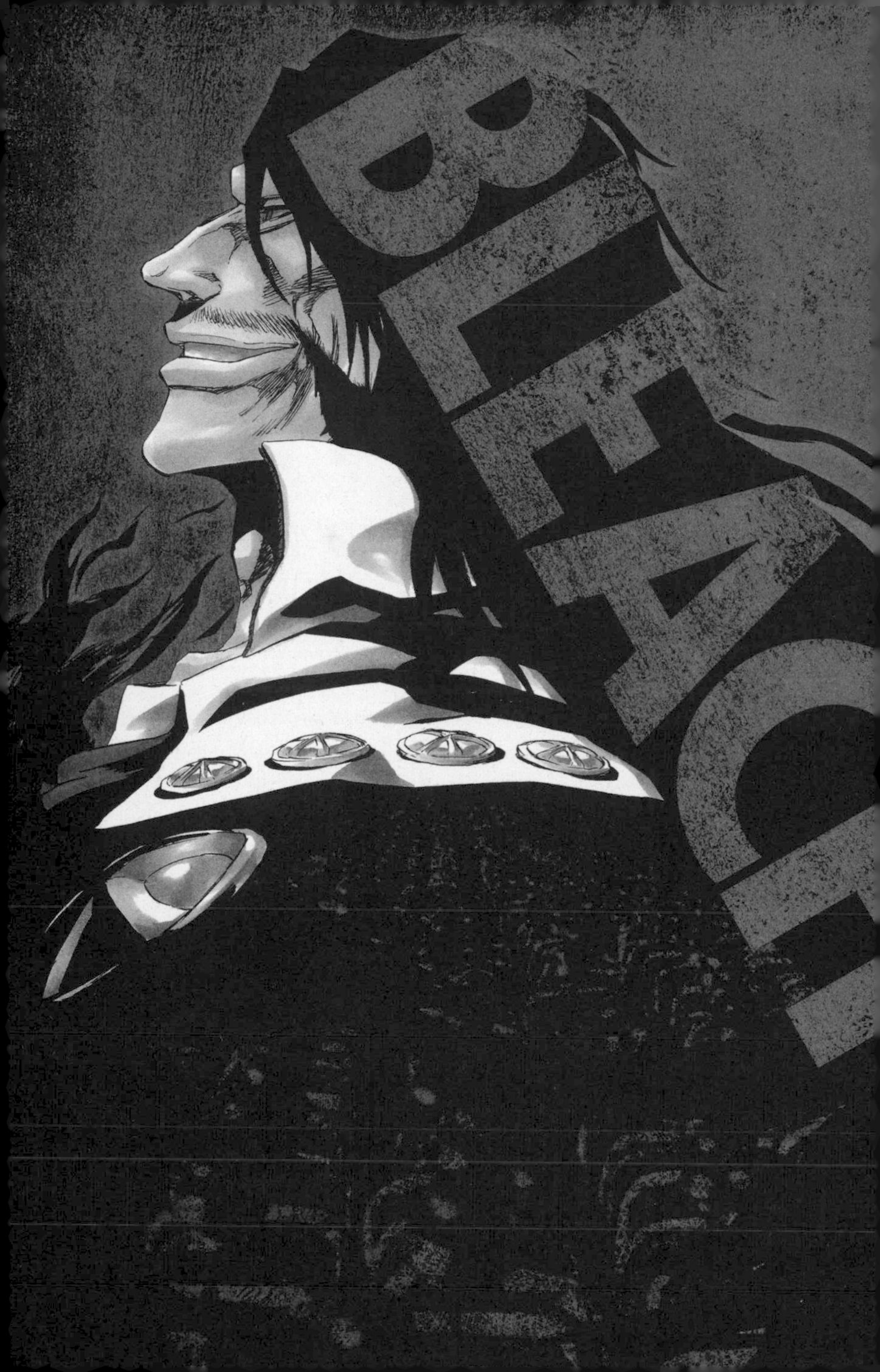
BLEACH

BLEACH
ブリーチ

READ THIS WAY

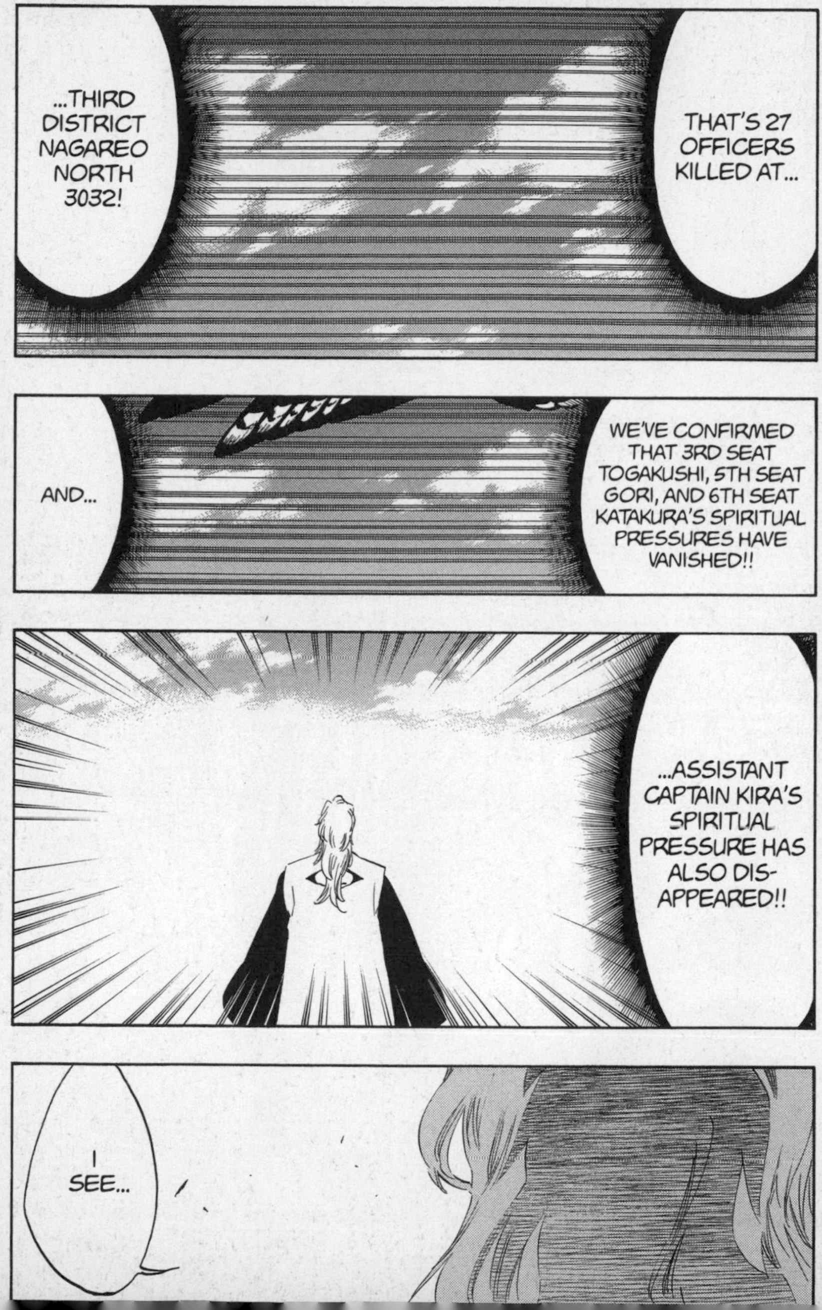
THAT'S 27 OFFICERS KILLED AT...
...THIRD DISTRICT NAGAREO NORTH 3032!
WE'VE CONFIRMED THAT 3RD SEAT TOGAKUSHI, 5TH SEAT GORI, AND 6TH SEAT KATAKURA'S SPIRITUAL PRESSURES HAVE VANISHED!!
AND...
...ASSISTANT CAPTAIN KIRA'S SPIRITUAL PRESSURE HAS ALSO DIS-APPEARED!!
I SEE...

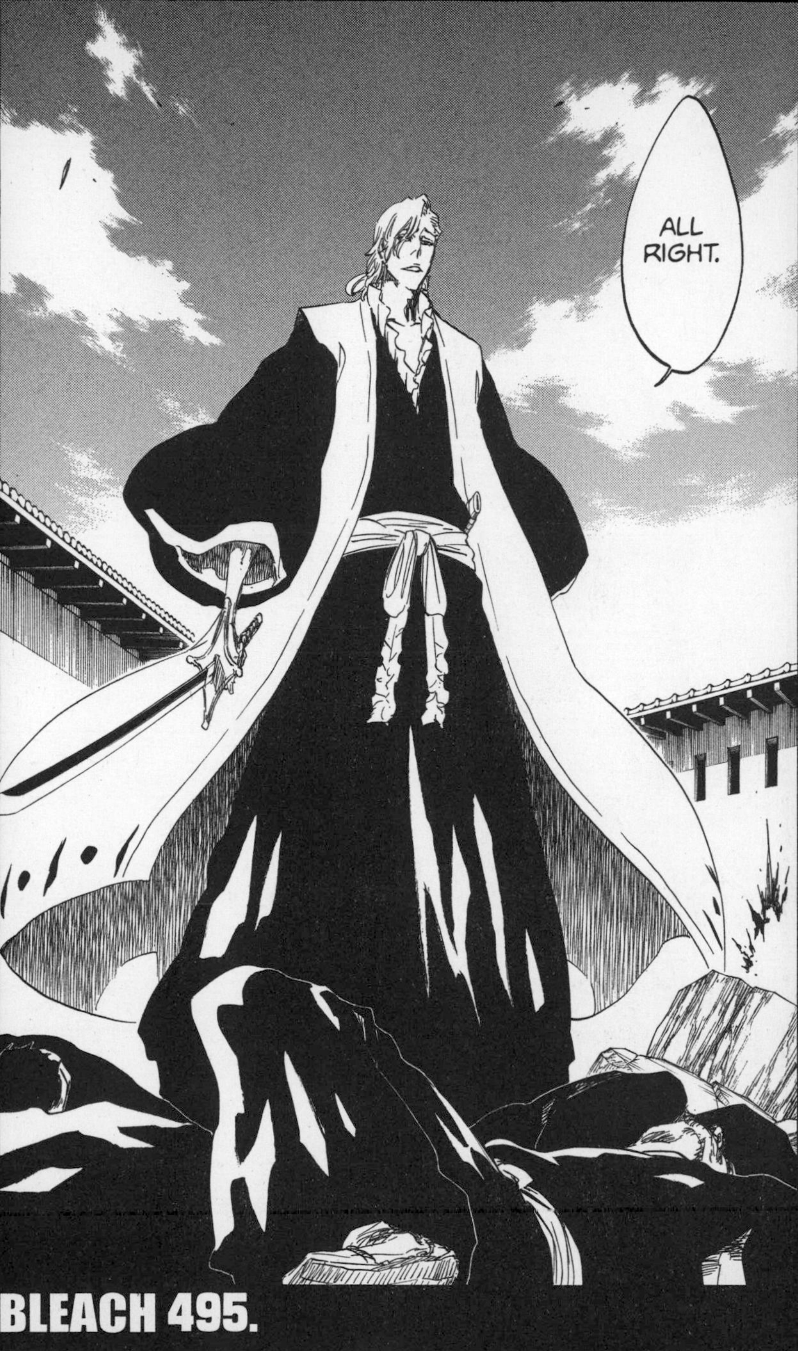
ALL RIGHT.

BLEACH 495.
Bleeding Guitar Blues

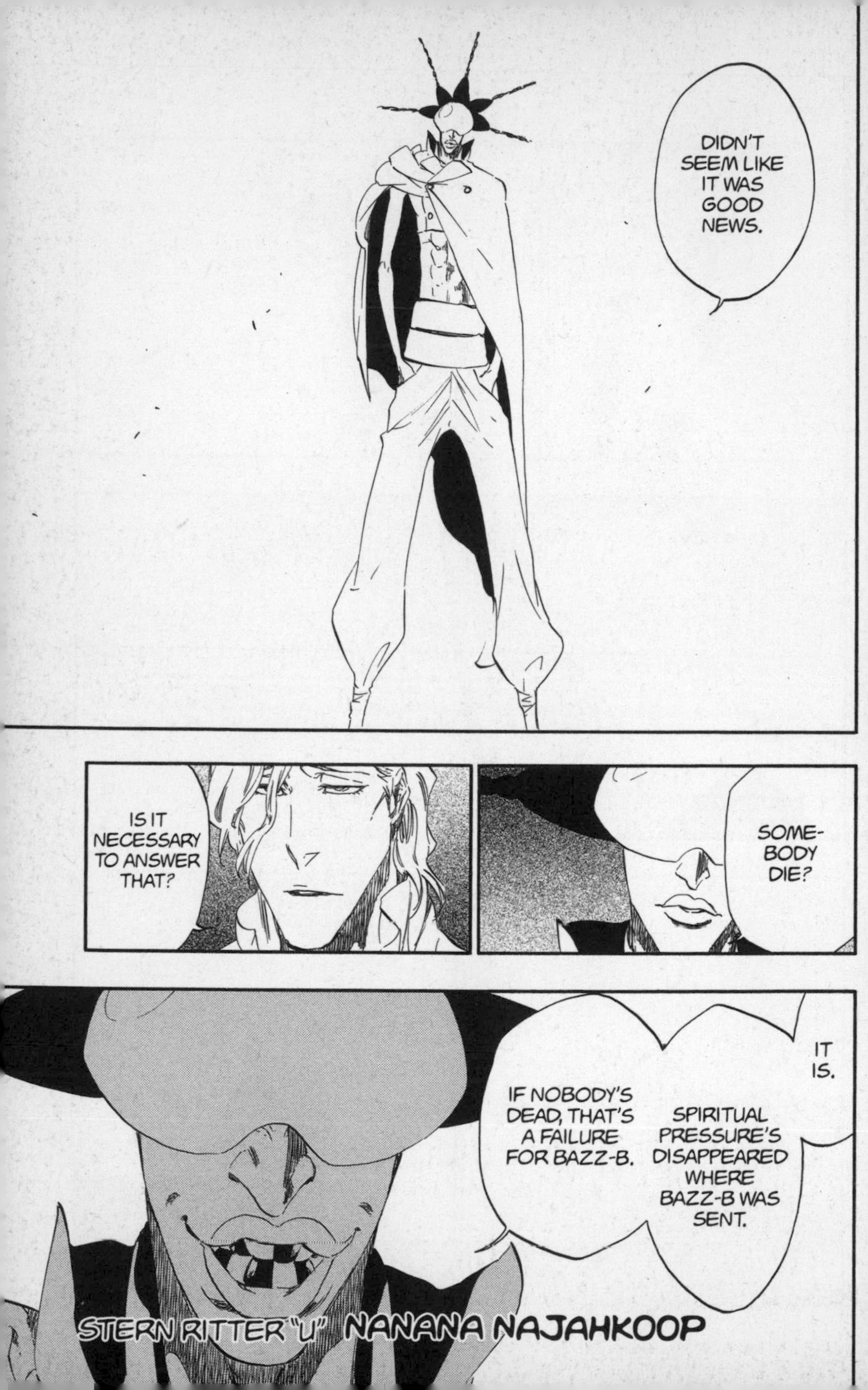
DIDN'T SEEM LIKE IT WAS GOOD NEWS.
SOME-BODY DIE?
IS IT NECESSARY TO ANSWER THAT?
IT IS.
SPIRITUAL PRESSURE'S DISAPPEARED WHERE BAZZ-B WAS SENT.
IF NOBODY'S DEAD, THAT'S A FAILURE FOR BAZZ-B.
STERN RITTER "U" NANANA NAJAHKOOP

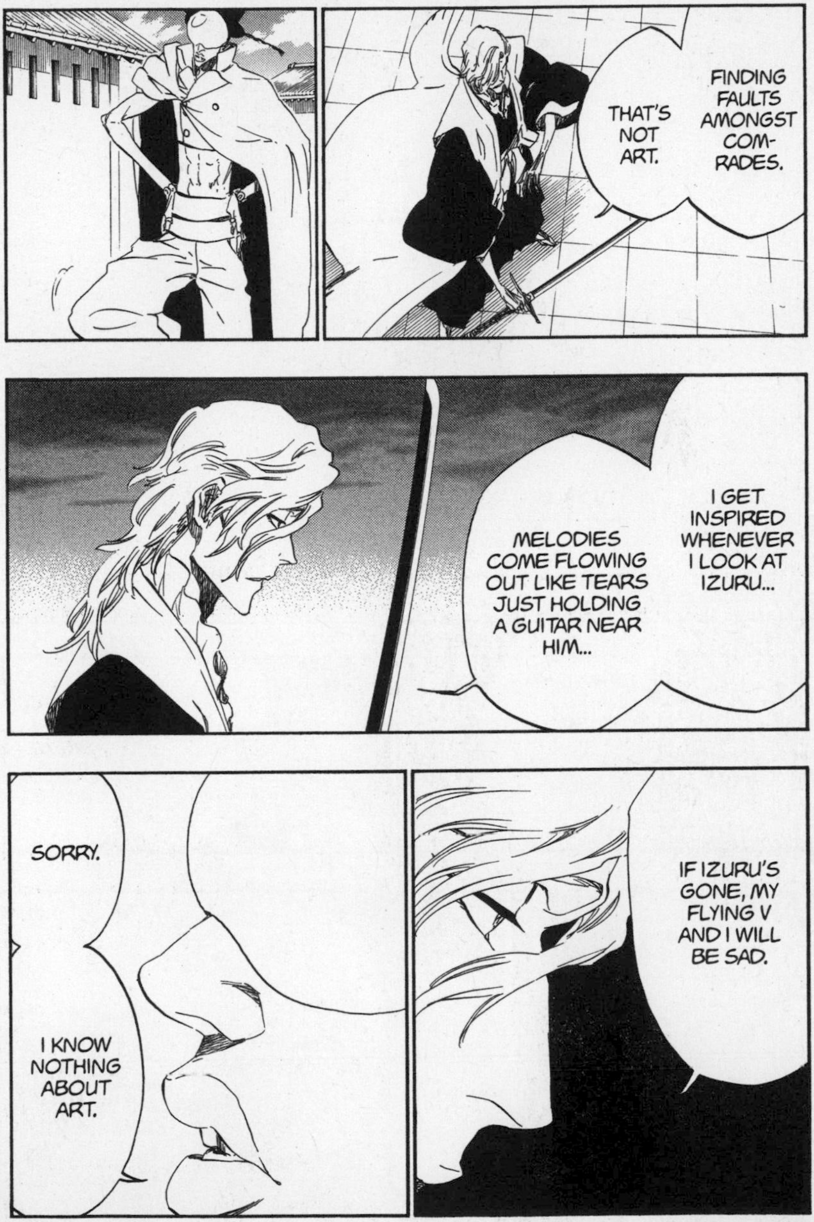
FINDING FAULTS AMONGST COM-RADES.
THAT'S NOT ART.
I GET INSPIRED WHENEVER I LOOK AT IZURU...
MELODIES COME FLOWING OUT LIKE TEARS JUST HOLDING A GUITAR NEAR HIM...
IF IZURU'S GONE, MY FLYING V AND I WILL BE SAD.
SORRY.
I KNOW NOTHING ABOUT ART.

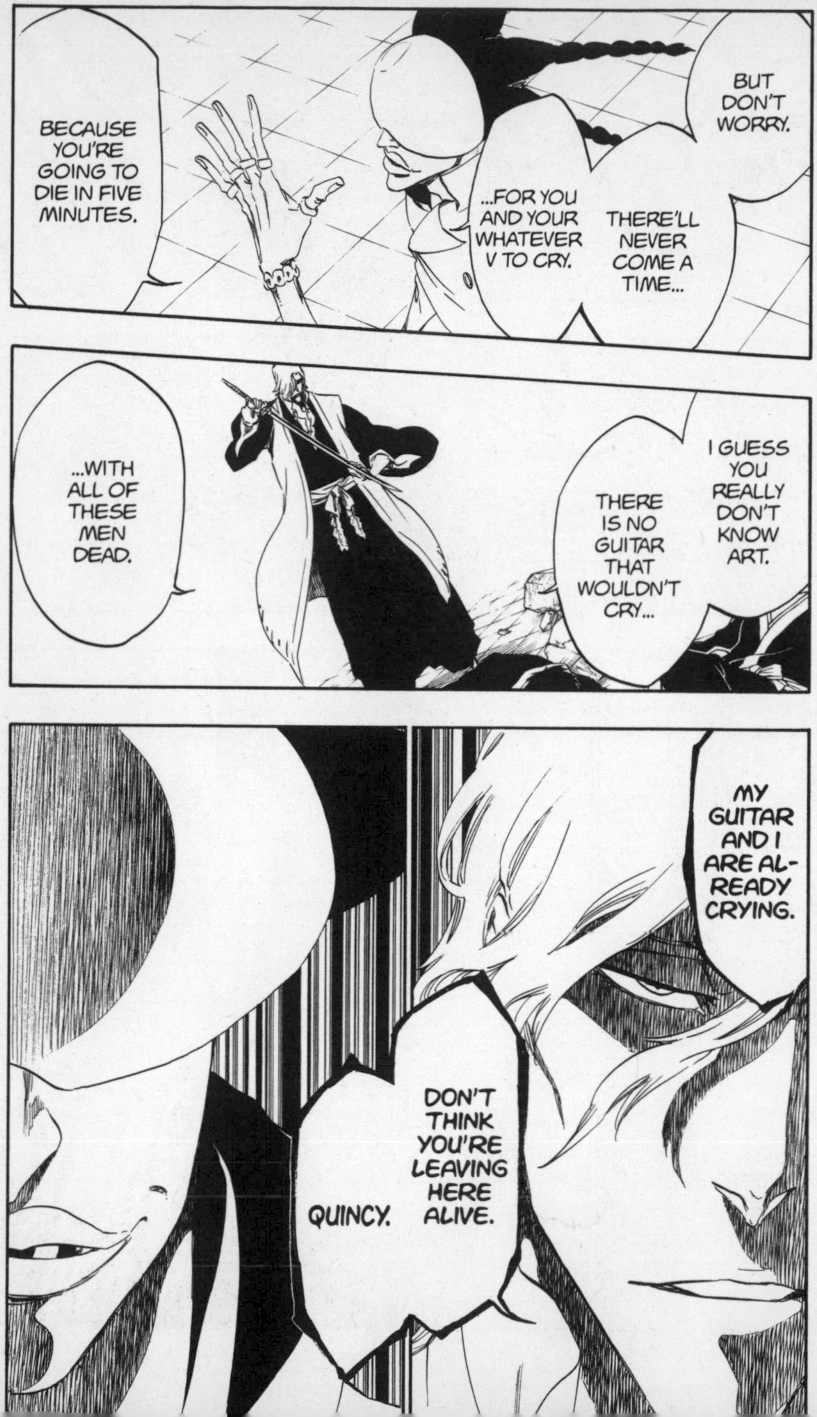
BUT DON'T WORRY.
THERE'LL NEVER COME A TIME...
...FOR YOU AND YOUR WHATEVER V TO CRY.
BECAUSE YOU'RE GOING TO DIE IN FIVE MINUTES.
I GUESS YOU REALLY DON'T KNOW ART.
THERE IS NO GUITAR THAT WOULDN'T CRY...
...WITH ALL OF THESE MEN DEAD.
MY GUITAR AND I ARE AL-READY CRYING.
DON'T THINK YOU'RE LEAVING HERE ALIVE.
QUINCY.

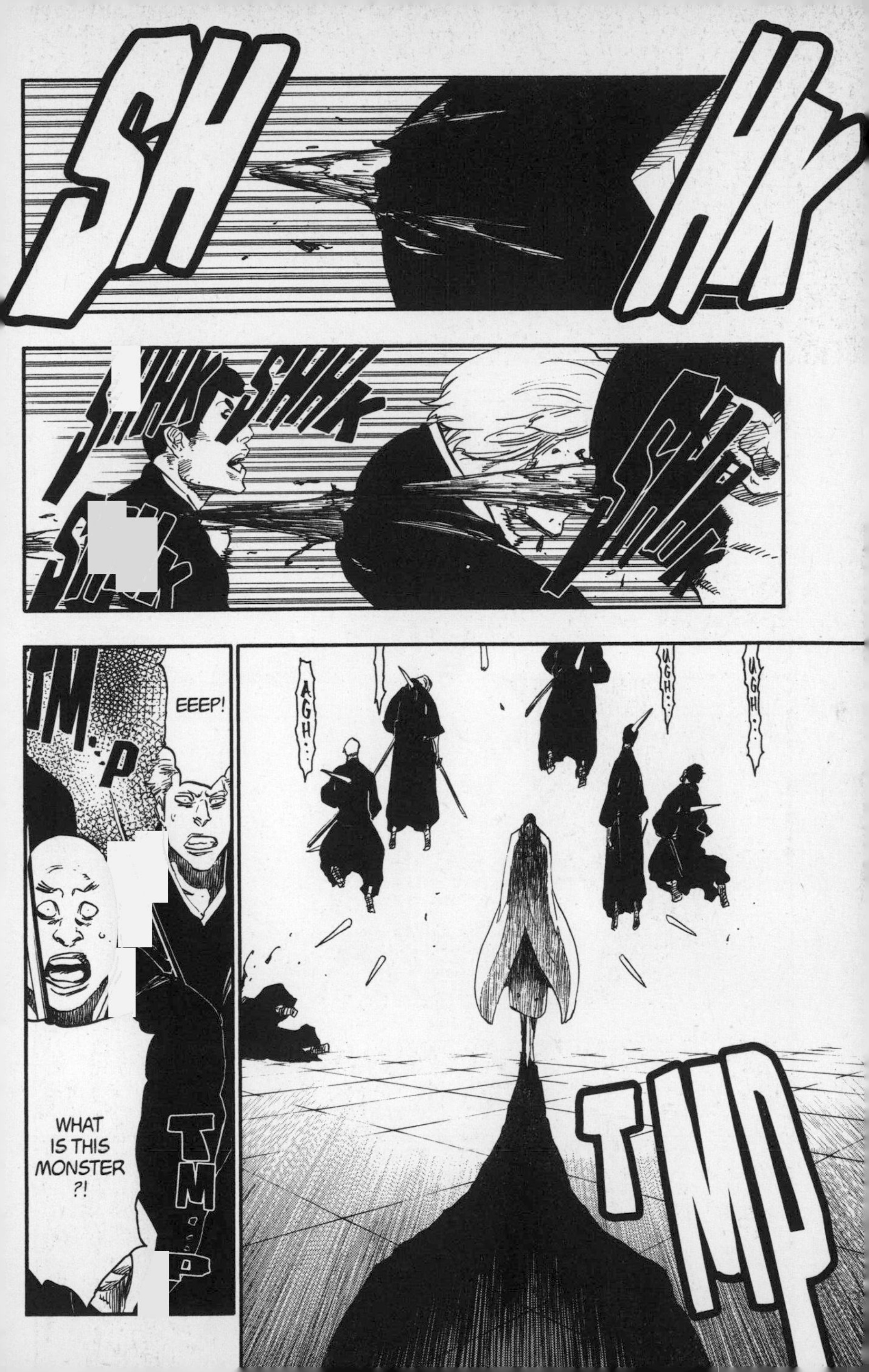

SHHK
SHHK
UGH...
UGH...
AGH...
TMP
EEEP!
WHAT IS THIS MONSTER?!
TMP

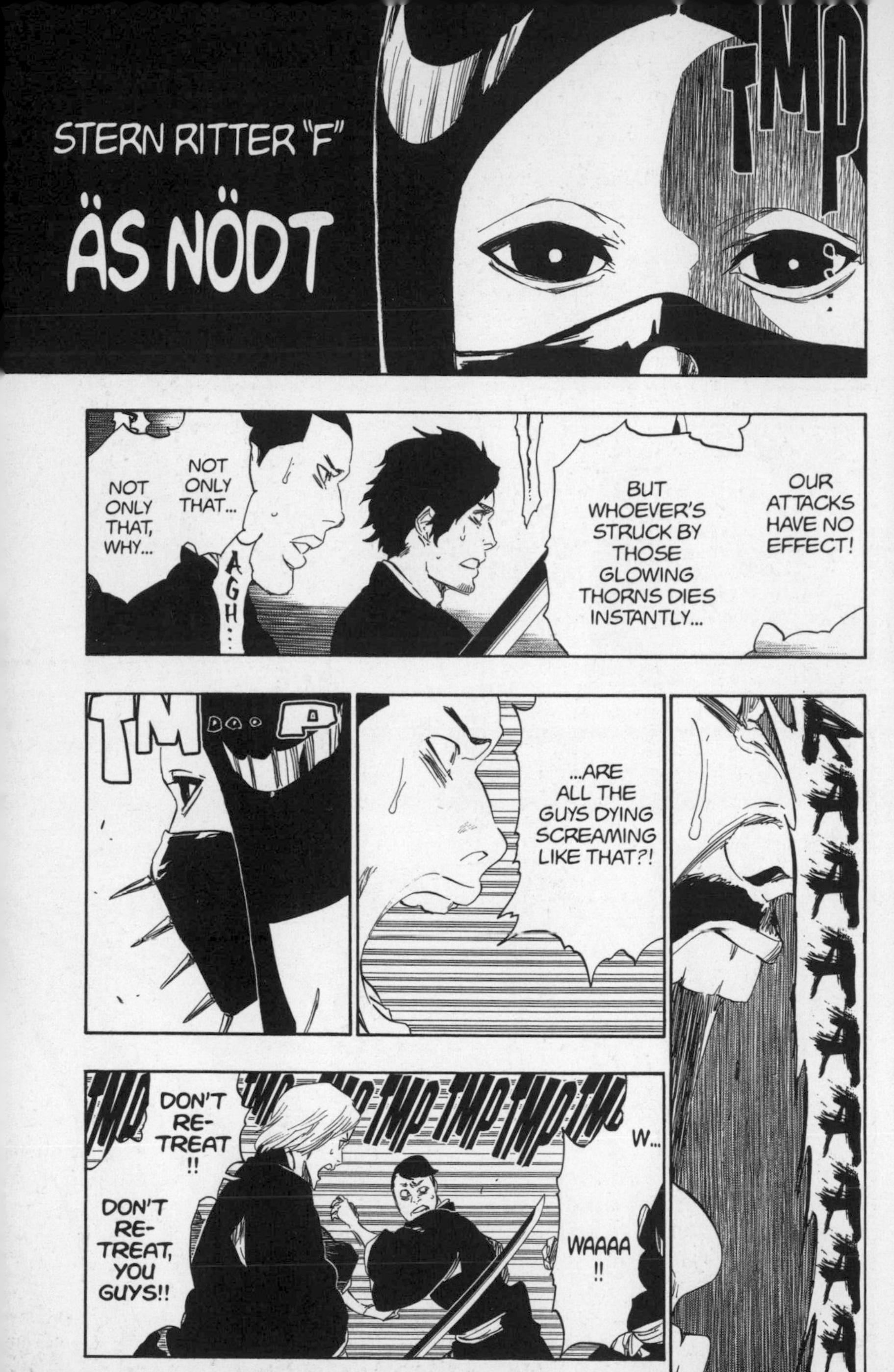
TMP
STERN RITTER "F"
ÄS NÖDT
OUR ATTACKS HAVE NO EFFECT!
BUT WHOEVER'S STRUCK BY THOSE GLOWING THORNS DIES INSTANTLY...
NOT ONLY THAT...
NOT ONLY THAT, WHY...
AGH...
RAAAAAAAAAAAA
...ARE ALL THE GUYS DYING SCREAMING LIKE THAT?!
TM...P
W...
WAAAA!!
TMP TMP TMP TMP TMP TMP
DON'T RE-TREAT!!
DON'T RE-TREAT, YOU GUYS!!

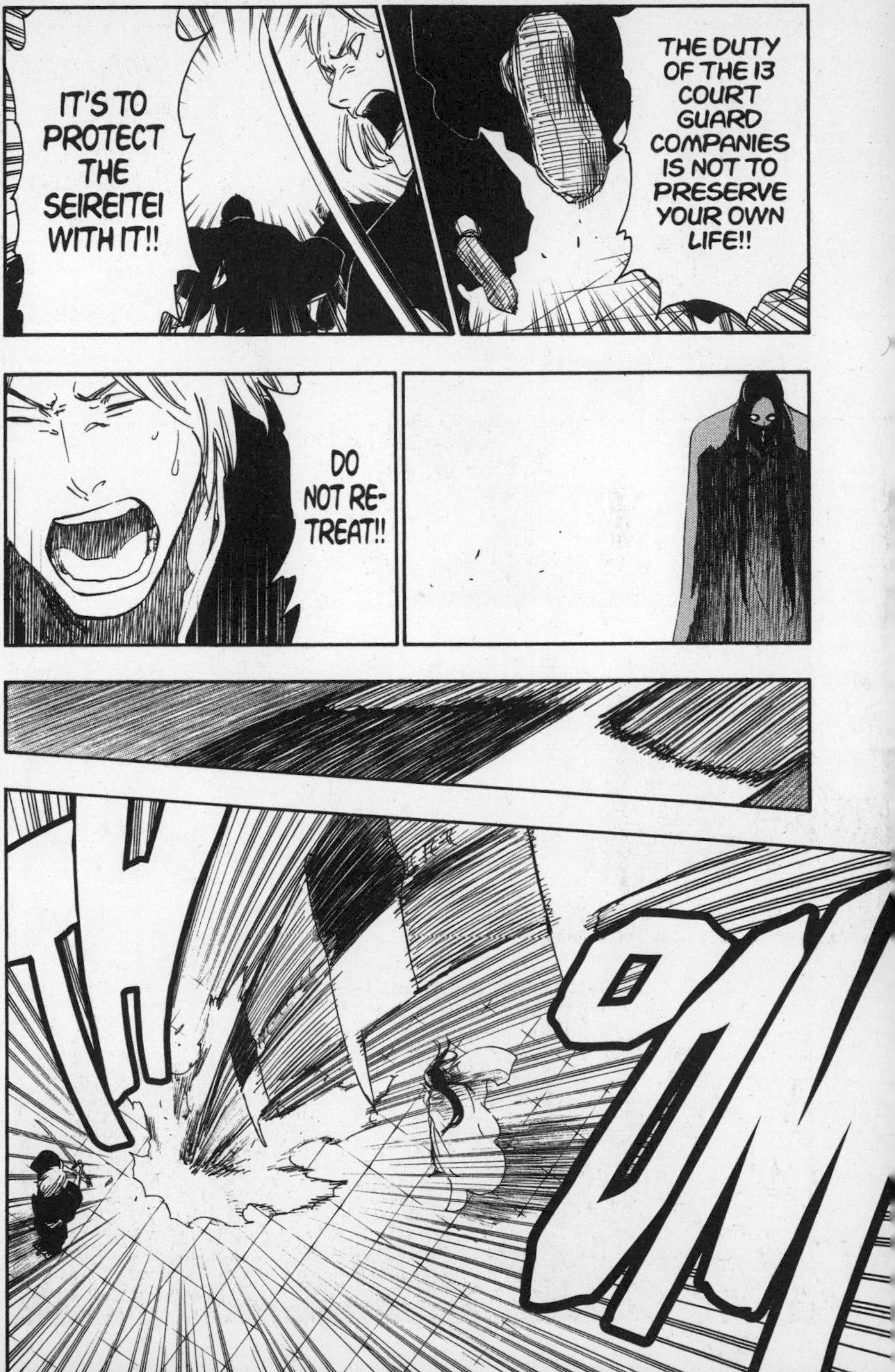
THE DUTY OF THE 13 COURT GUARD COMPANIES IS NOT TO PRESERVE YOUR OWN LIFE!!
IT'S TO PROTECT THE SEIREITEI WITH IT!!
DO NOT RE-TREAT!!

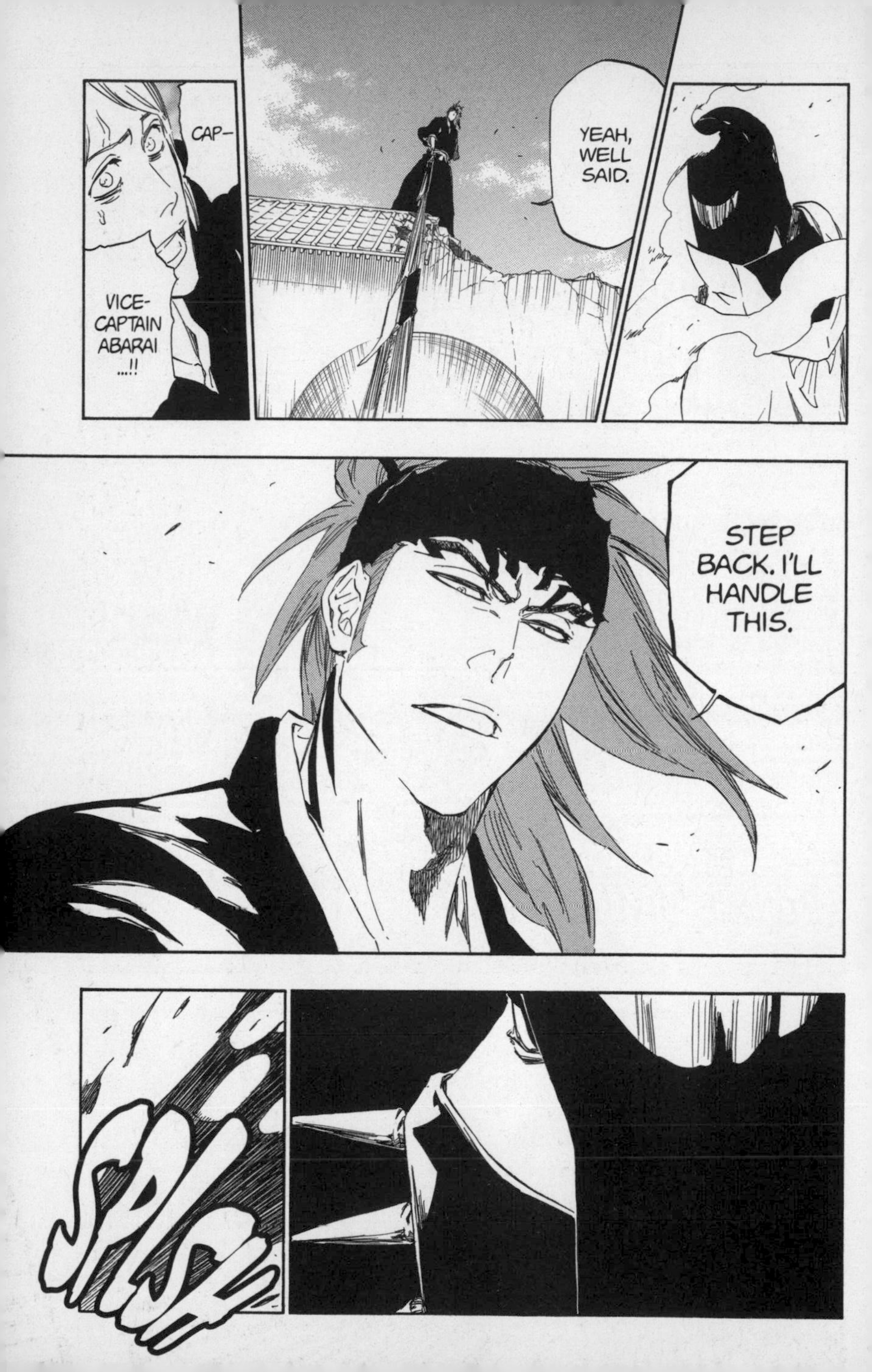
YEAH, WELL SAID.
CAP—
VICE-CAPTAIN ABARAI ....!!
STEP BACK. I'LL HANDLE THIS.
SPISH

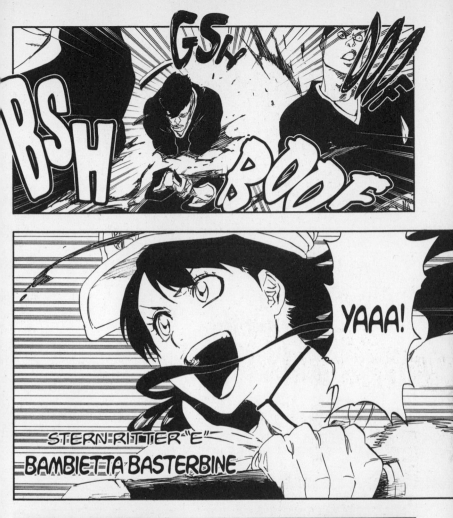

YAAA!

STERN RITTER "E"
BAMBIETTA BASTERBINE

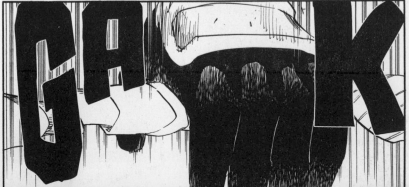

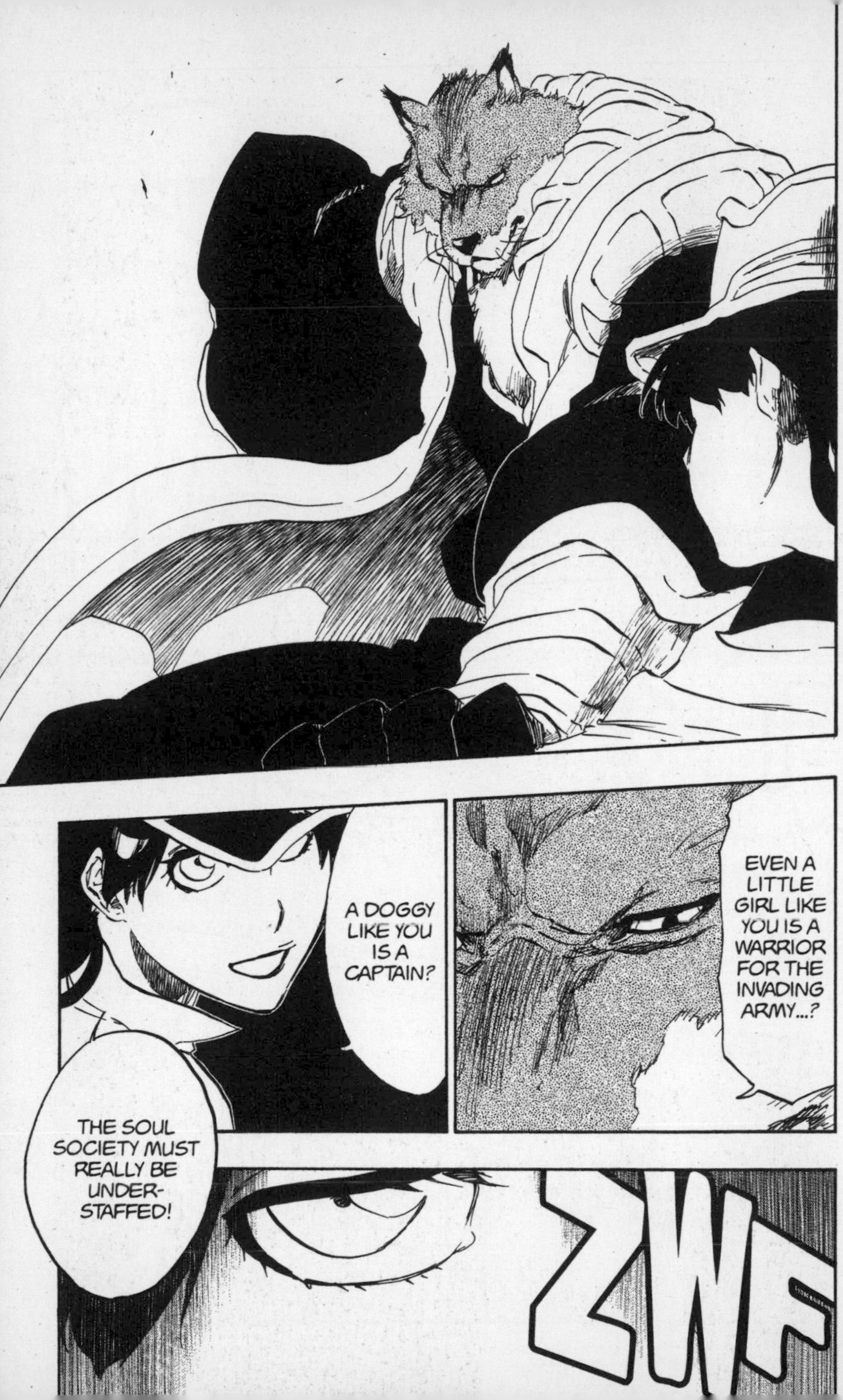
EVEN A LITTLE GIRL LIKE YOU IS A WARRIOR FOR THE INVADING ARMY...?
A DOGGY LIKE YOU IS A CAPTAIN?
THE SOUL SOCIETY MUST REALLY BE UNDER-STAFFED!
ZWF

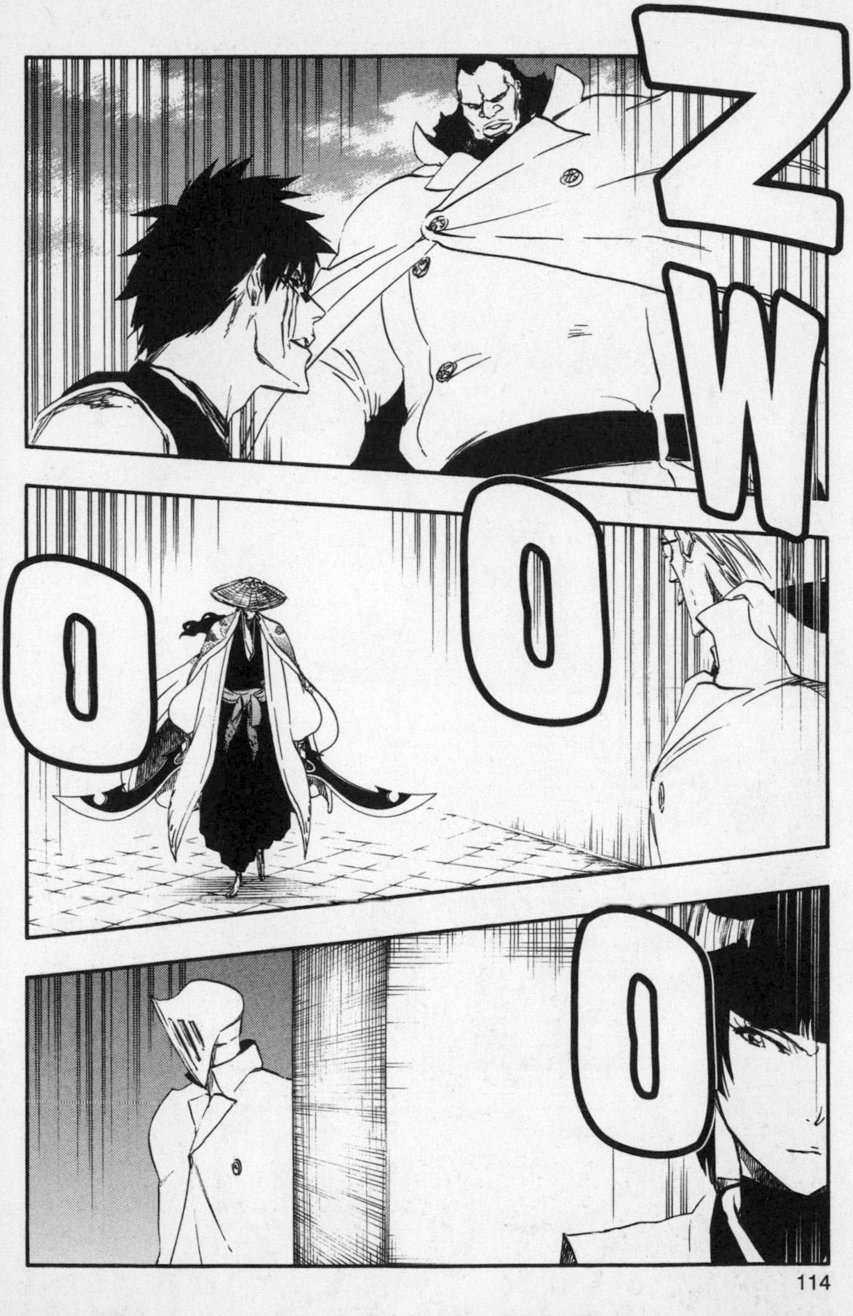
ZWOOO

READ THIS WAY

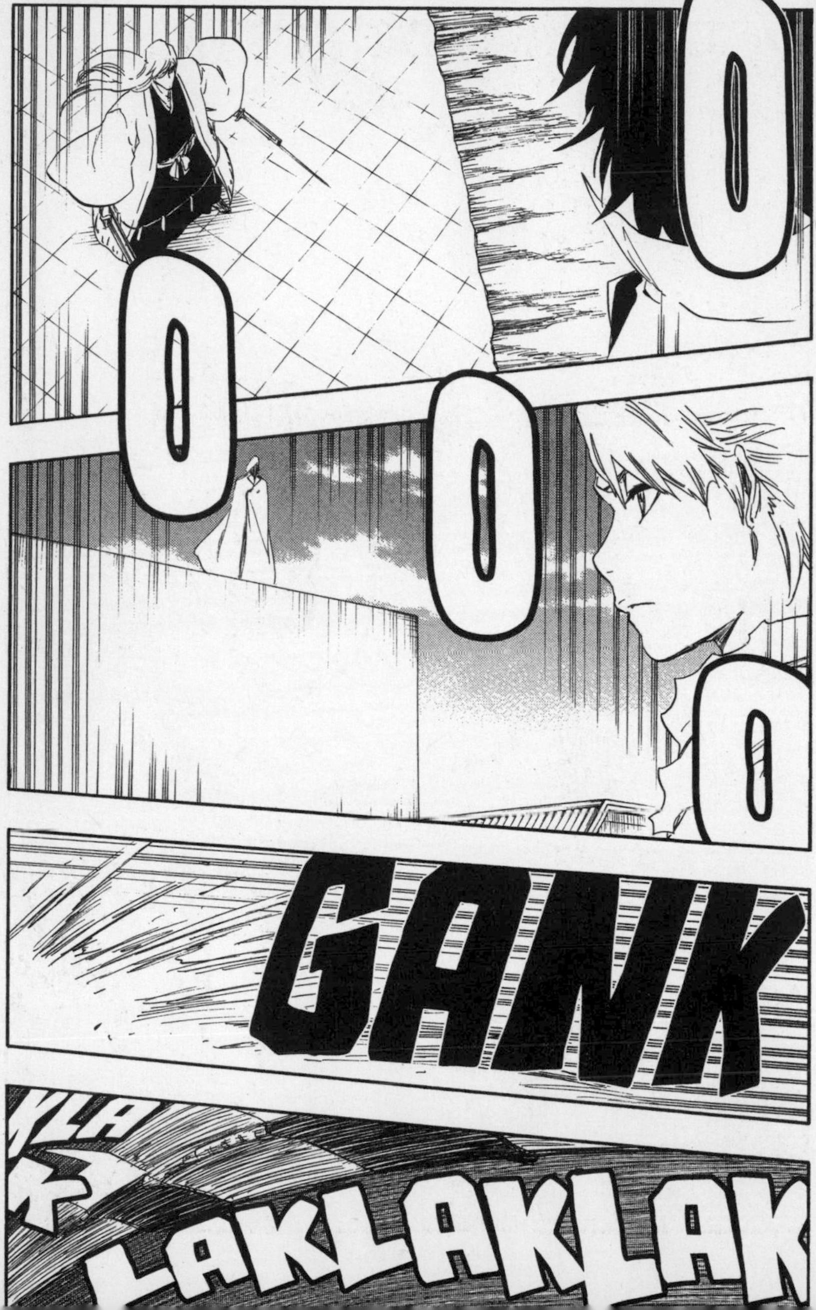

OOOO
GANK
KLA
LAKLAKLAK

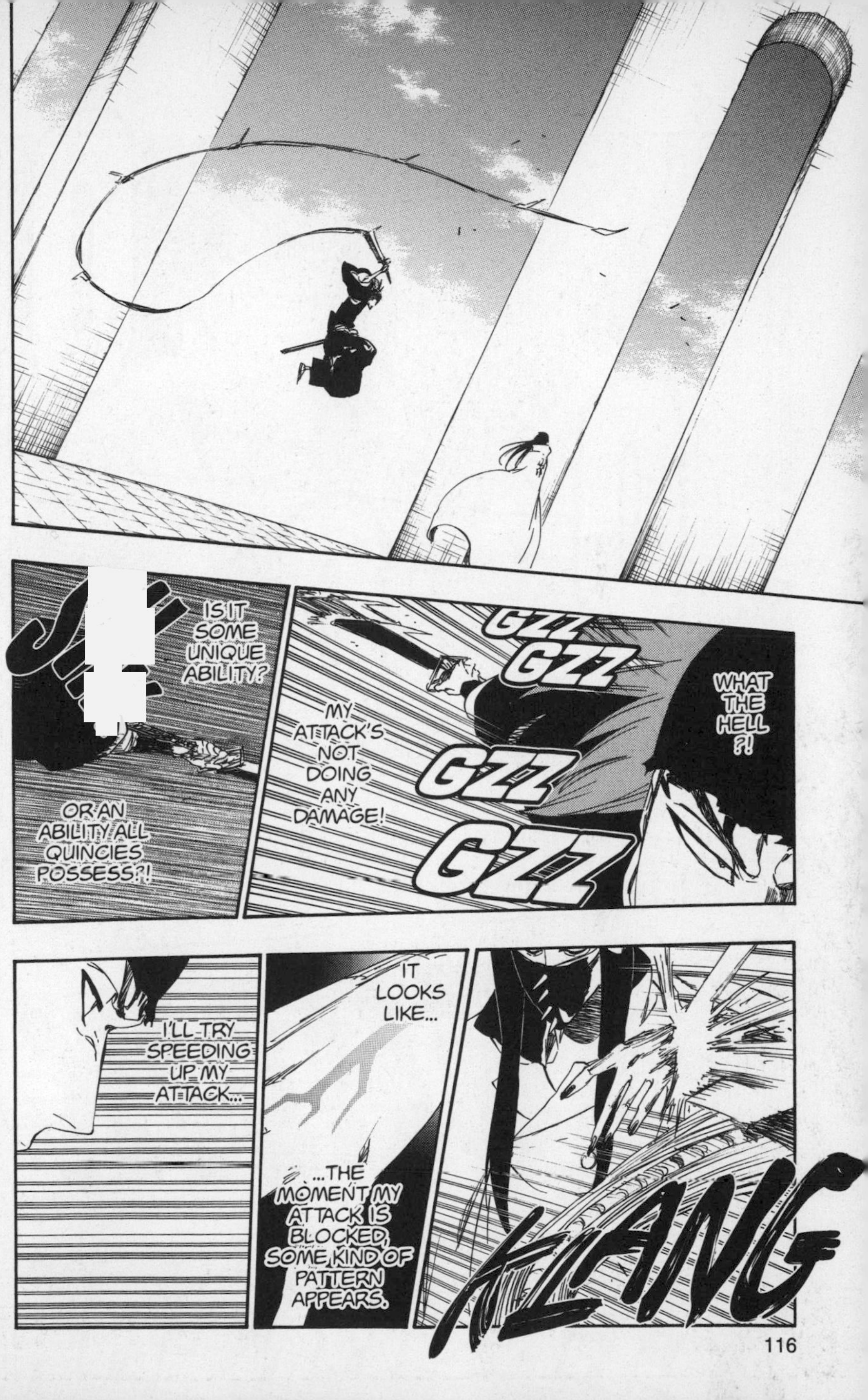
WHAT THE HELL ?!
GZZ GZZ
MY ATTACK'S NOT DOING ANY DAMAGE!
GZZ
GZZ
IS IT SOME UNIQUE ABILITY?
OR AN ABILITY ALL QUINCIES POSSESS?!
KLANG
IT LOOKS LIKE...
...THE MOMENT MY ATTACK IS BLOCKED, SOME KIND OF PATTERN APPEARS.
I'LL TRY SPEEDING UP MY ATTACK...

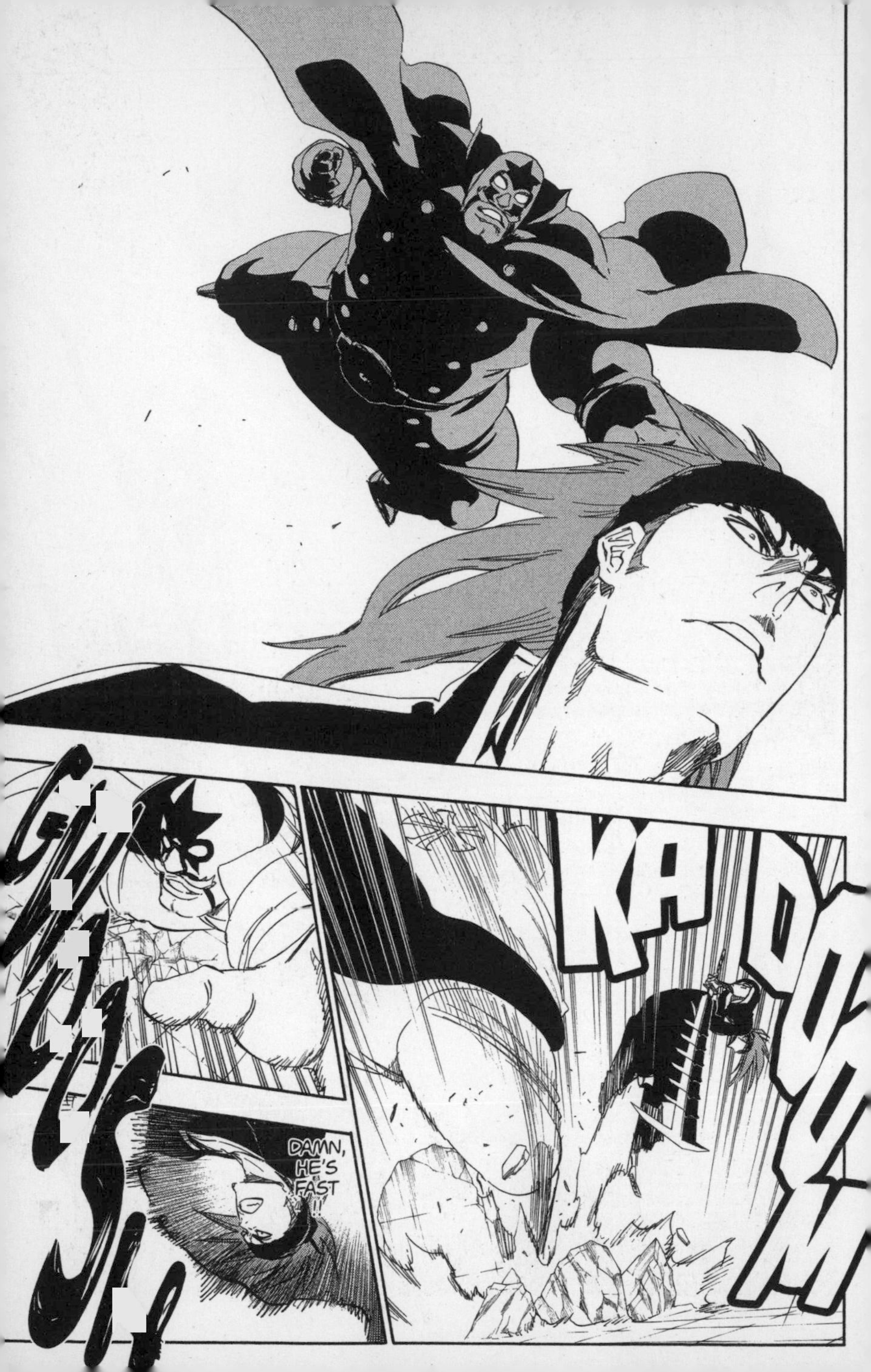
DAMN, HE'S FAST!!

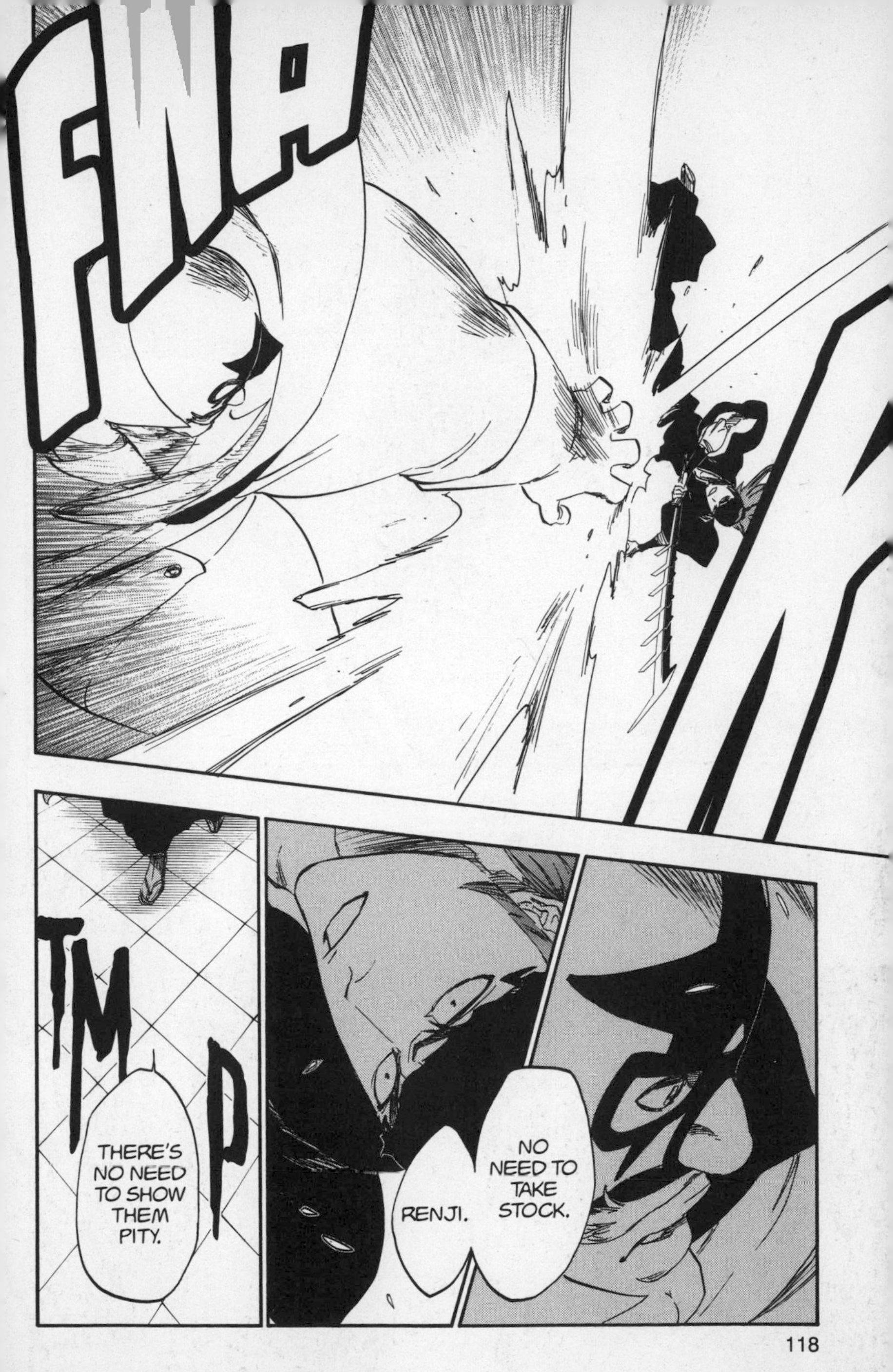
FWA
NO NEED TO TAKE STOCK.
RENJI.
TMP
THERE'S NO NEED TO SHOW THEM PITY.

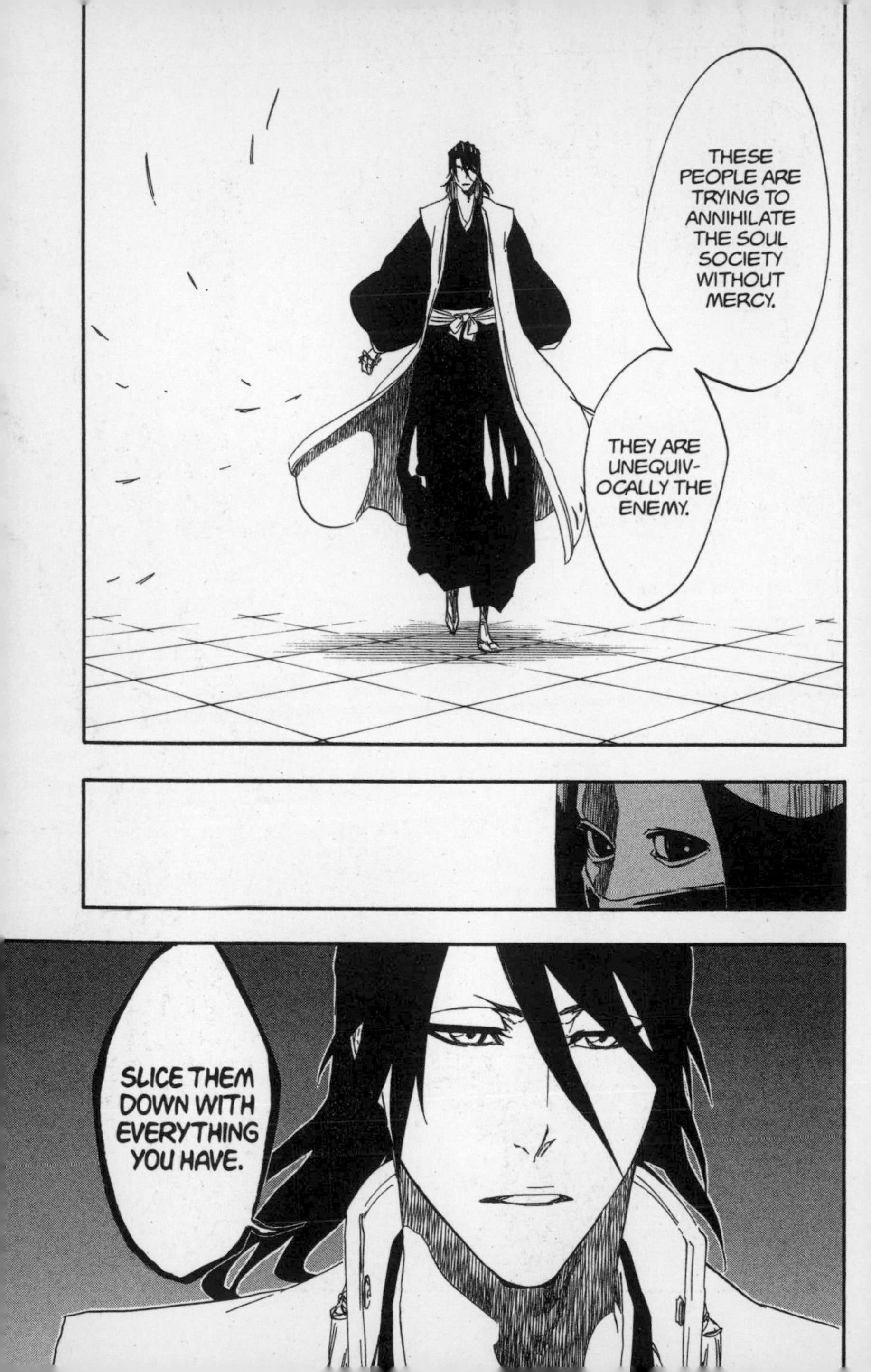
THESE PEOPLE ARE TRYING TO ANNIHILATE THE SOUL SOCIETY WITHOUT MERCY.
THEY ARE UNEQUIV-OCALLY THE ENEMY.
SLICE THEM DOWN WITH EVERYTHING YOU HAVE.

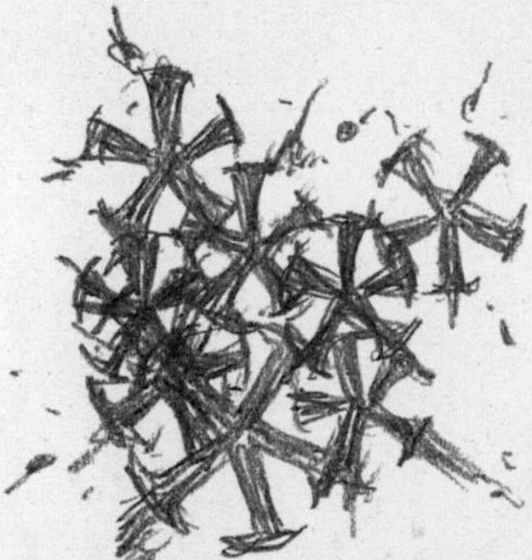

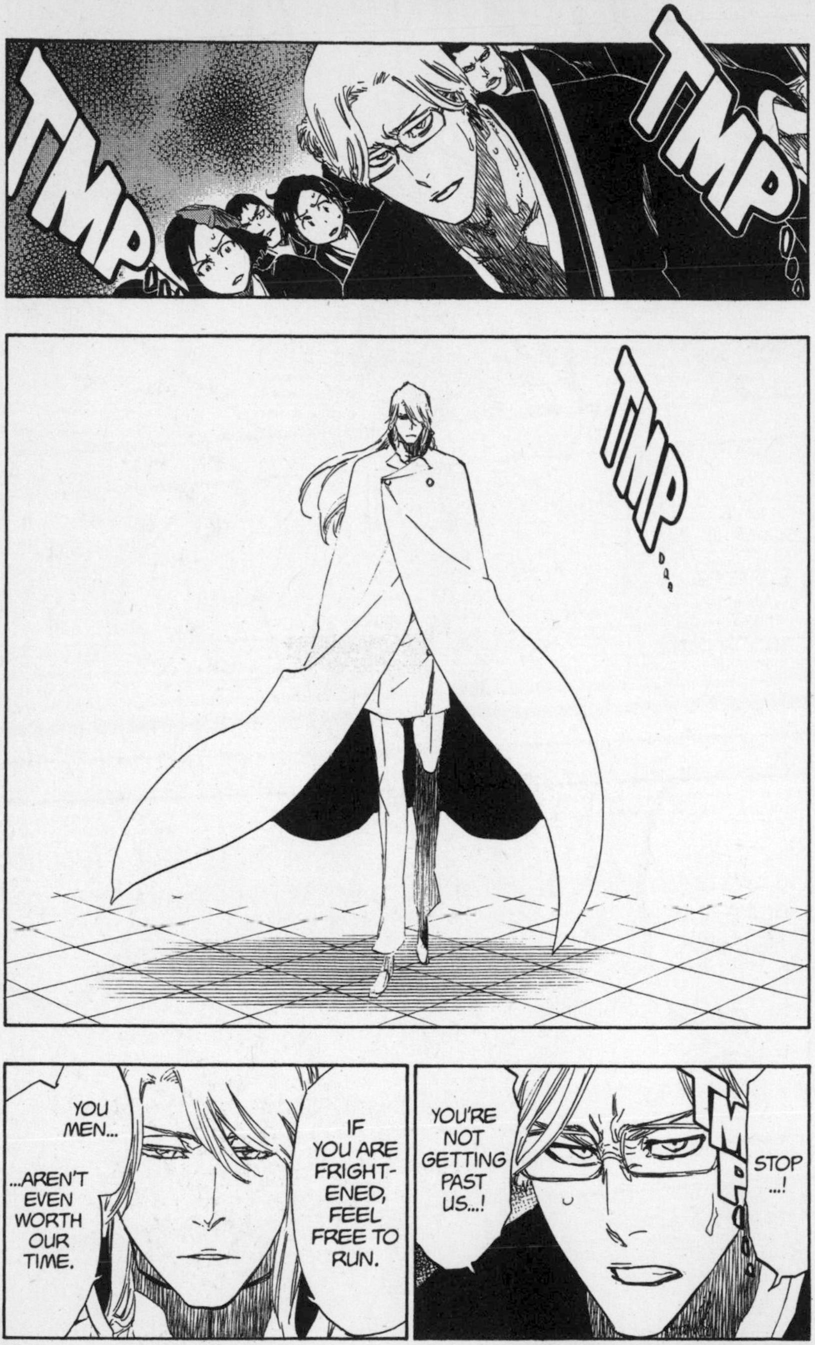
TMP...
TMP...
TMP...
TMP...
STOP ...!
YOU'RE NOT GETTING PAST US...!
IF YOU ARE FRIGHT- ENED, FEEL FREE TO RUN.
YOU MEN...
...AREN'T EVEN WORTH OUR TIME.

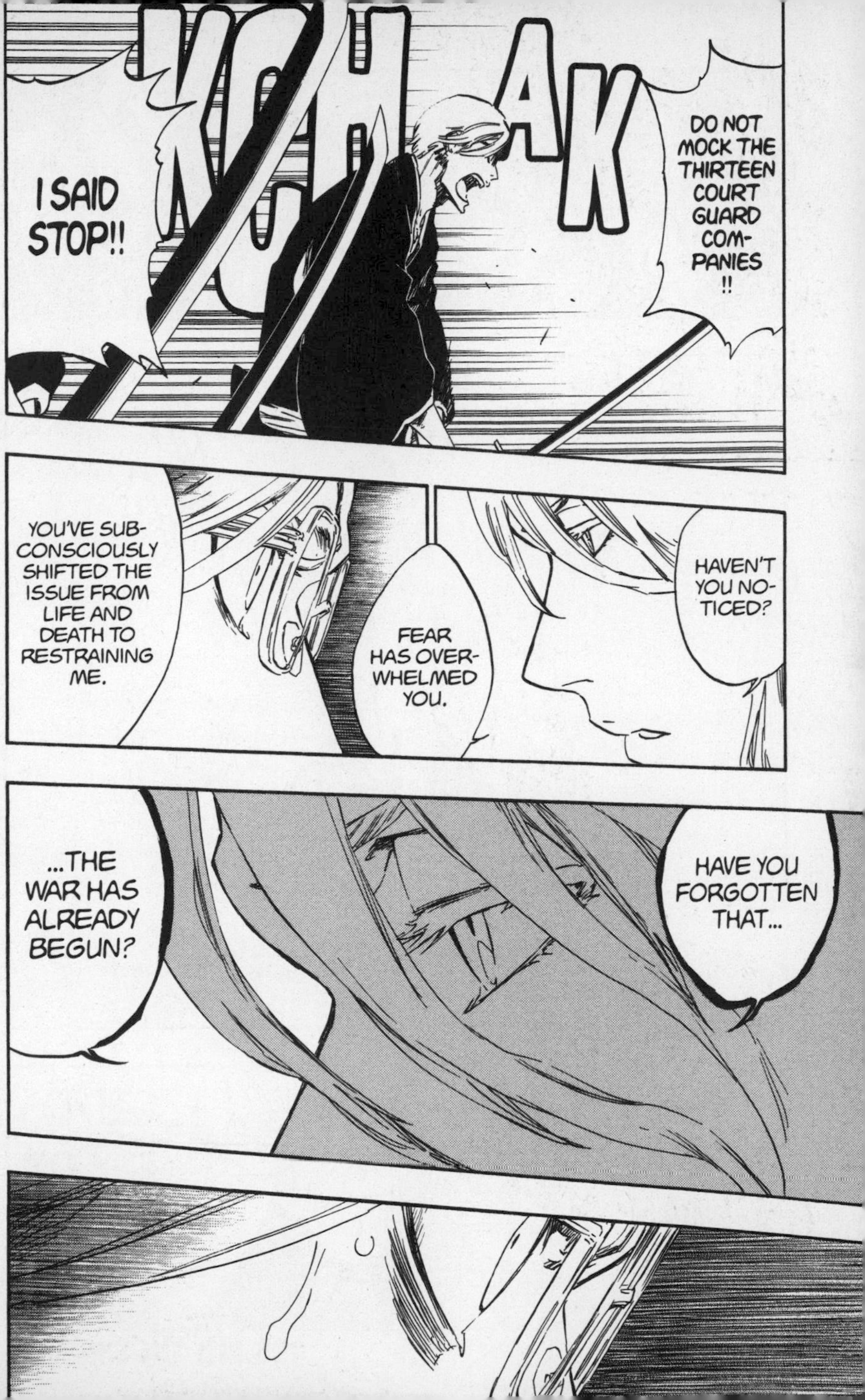
KCHAK
DO NOT MOCK THE THIRTEEN COURT GUARD COM-PANIES!!
I SAID STOP!!
HAVEN'T YOU NO-TICED?
FEAR HAS OVER-WHELMED YOU.
YOU'VE SUB-CONSCIOUSLY SHIFTED THE ISSUE FROM LIFE AND DEATH TO RESTRAINING ME.
HAVE YOU FORGOTTEN THAT...
...THE WAR HAS ALREADY BEGUN?

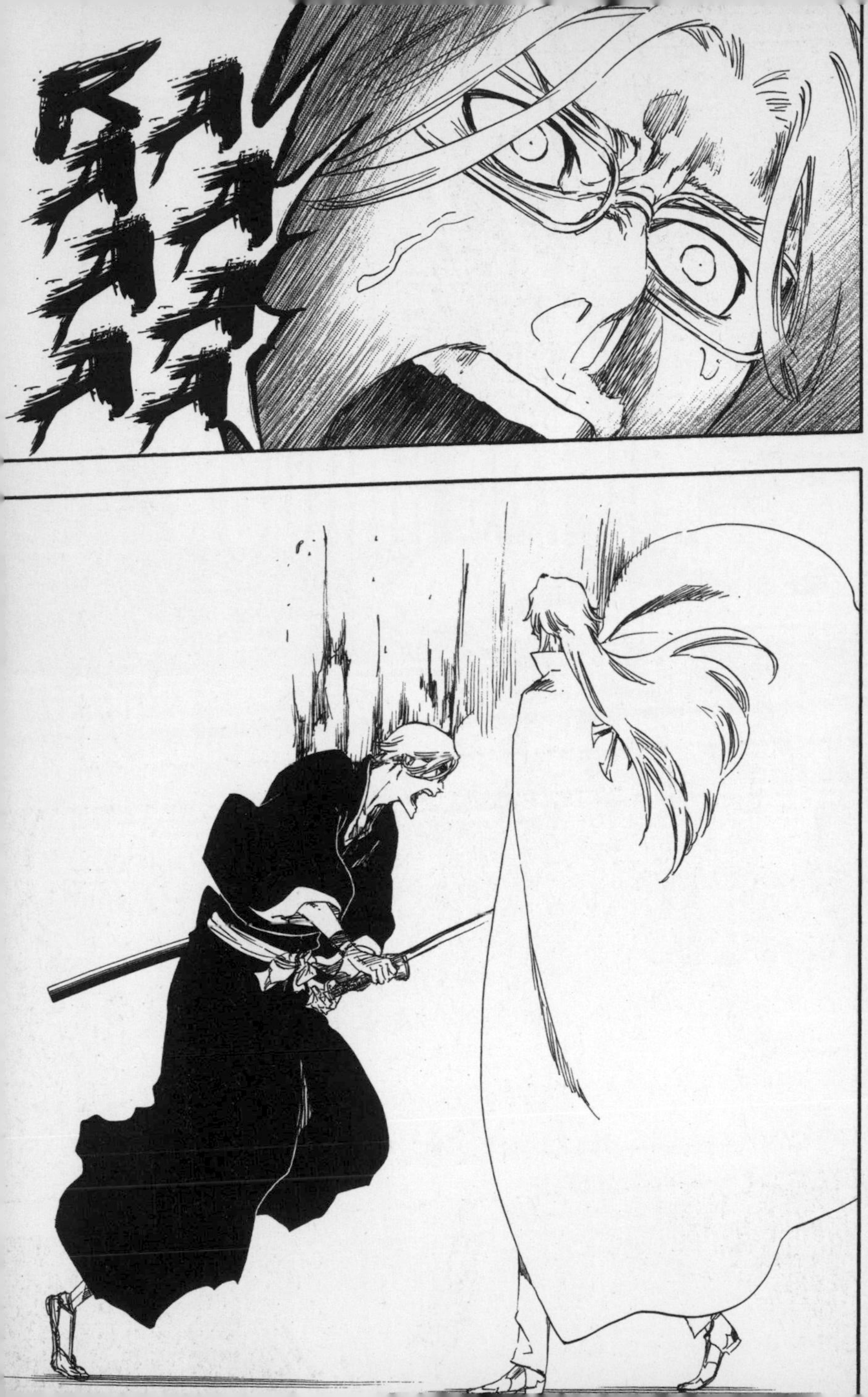
カカカカ
タカカカ

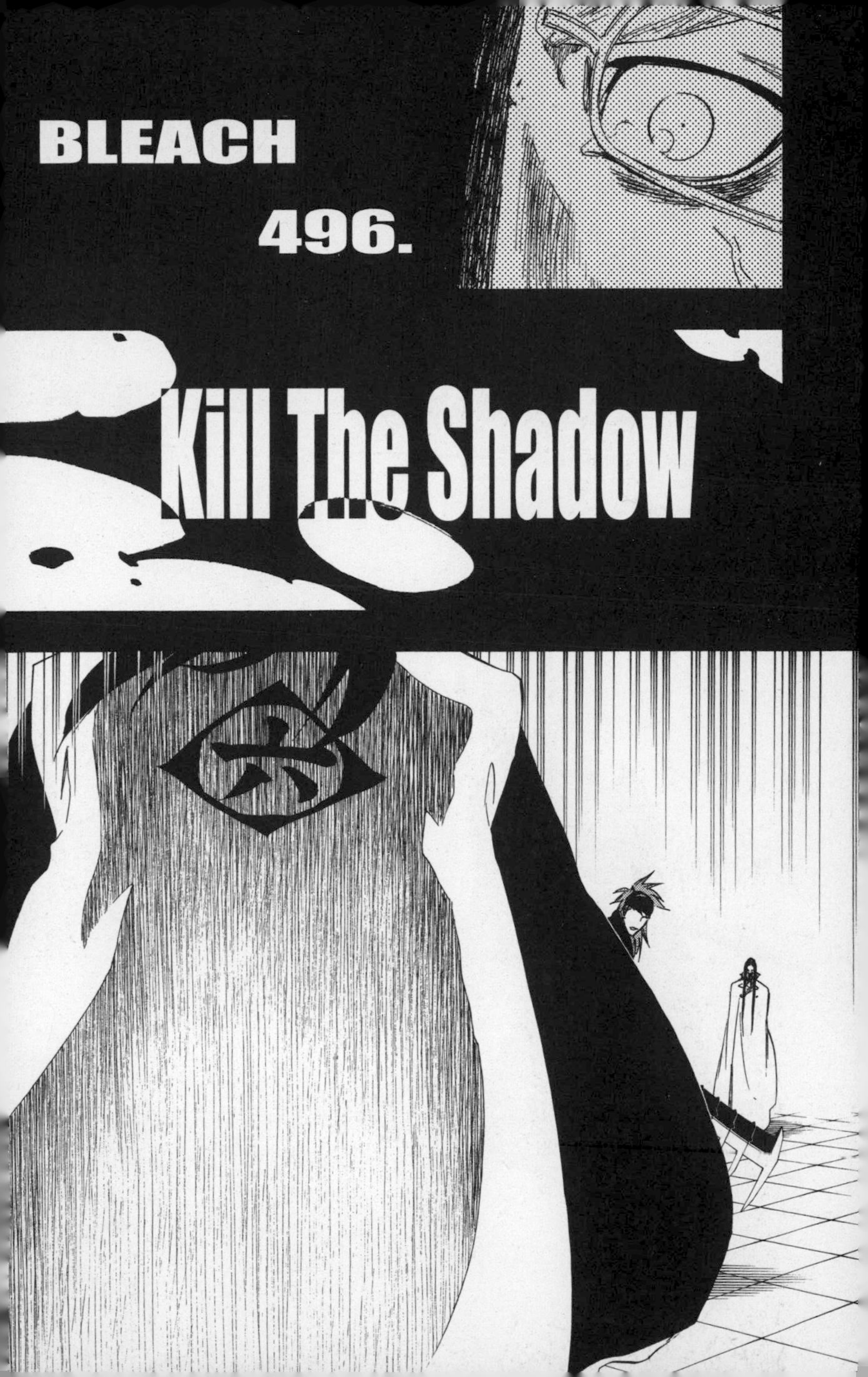
BLEACH
496.
Kill The Shadow

READ THIS WAY

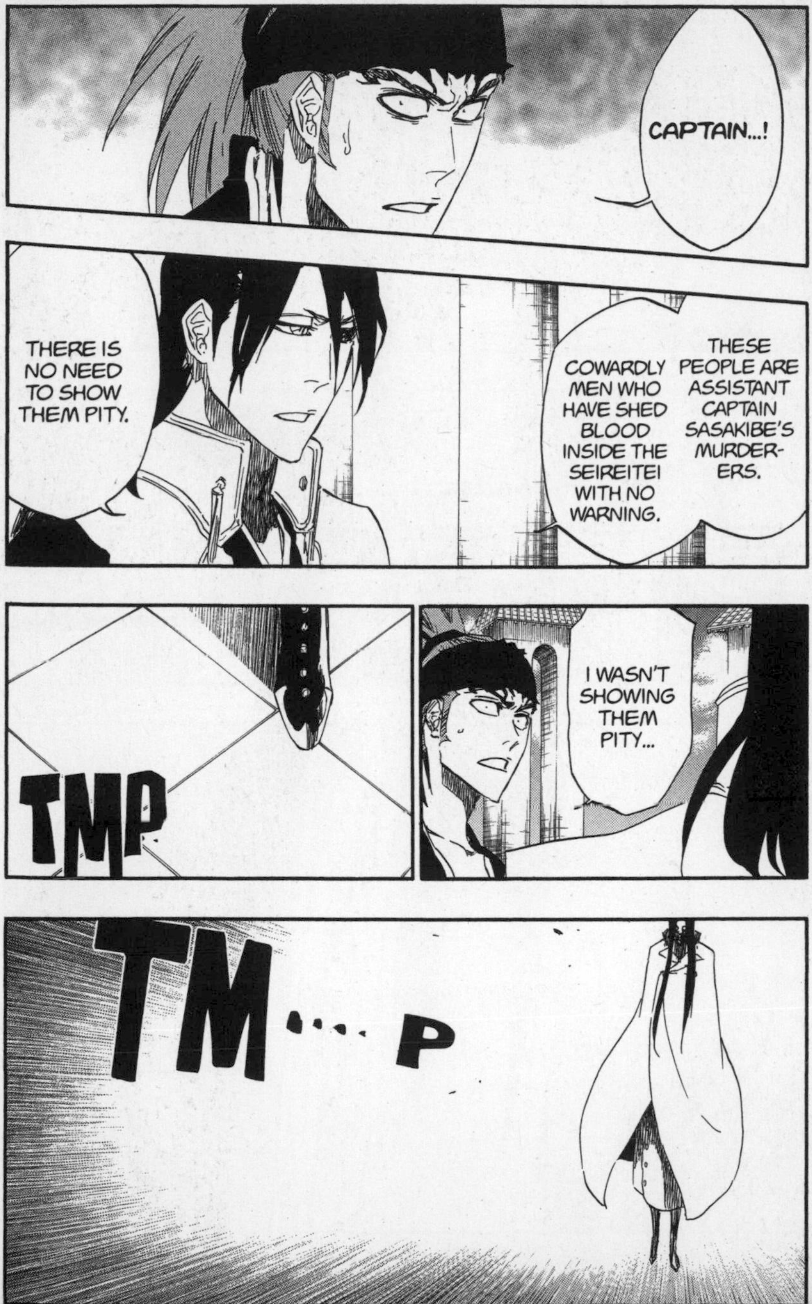
CAPTAIN...!
THESE PEOPLE ARE ASSISTANT CAPTAIN SASAKIBE'S MURDER-ERS.
COWARDLY MEN WHO HAVE SHED BLOOD INSIDE THE SEIREITEI WITH NO WARNING.
THERE IS NO NEED TO SHOW THEM PITY.
I WASN'T SHOWING THEM PITY...
TMP
TM...P

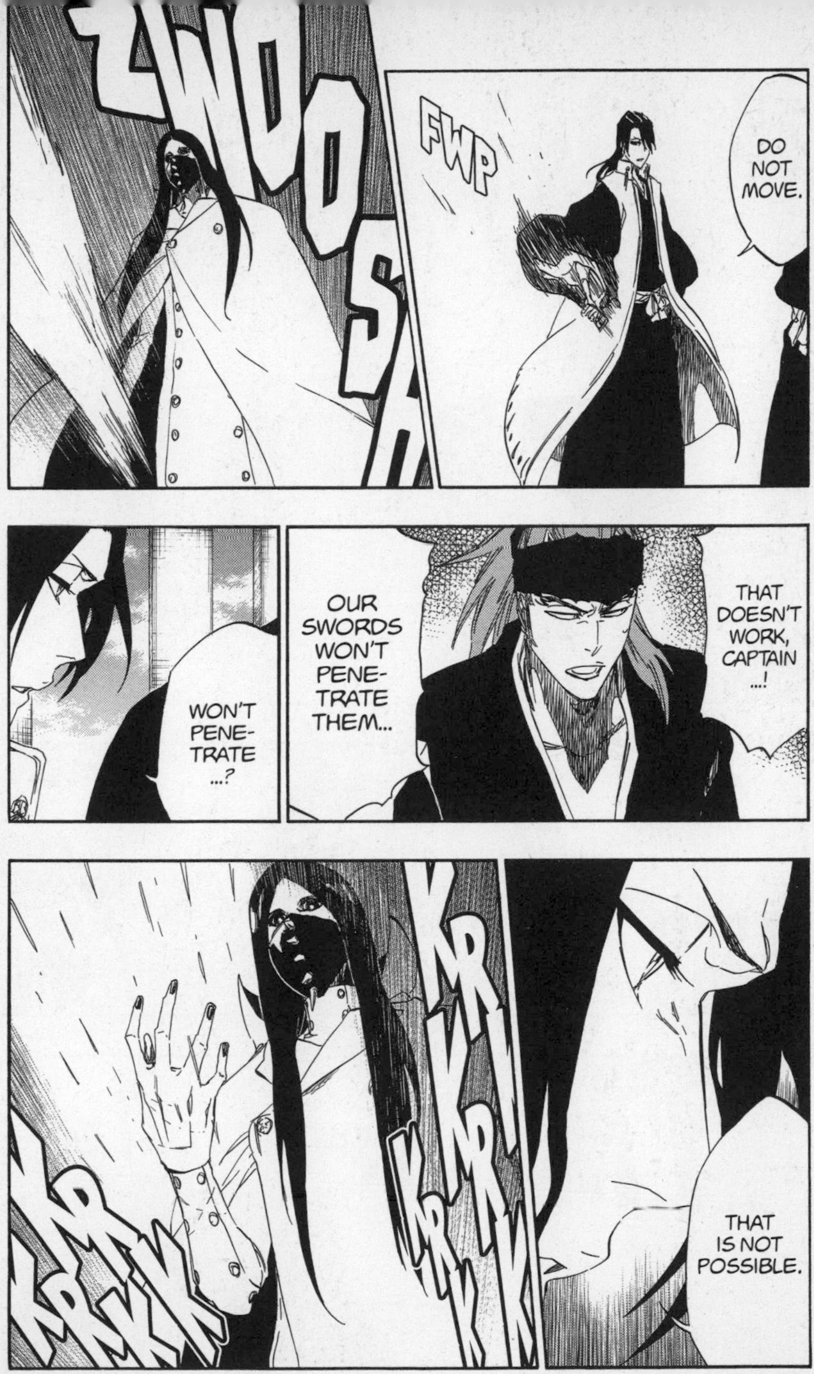
FWP
DO NOT MOVE.
ZWOOSH
THAT DOESN'T WORK, CAPTAIN...!
OUR SWORDS WON'T PENETRATE THEM...
WON'T PENETRATE...?
THAT IS NOT POSSIBLE.

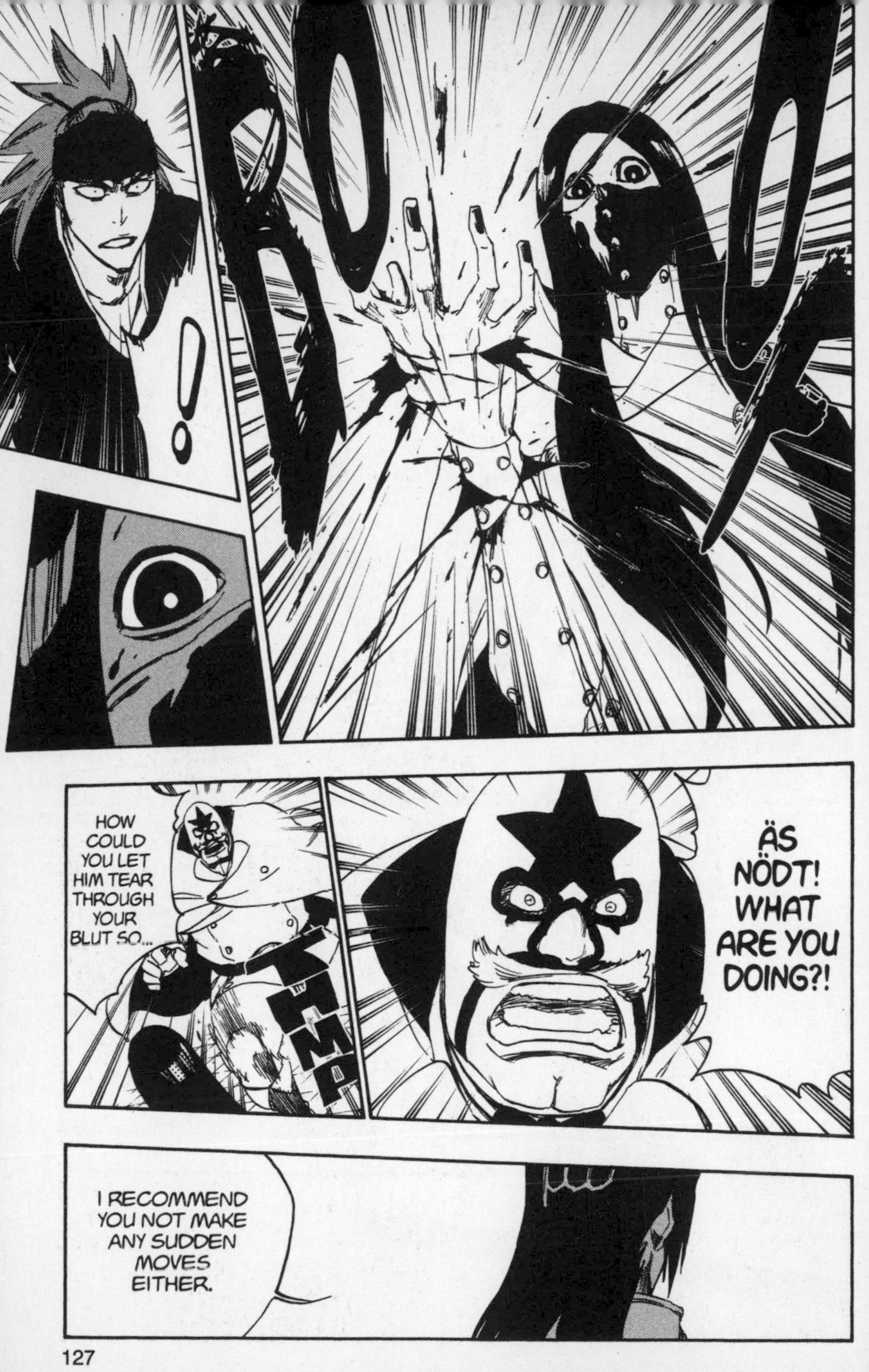
ÄS NÖDT! WHAT ARE YOU DOING?!
HOW COULD YOU LET HIM TEAR THROUGH YOUR BLUT SO...
I RECOMMEND YOU NOT MAKE ANY SUDDEN MOVES EITHER.

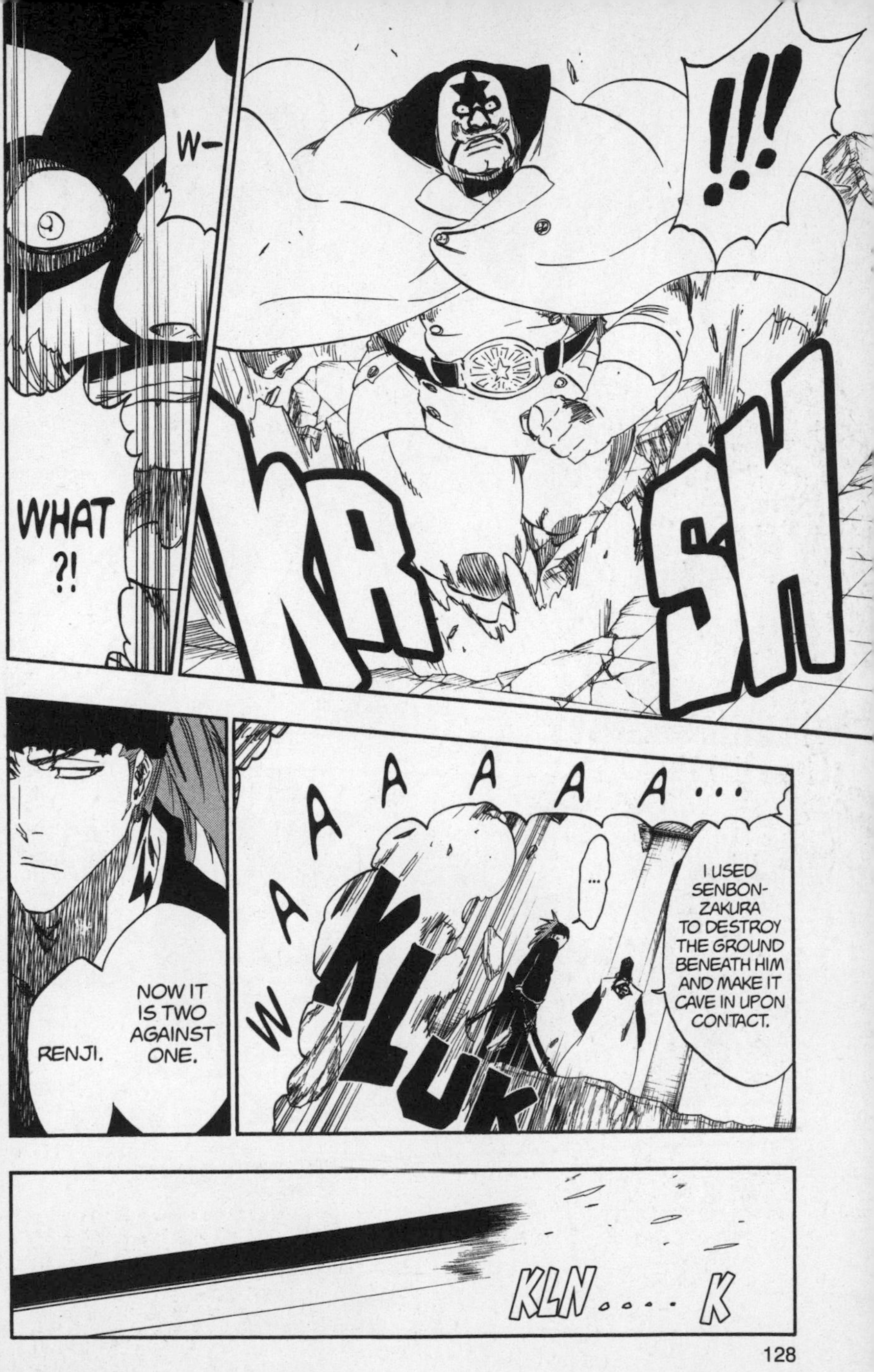
!!!
RA SH
W-
WHAT ?!
WAAAAAAA...
KLUK
...
I USED SENBON-ZAKURA TO DESTROY THE GROUND BENEATH HIM AND MAKE IT CAVE IN UPON CONTACT.
NOW IT IS TWO AGAINST ONE.
RENJI.
KLN... K

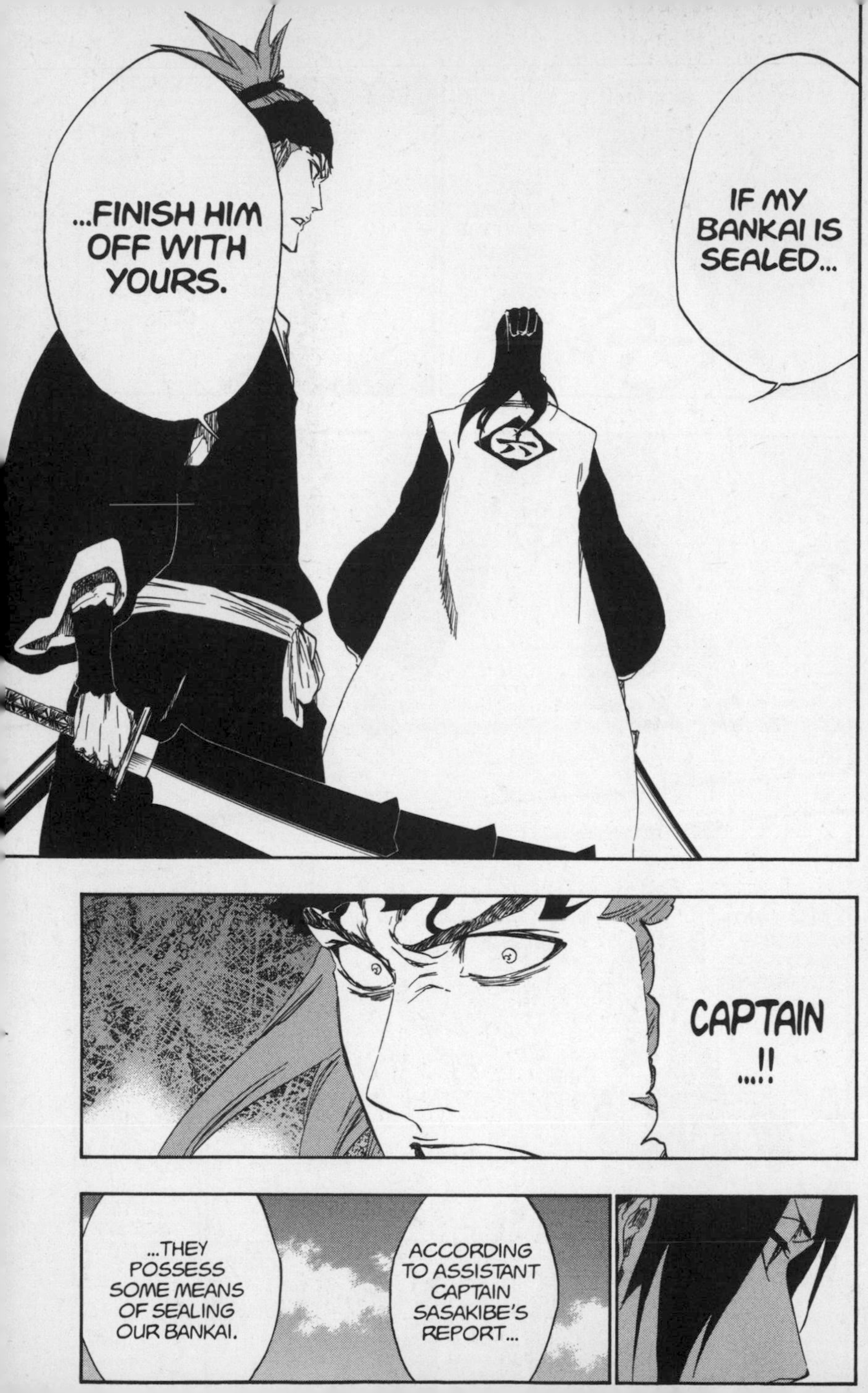
IF MY BANKAI IS SEALED...
...FINISH HIM OFF WITH YOURS.
CAPTAIN ...!!
ACCORDING TO ASSISTANT CAPTAIN SASAKIBE'S REPORT...
...THEY POSSESS SOME MEANS OF SEALING OUR BANKAI.

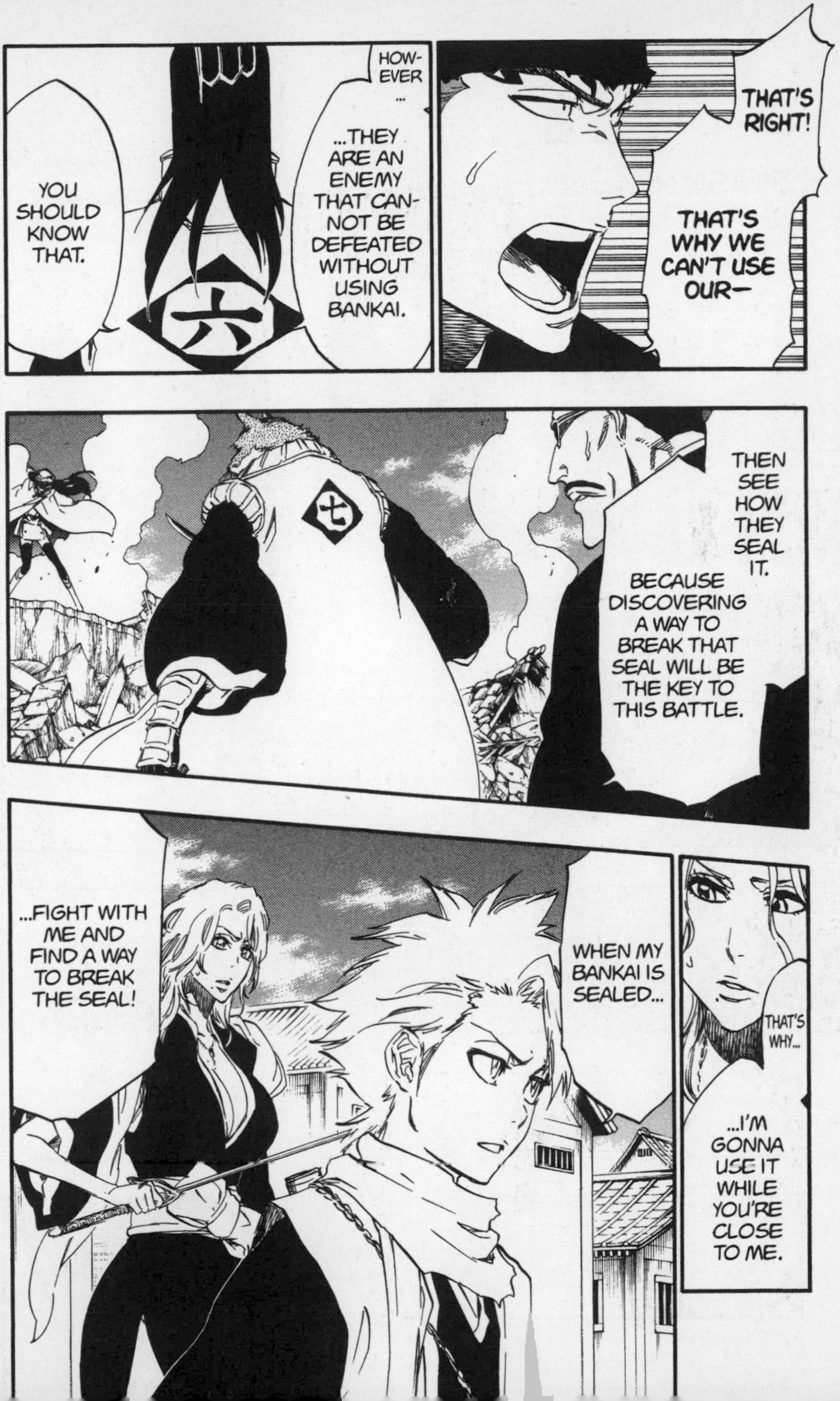
THAT'S RIGHT!
THAT'S WHY WE CAN'T USE OUR—
HOW-EVER ...
...THEY ARE AN ENEMY THAT CAN-NOT BE DEFEATED WITHOUT USING BANKAI.
YOU SHOULD KNOW THAT.
THEN SEE HOW THEY SEAL IT.
BECAUSE DISCOVERING A WAY TO BREAK THAT SEAL WILL BE THE KEY TO THIS BATTLE.
THAT'S WHY...
...I'M GONNA USE IT WHILE YOU'RE CLOSE TO ME.
WHEN MY BANKAI IS SEALED...
...FIGHT WITH ME AND FIND A WAY TO BREAK THE SEAL!

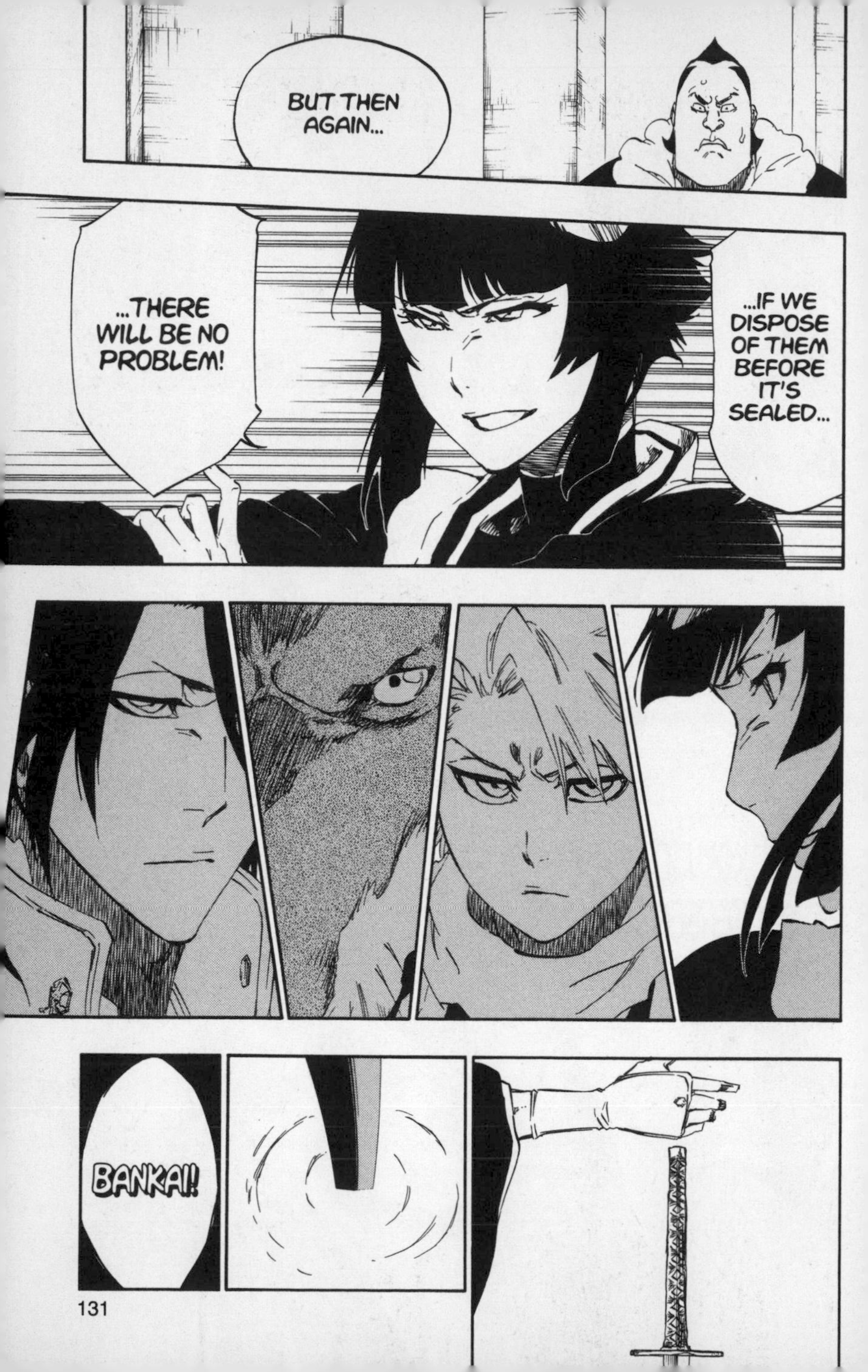
BUT THEN AGAIN...
...IF WE DISPOSE OF THEM BEFORE IT'S SEALED...
...THERE WILL BE NO PROBLEM!
BANKAI!

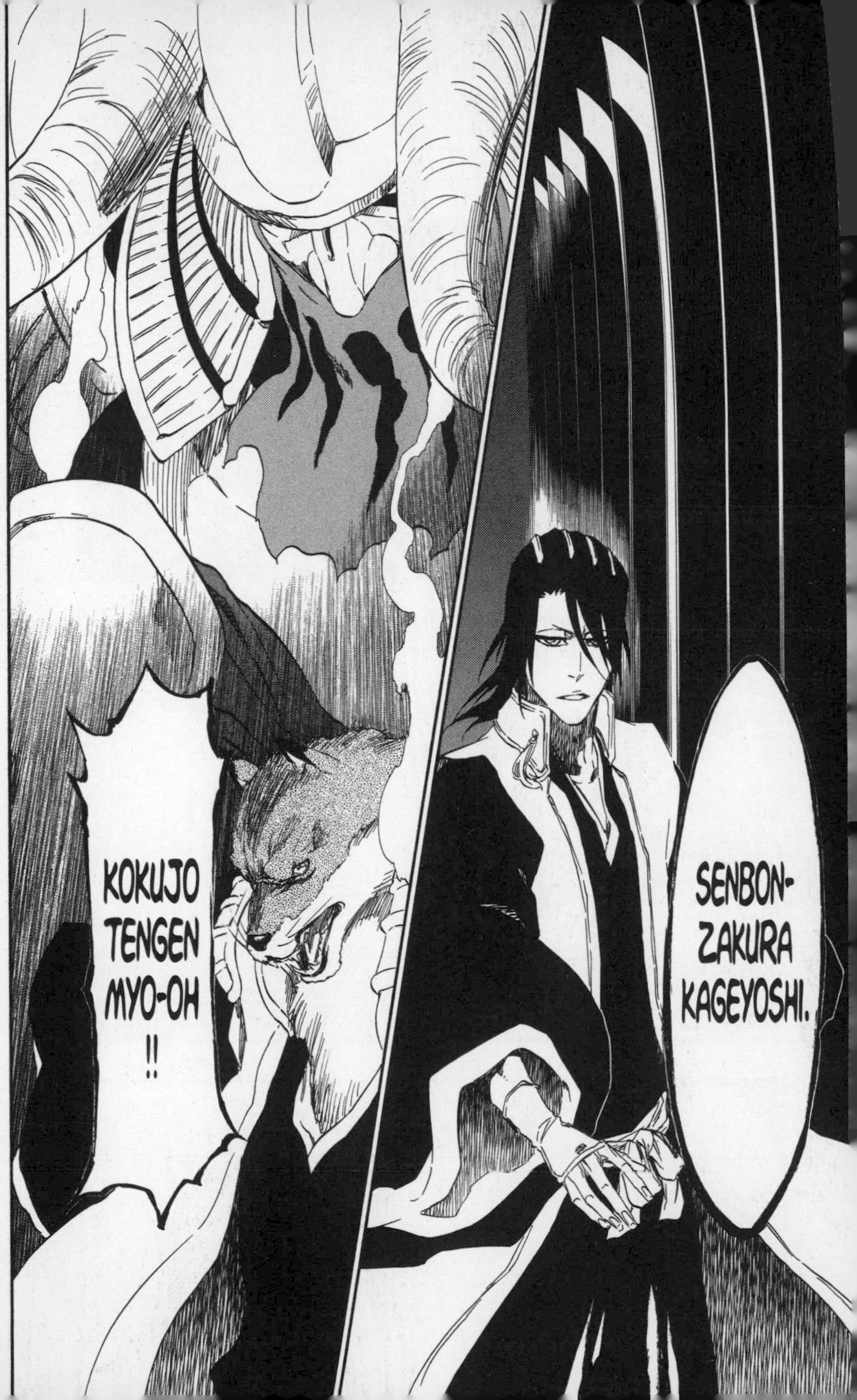
SENBON-
ZAKURA
KAGEYOSHI.
KOKUJO
TENGEN
MYO-OH
!!

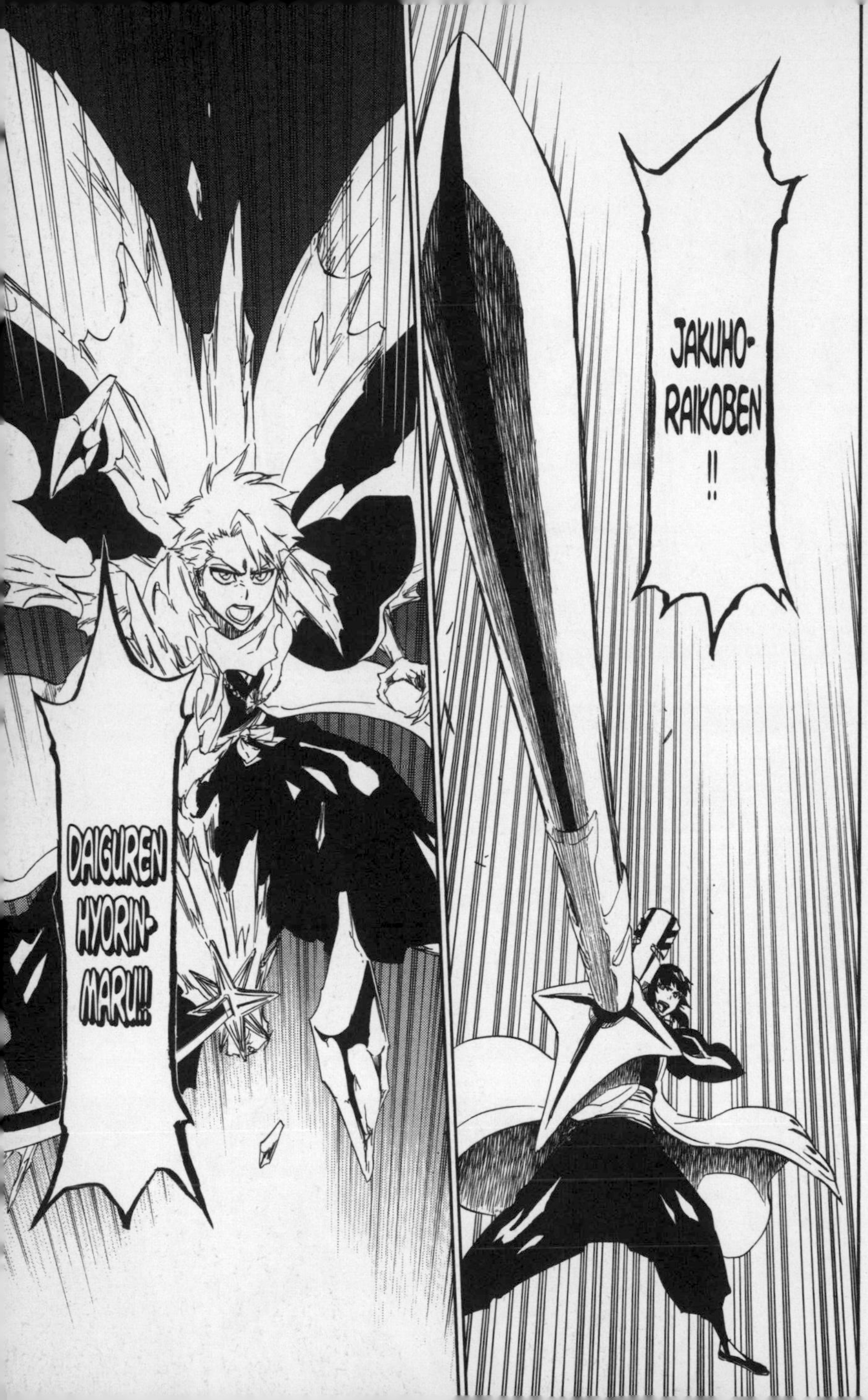
JAKUHO-RAIKOBEN!!
DAIGUREN HYORIN-MARU!!!

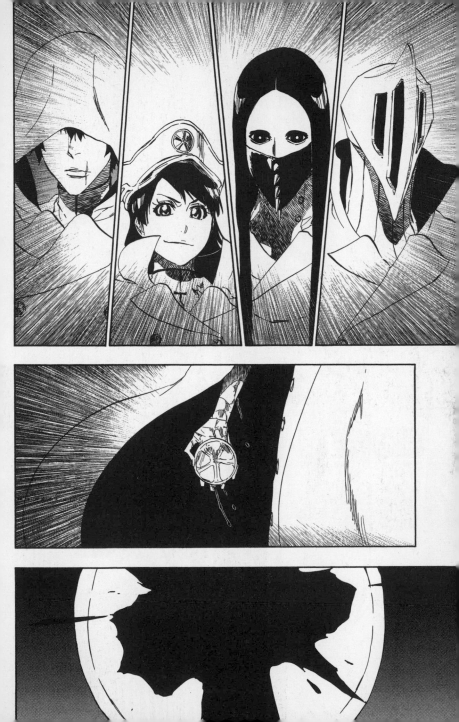

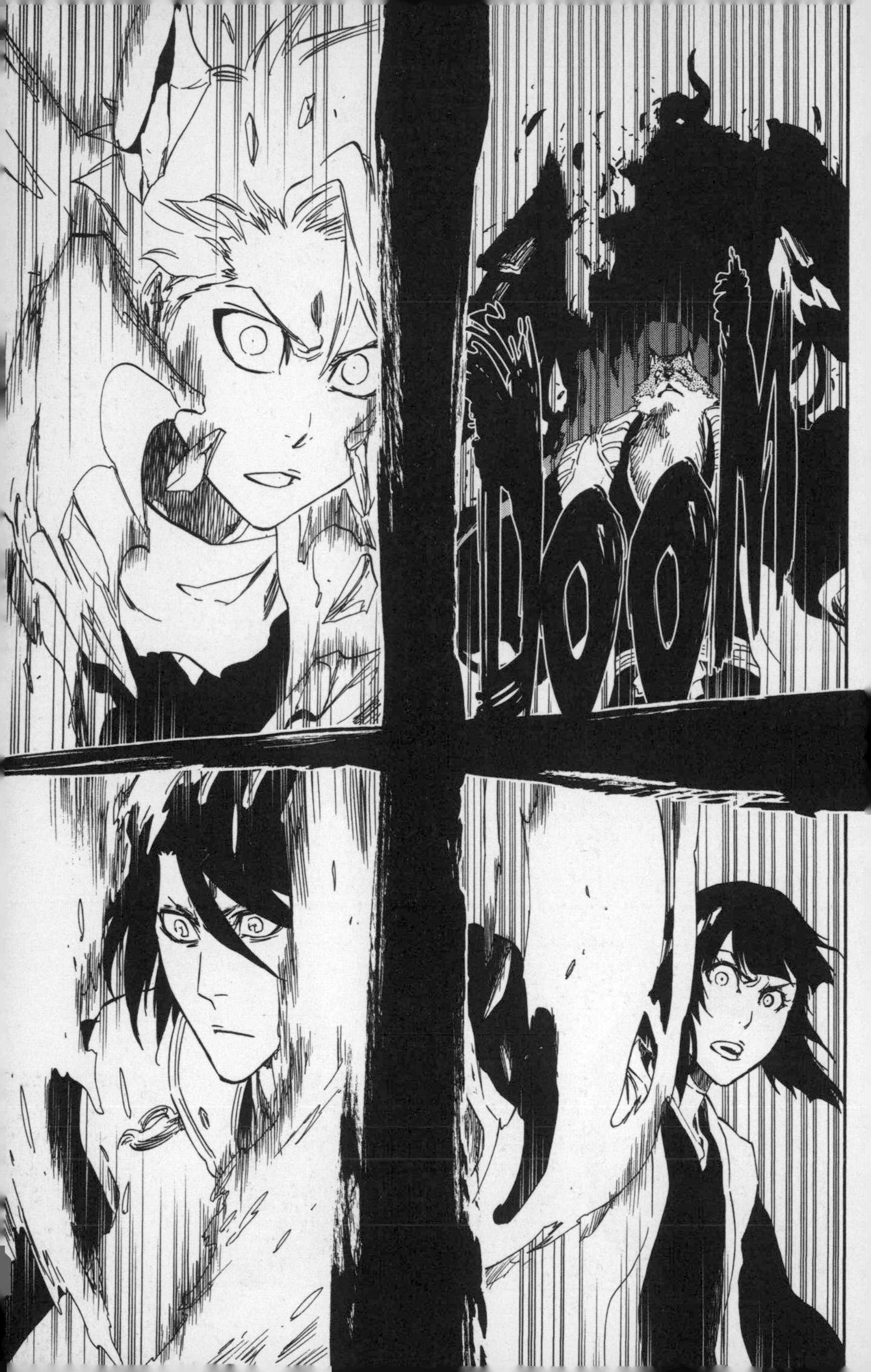
DOOOM

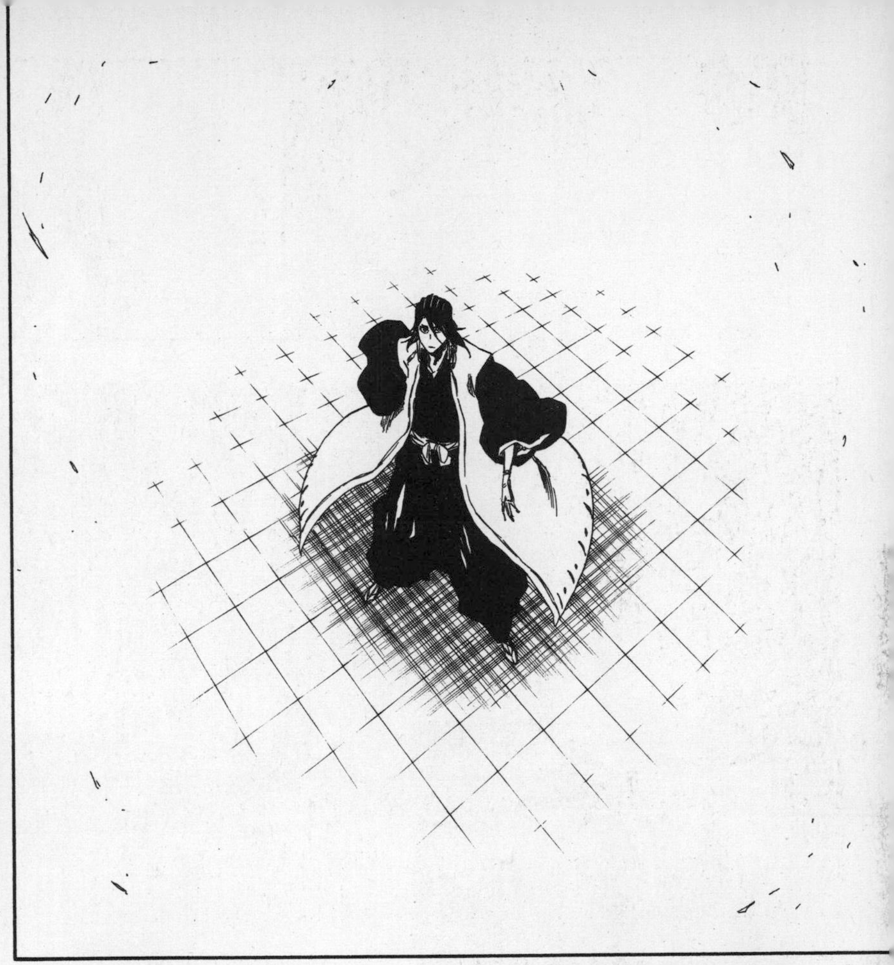
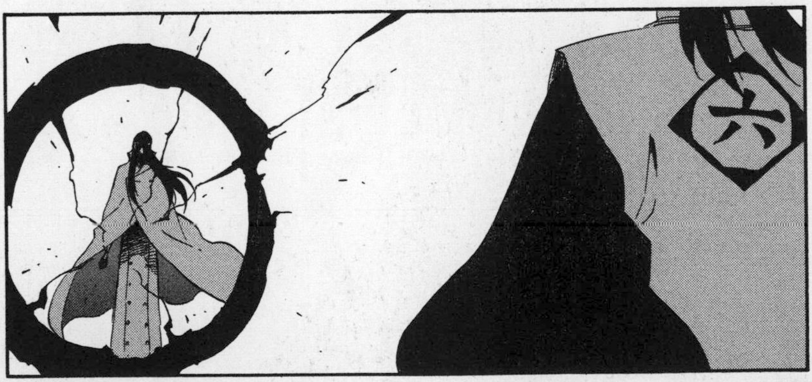
六

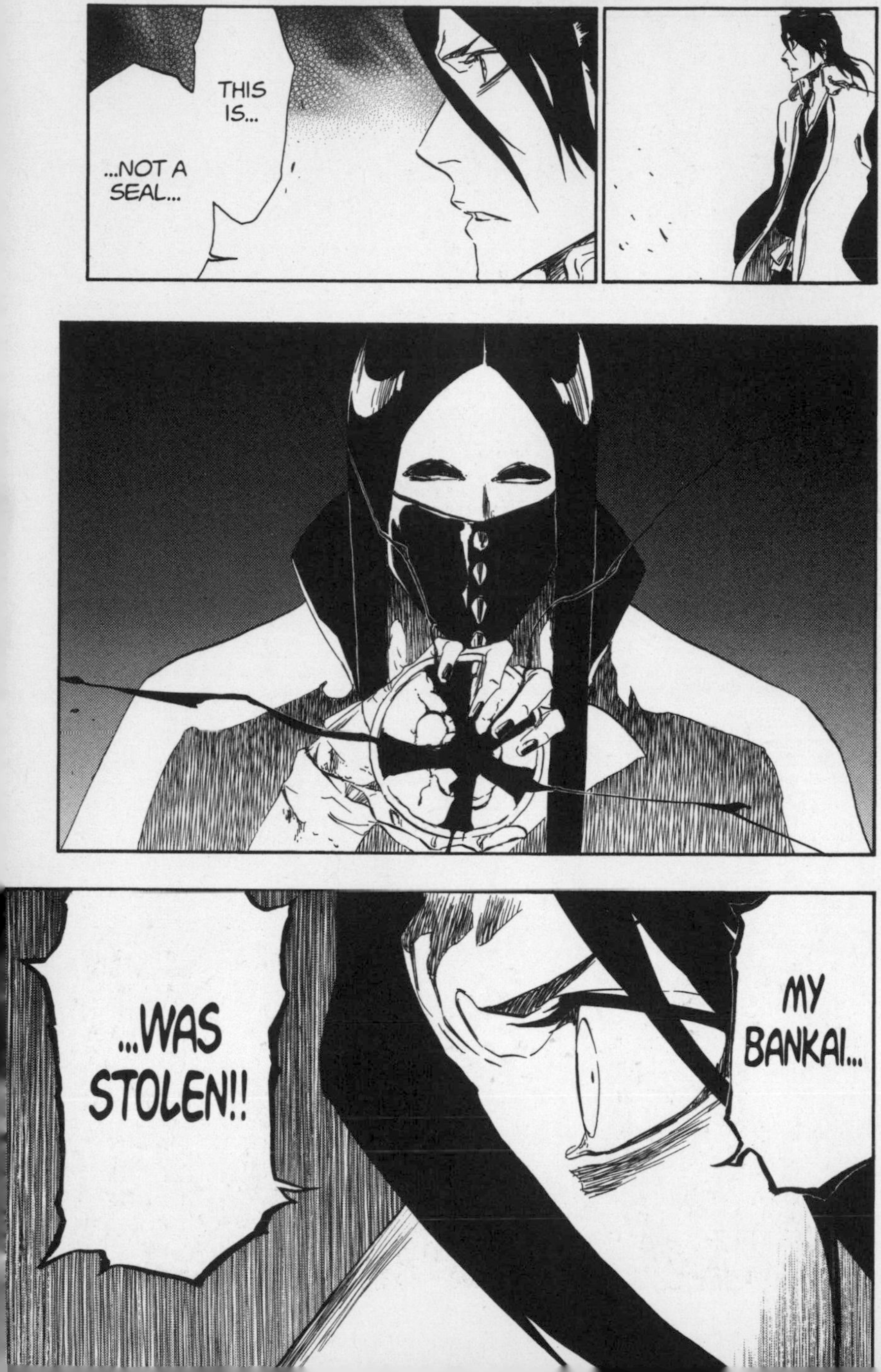
THIS IS...
...NOT A SEAL...
MY BANKAI...
...WAS STOLEN!!

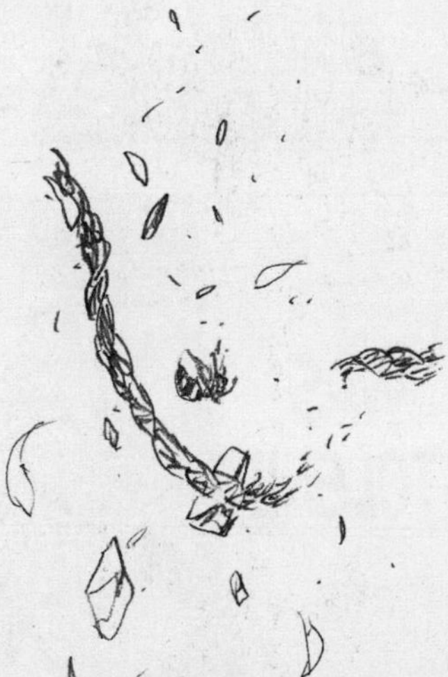

497.KILL THE SHADOW 2

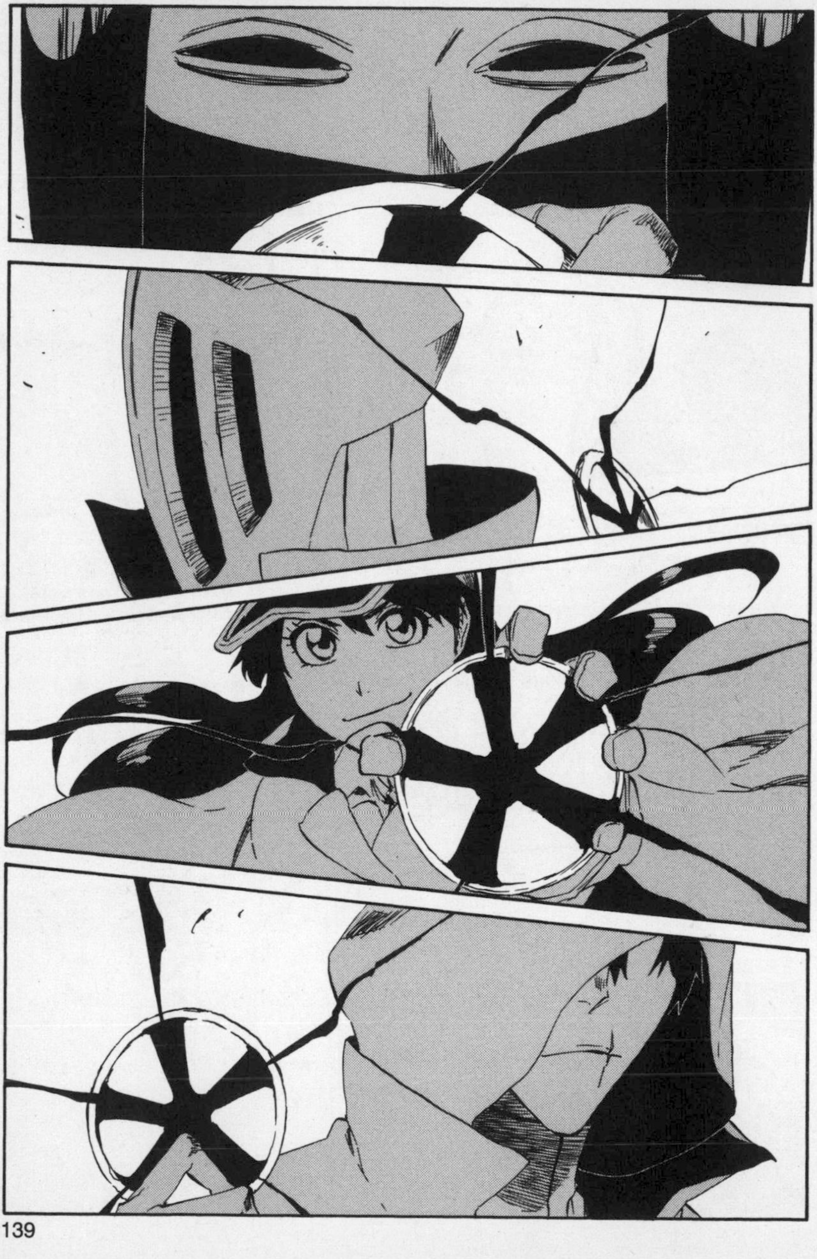

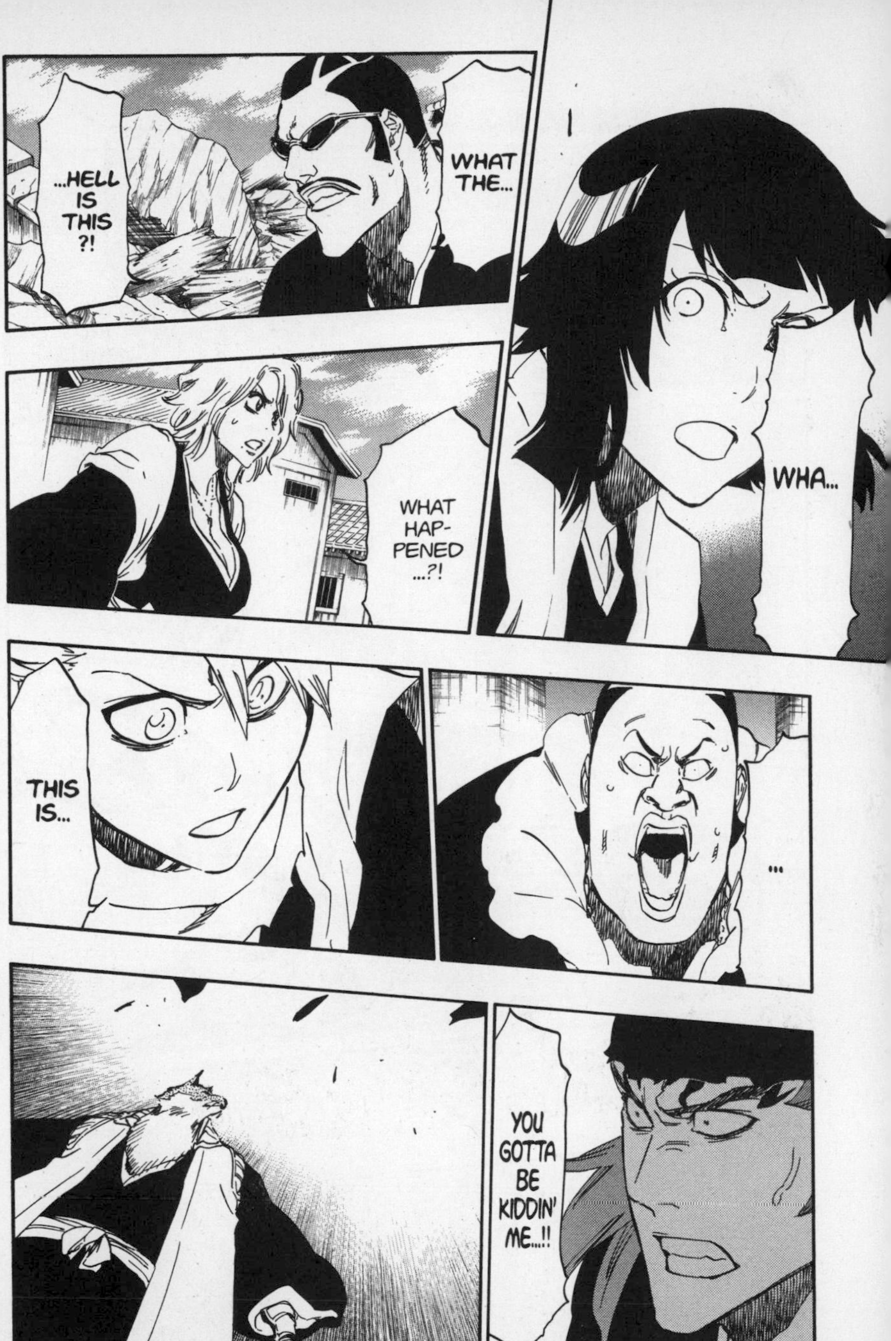
WHA...
WHAT THE...
...HELL IS THIS ?!
WHAT HAP-PENED ...?!
...
THIS IS...
YOU GOTTA BE KIDDIN' ME...!!

READ THIS WAY

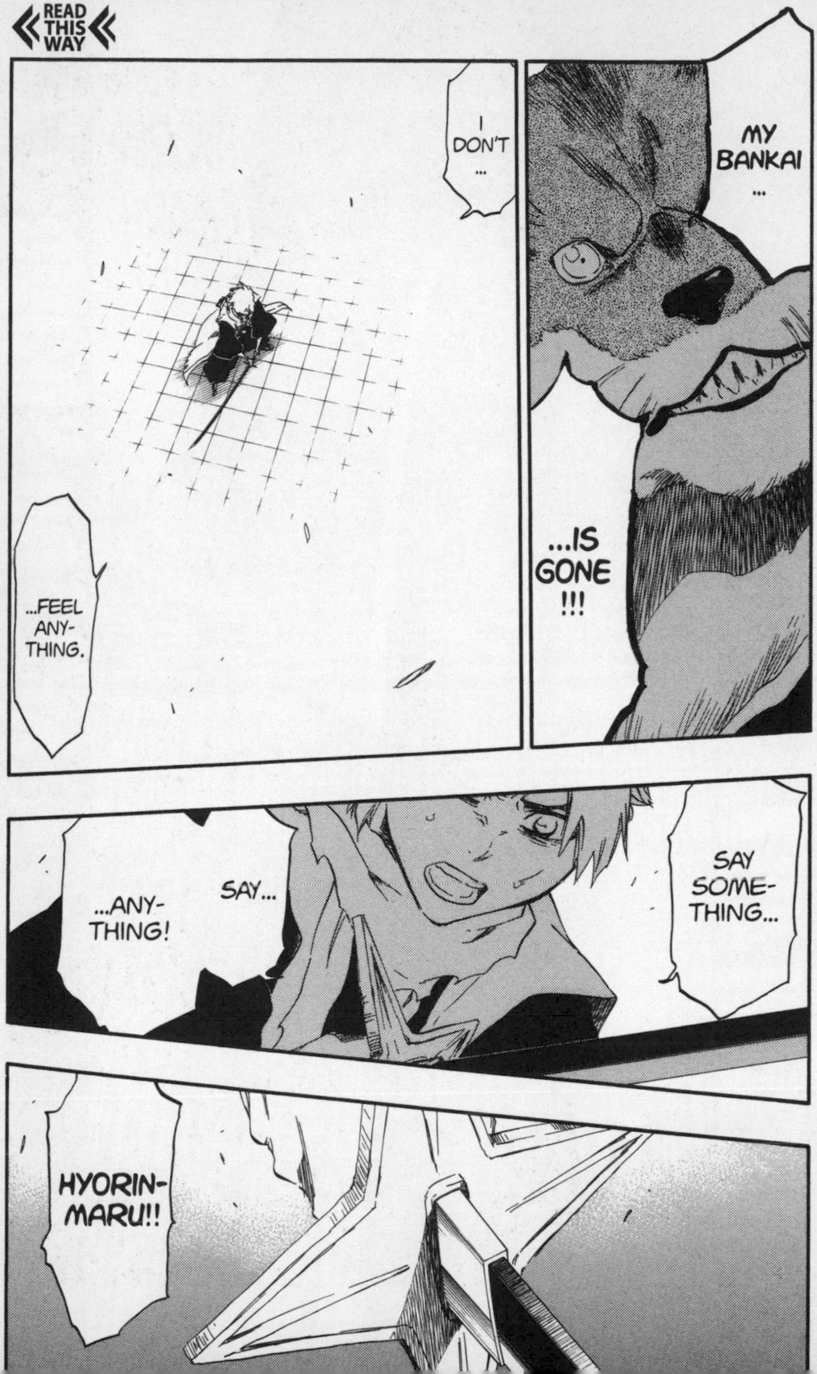
MY BANKAI ...
...IS GONE !!!
I DON'T ...
...FEEL ANY-THING.
SAY SOME-THING...
SAY...
...ANY-THING!
HYORIN-MARU!!

BLEACH 497. Kill The Shadow 2

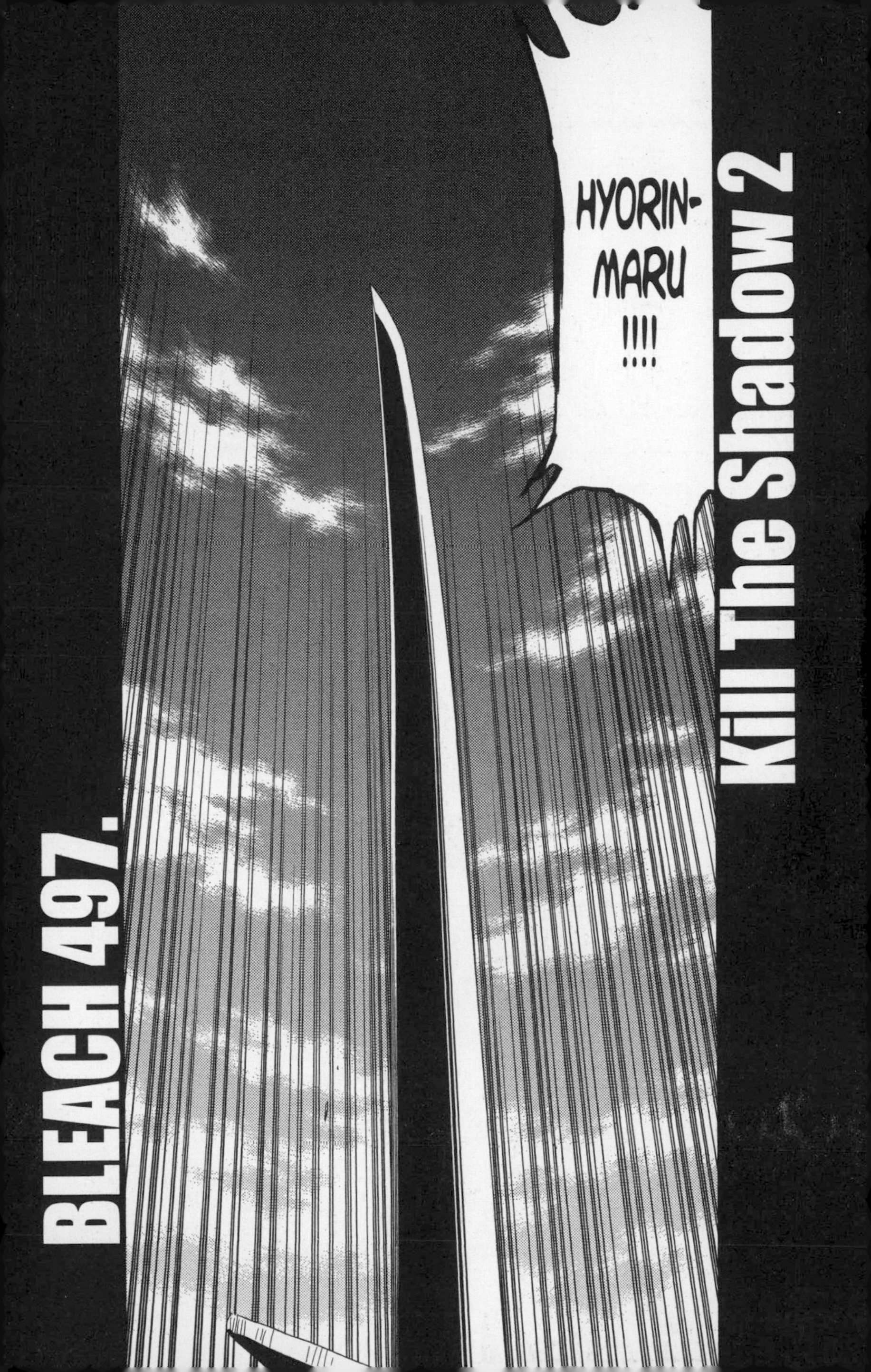
HYORIN-MARU !!!!

READ THIS WAY

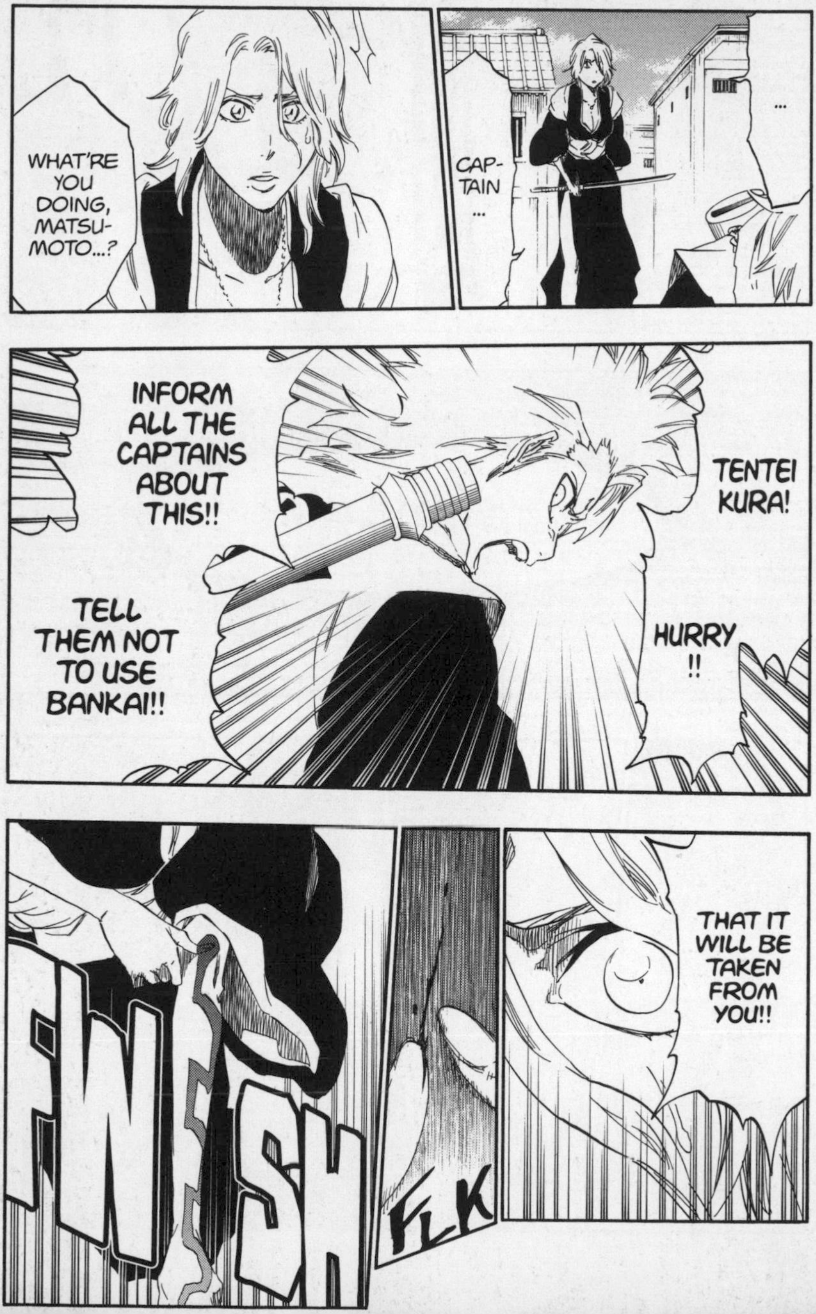
...
CAPTAIN...
WHAT'RE YOU DOING, MATSUMOTO...?
TENTEI KURA!
HURRY!!
INFORM ALL THE CAPTAINS ABOUT THIS!!
TELL THEM NOT TO USE BANKAI!!
THAT IT WILL BE TAKEN FROM YOU!!
FLK
FWISH

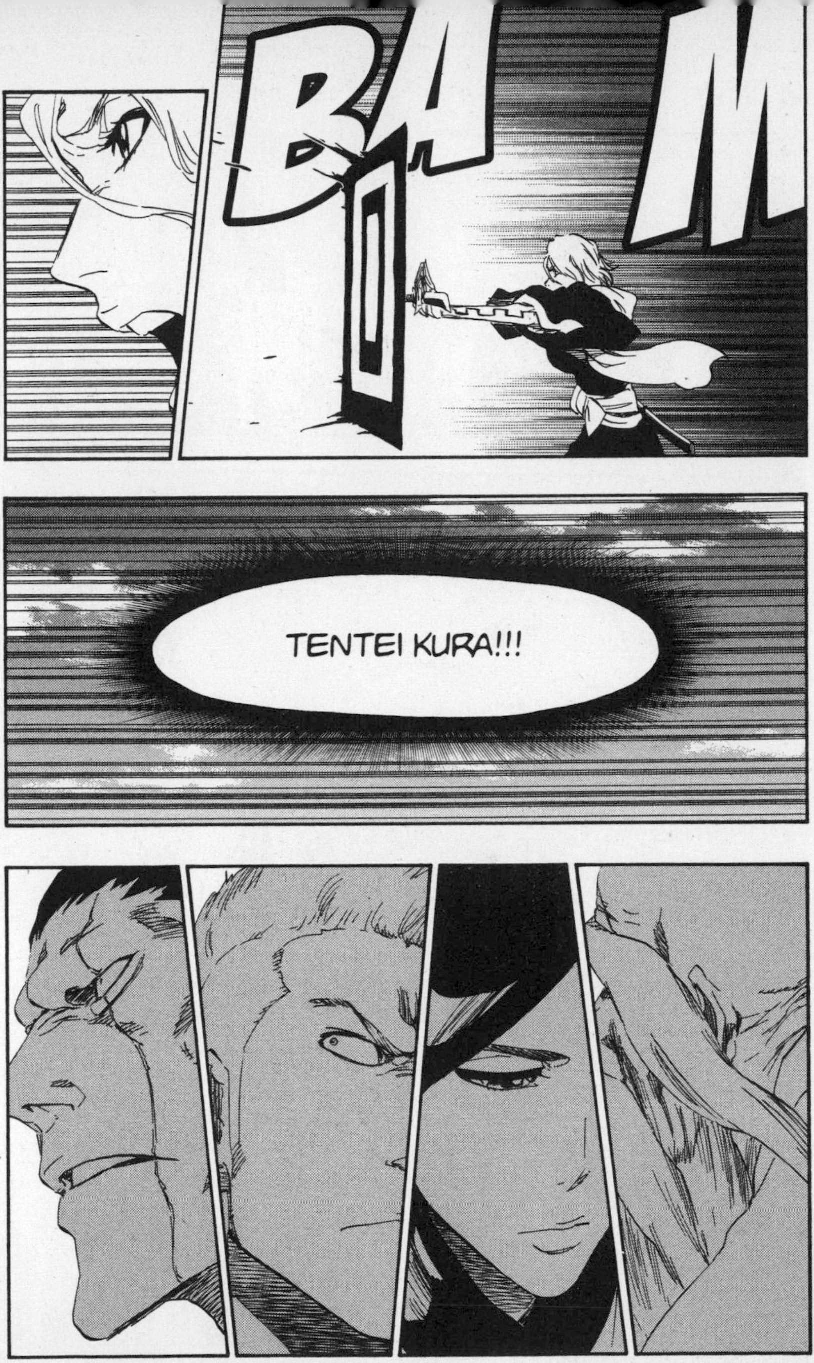
BAM
TENTEI KURA!!!

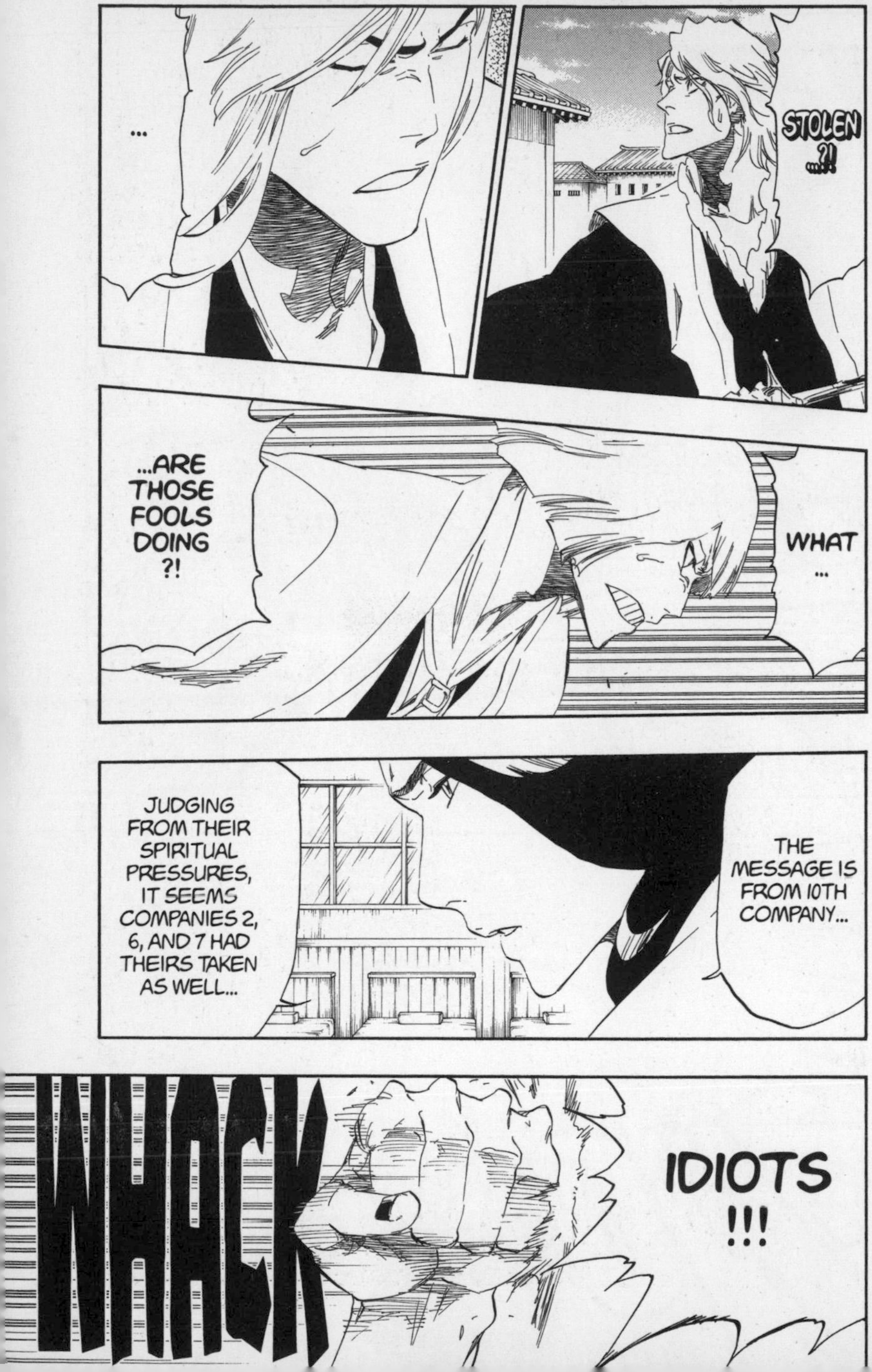
STOLEN ...?!
...
WHAT ...
...ARE THOSE FOOLS DOING ?!
THE MESSAGE IS FROM 10TH COMPANY...
JUDGING FROM THEIR SPIRITUAL PRESSURES, IT SEEMS COMPANIES 2, 6, AND 7 HAD THEIRS TAKEN AS WELL...
IDIOTS !!!
WHACK

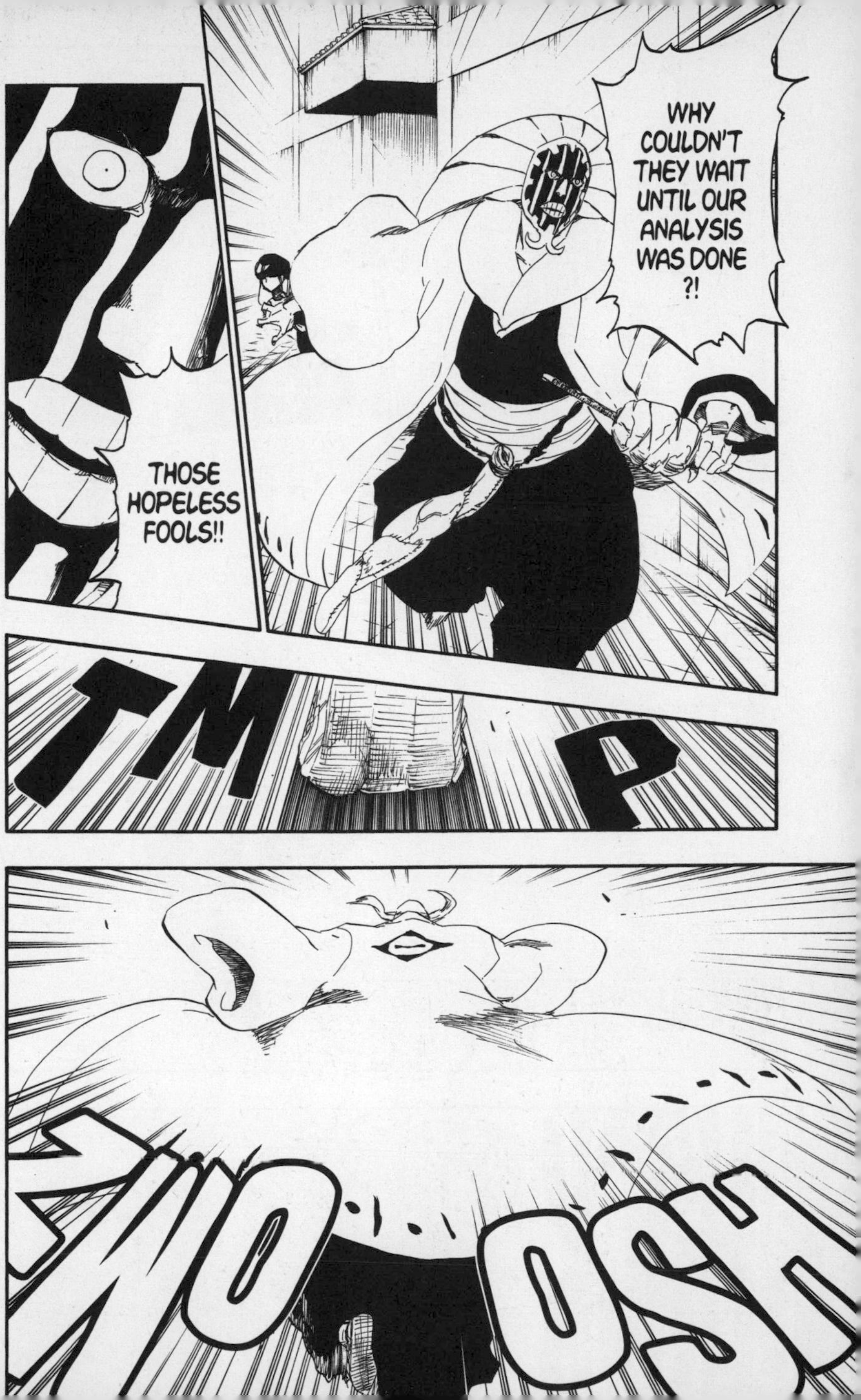
WHY COULDN'T THEY WAIT UNTIL OUR ANALYSIS WAS DONE ?!
THOSE HOPELESS FOOLS!!

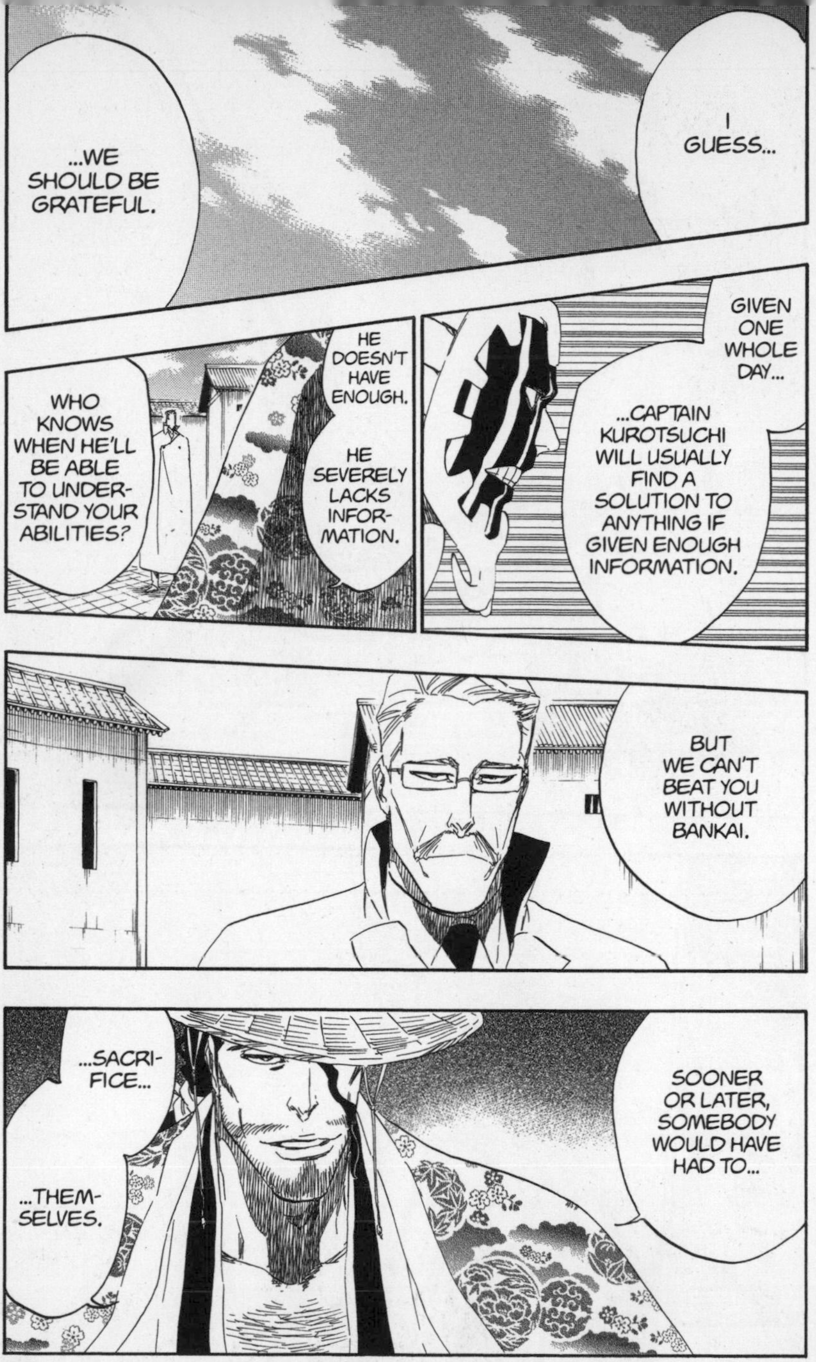
I GUESS...
...WE SHOULD BE GRATEFUL.
GIVEN ONE WHOLE DAY...
...CAPTAIN KUROTSUCHI WILL USUALLY FIND A SOLUTION TO ANYTHING IF GIVEN ENOUGH INFORMATION.
HE DOESN'T HAVE ENOUGH.
HE SEVERELY LACKS INFOR-MATION.
WHO KNOWS WHEN HE'LL BE ABLE TO UNDER-STAND YOUR ABILITIES?
BUT WE CAN'T BEAT YOU WITHOUT BANKAI.
SOONER OR LATER, SOMEBODY WOULD HAVE HAD TO...
...SACRI-FICE...
...THEM-SELVES.

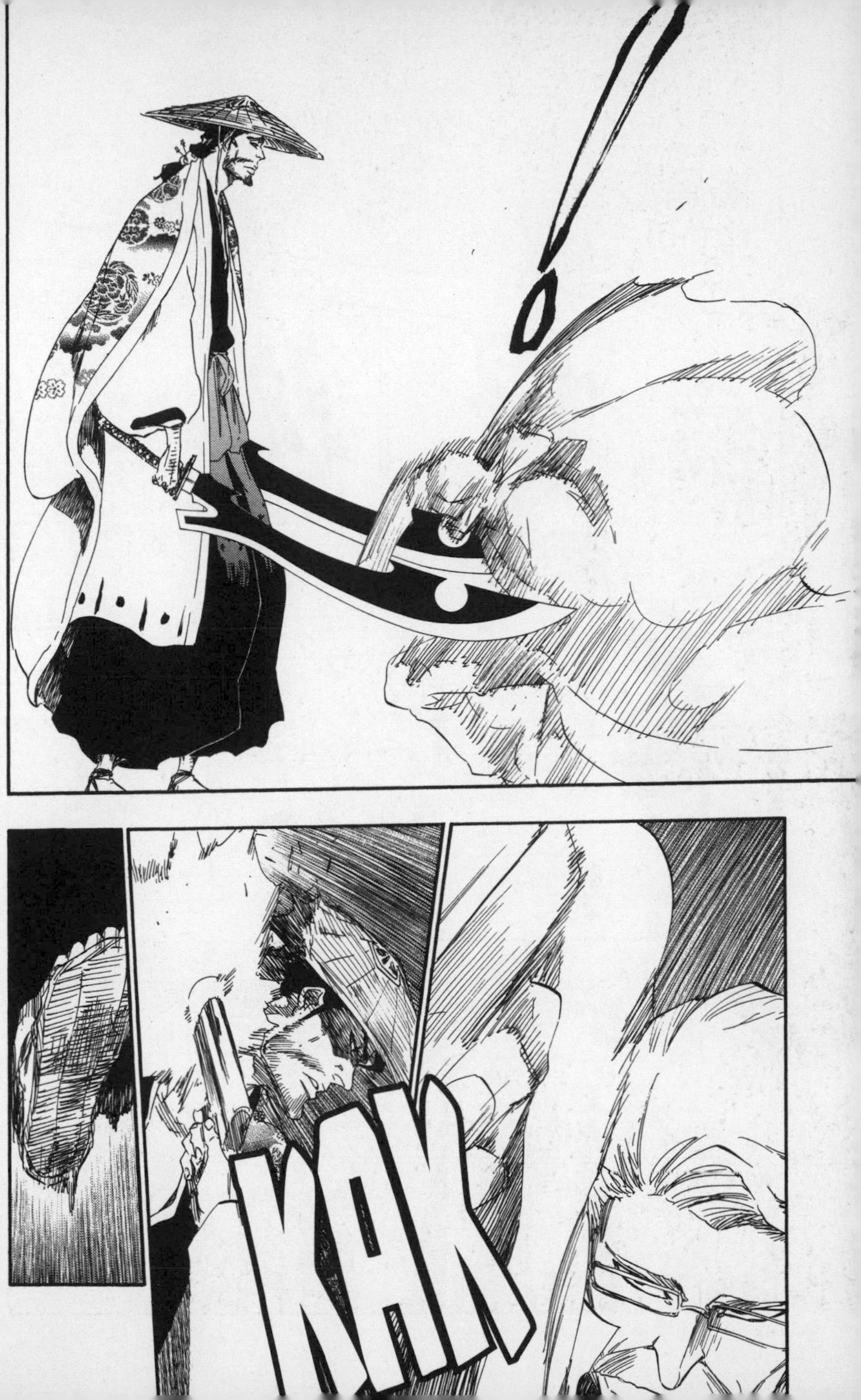
KAK

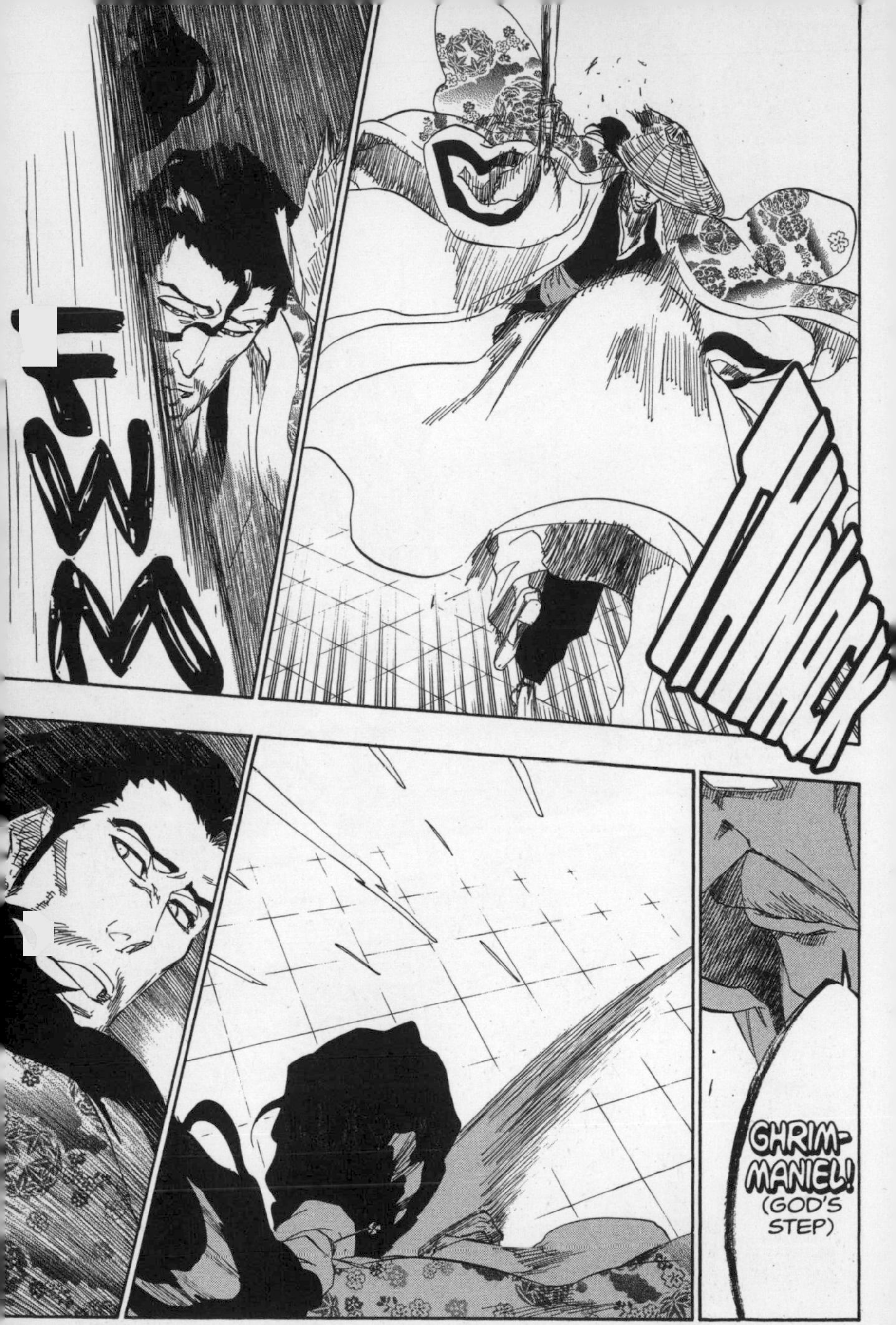
THWACK
FWM
GHRIM-
MANIEL!
(GOD'S
STEP)

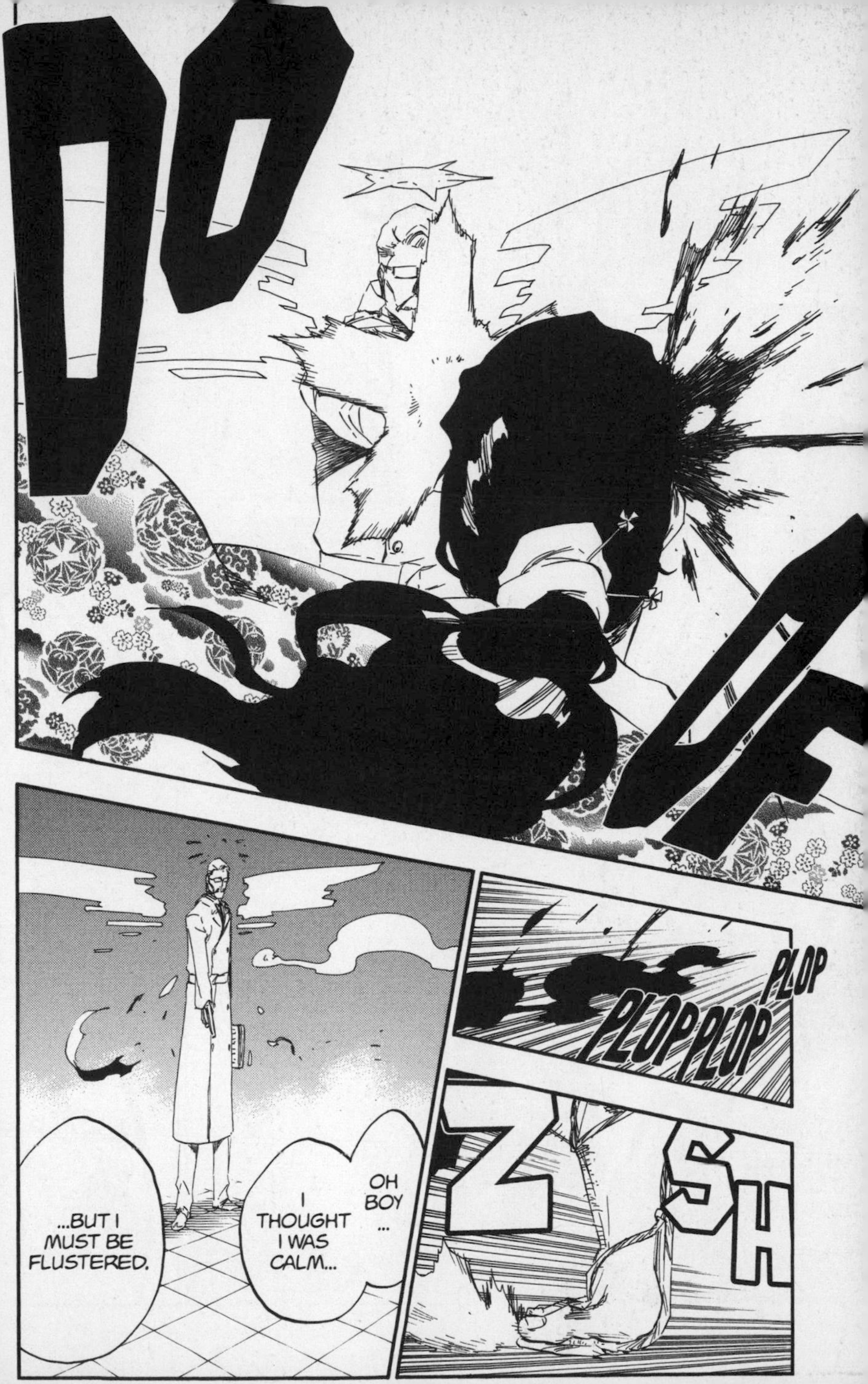
DO
PLOP PLOP PLOP
ZSH
OH BOY ...
I THOUGHT I WAS CALM...
...BUT I MUST BE FLUSTERED.

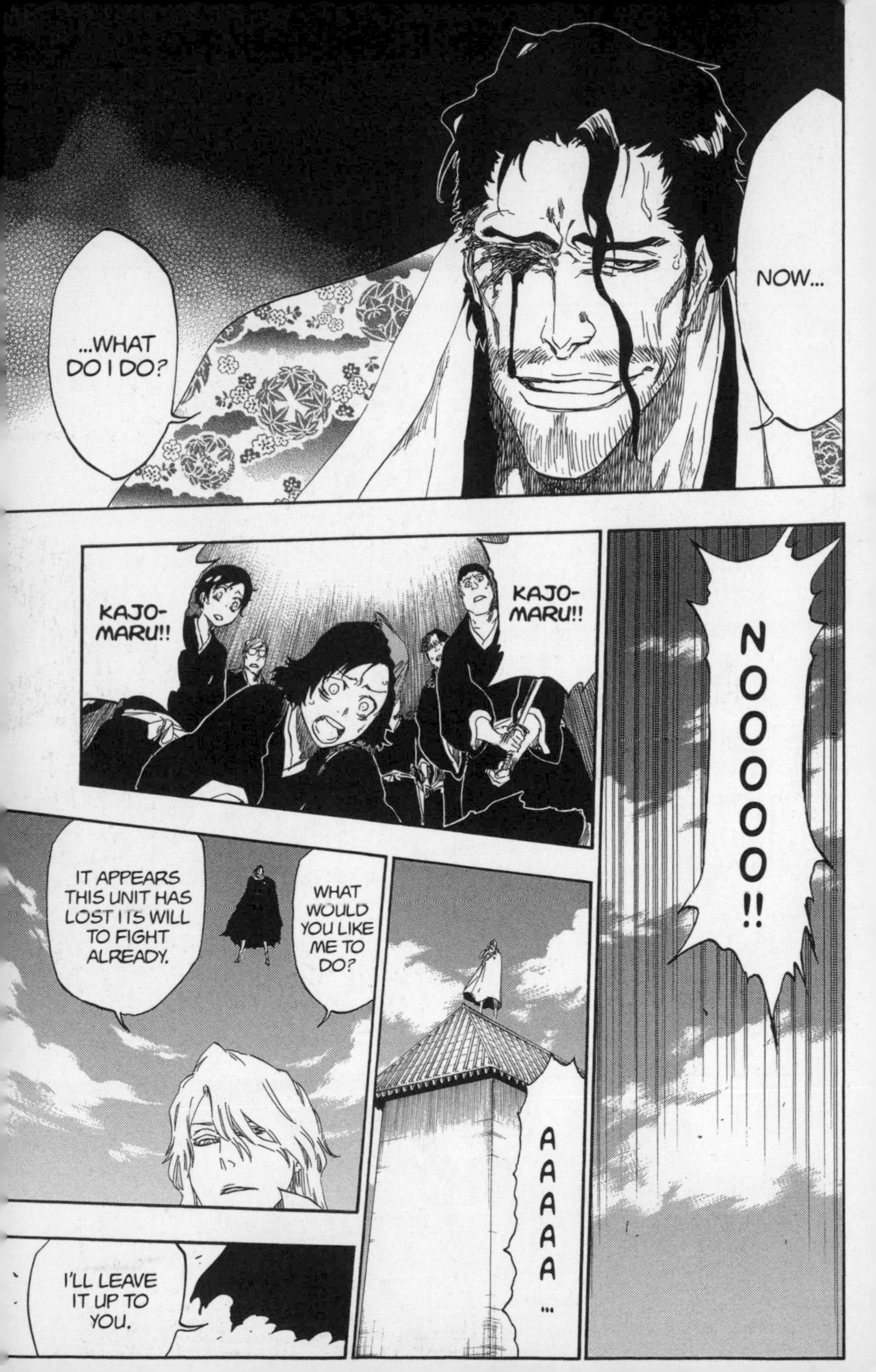
NOW...
...WHAT DO I DO?
NOOOOOO!!
KAJO-MARU!!
KAJO-MARU!!
AAAAA...
IT APPEARS THIS UNIT HAS LOST ITS WILL TO FIGHT ALREADY.
WHAT WOULD YOU LIKE ME TO DO?
I'LL LEAVE IT UP TO YOU.

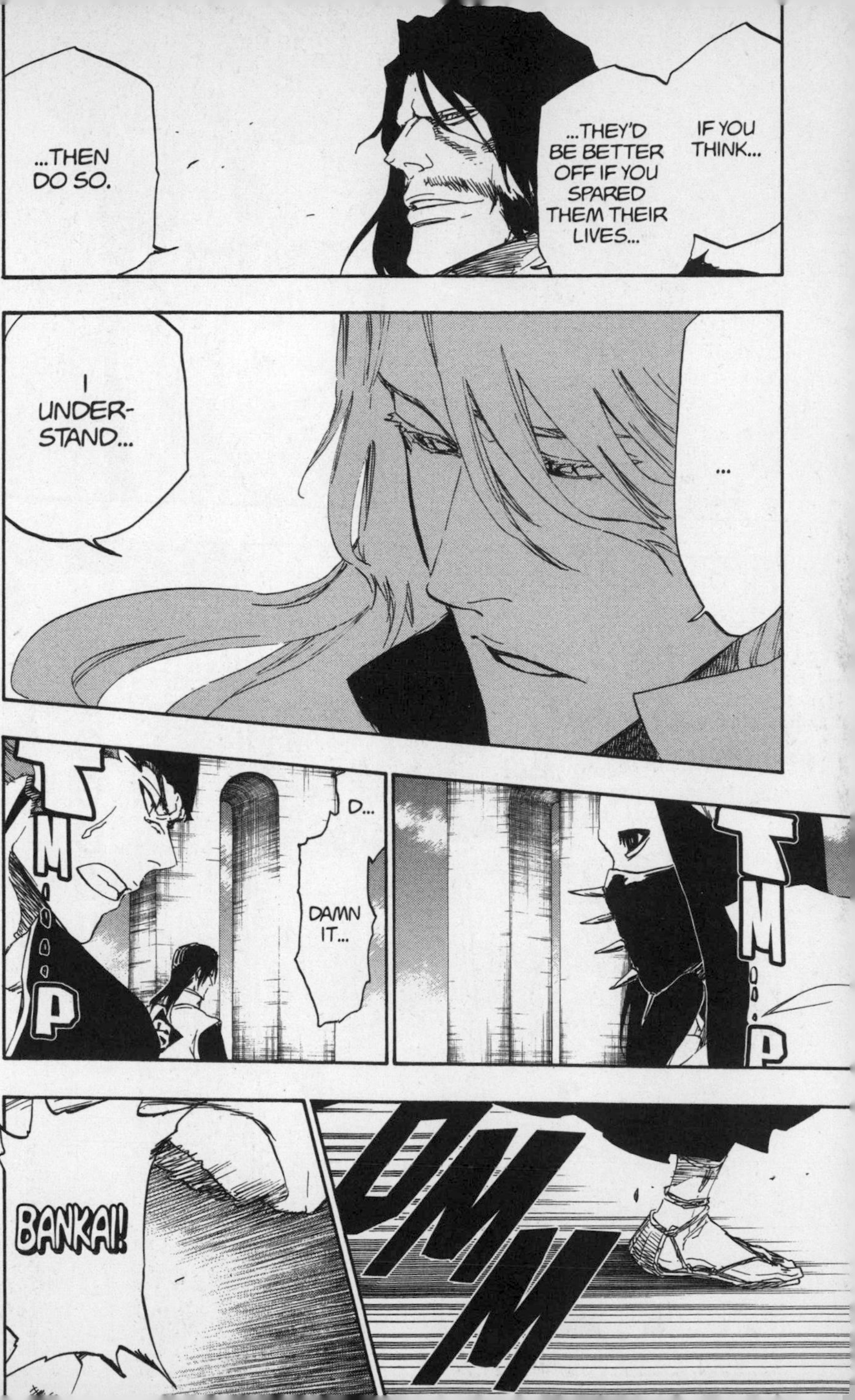
IF YOU THINK...
...THEY'D BE BETTER OFF IF YOU SPARED THEM THEIR LIVES...
...THEN DO SO.
...
I UNDER-STAND...
TMP
TMP
D...
DAMN IT...
DMM
BANKAI!

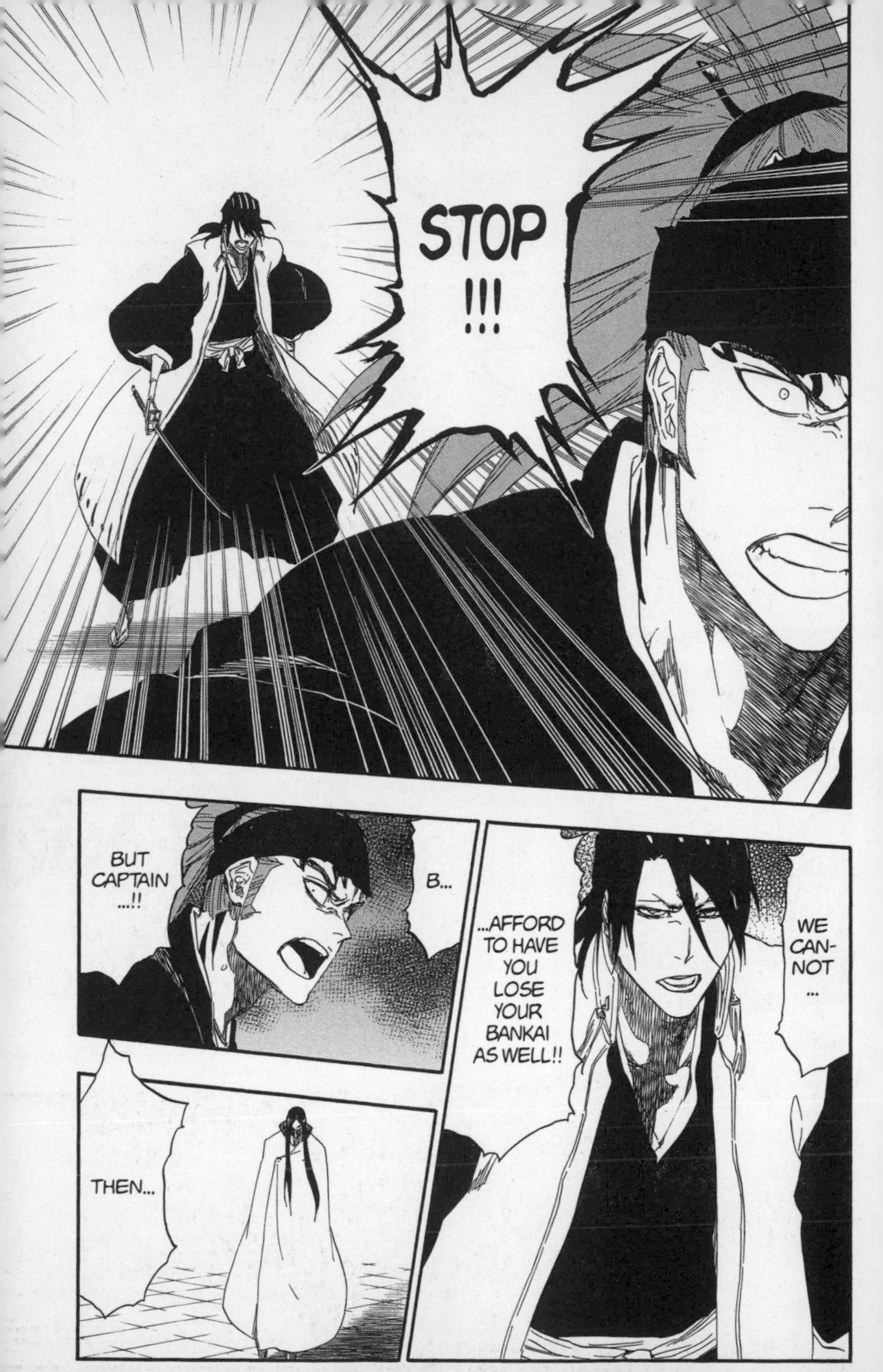
STOP !!!
WE CAN-NOT ...
...AFFORD TO HAVE YOU LOSE YOUR BANKAI AS WELL!!
B...
BUT CAPTAIN ...!!
THEN...

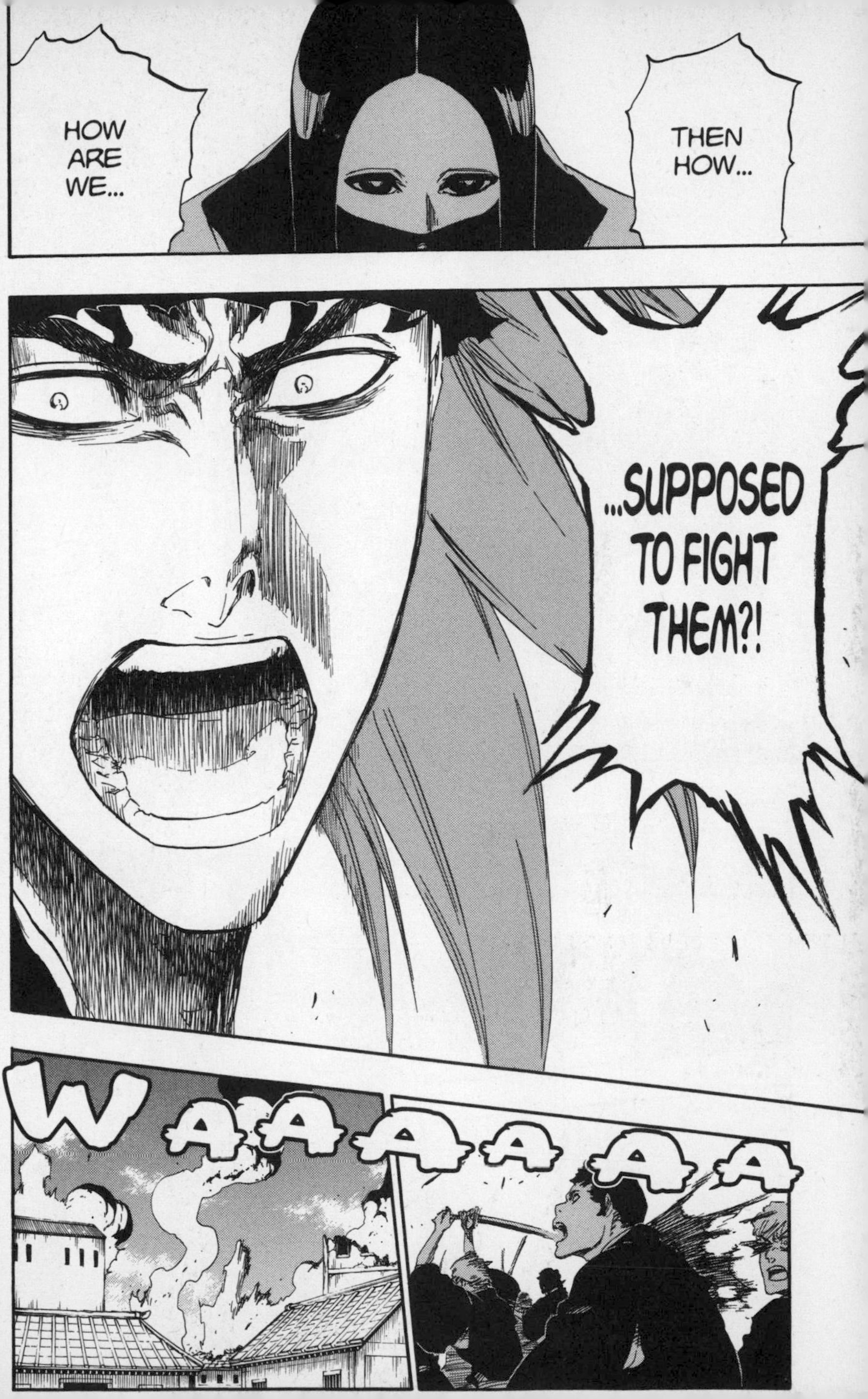
THEN HOW...
HOW ARE WE...
...SUPPOSED TO FIGHT THEM?!
WAAAAAAA

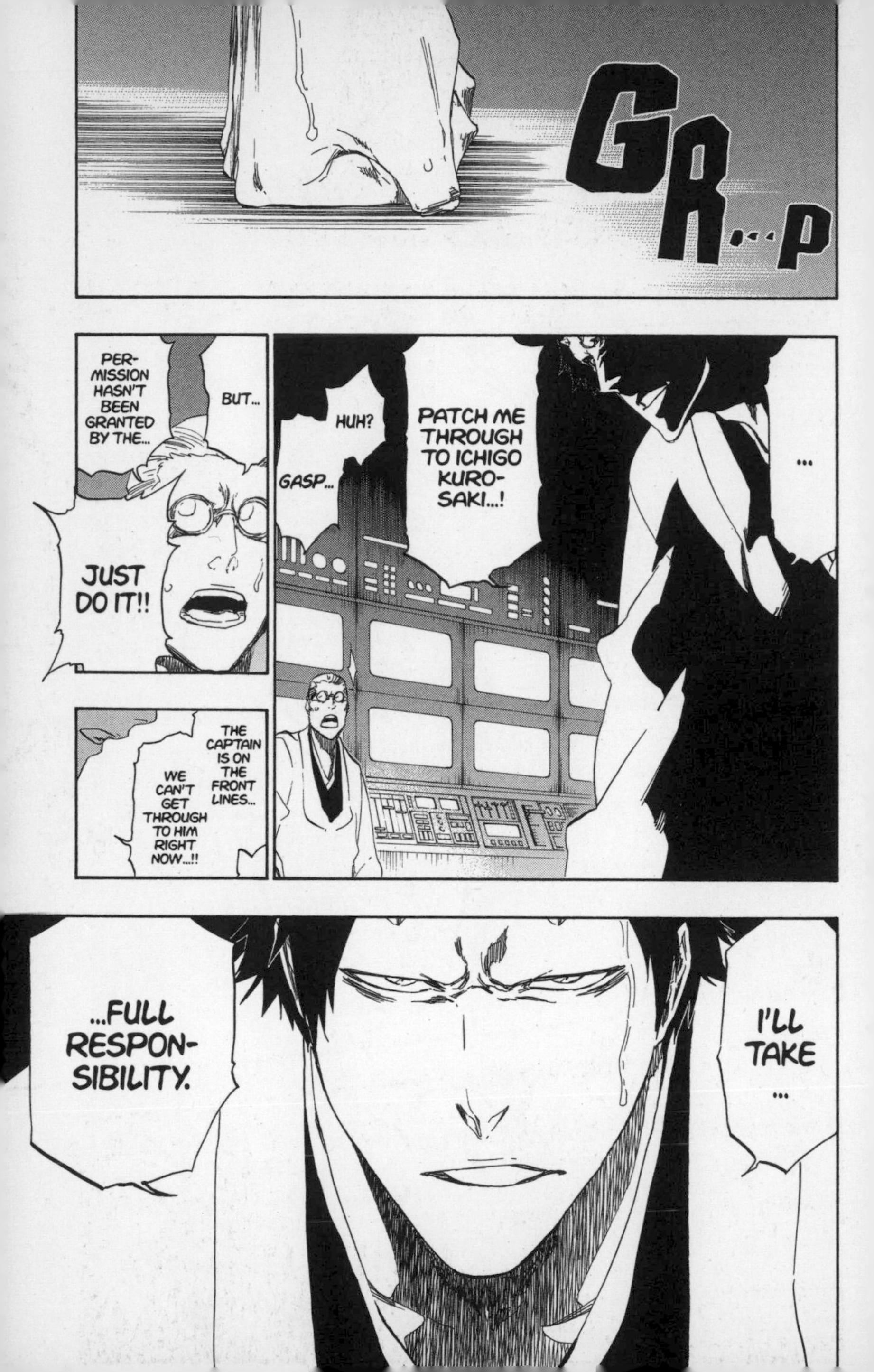
GR...P
...
PATCH ME THROUGH TO ICHIGO KUROSAKI...!
HUH?
GASP...
BUT...
PERMISSION HASN'T BEEN GRANTED BY THE...
JUST DO IT!!
THE CAPTAIN IS ON THE FRONT LINES...
WE CAN'T GET THROUGH TO HIM RIGHT NOW...!!
I'LL TAKE...
...FULL RESPONSIBILITY.

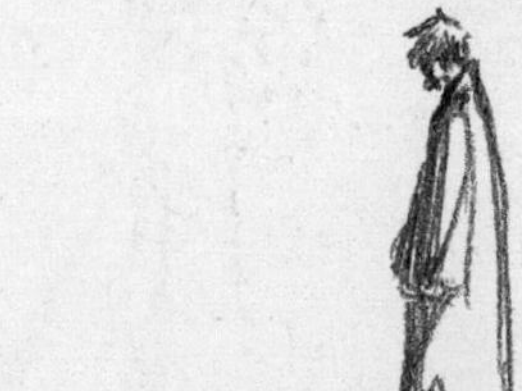

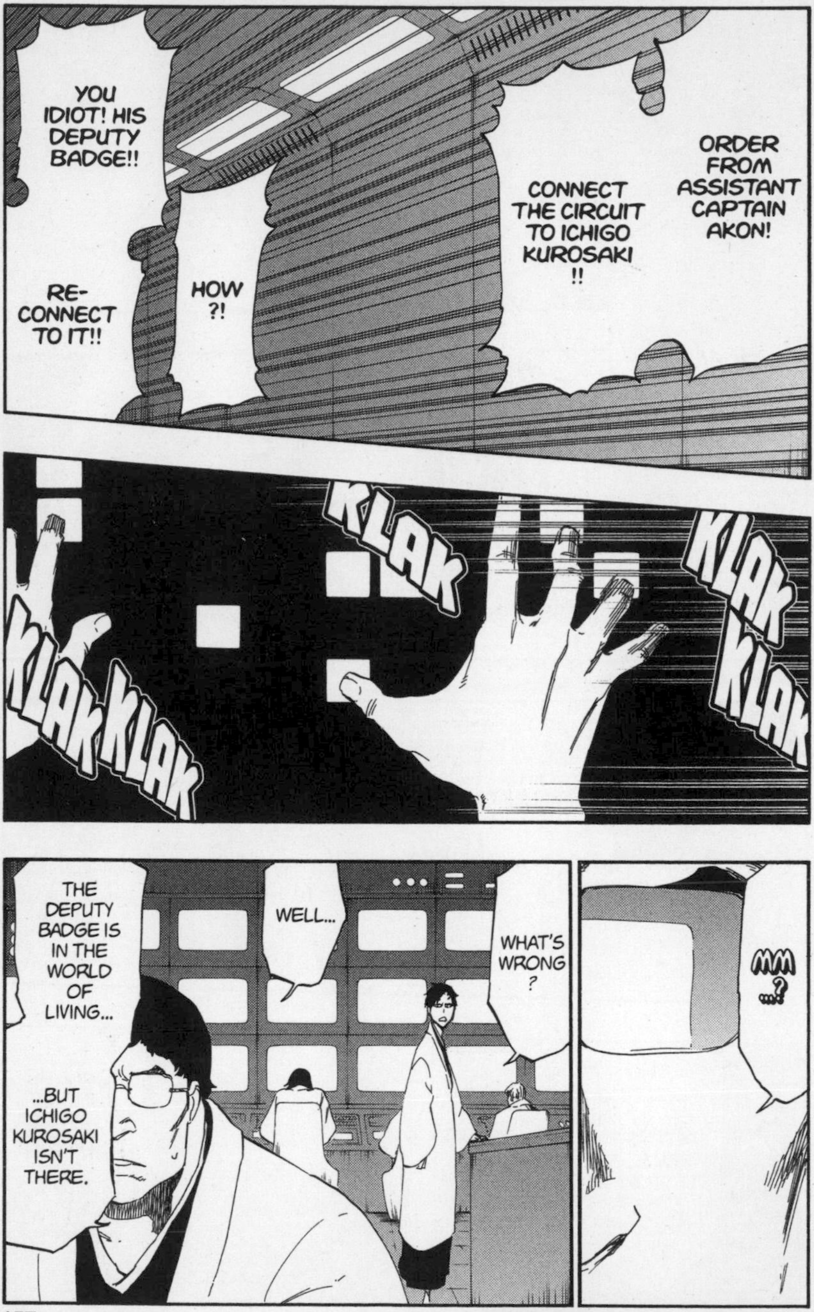
ORDER FROM ASSISTANT CAPTAIN AKON!
CONNECT THE CIRCUIT TO ICHIGO KUROSAKI !!
HOW ?!
YOU IDIOT! HIS DEPUTY BADGE!!
RE-CONNECT TO IT!!
KLAK
KLAK KLAK
KLAK KLAK KLAK
MM ...?
WHAT'S WRONG ?
WELL...
THE DEPUTY BADGE IS IN THE WORLD OF LIVING...
...BUT ICHIGO KUROSAKI ISN'T THERE.

498. THE DARK RESCUER

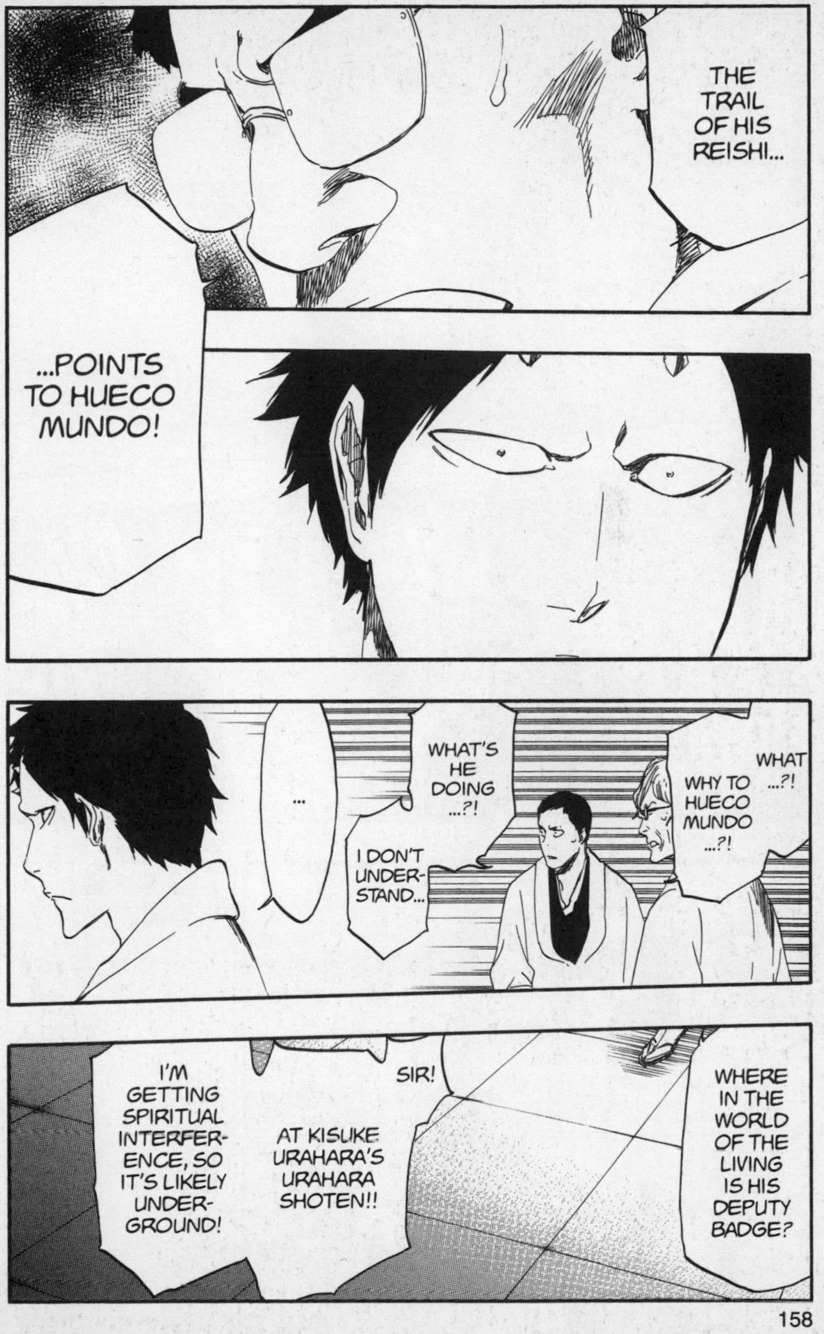
THE TRAIL OF HIS REISHI...
...POINTS TO HUECO MUNDO!
WHAT ...?!
WHY TO HUECO MUNDO ...?!
WHAT'S HE DOING ...?!
I DON'T UNDER-STAND...
...
WHERE IN THE WORLD OF THE LIVING IS HIS DEPUTY BADGE?
SIR!
AT KISUKE URAHARA'S URAHARA SHOTEN!!
I'M GETTING SPIRITUAL INTERFER-ENCE, SO IT'S LIKELY UNDER-GROUND!

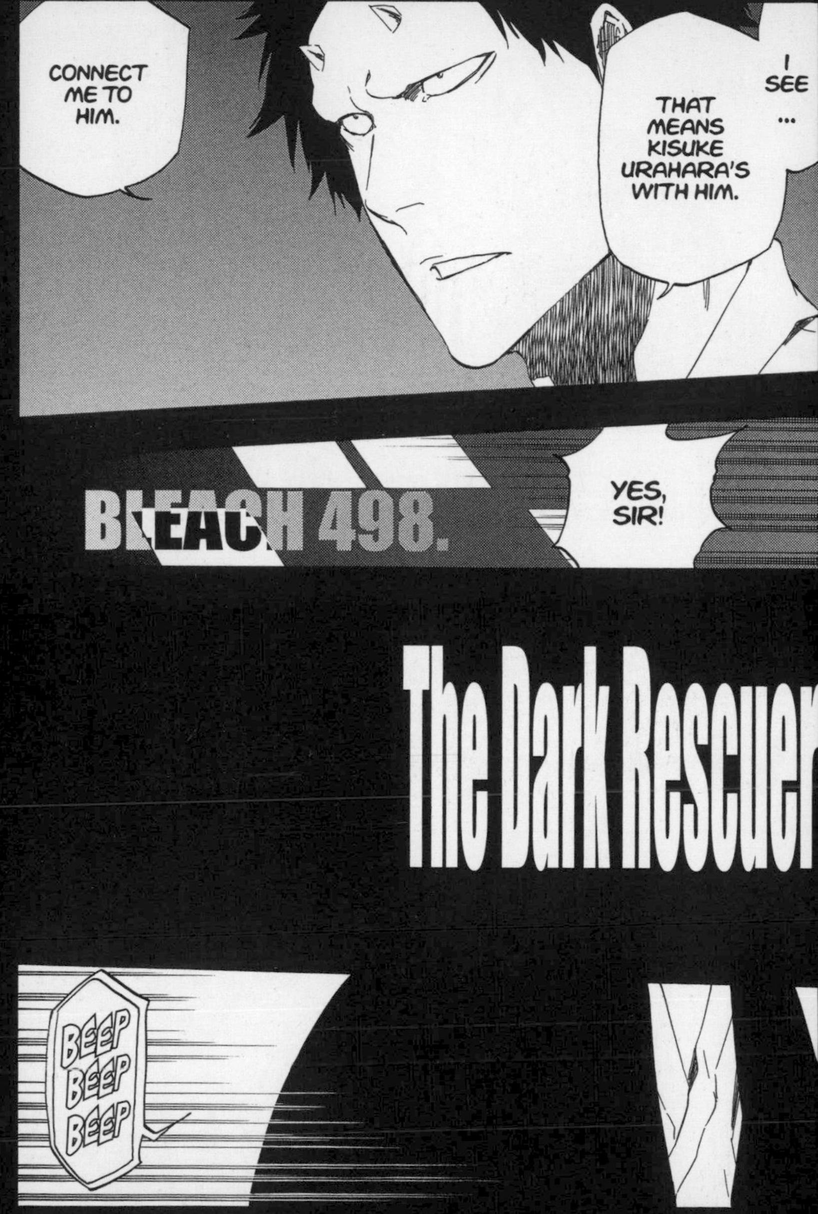
I SEE...
THAT MEANS KISUKE URAHARA'S WITH HIM.
CONNECT ME TO HIM.
YES, SIR!
BLEACH 498.
The Dark Rescuer
BEEP BEEP BEEP

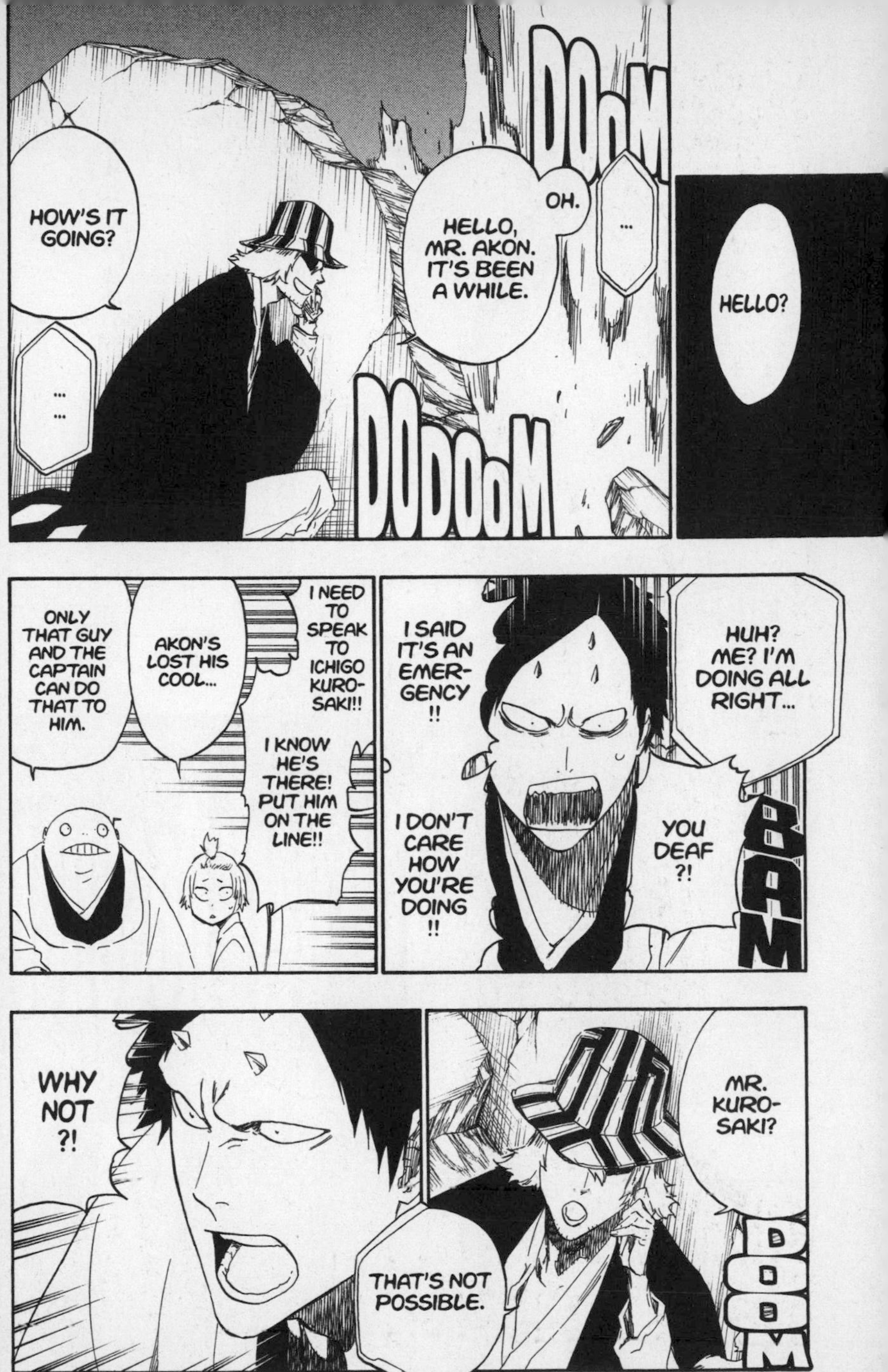
HELLO?
...
DOOM
OH.
HELLO, MR. AKON. IT'S BEEN A WHILE.
DODOOM
HOW'S IT GOING?
... ...
HUH? ME? I'M DOING ALL RIGHT...
BAM
YOU DEAF ?!
I SAID IT'S AN EMERGENCY !!
I DON'T CARE HOW YOU'RE DOING !!
I NEED TO SPEAK TO ICHIGO KUROSAKI!!
I KNOW HE'S THERE! PUT HIM ON THE LINE!!
AKON'S LOST HIS COOL...
ONLY THAT GUY AND THE CAPTAIN CAN DO THAT TO HIM.
MR. KUROSAKI?
DOOM
THAT'S NOT POSSIBLE.
WHY NOT ?!

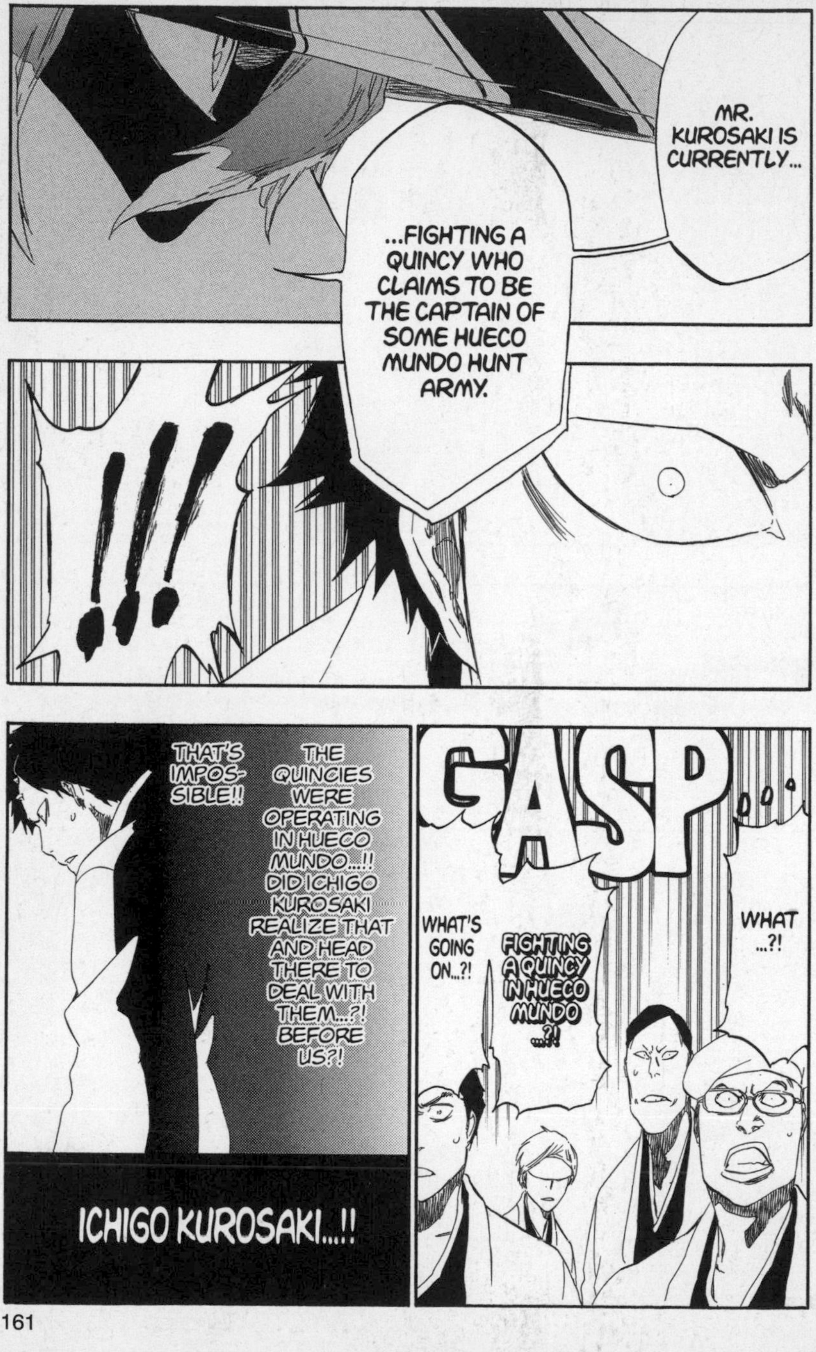
MR. KUROSAKI IS CURRENTLY...
...FIGHTING A QUINCY WHO CLAIMS TO BE THE CAPTAIN OF SOME HUECO MUNDO HUNT ARMY.
!!!
GASP...
WHAT ...?!
FIGHTING A QUINCY IN HUECO MUNDO ...?!
WHAT'S GOING ON...?!
THE QUINCIES WERE OPERATING IN HUECO MUNDO...!! DID ICHIGO KUROSAKI REALIZE THAT AND HEAD THERE TO DEAL WITH THEM...?! BEFORE US?!
THAT'S IMPOS-SIBLE!!
ICHIGO KUROSAKI...!!

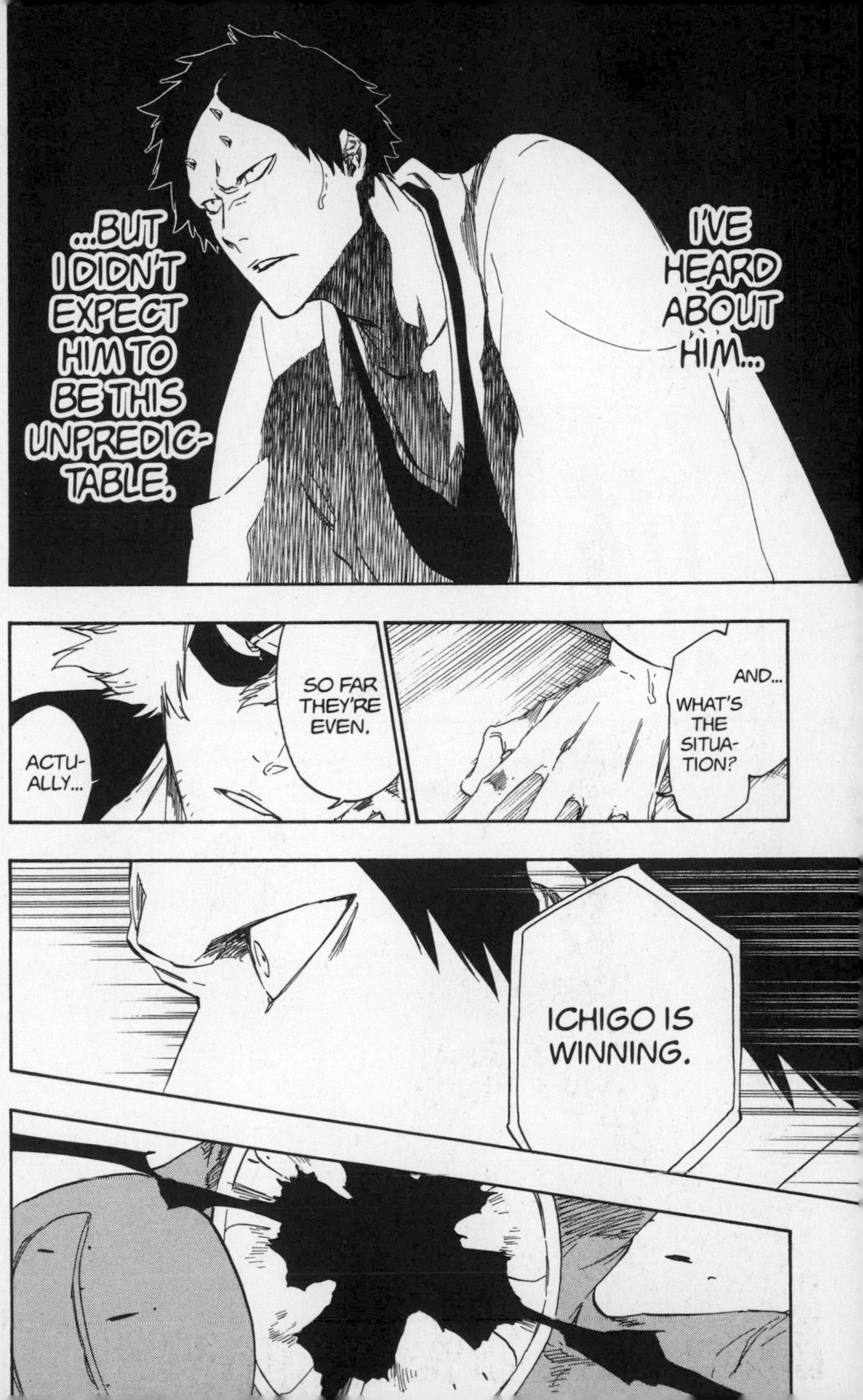
I'VE HEARD ABOUT HIM...
...BUT I DIDN'T EXPECT HIM TO BE THIS UNPREDIC-TABLE.
AND... WHAT'S THE SITUA-TION?
SO FAR THEY'RE EVEN.
ACTU-ALLY...
ICHIGO IS WINNING.

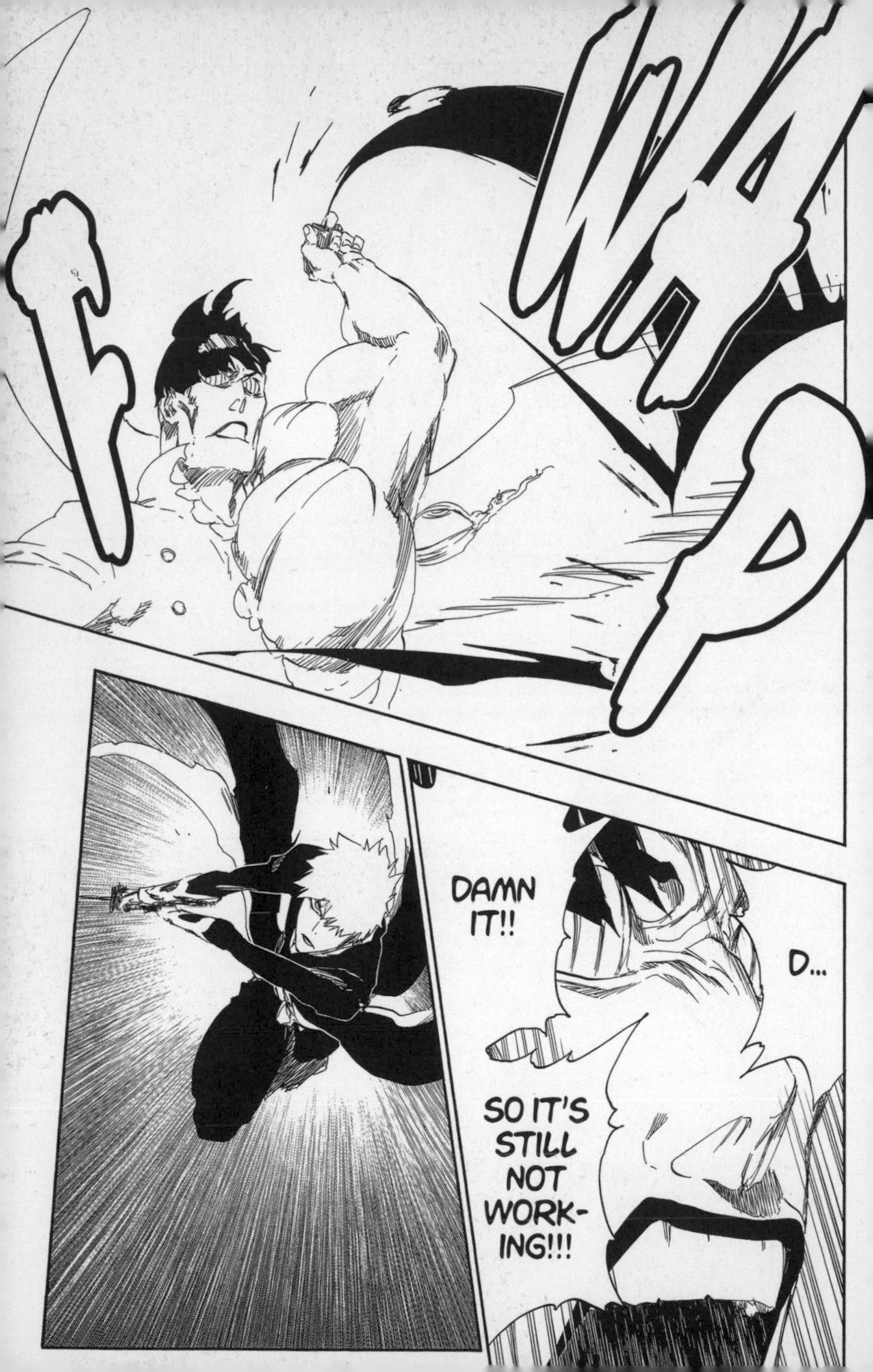
WHAP
DAMN IT!!
D...
SO IT'S STILL NOT WORKING!!!

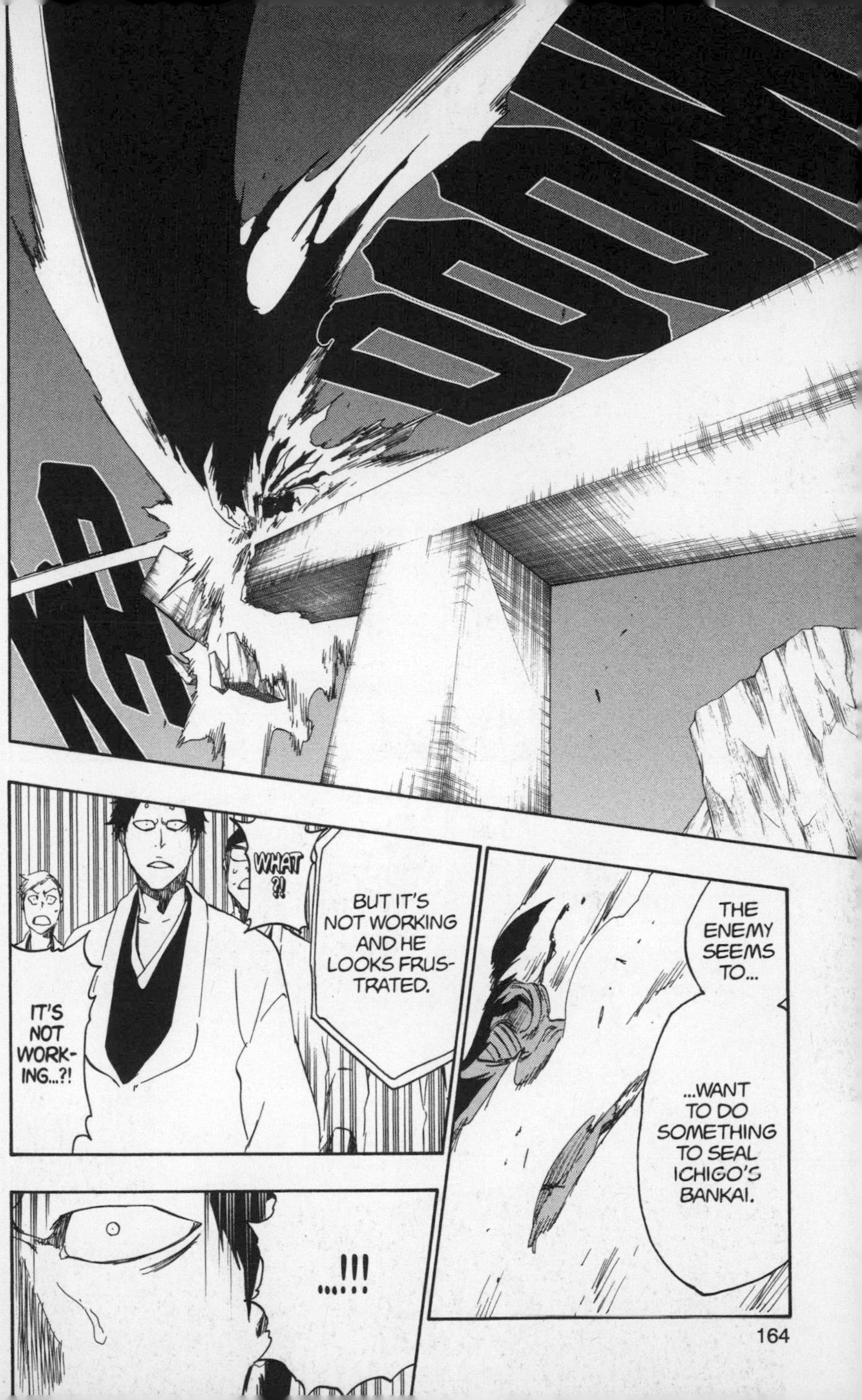
THE ENEMY SEEMS TO...
...WANT TO DO SOMETHING TO SEAL ICHIGO'S BANKAI.
BUT IT'S NOT WORKING AND HE LOOKS FRUS-TRATED.
WHAT ?!
IT'S NOT WORKING...?!
...!!!

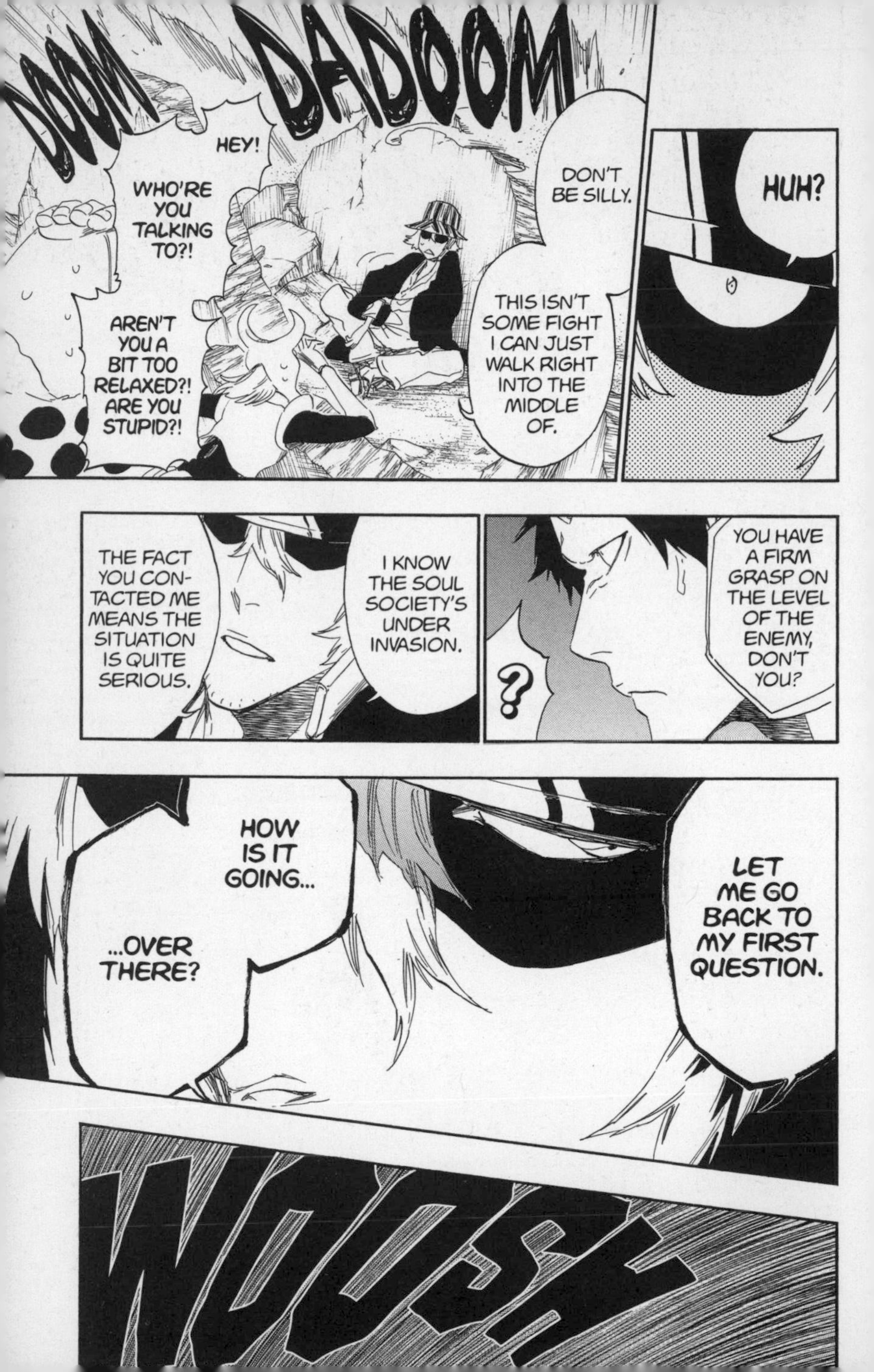
HUH?
DADOOM
DON'T BE SILLY.
THIS ISN'T SOME FIGHT I CAN JUST WALK RIGHT INTO THE MIDDLE OF.
DOOM
HEY!
WHO'RE YOU TALKING TO?!
AREN'T YOU A BIT TOO RELAXED?! ARE YOU STUPID?!
YOU HAVE A FIRM GRASP ON THE LEVEL OF THE ENEMY, DON'T YOU?
?
I KNOW THE SOUL SOCIETY'S UNDER INVASION.
THE FACT YOU CONTACTED ME MEANS THE SITUATION IS QUITE SERIOUS.
LET ME GO BACK TO MY FIRST QUESTION.
HOW IS IT GOING...
...OVER THERE?

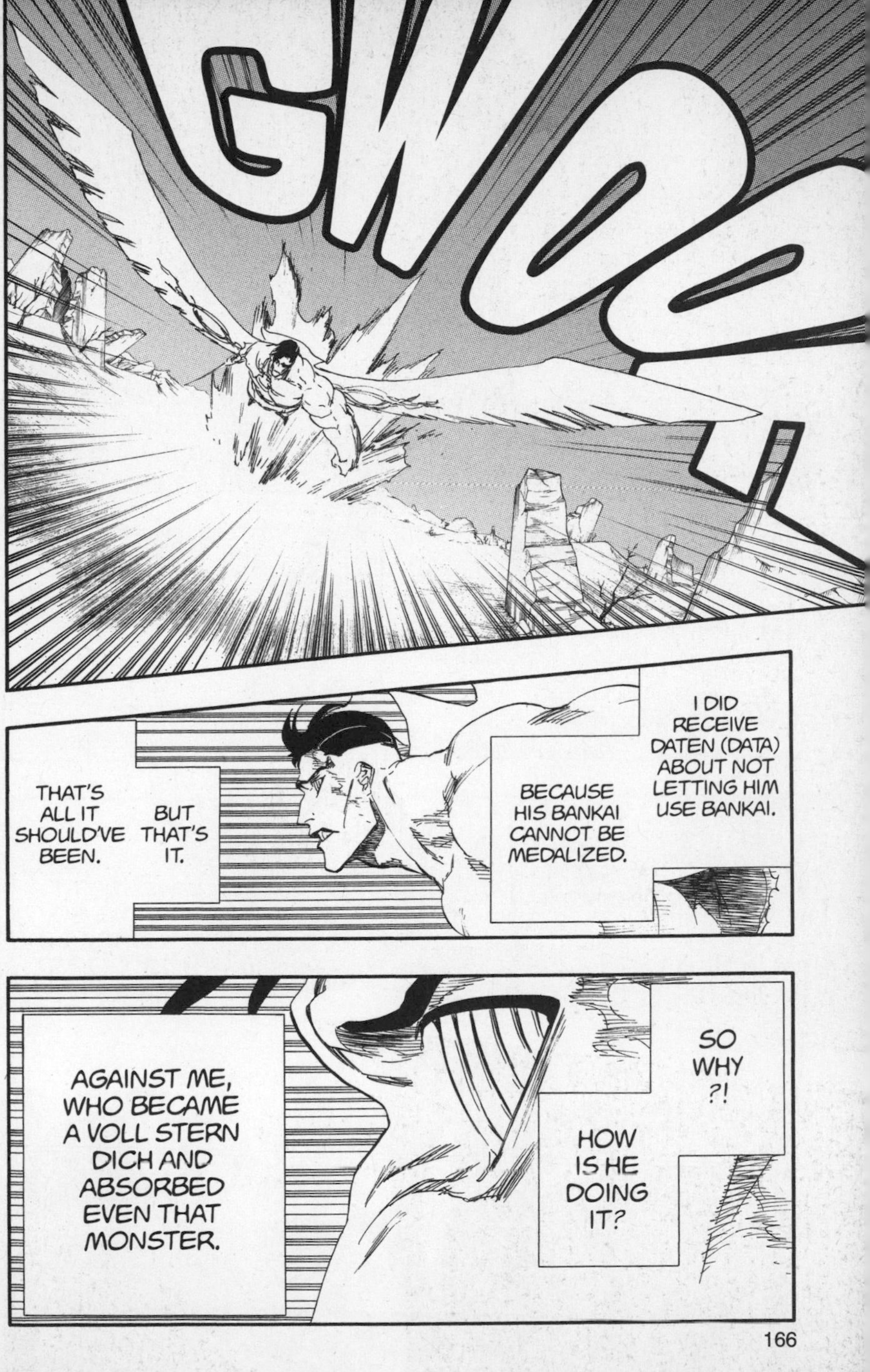
GWOO
I DID RECEIVE DATEN (DATA) ABOUT NOT LETTING HIM USE BANKAI.
BECAUSE HIS BANKAI CANNOT BE MEDALIZED.
BUT THAT'S IT.
THAT'S ALL IT SHOULD'VE BEEN.
SO WHY?!
HOW IS HE DOING IT?
AGAINST ME, WHO BECAME A VOLL STERN DICH AND ABSORBED EVEN THAT MONSTER.

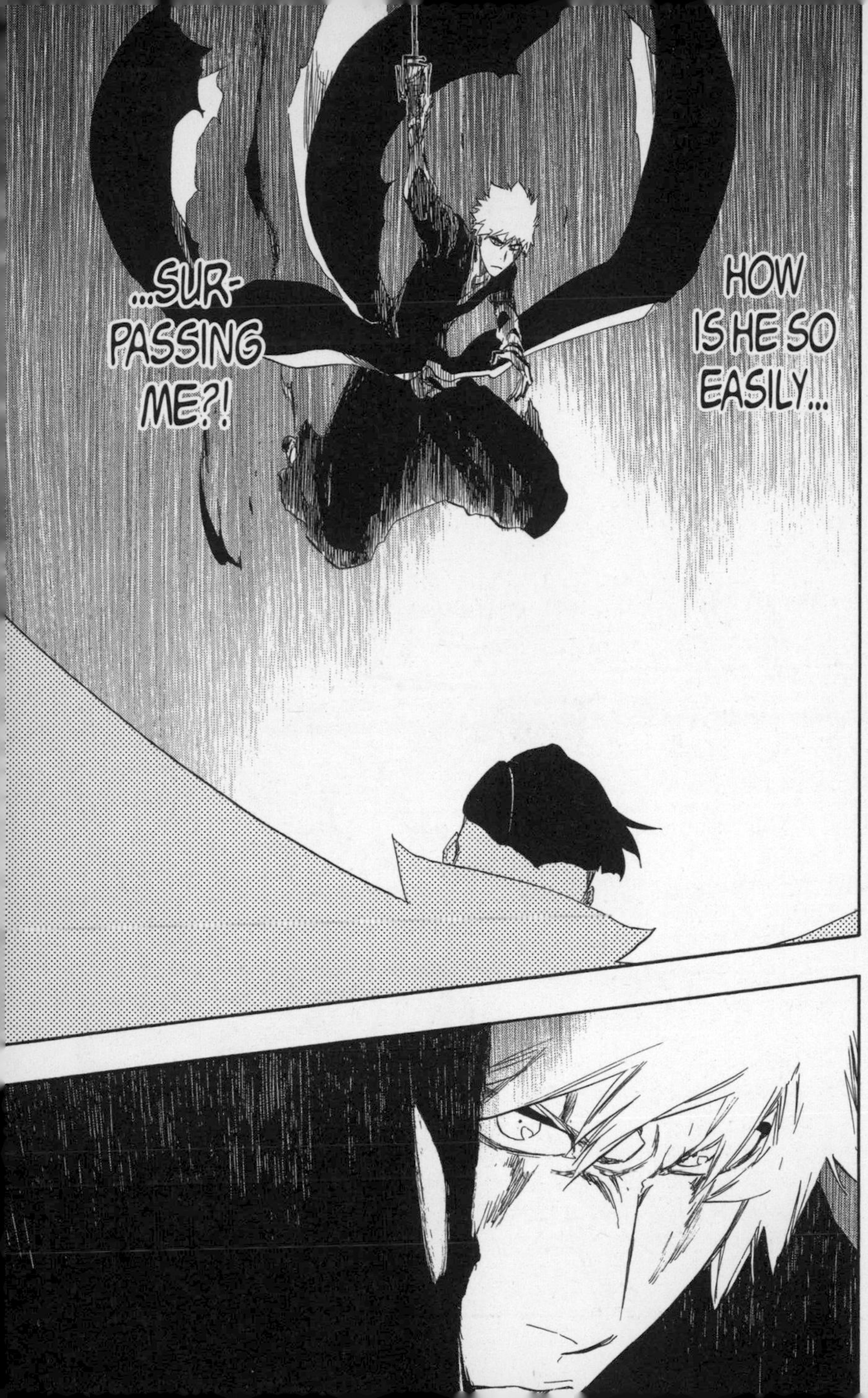
HOW IS HE SO EASILY...
...SUR-PASSING ME?!

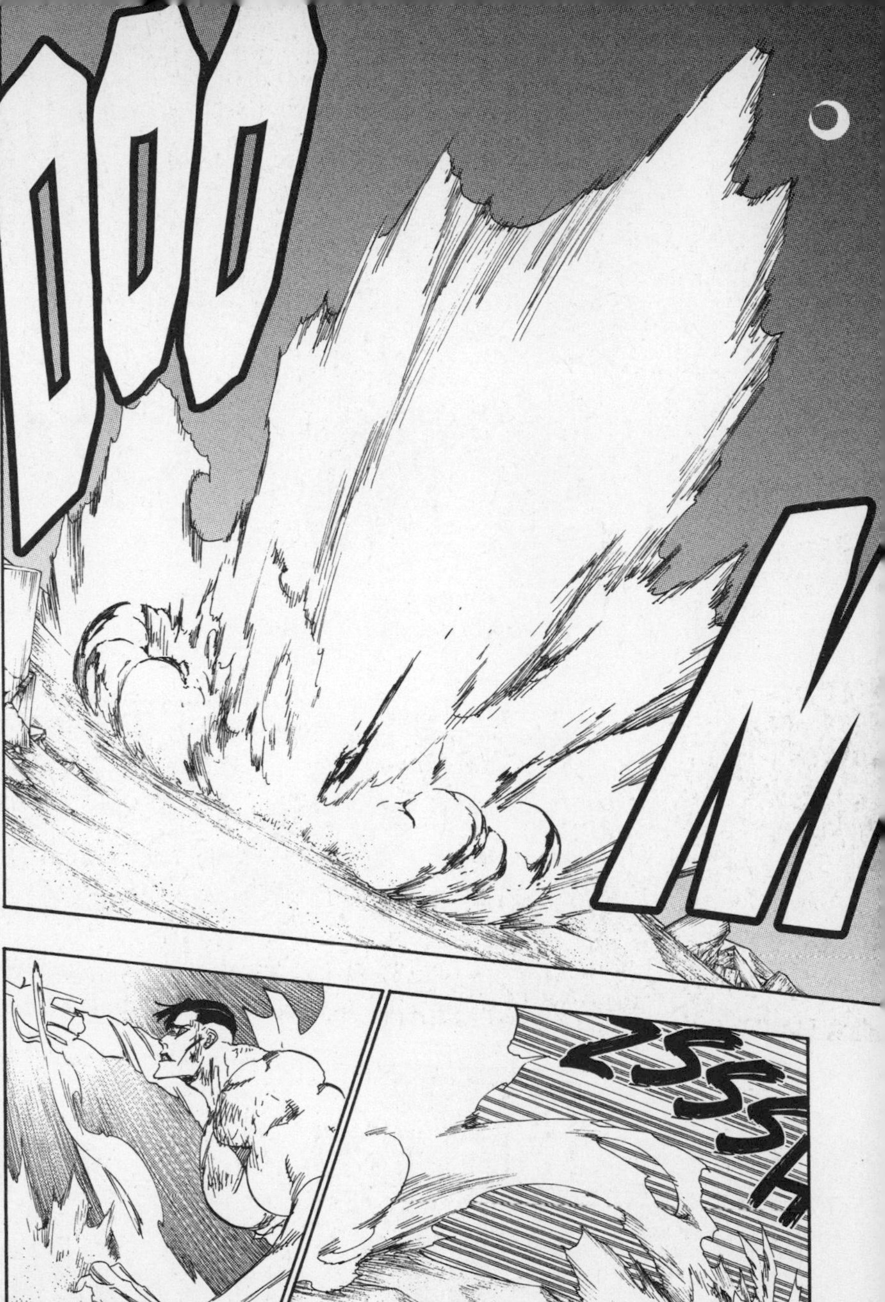
DOOM
ZSSH

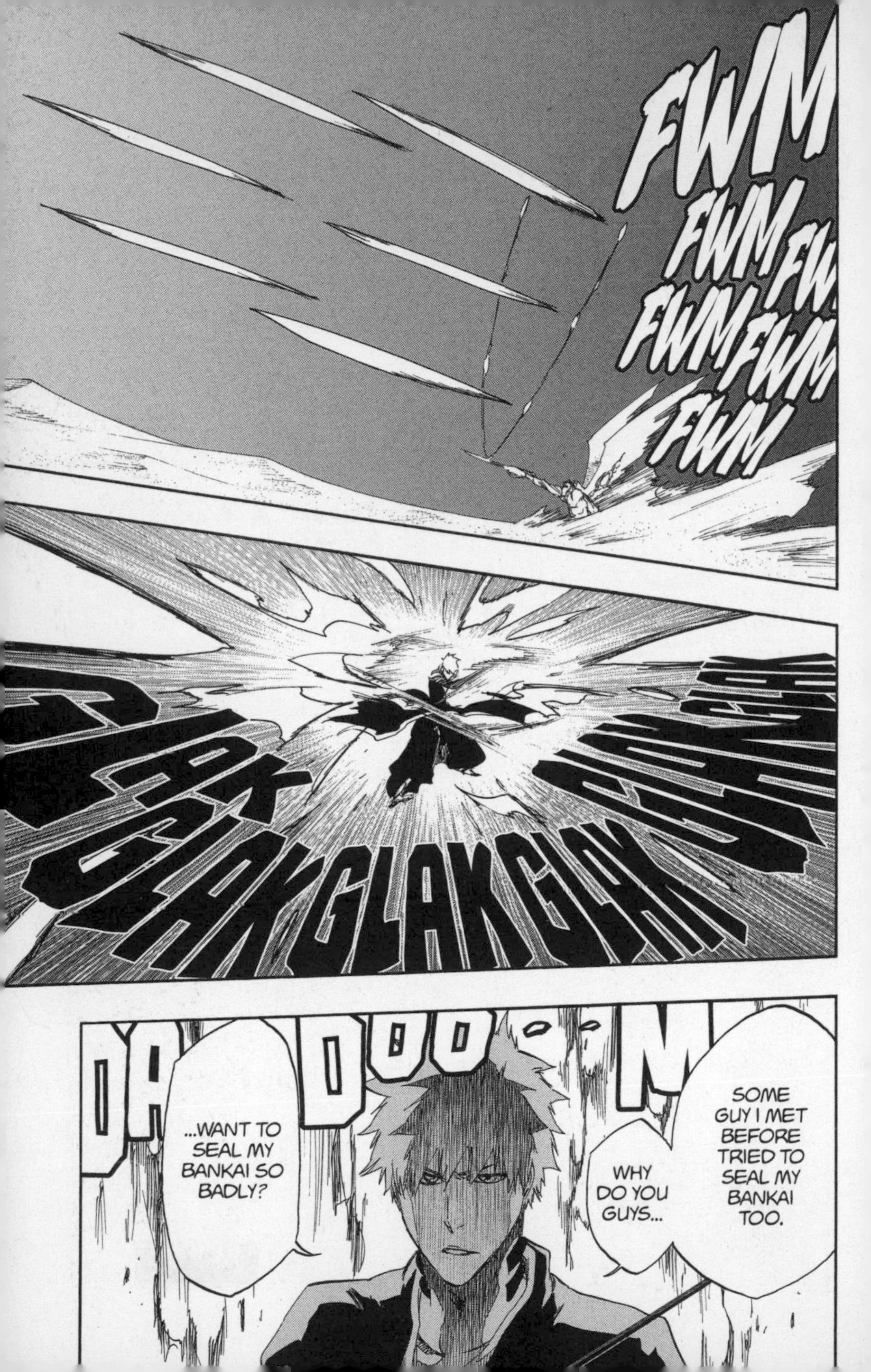
FWM
FWM
FWM
FWM
FWM
SOME GUY I MET BEFORE TRIED TO SEAL MY BANKAI TOO.
WHY DO YOU GUYS...
...WANT TO SEAL MY BANKAI SO BADLY?

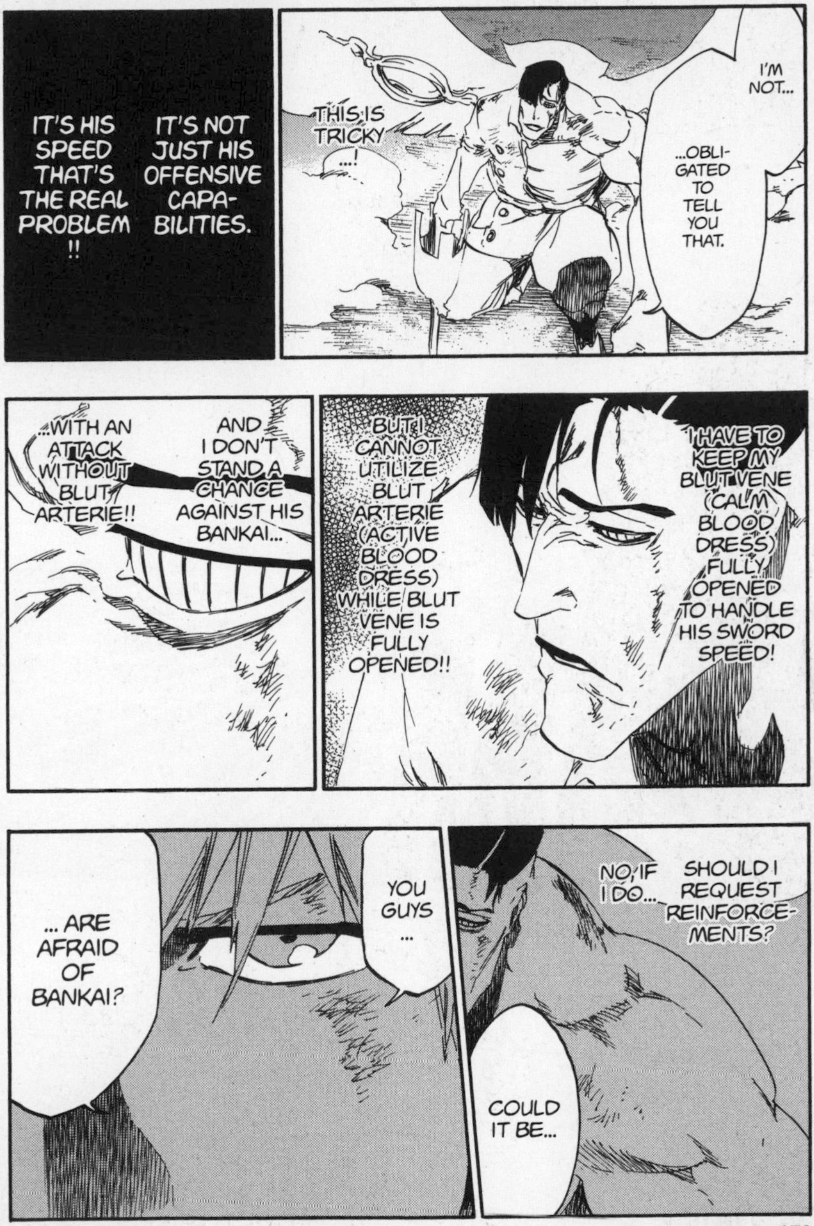
I'M NOT...
...OBLIGATED TO TELL YOU THAT.
THIS IS TRICKY ....!
IT'S NOT JUST HIS OFFENSIVE CAPABILITIES.
IT'S HIS SPEED THAT'S THE REAL PROBLEM !!
I HAVE TO KEEP MY BLUT VENE (CALM BLOOD DRESS) FULLY OPENED TO HANDLE HIS SWORD SPEED!
BUT I CANNOT UTILIZE BLUT ARTERIE (ACTIVE BLOOD DRESS) WHILE BLUT VENE IS FULLY OPENED!!
AND I DON'T STAND A CHANCE AGAINST HIS BANKAI...
...WITH AN ATTACK WITHOUT BLUT ARTERIE!!
SHOULD I REQUEST REINFORCEMENTS?
NO, IF I DO...
COULD IT BE...
YOU GUYS ...
... ARE AFRAID OF BANKAI?

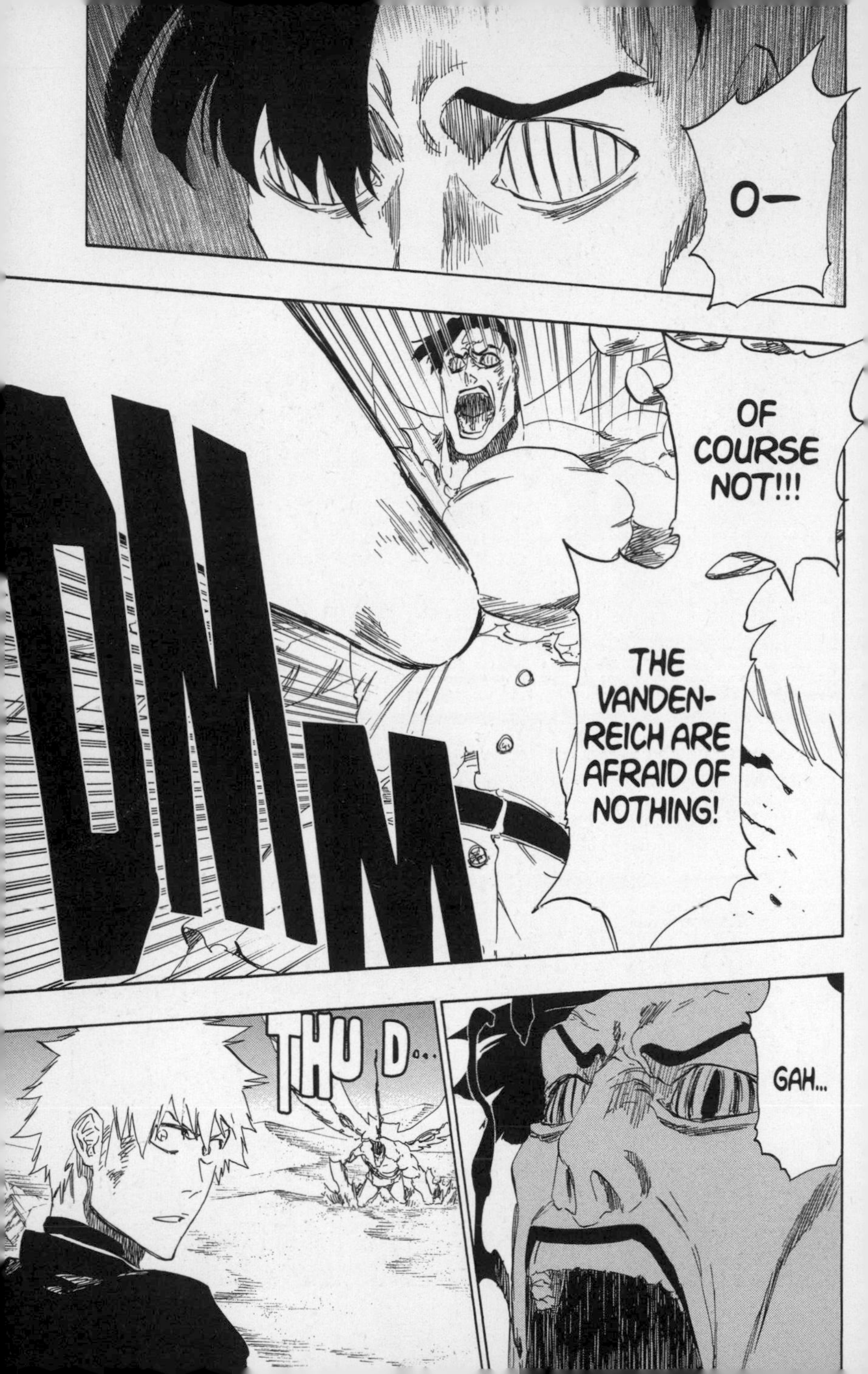
O—
OF COURSE NOT!!!
THE VANDEN-REICH ARE AFRAID OF NOTHING!
DMM
GAH...
THUD...

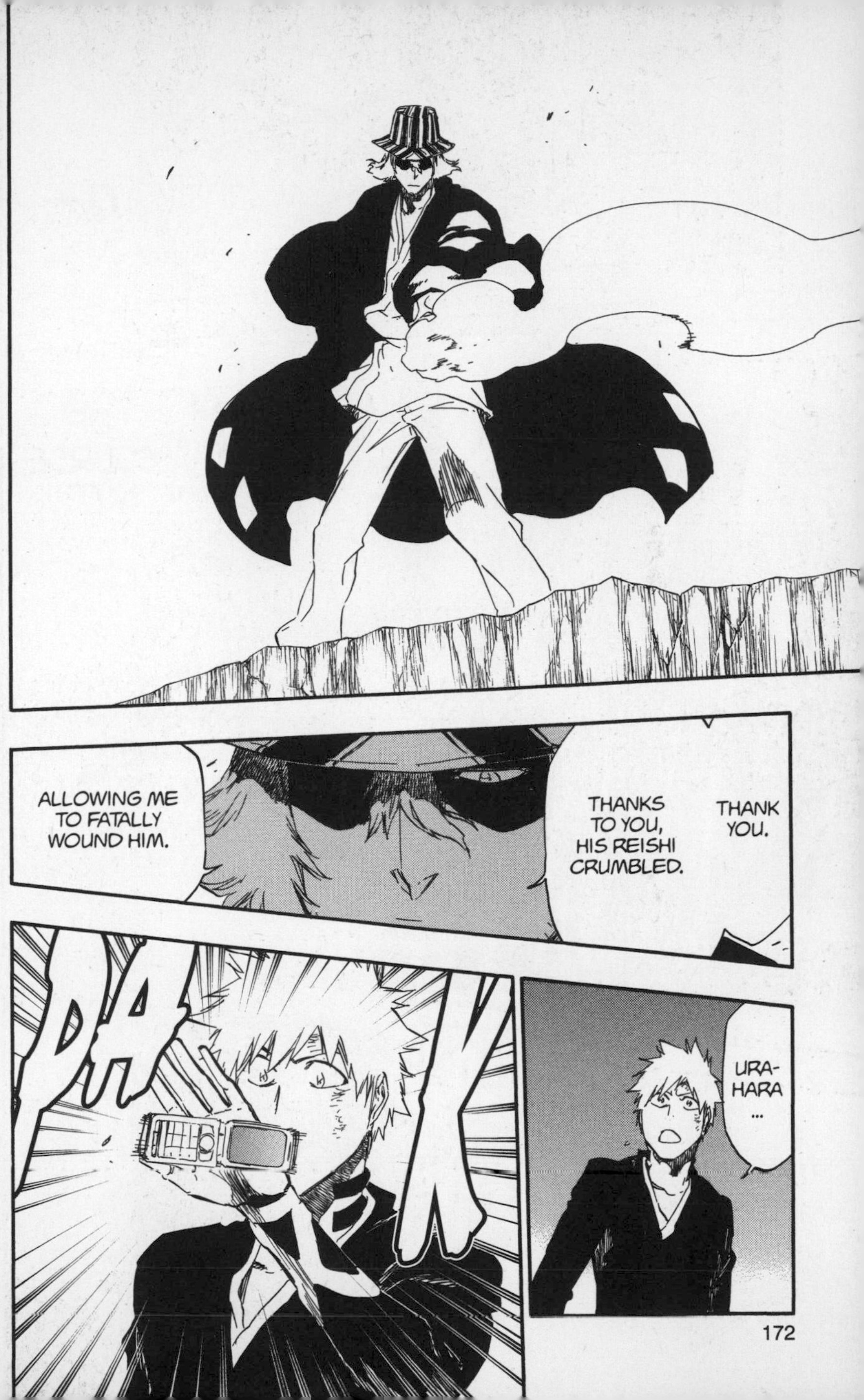
THANK YOU.
THANKS TO YOU, HIS REISHI CRUMBLED.
ALLOWING ME TO FATALLY WOUND HIM.
URA-HARA ...

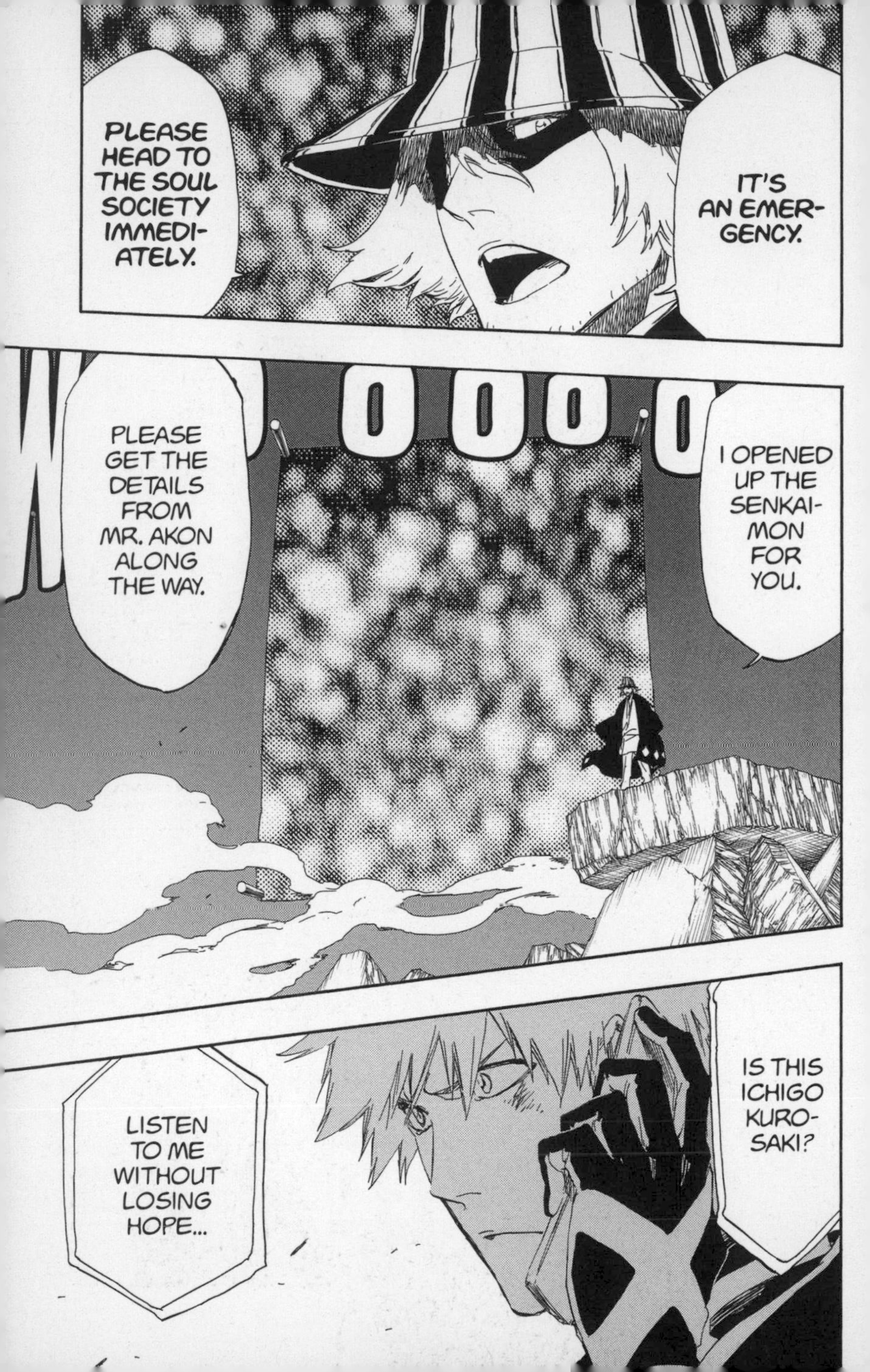
IT'S AN EMERGENCY.
PLEASE HEAD TO THE SOUL SOCIETY IMMEDIATELY.
I OPENED UP THE SENKAIMON FOR YOU.
PLEASE GET THE DETAILS FROM MR. AKON ALONG THE WAY.
IS THIS ICHIGO KUROSAKI?
LISTEN TO ME WITHOUT LOSING HOPE...

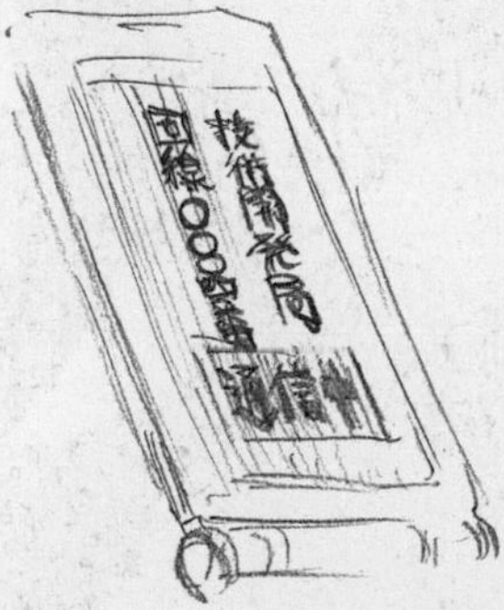
技術開発局

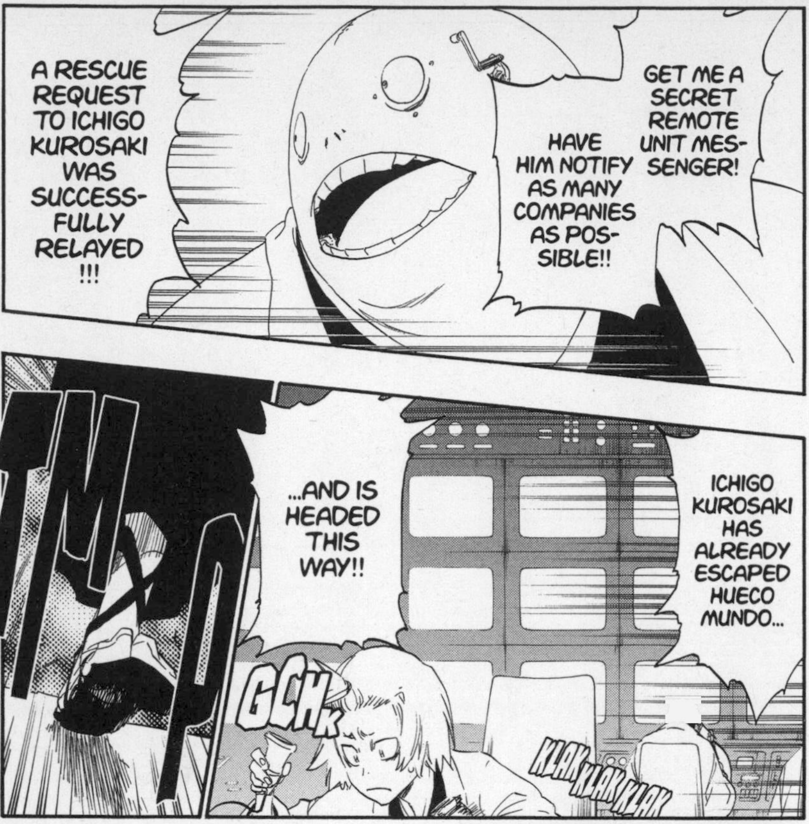
GET ME A SECRET REMOTE UNIT MES-SENGER!
HAVE HIM NOTIFY AS MANY COMPANIES AS POS-SIBLE!!
A RESCUE REQUEST TO ICHIGO KUROSAKI WAS SUCCESS-FULLY RELAYED !!!
ICHIGO KUROSAKI HAS ALREADY ESCAPED HUECO MUNDO...
KLAK KLAK KLAK
...AND IS HEADED THIS WAY!!
GCHK
TMP

499.RESCUER IN THE DARK

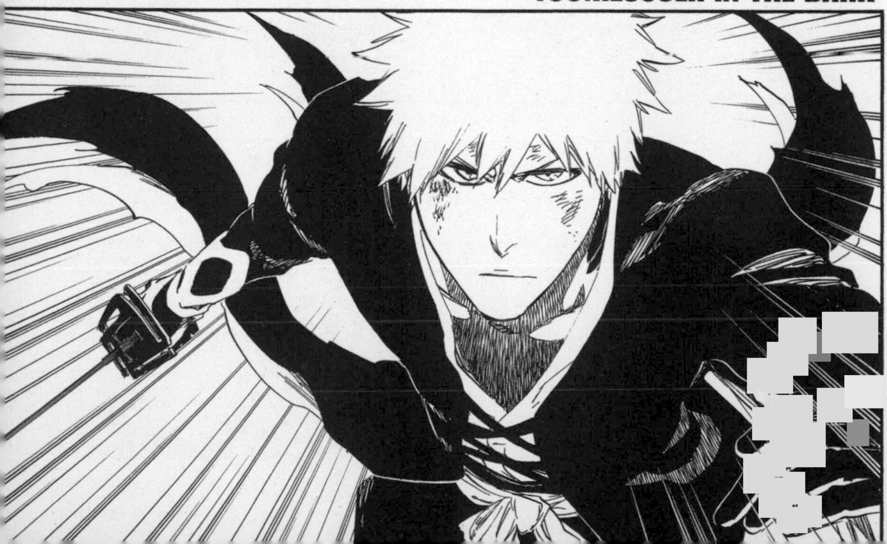

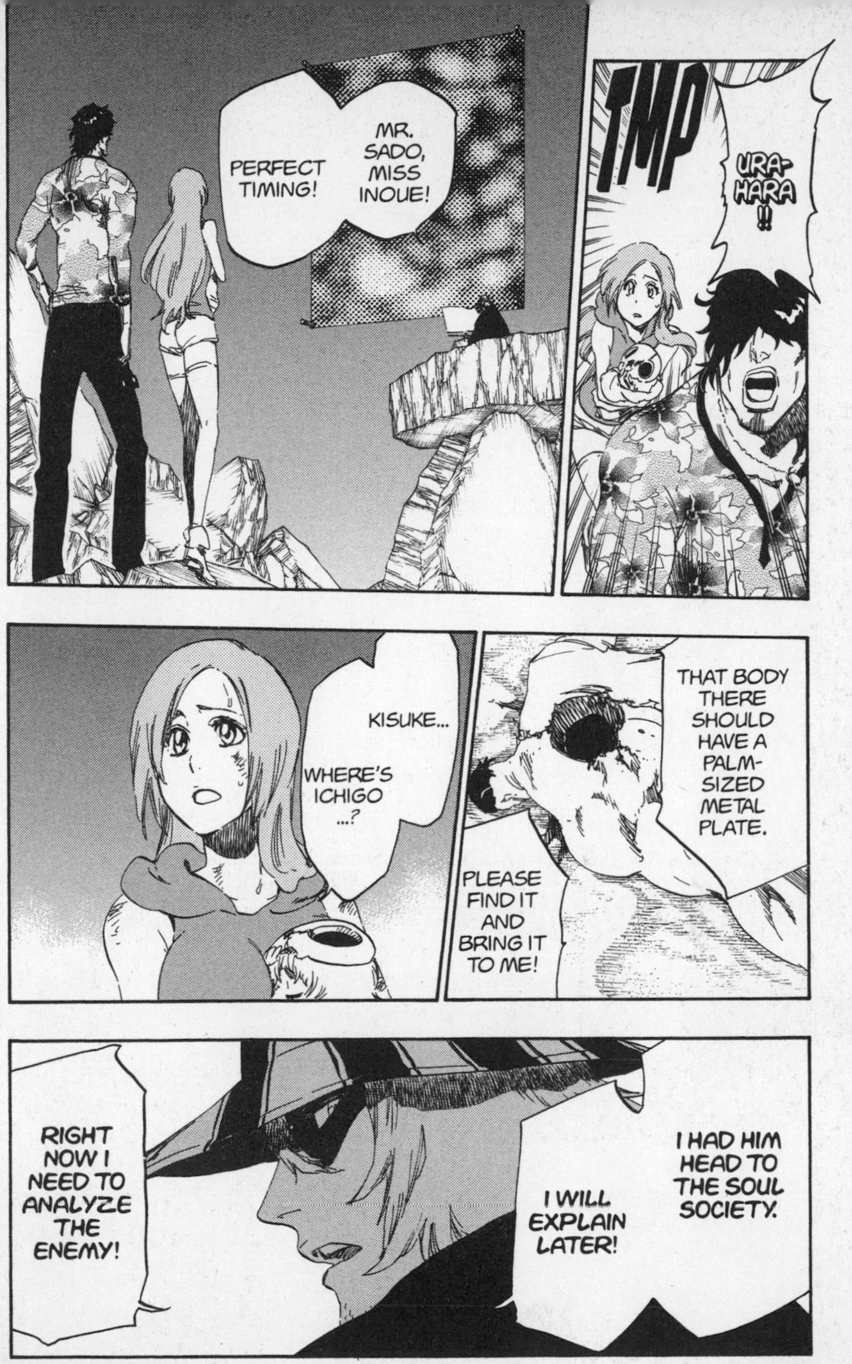
TMP
URA-HARA!!
MR. SADO, MISS INOUE!
PERFECT TIMING!
THAT BODY THERE SHOULD HAVE A PALM-SIZED METAL PLATE.
PLEASE FIND IT AND BRING IT TO ME!
KISUKE...
WHERE'S ICHIGO ...?
I HAD HIM HEAD TO THE SOUL SOCIETY.
I WILL EXPLAIN LATER!
RIGHT NOW I NEED TO ANALYZE THE ENEMY!

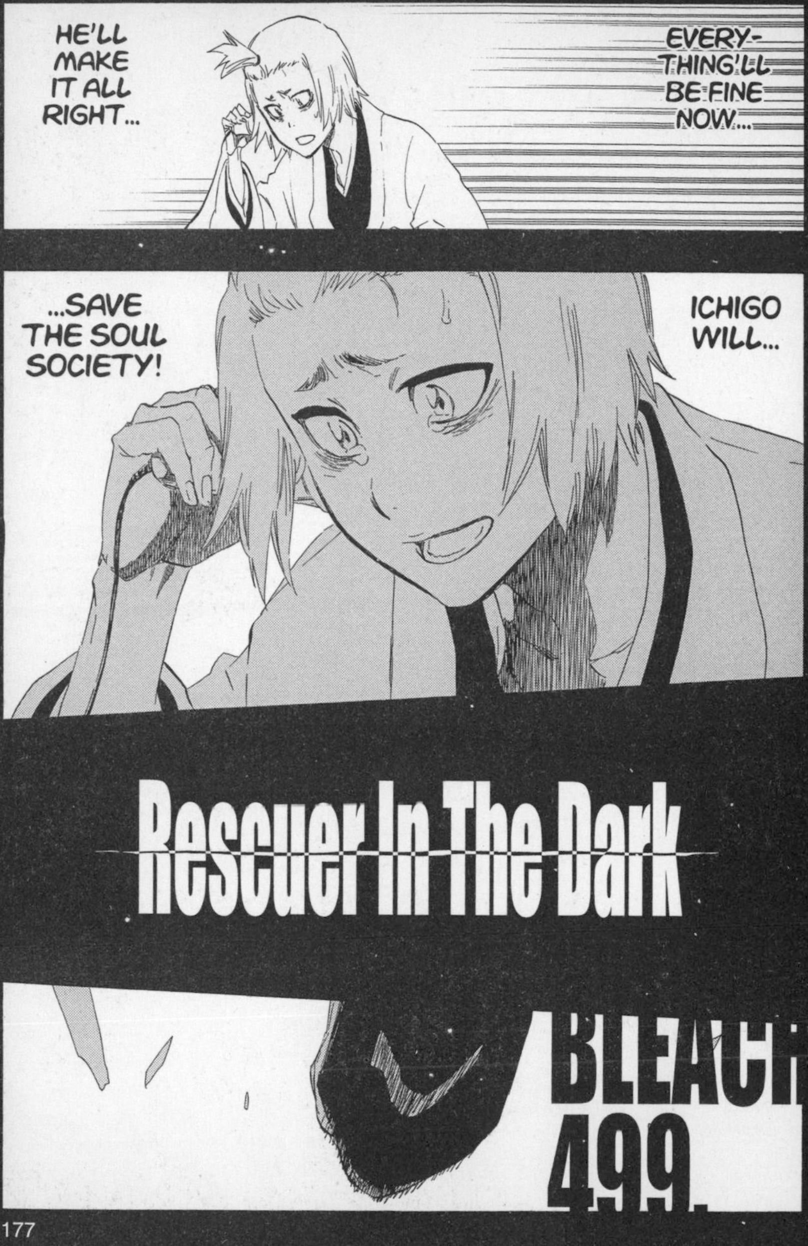
EVERY-THING'LL BE FINE NOW...
HE'LL MAKE IT ALL RIGHT...
ICHIGO WILL...
...SAVE THE SOUL SOCIETY!
Rescuer In The Dark
BLEACH 499.

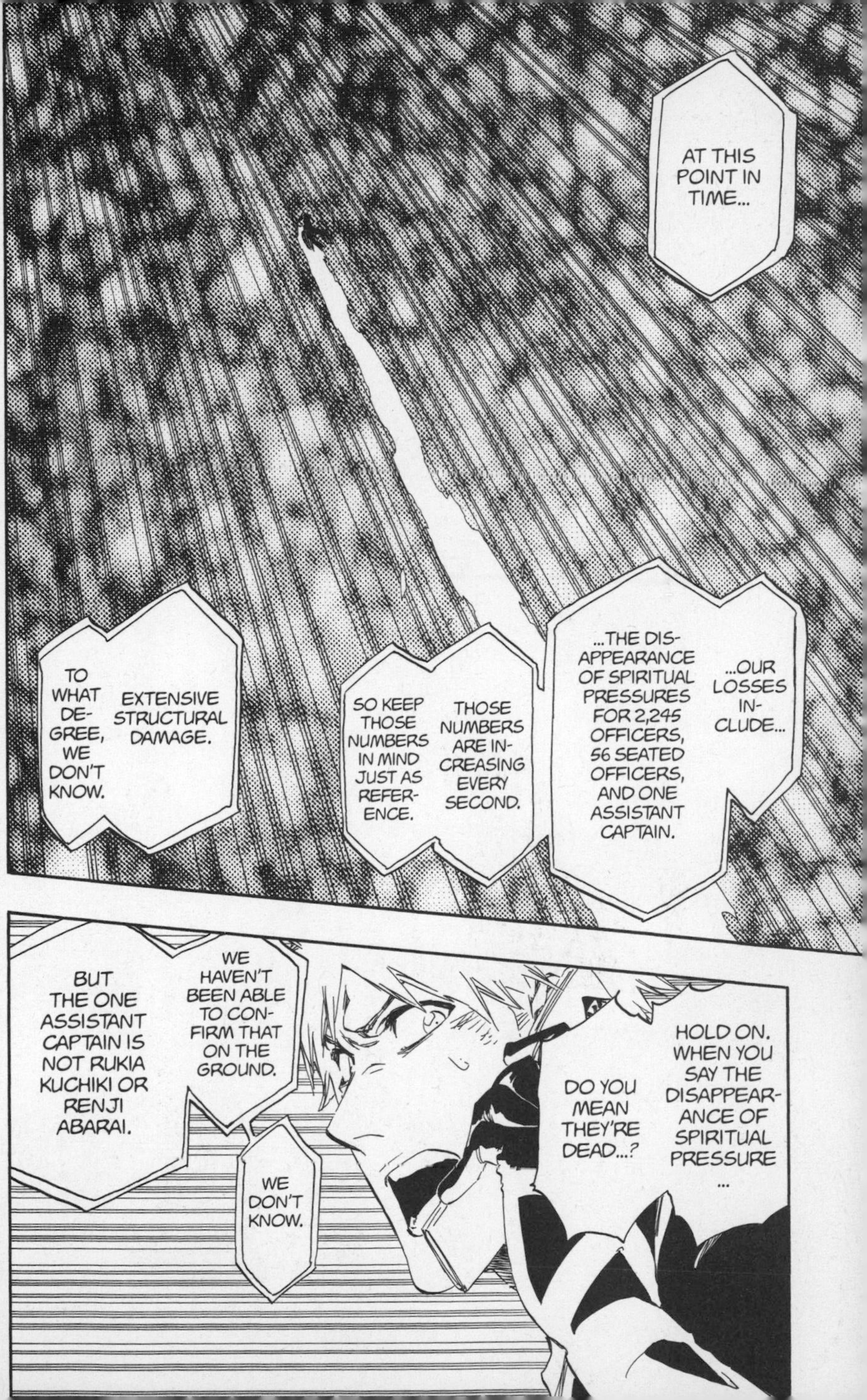
AT THIS POINT IN TIME...
...OUR LOSSES INCLUDE...
...THE DISAPPEARANCE OF SPIRITUAL PRESSURES FOR 2,245 OFFICERS, 56 SEATED OFFICERS, AND ONE ASSISTANT CAPTAIN.
THOSE NUMBERS ARE INCREASING EVERY SECOND.
SO KEEP THOSE NUMBERS IN MIND JUST AS REFERENCE.
EXTENSIVE STRUCTURAL DAMAGE.
TO WHAT DEGREE, WE DON'T KNOW.
HOLD ON. WHEN YOU SAY THE DISAPPEARANCE OF SPIRITUAL PRESSURE...
DO YOU MEAN THEY'RE DEAD...?
WE DON'T KNOW.
WE HAVEN'T BEEN ABLE TO CONFIRM THAT ON THE GROUND.
BUT THE ONE ASSISTANT CAPTAIN IS NOT RUKIA KUCHIKI OR RENJI ABARAI.

READ THIS WAY

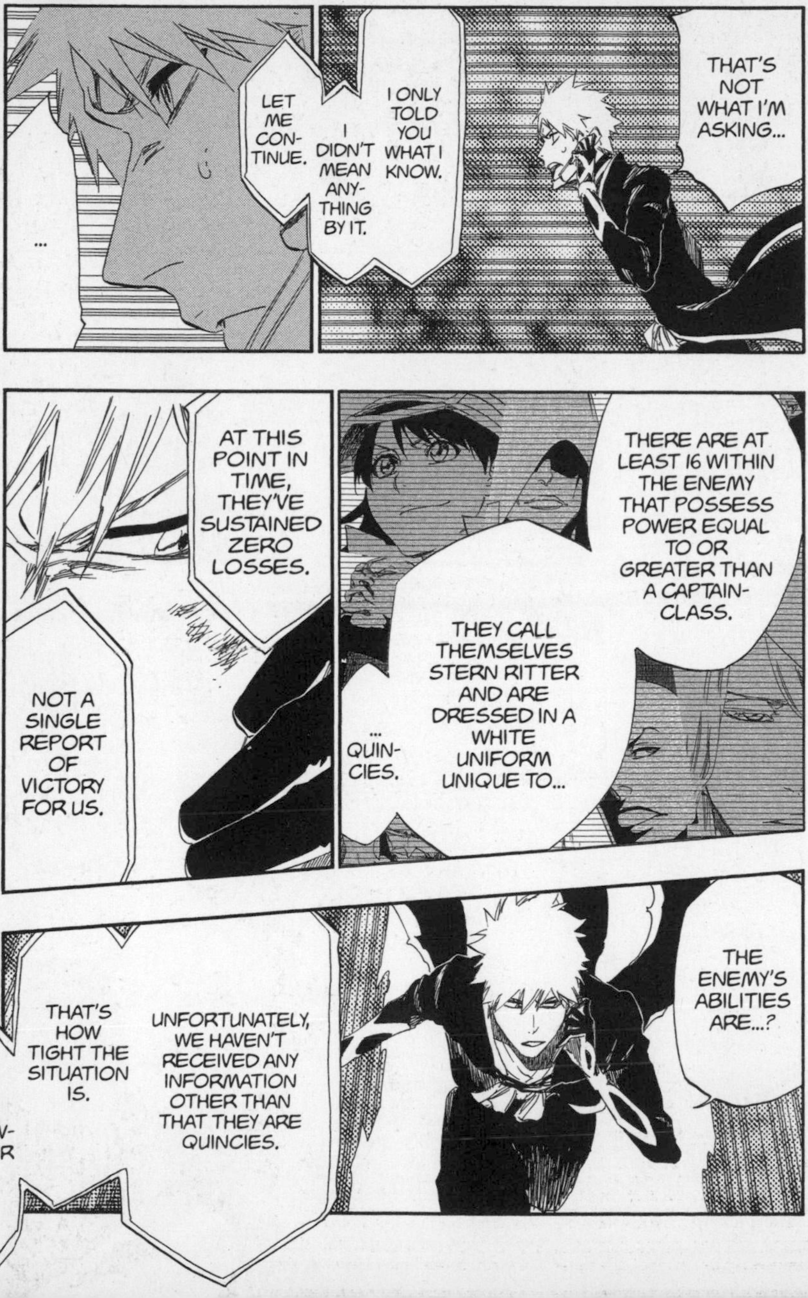
THAT'S NOT WHAT I'M ASKING...
I ONLY TOLD YOU WHAT I KNOW.
I DIDN'T MEAN ANYTHING BY IT.
LET ME CONTINUE.
...
THERE ARE AT LEAST 16 WITHIN THE ENEMY THAT POSSESS POWER EQUAL TO OR GREATER THAN A CAPTAIN-CLASS.
THEY CALL THEMSELVES STERN RITTER AND ARE DRESSED IN A WHITE UNIFORM UNIQUE TO...
... QUINCIES.
AT THIS POINT IN TIME, THEY'VE SUSTAINED ZERO LOSSES.
NOT A SINGLE REPORT OF VICTORY FOR US.
THE ENEMY'S ABILITIES ARE...?
UNFORTUNATELY, WE HAVEN'T RECEIVED ANY INFORMATION OTHER THAN THAT THEY ARE QUINCIES.
THAT'S HOW TIGHT THE SITUATION IS.
HOWEVER ...

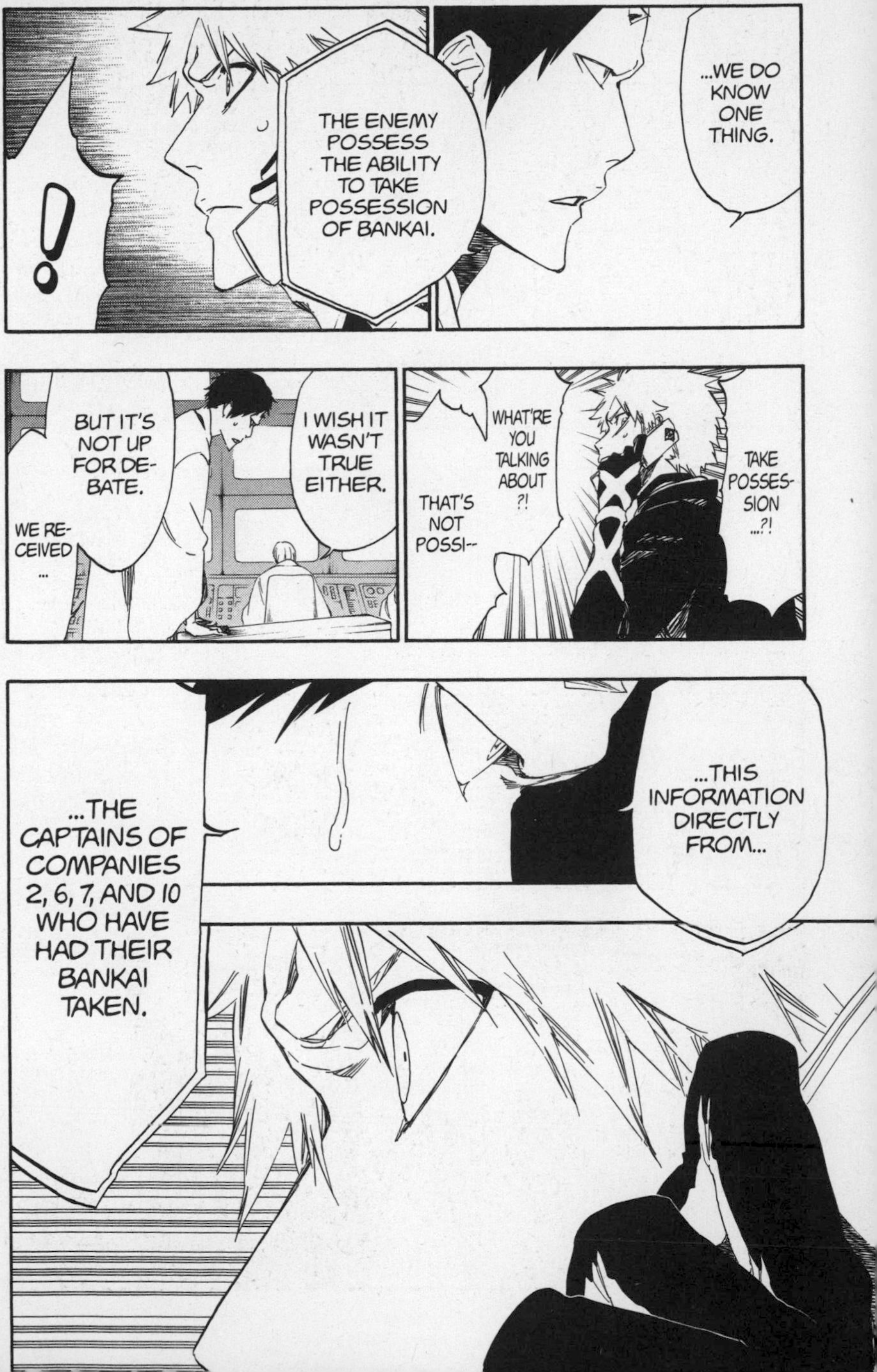
...WE DO KNOW ONE THING.
THE ENEMY POSSESS THE ABILITY TO TAKE POSSESSION OF BANKAI.
!
TAKE POSSES-SION ...?!
WHAT'RE YOU TALKING ABOUT ?!
THAT'S NOT POSSI--
I WISH IT WASN'T TRUE EITHER.
BUT IT'S NOT UP FOR DE-BATE.
WE RE-CEIVED ...
...THIS INFORMATION DIRECTLY FROM...
...THE CAPTAINS OF COMPANIES 2, 6, 7, AND 10 WHO HAVE HAD THEIR BANKAI TAKEN.

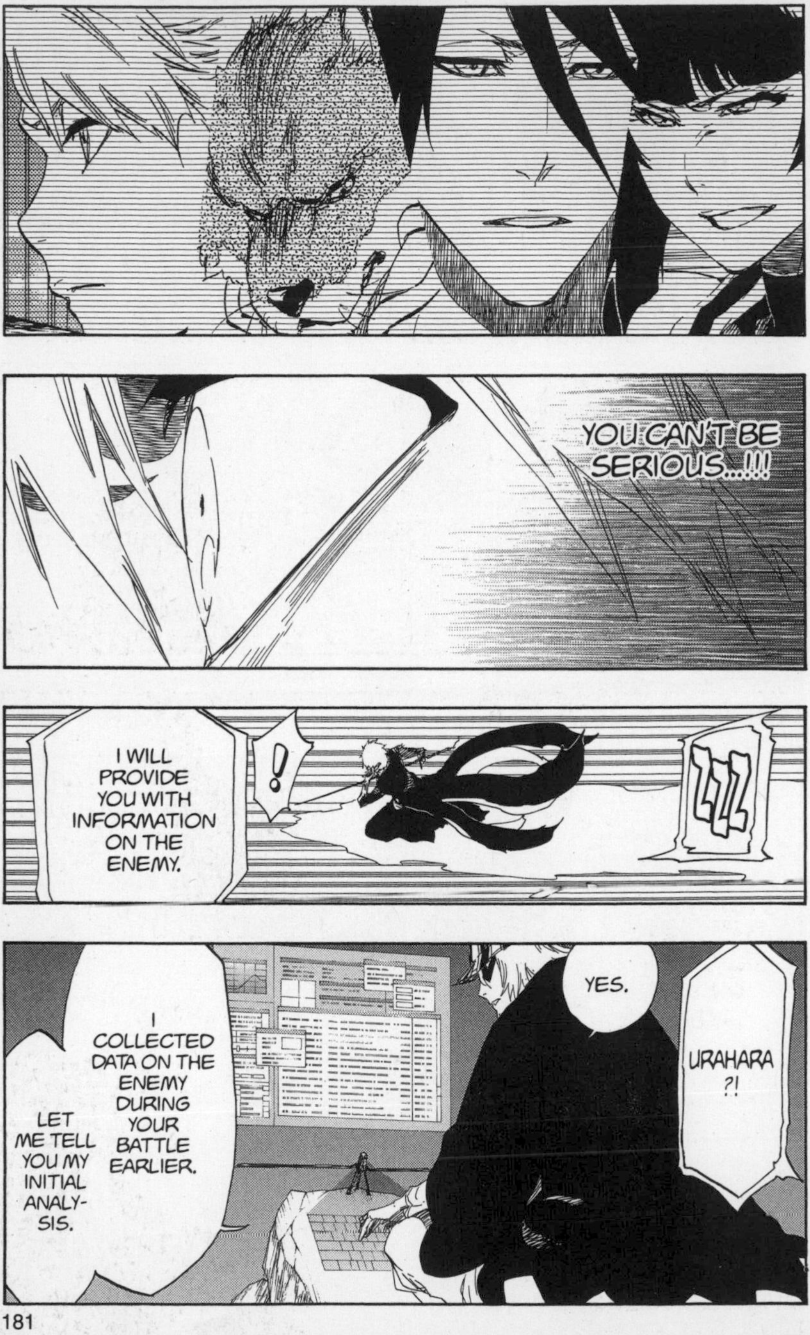
YOU CAN'T BE SERIOUS...!!!
ZZZ
!
I WILL PROVIDE YOU WITH INFORMATION ON THE ENEMY.
URAHARA?!
YES.
I COLLECTED DATA ON THE ENEMY DURING YOUR BATTLE EARLIER.
LET ME TELL YOU MY INITIAL ANALY-SIS.

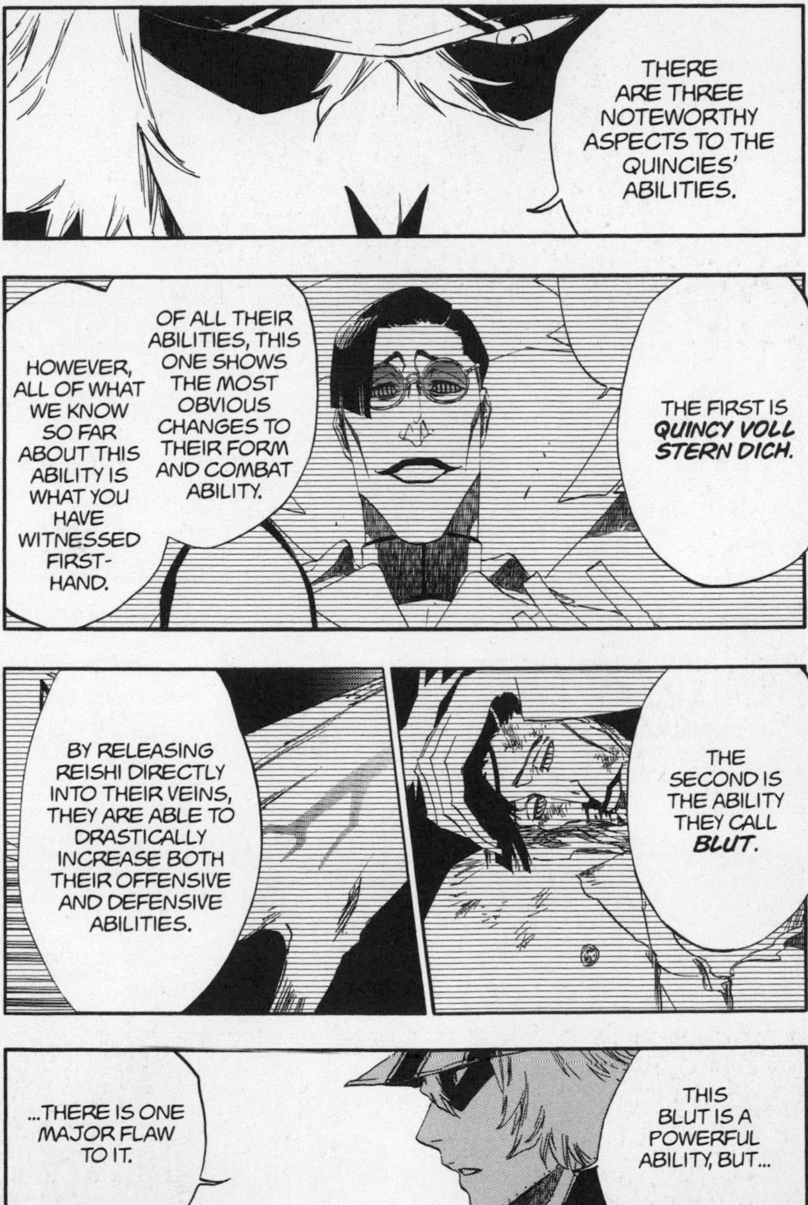
THERE ARE THREE NOTEWORTHY ASPECTS TO THE QUINCIES' ABILITIES.
THE FIRST IS ***QUINCY VOLL STERN DICH.***
OF ALL THEIR ABILITIES, THIS ONE SHOWS THE MOST OBVIOUS CHANGES TO THEIR FORM AND COMBAT ABILITY.
HOWEVER, ALL OF WHAT WE KNOW SO FAR ABOUT THIS ABILITY IS WHAT YOU HAVE WITNESSED FIRST-HAND.
THE SECOND IS THE ABILITY THEY CALL ***BLUT***.
BY RELEASING REISHI DIRECTLY INTO THEIR VEINS, THEY ARE ABLE TO DRASTICALLY INCREASE BOTH THEIR OFFENSIVE AND DEFENSIVE ABILITIES.
THIS BLUT IS A POWERFUL ABILITY, BUT...
...THERE IS ONE MAJOR FLAW TO IT.

READ THIS WAY

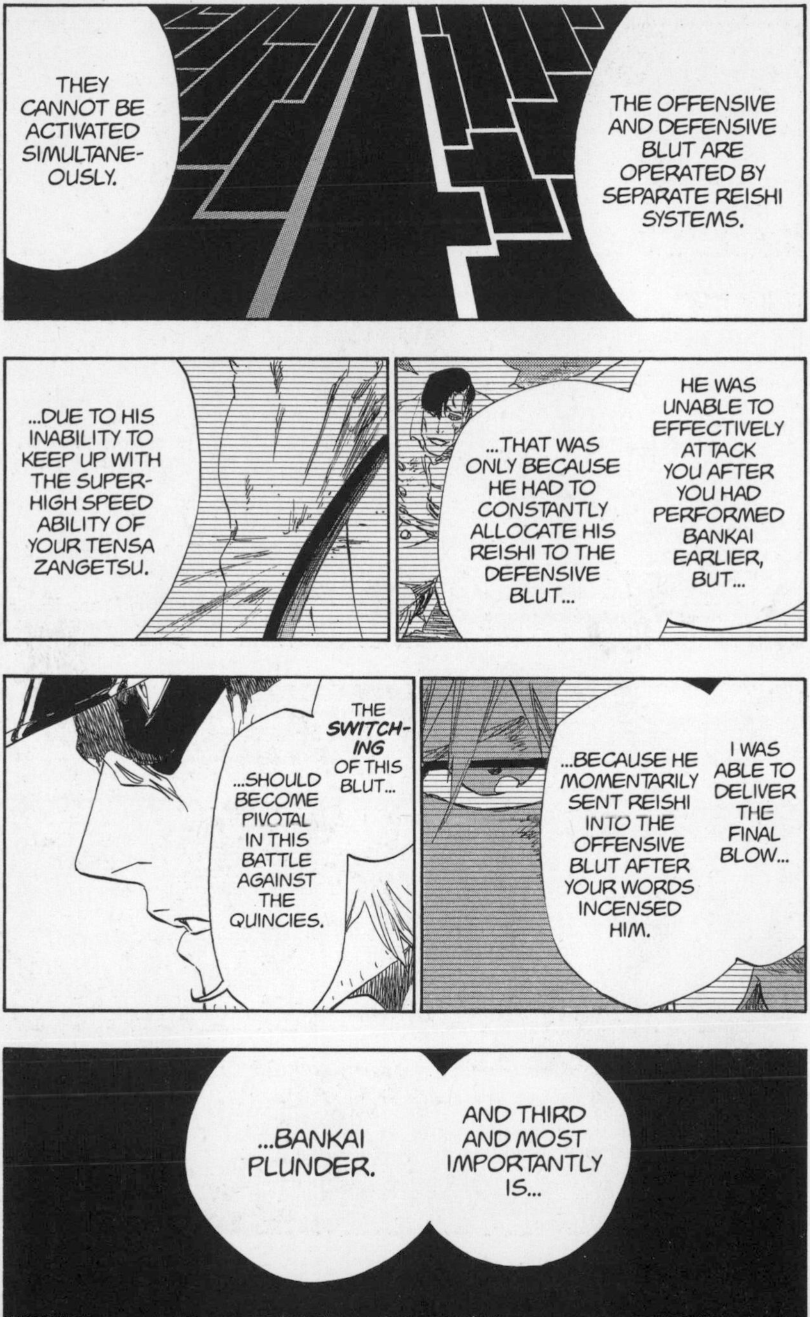
THE OFFENSIVE AND DEFENSIVE BLUT ARE OPERATED BY SEPARATE REISHI SYSTEMS.
THEY CANNOT BE ACTIVATED SIMULTANE-OUSLY.
HE WAS UNABLE TO EFFECTIVELY ATTACK YOU AFTER YOU HAD PERFORMED BANKAI EARLIER, BUT...
...THAT WAS ONLY BECAUSE HE HAD TO CONSTANTLY ALLOCATE HIS REISHI TO THE DEFENSIVE BLUT...
...DUE TO HIS INABILITY TO KEEP UP WITH THE SUPER-HIGH SPEED ABILITY OF YOUR TENSA ZANGETSU.
I WAS ABLE TO DELIVER THE FINAL BLOW...
...BECAUSE HE MOMENTARILY SENT REISHI INTO THE OFFENSIVE BLUT AFTER YOUR WORDS INCENSED HIM.
THE *SWITCHING* OF THIS BLUT...
...SHOULD BECOME PIVOTAL IN THIS BATTLE AGAINST THE QUINCIES.
AND THIRD AND MOST IMPORTANTLY IS...
...BANKAI PLUNDER.

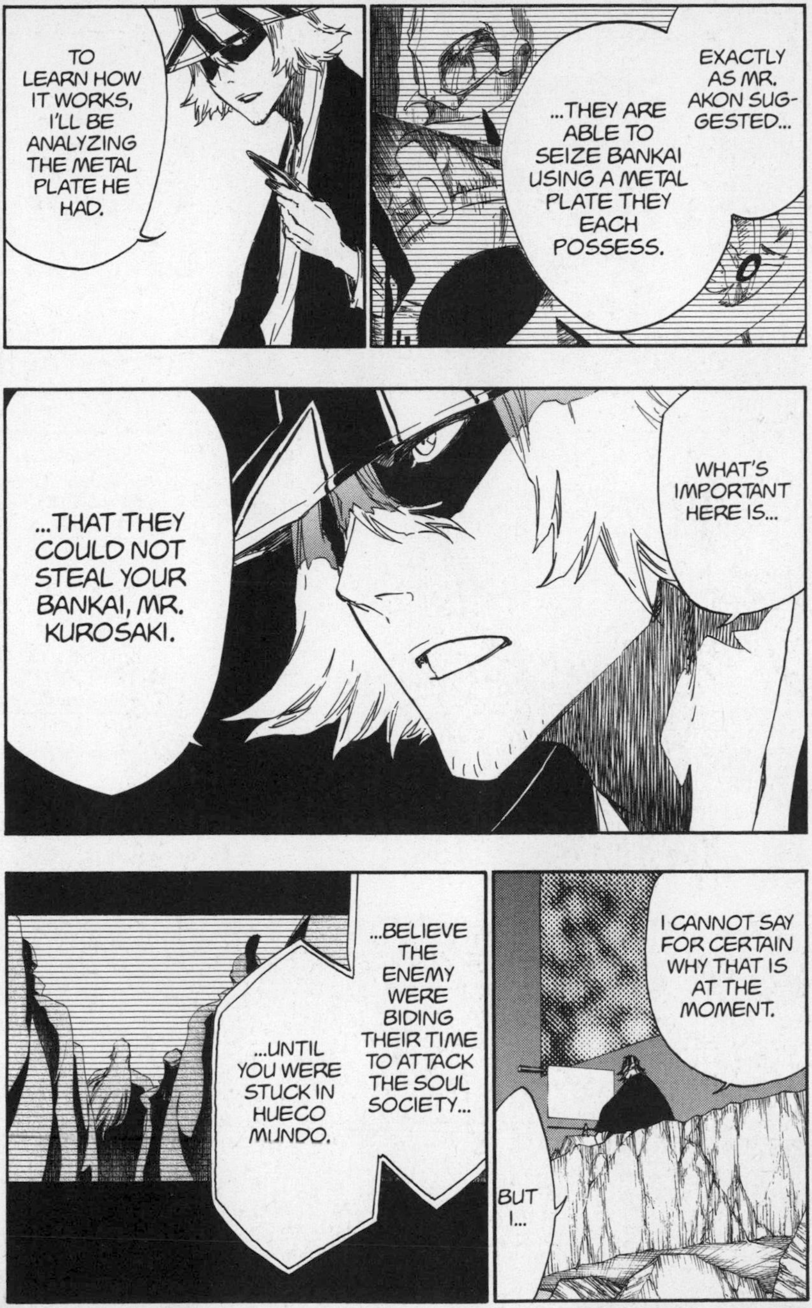
EXACTLY AS MR. AKON SUGGESTED...
...THEY ARE ABLE TO SEIZE BANKAI USING A METAL PLATE THEY EACH POSSESS.
TO LEARN HOW IT WORKS, I'LL BE ANALYZING THE METAL PLATE HE HAD.
WHAT'S IMPORTANT HERE IS...
...THAT THEY COULD NOT STEAL YOUR BANKAI, MR. KUROSAKI.
I CANNOT SAY FOR CERTAIN WHY THAT IS AT THE MOMENT.
BUT I...
...BELIEVE THE ENEMY WERE BIDING THEIR TIME TO ATTACK THE SOUL SOCIETY...
...UNTIL YOU WERE STUCK IN HUECO MUNDO.

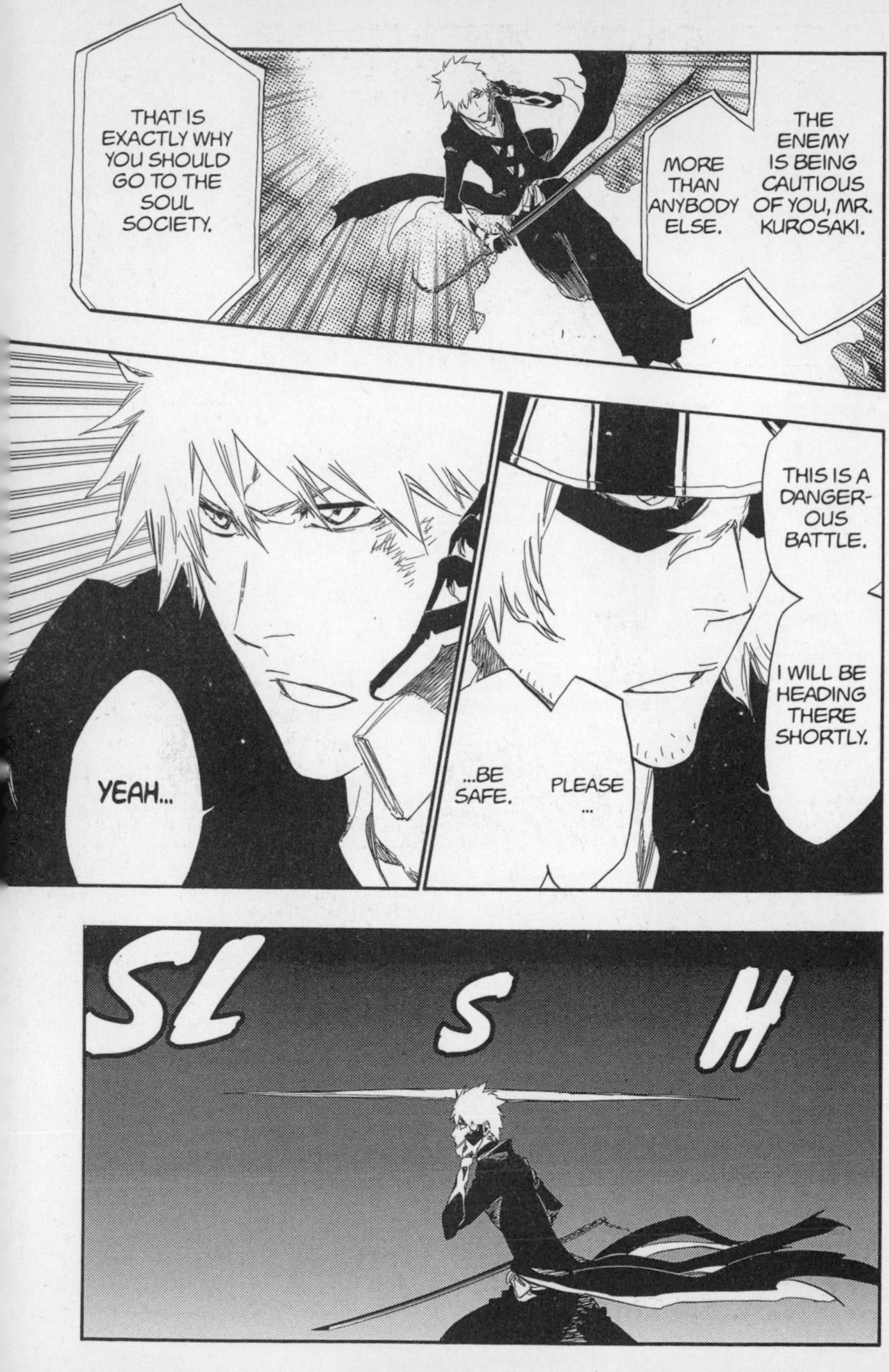
THE ENEMY IS BEING CAUTIOUS OF YOU, MR. KUROSAKI.
MORE THAN ANYBODY ELSE.
THAT IS EXACTLY WHY YOU SHOULD GO TO THE SOUL SOCIETY.
THIS IS A DANGER-OUS BATTLE.
I WILL BE HEADING THERE SHORTLY.
PLEASE ...
...BE SAFE.
YEAH...
SL S H

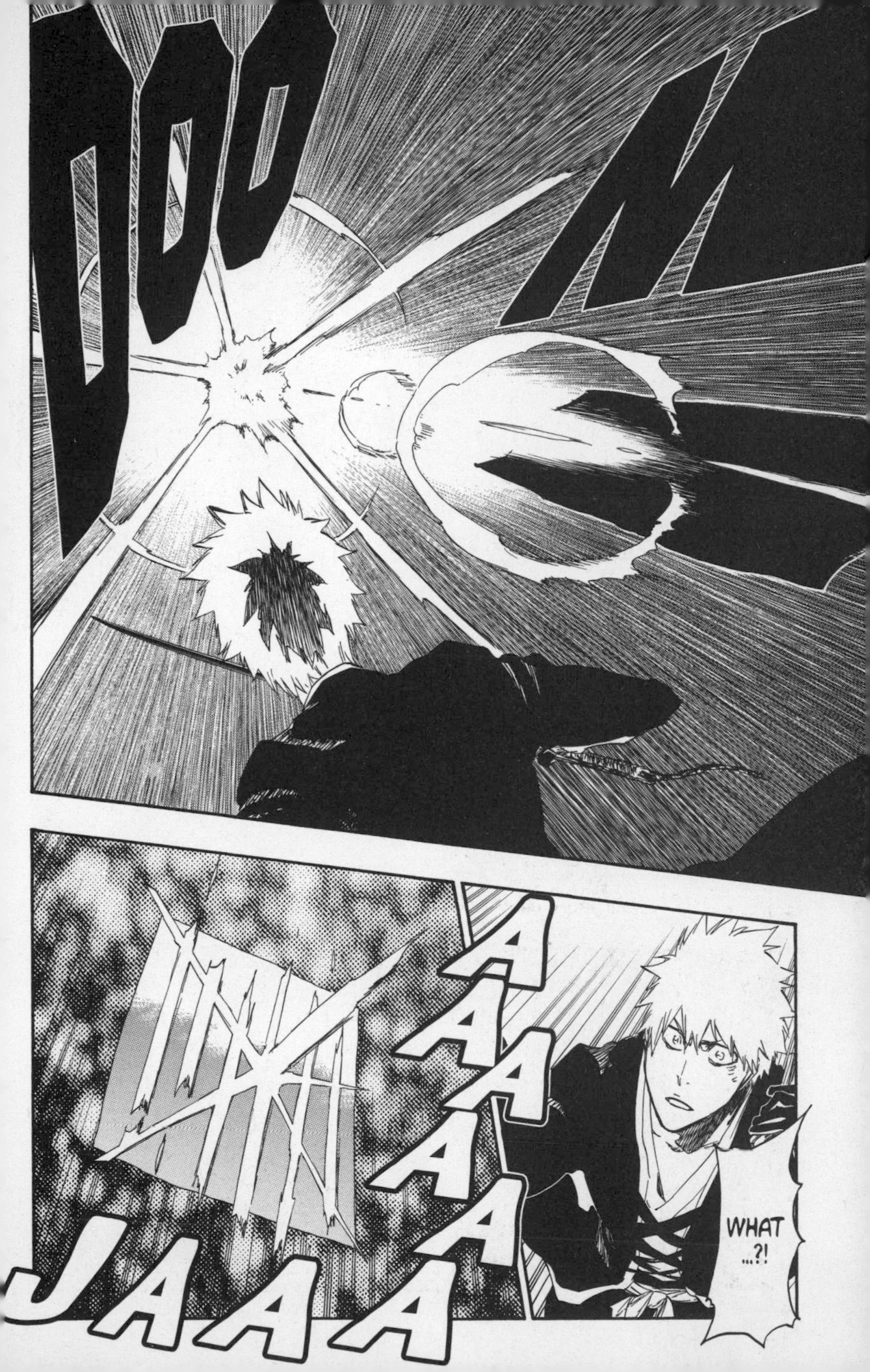
WHAT ...?!

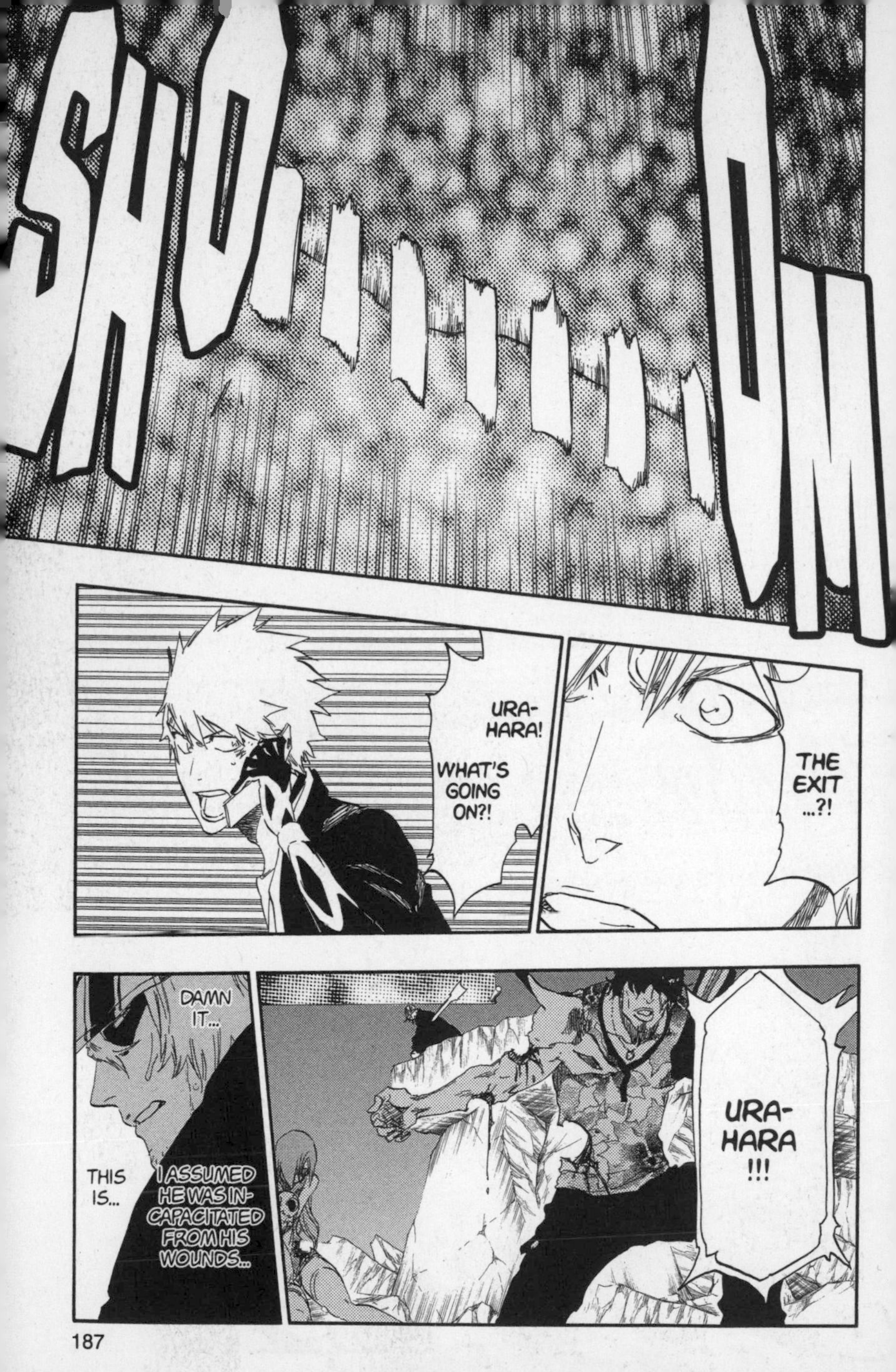
SHOOOOOOOM
THE EXIT ...?!
URA-HARA!
WHAT'S GOING ON?!
URA-HARA !!!
DAMN IT...
I ASSUMED HE WAS IN-CAPACITATED FROM HIS WOUNDS...
THIS IS...

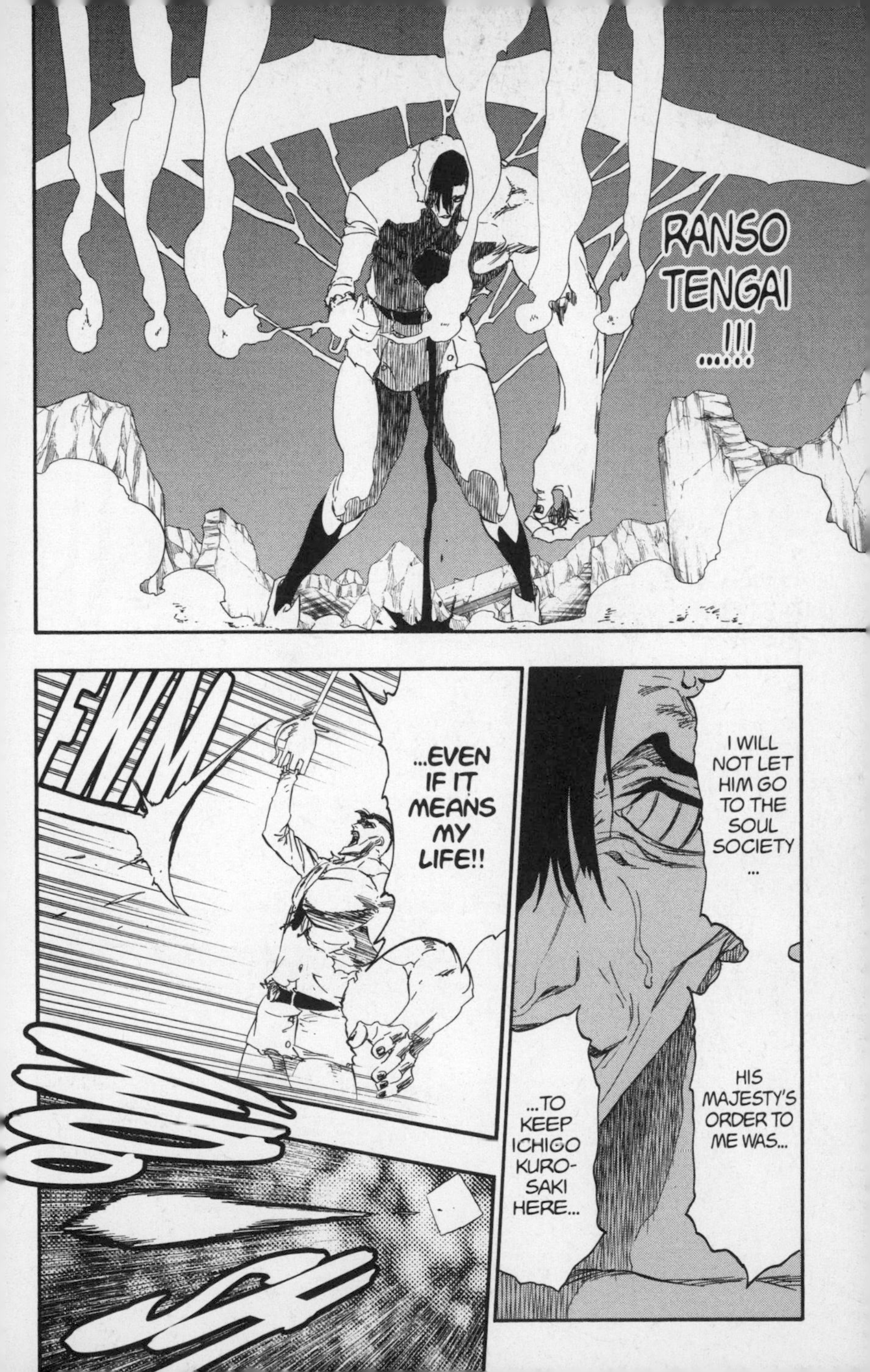
RANSO TENGAI ...!!!
I WILL NOT LET HIM GO TO THE SOUL SOCIETY ...
HIS MAJESTY'S ORDER TO ME WAS...
...TO KEEP ICHIGO KURO-SAKI HERE...
...EVEN IF IT MEANS MY LIFE!!

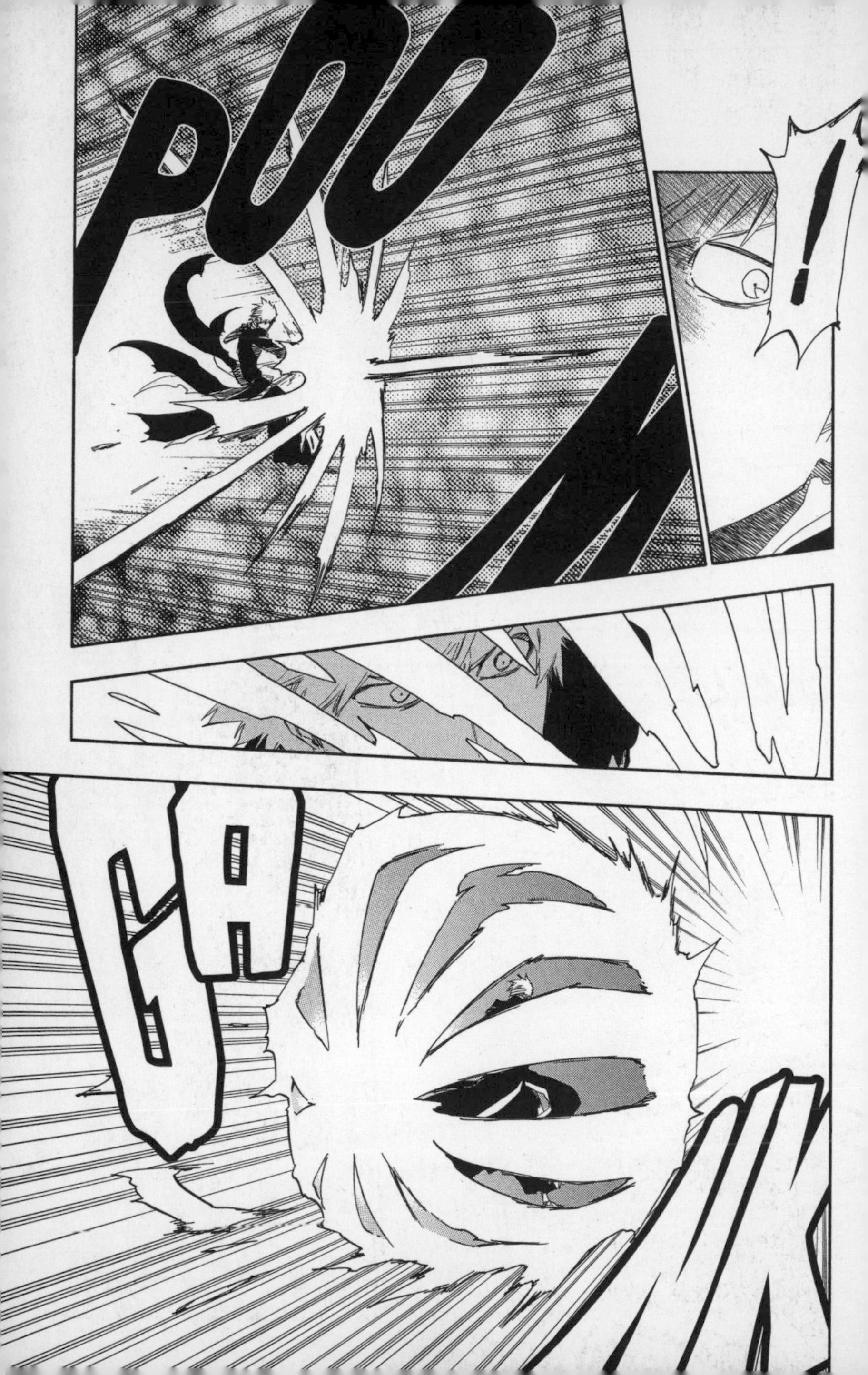

!
POOM
CHA

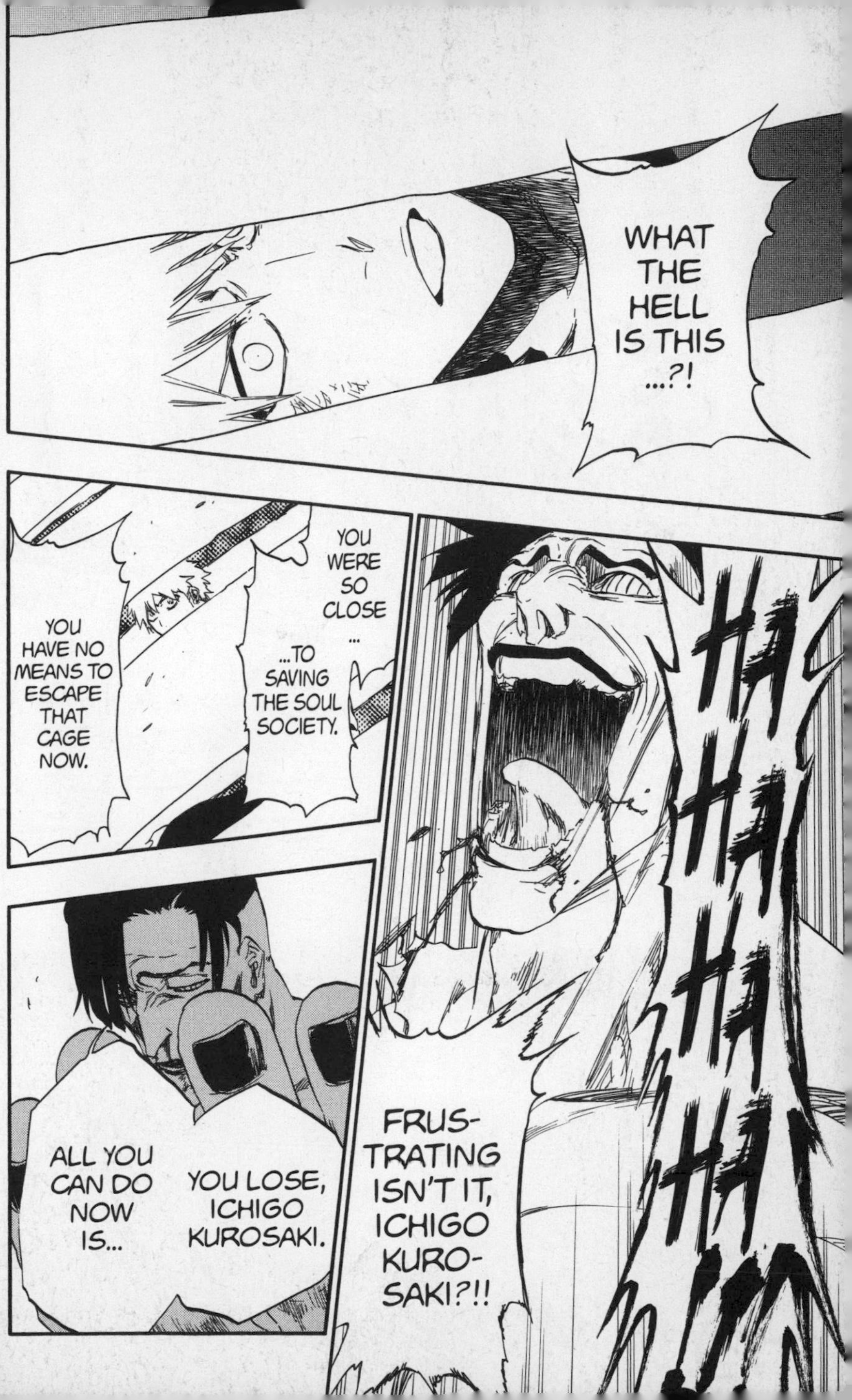
WHAT THE HELL IS THIS ...?!
HA HA HA HA HA HA
FRUS-TRATING ISN'T IT, ICHIGO KURO-SAKI?!!
YOU WERE SO CLOSE ...
...TO SAVING THE SOUL SOCIETY.
YOU HAVE NO MEANS TO ESCAPE THAT CAGE NOW.
YOU LOSE, ICHIGO KUROSAKI.
ALL YOU CAN DO NOW IS...

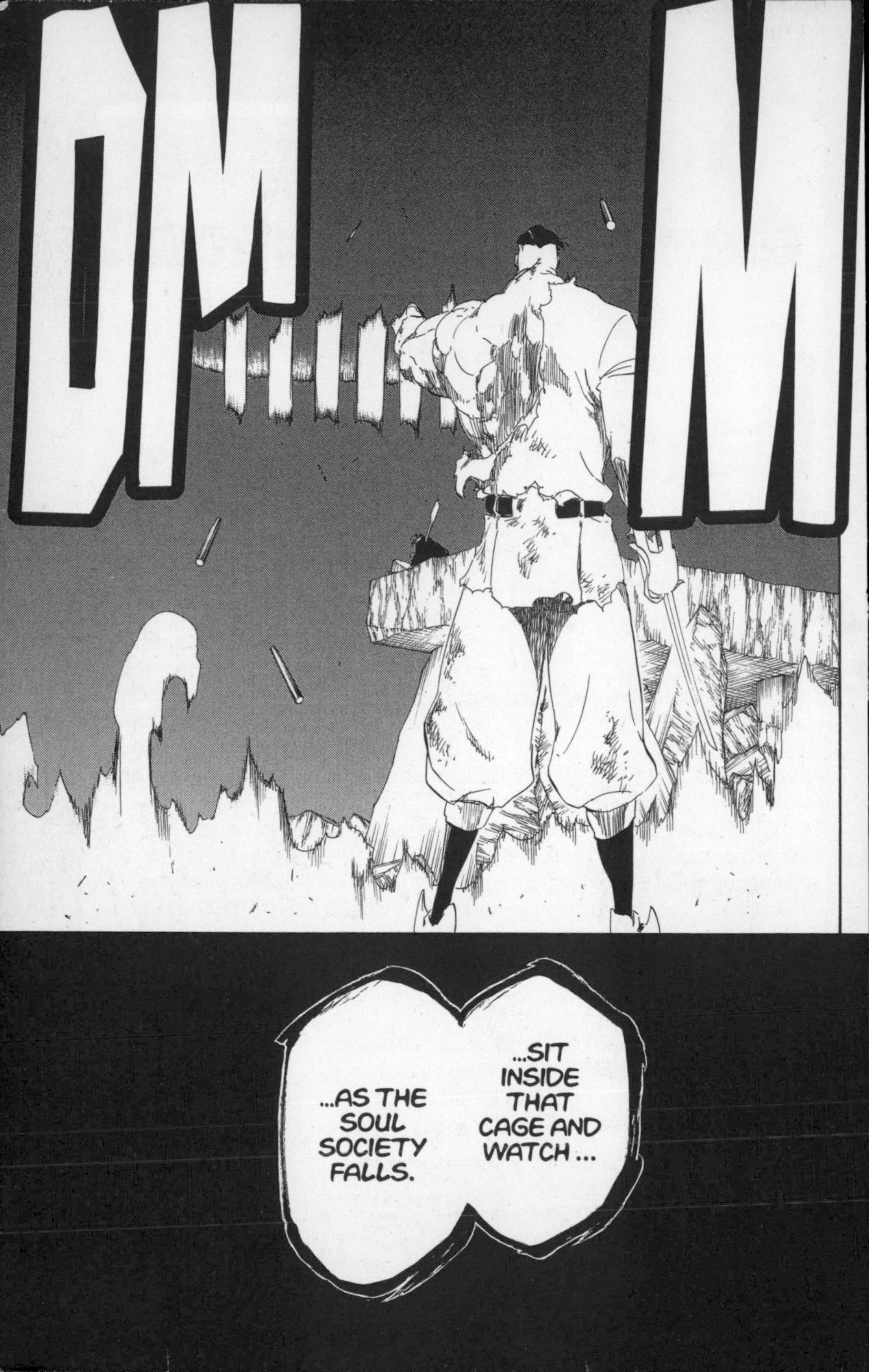
DM......M
...SIT INSIDE THAT CAGE AND WATCH ...
...AS THE SOUL SOCIETY FALLS.

You're Reading in the Wrong Direction!!

Whoops! Guess what? You're starting at the wrong end of the comic!

…It's true! In keeping with the original Japanese format, **Bleach** is meant to be read from right to left, starting in the upper-right corner.

Unlike English, which is read from left to right, Japanese is read from right to left, meaning that action, sound effects and word-balloon order are completely reversed… something which can make readers unfamiliar with Japanese feel pretty backwards themselves. For this reason, manga or Japanese comics published in the U.S. in English have sometimes been published "flopped"—that is, printed in exact reverse order, as though seen from the other side of a mirror.

By flopping pages, U.S. publishers can avoid confusing readers, but the compromise is not without its downside. For one thing, a character in a flopped manga series who once wore in the original Japanese version a T-shirt emblazoned with "M A Y" (as in "the merry month of") now wears one which reads "Y A M"! Additionally, many manga creators in Japan are themselves unhappy with the process, as some feel the mirror-imaging of their art skews their original intentions.

We are proud to bring you Tite Kubo's **Bleach** in the original unflopped format. For now, though, turn to the other side of the book and let the adventure begin…!

—Editor

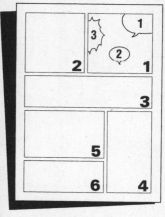

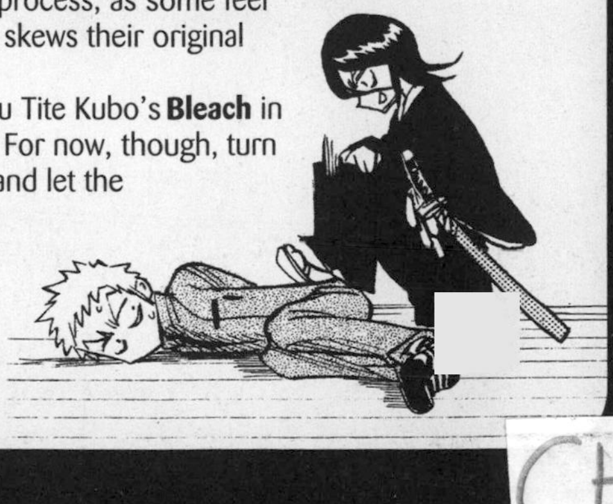